LYNCHING IN VIRGINIA

The American South Series

ELIZABETH R. VARON AND ORVILLE VERNON BURTON, EDITORS

LYNCHING IN VIRGINIA

Racial Terror and Its Legacy

EDITED BY GIANLUCA DE FAZIO

UNIVERSITY OF VIRGINIA PRESS

Charlottesville and London

The University of Virginia Press is situated on the traditional lands of the Monacan Nation, and the Commonwealth of Virginia was and is home to many other Indigenous people. We pay our respect to all of them, past and present. We also honor the enslaved African and African American people who built the University of Virginia, and we recognize their descendants. We commit to fostering voices from these communities through our publications and to deepening our collective understanding of their histories and contributions.

UNIVERSITY OF VIRGINIA PRESS
© 2024 by the Rector and Visitors of the University of Virginia
All rights reserved
Printed in the United States of America on acid-free paper

First published 2024

1 3 5 7 9 8 6 4 2

Library of Congress Cataloging-in-Publication Data
Names: De Fazio, Gianluca, editor.
Title: Lynching in Virginia : racial terror and its legacy / edited by Gianluca De Fazio.
Other titles: American South series.
Description: Charlottesville : University of Virginia Press, 2024. | Series: The American South series | Includes bibliographical references and index.
Identifiers: LCCN 2024007402 (print) | LCCN 2024007403 (ebook) | ISBN 9780813951164 (paperback ; acid-free paper) | ISBN 9780813951157 (hardcover ; acid-free paper) | ISBN 9780813951171 (ebook)
Subjects: LCSH: Lynching—Virginia—History—19th century. | Lynching—Virginia—History—20th century. | Lynching—Government policy—Virginia. | African Americans—Segregation—Virginia. | Lynching victims—Virginia—History. | Virginia—Race relations—History. | BISAC: SOCIAL SCIENCE / Ethnic Studies / American / African American & Black Studies | HISTORY / United States / State & Local / South (AL, AR, FL, GA, KY, LA, MS, NC, SC, TN, VA, WV)
Classification: LCC HV6465.V8 L85 2024 (print) | LCC HV6465.V8 (ebook) |
DDC 362.88/9309755—dc23/eng/20240318
LC record available at https://lccn.loc.gov/2024007402
LC ebook record available at https://lccn.loc.gov/2024007403

Cover design: David Drummond

This book is dedicated to the victims of racial terror
and those who strive to honor their memory.

CONTENTS

ACKNOWLEDGMENTS ix

Introduction: Lynching and Racial Terror in Virginia 1

PART I. NEWSPAPERS AND LYNCHING NARRATIVES 19

Impossible Love: An Interracial Romance
in Post-Reconstruction Virginia 25
JIM HALL

"You Shudder at the Picture": The *Richmond Planet* and the Lynching
of Three Black Miners in Clifton Forge in 1891 45
DOLORES FLAMIANO

PART II. LYNCHING IN SOUTHWEST VIRGINIA 67

Lynchings in Southwest Virginia, 1883–1927 73
JAMES WILLIAM HAGY

Justice and Injustice in the Coalfields:
Lynchings in Wise County 103
TOM COSTA AND ZOE CRIHFIELD

PART III. THE STATE RESPONSE TO LYNCHING 123

Faces of O'Ferrall: Virginia's Antilynching Governor
in the Jim Crow Era 129
CHARLES T. BLAIR

How "Judge Lynch" Influenced Virginia Courts,
Lawmakers, and Journalists   150
DALE BRUMFIELD

Uneven Justice: The Origin and Practice of Legalized Lynch Law
in Jim Crow Virginia   173
KEVIN HEGG

Six Sham Trials: Judge George Anderson and Jim Crow
in Alleghany and Botetourt County Courts   197
JOSH HOWARD

PART IV. COLLECTIVE MEMORY AND MEMORIALIZATION OF LYNCHING VICTIMS   221

The Train at Wood's Crossing   227
BRENDAN WOLFE

Public History as Activism: Helping a Community Come
to Terms with Racial Violence   253
ANDREA DOUGLAS

Restoring History: Writing the Narratives of
Alexandria's Two Documented Lynchings   272
MADDY MCCOY, FARAR ELLIOTT, SUSAN K. FLINN, ANN MARIE HAY,
ELIZABETH LOCKWOOD, CHRISTOPHER MILKO, AND ROB TAYLOR

Conclusion: The Legacy of Lynching in Virginia Today   295
GIANLUCA DE FAZIO

An Afterword   299
W. FITZHUGH BRUNDAGE

NOTES ON CONTRIBUTORS   303
INDEX   307

ACKNOWLEDGMENTS

My interest in lynching in the US South started more than a decade ago when I was a graduate student in Sociology at Emory University in Atlanta. My then dissertation advisor, and now mentor and friend, Roberto Franzosi, recruited me to be a research assistant for his project on lynching in Georgia. Roberto taught me how to design, organize, and conduct large-scale projects, as well as to train undergraduate research teams and develop meticulous research protocols. More importantly, though, Roberto constantly reminded me that behind those hundreds of articles were the stories of real people who had suffered unimaginable terror and who should not be forgotten. Stefania Vicari, also a research assistant on that project, was a constant source of motivation and unshakeable friendship. Thank you both for what you have taught me through the years.

When I moved to Virginia to join the Justice Studies Department at James Madison University in 2014, I was incredibly lucky to find a nurturing intellectual environment and colleagues who soon became a second family. When I first came up with the idea of building a digital project on lynching in Virginia, Glenn Hastedt, who was then head of the department, immediately supported my plan and gave me the opportunity to teach an advanced research course to start collecting data. Since that first course in spring 2017, several undergraduate research teams have examined an extraordinarily difficult topic with passion and engagement. All the primary sources that populate the Racial Terror: Lynching in Virginia website are the direct product of the students' work. The current head of the department, Peggy Plass, has eagerly championed my efforts to put together and edit this volume.

Through several grants, the Office of the Provost and the College of Art and Letters at JMU have provided financial support for both the digital project and this book.

The Racial Terror digital project would never have taken place without the extraordinary support of JMU Libraries, especially its Head of Digital Projects, Kevin Hegg. Kevin not only designed and implemented the website, he constantly pushed me to embrace new research directions and ideas. Zeyu Ju, Daroon Jalil, and Howard Carrier were instrumental in setting up the early phases of the digital project.

I owe an intellectual debt to the contributors to this volume and the many conversations we had about lynching in Virginia. I am indebted as well as to other scholars of racial violence, especially E. M. Beck, Seth Kotch, Elijah Gaddis, and Steve Reich.

Nadine Zimmerli, the acquisition editor at UVA Press, firmly believed and advocated for this project since its inception. Throughout the reviewing and editing process, Nadine was always sympathetic and encouraging. Fernando Campos helped me to navigate the production process with patience and professionalism. I want also to thank Fitz Brundage for his generosity in reviewing the manuscript and providing invaluable feedback; his comments forced me to sharpen the focus of the volume and make a much more cogent argument on what makes lynching in Virginia such an important topic for both academics and the general public.

Last, but not least, since my years at Emory, Heather has been my best friend and both intellectual and life partner. Thank you for your unwavering support during this project and beyond. Sabina and Noah make everything worthwhile.

LYNCHING IN VIRGINIA

INTRODUCTION

LYNCHING AND RACIAL TERROR IN VIRGINIA

Benjamin Thomas was only sixteen years old when he was summarily accused of attempting to assault an eight-year-old white girl in Alexandria, Virginia, on August 7, 1899. News about the alleged attempted assault and Thomas's arrest quickly spread across town, provoking very different reactions across the racial divide. Remembering well how Joseph McCoy, another Black youth accused of outraging two young white ladies, had been lynched two years earlier, the Alexandrian Black community mobilized to prevent another lynching. A group of African American men offered to aid Mayor Simpson and local police officers to defend the jail from a possible attack by white mobs, but the authorities refused the offer. Moreover, indignant at the suggestion that a mob would try to lynch Thomas, the police arrested several of the Black men because of their "disorderly behavior." The *Richmond Planet* would later editorialize: "Was there ever a greater parody upon justice than the sight of citizens of Alexandria—colored citizens hauled before a white mayor and fined $20 for doing their duty? Mayor Simpson is a disgrace to the office. He, a sworn official of the law fining other citizens who were anxious to see the laws upheld."[1]

Meanwhile, many local whites were following a well-known script that exacted a quick and lethal response to the alleged attack on an "innocent white girl." Attempted rape was a crime punishable with the death penalty in Virginia, and Thomas was already in custody awaiting trial. However, for the enraged white populace, "letting the law take its course" was not a satisfactory option. To add to the rage of white Alexandrians, the Black community's efforts to protect Thomas further incensed the crowds. Following the arrest and quick trial of the "disorderly" and "riotous" Black men, rumors of an impending armed Black uprising swirled around the city, fueling the feverish paranoia that Black men were planning to arm themselves and kill white residents. On the evening of August 8, "Chief of Police Webster, with a force of four regular officers and twenty sworn citizens, was detailed to guard the prisoner. Meanwhile, as time advanced, the situation became easy to read. Every gun shop and hardware store in town was visited, and in a short while it was impossible to find a spare weapon anywhere. Citizens walked the streets with protruding pockets, and many went so far as to shoulder rifles and shotguns."[2]

While the previous day Mayor Simpson had rejected the notion that the local jail might be in danger, reserving his scorn for the Black citizens that had offered their help, he now found himself trying to placate the white mob outside of the jail. The mayor addressed the crowd with these words: "Fellow citizens, if you will disperse and go away quietly, I will promise you that a court will be convened today and a true bill found by the grand jury. If this is not done, I will give you my word, as a man of honor, *that I will personally lead a mob tomorrow night to lynch Thomas*" (emphasis added).[3] The white mob of 500 to 2,000 people, however, was not impressed with the mayor's promise of a sham trial and a delayed execution; mob justice required a swift, lethal, and brutal response. After attacking the jail with a battering ram and axes, the mob eventually was able to get inside and take Benjamin Thomas from his cell. The enraged white crowd took Thomas outside with a rope around his neck, and, after beating him repeatedly, they brought him to Leadbeater Corner. There, the mob first hung Thomas to a lamppost and then riddled his body with bullets, leaving his body hanging "as a terrible warning" to the Black community, as some of the spectators to the lynching collected souvenirs at the scene.[4]

Several newspapers had reported that the most prominent citizens of Alexandria had participated to the lynching; however, the coroner's inquiry was unable to identify any of the lynchers. Nobody was ever indicted, let alone convicted, for the lynching of Benjamin Thomas. While heavily criticized in the Black press, Alexandria authorities suffered no consequences for their failure to prevent a lynching or investigate the mob. On the contrary, white newspapers lionized and praised their alleged heroic efforts to (unsuccessfully) defend the jail. In a defiant display of Black resistance and protest against the lynching, Benjamin Thomas's mother, Elizabeth, "refused to receive [his] remains at her home. She could not bear to look upon her boy, she said, and would have nothing to do with his funeral."[5]

On August 8, 2020, the 121st anniversary of the lynching of Benjamin Thomas, the mayor and the sheriff of Alexandria laid a wreath at the corner where Thomas was hanged, as part of a remembrance project to honor the two Black youths who were cruelly lynched in the late 1890s.[6] Benjamin Thomas was just one of the 115 people who were lynched in Virginia between 1866 and 1932, as documented in the digital history project Racial Terror: Lynching in Virginia. The murder of Thomas is also one of the several lynchings that are now being publicly discussed and memorialized as a part of a sweeping reckoning with the history of racialized terror in the United States. For far too long, stories of lynching and their impact on Black families and communities have been neglected and purged from both collective and institutional memories. History textbooks and curricula have typically overlooked lynchings as a tool of enforcing white supremacy and controlling Black communities through terror.[7] To address this gap, in 2020, the Virginia Board of Education approved the recommendation by the Commission on African American History Education to add "content about the history of lynching in America to the high school Virginia and U.S. History course."[8] While it is currently unclear if and how this recommendation will be implemented, K–12 teachers will find that this volume provides valuable resources to incorporate lynching in their lessons plans.[9]

Over the past several years, I have developed the digital history project Racial Terror: Lynching in Virginia to document with primary sources all the lynchings that took place in the Commonwealth since the end of the Civil War. The website provides more than nine hundred newspaper articles reporting on Virginia lynchings and offers brief narratives for each documented lynching victim.[10] I have also been involved in a local community remembrance project in Harrisonburg, Virginia, to memorialize the 1878 lynching of Charlotte Harris in Rockingham County; in September 2020 a historical marker was unveiled in downtown Harrisonburg to honor her memory.[11] Behind this project are both scholarly and community-oriented efforts to unveil and disseminate the stories of lynching that had been forgotten and expunged from collective and institutional memories across Virginia. Making these stories available to researchers and the public alike, I strive to provide a more complete history of racial violence and terror in

Virginia—an uncomfortable aspect of our history that should inform contemporary debates on how we think about our past and address the legacy of racial violence. In line with the underlying spirit of my research and public agenda, I envision this book as an additional way to advance original research on lynching in Virginia, as well as to inform the general public about the legacy of racial terror in the Old Dominion.

This volume brings together interdisciplinary contributions from historians, social scientists, journalists, activists, students, and civic-minded citizens who have been researching the histories of racial terror in Virginia. I deliberately invited a variety of academic and nonacademic voices and perspectives to clarify the role of lynching in shaping Jim Crow Virginia and examine its legacy today. At its most basic level, this volume offers in-depth investigations of some of the lynchings that took place in Jim Crow Virginia and situates them within their social and political context. By divulging these stories, this project aims to counter the collective amnesia that local communities very often suffer about their past; it also aims to restore the dignity of the people who were brutally murdered. The simple act of discussing past lynchings is a first step towards restoring the truth of how racialized terrorism affected many local Virginia communities and how those episodes were often soon forgotten by the white community and removed from collective memory. Black communities, on the other hand, did not have the luxury to forget these atrocities and the constant threat of violence and intimidation against them. By disseminating these stories, this volume embraces the objective of community-oriented public history to spark further research, education, and remembrance initiatives across Virginia, where many other lynching stories have not yet been told and widely shared.

The essays in this volume, however, go beyond storytelling: they collectively provide a thorough examination of how lynchings (and other forms of racial terror) impacted Virginia from the end of Reconstruction well into the 1930s, when the spectacle of lynching became increasingly unacceptable. For instance, this project explores the contested coverage of mob violence in white and Black newspapers and the struggle over the meaning of lynching; it also examines the evolving state response to mob violence, highlighting how governors, courts, judges, and the legal system as a whole shaped racial terror in the Commonwealth. Authorities had the duty and capacity to prevent lynchings or punish the lynchers most of the time; however, for decades they often refused to do so. While the chapters cover episodes of mob violence all over Virginia, special attention is dedicated to examining the puzzle of why lynchings were concentrated in the southwest portion of the state, a lightly populated area with no plantation economy, where one would expect few cases of racial terror.

Overall, this book suggests an interpretation of race relations in the Commonwealth that challenges certain aspects of the narrative that Virginia, in contrast with other Deep South states, displayed lower levels of racial conflict and subjugation. By situating lynching within the larger spectrum of racialized violence, several chapters connect completed lynchings with lynching threats and capital punishment, unveiling how Black communities were the targets of pervasive, coercive racial control. With its long history of using the death penalty as an instrument of racial repression, Virginia represents an ideal case to investigate how racial terror has been historically unleashed under a variety of both legal and extralegal means, of which lynching was the most visible.[12]

Finally, this volume examines the collective memory of lynching in Virginia—its legacy—and how communities are memorializing lynching episodes amid a national reckoning with our past of racial terrorism. In the past few years, a host of initiatives across Virginia started to recognize this past through historical markers, commemorations, proclamations, pilgrimages, and other events geared towards remembering the people who were lynched. Several contributors to this volume were directly involved in these local initiatives, and in their essays they discuss the collective and institutional projects implemented in Charlottesville and Alexandria to restore the collective memory of lynching victims; describe the challenges they faced in their own efforts at commemoration; and offer suggestions on how to move forward in dealing with the legacy of racial terror killings in Virginia. Connecting past racial violence with contemporary issues like mass incarceration, police brutality, white supremacist violence, and controversies over Confederate monuments, these essays make painfully clear the need to revisit the often white-washed stories that local communities tell about themselves and to develop practices to construct more inclusive narratives and landscapes in Virginia and elsewhere.

Lynching in Virginia

The history of lynching is intertwined with the history of Virginia. Most historians agree that the word "lynching," and its derivative terms "Lynch Law" and "Judge Lynch," originated in Virginia during the Revolutionary War.[13] The term "lynching," indicating an extralegal execution conducted by a mob against a perceived threat to the community, can in fact be traced back to Col. Charles Lynch of Bedford County. In the 1780s Lynch and other members of the patriot militias had set up extralegal trials to prosecute and punish alleged loyalists siding with the British Crown. During the chaos produced by the war, common bandits and criminals were also subjected to Lynch Law. These extralegal trials, presided over by Judge Lynch, often resulted in harsh sentences for the accused, and, at times, in the hanging of the alleged traitor or criminal.[14] While this form of "revolutionary justice" subsided at the end of the war, the idea of people having the right to take the law into their own hands "emerged as a powerful rationale for extralegal violence against those deemed to be enemies of the public good" in the United States.[15]

For the next several decades, the term "lynching" indicated a form of "popular justice" meted out against perceived threats to the community. Summary extralegal executions proliferated, especially in the Far West, where lynching became associated with the violent rituals of "frontier justice." Most victims of mob violence in the West in the first half of the nineteenth century tended to be white, while in the mid-1800s vigilante justice in the Southwest often targeted Mexicans and Mexican Americans.[16] It was only after the Civil War and the end of Reconstruction that lynching took on the current racialized understanding of the term: terror killings targeting primarily African American men in the Jim Crow South. To be sure, lethal mob violence against Blacks did occur both inside and outside of the South during Reconstruction and even in earlier decades. For instance, at least nine men were lynched in Virginia between 1866 and 1871, all of them Black, except for one white victim;[17] in states like Kansas and Kentucky, anti-Black mob violence surged during Reconstruction.[18] Historians have now recognized that while the overwhelming majority of lynchings took place in Jim Crow South, the practice did not represent a unique Southern phenomenon, nor can it be seen as an indicator of "negative exceptionalism."[19]

This book, however, focuses on lynching in Virginia after the end of Reconstruction, as this is the period during which racial terror killings became a widespread practice within the larger Jim Crow system of coercion and oppression against Black communities. The frequency of lynching and its increasingly extensive coverage in newspapers cemented the prominence of lethal mob violence as a tool of racial control and white supremacy. After the end of Reconstruction, lynching entered the political and cultural discourse as a peculiar phenomenon associated with the Deep South; for decades, white southern politicians and the press worked tirelessly to defend and legitimize lynch mobs as necessary to defend white women from "Black rapists." But lynching also became a central object of reporting and revulsion in the Black press, with courageous journalists and activists like Ida B. Wells and John Mitchell Jr. leading the campaign to denounce the barbarism of lynching and seeking federal intervention to stop mob violence against African American communities.[20] It is within this political, legal, and discursive context that racialized terrorism in Virginia is investigated in this book.

For our purposes here, we rely on the definition of lynching that was elaborated in 1940 at a NAACP meeting with other antilynching organizations at the Tuskegee Institute in Alabama. For an event to qualify as a lynching, four conditions have to be met: 1) there needs to be evidence that a person was killed; 2) the person was killed illegally; 3) a group of at least three individuals was responsible for the death; 4) the group acted under the pretext of service to justice, honor, or tradition.[21] While this definition was the result of a compromise among various antilynching organizations and presents several limitations, scholars across disciplines have adopted it to guide their research.[22] It is important to note that even though the modality of lynchings varied across the Jim Crow South—from spectacle events with thousands of participants to secretive killings in the dead of night—almost all these incidents shared some basic traits. Lynching in the post-Reconstruction South typically involved a lethal punishment for someone who was accused of having committed a crime, or just for violating racial etiquette, with an utter disregard for due process and fundamental rights. Lynchings were also a tool of racial repression and white supremacy, as they were meant not just to eliminate an alleged threat to the (white) community, but, crucially, to intimidate and terrorize Black people. Relatedly, lynchers could rely on a certain level of support from the local (white) community, as well as virtual impunity from the legal and political system. While there is not a unified inventory of how many lynchings took place in the United States, various estimates indicate that probably between three and four thousand Black people were lynched in the Jim Crow South between the end of Reconstruction and the 1940s.[23]

On the website Racial Terror: Lynching in Virginia, I documented 115 people who were lynched between 1866 and 1932 across fifty-seven counties in the Old Dominion. The majority of lynching victims were Black men (93 out of 115, or 82 percent), while 20 victims were white men (17 percent). Two women, one Black, Charlotte Harris, and one white, Peb Falls, were also lynched, both in Rockingham County. This count is certainly an underestimation of the real number of lynching victims in Virginia, as inventories rely on newspaper reports to identify lynching events.[24] Many episodes of lethal mob violence were not covered in the press, or the newspapers that might have reported them do not exist anymore and were never preserved or archived. Without these sources, lynching events cannot be properly documented and added to inventories of mob violence. While the number of lynching victims is thus undercounted,[25] inventories are nonetheless a critical tool for tracking the extent of lethal mob violence over time and assessing variation across states and counties.

In contemporary public discourse, lynching often evokes the atrocities of the Deep South, as some of the most infamous cases took place in states like Georgia (for instance, the torturing and lynching of Sam Hose in 1899, or the quadruple Moore's Ford lynching in 1946), or Texas (the 1893 spectacle lynching of Henry Smith in Paris, Texas, before a crowd of several thousand people). Notwithstanding the fact that the practice of lynching originated in revolutionary Virginia, the Old Dominion is rarely associated with the racialized terrorism that pervaded the Deep South. Until very recently, the issue of lynching would never surface in the way Virginia celebrates and discusses its own past. This gap is also reflected in the lynching scholarship.[26] The comparison of Georgia and Virginia in *Lynching in the New South* by historian Fitz Brundage is one the most important historical analyses of southern lynchings, but it also represents an exception to the relative neglect of the Commonwealth in academic investigations of lynching.[27] This partial neglect is not without reasons: there were comparatively fewer lynchings in Virginia than in the rest of the South—sociologists Stewart Tolnay and E. M. Beck catalogued 458 lynchings in Georgia and 538 in Mississippi between 1882 and 1930.[28] Only rarely did lynchings in Virginia turn into spectacular events with massive crowds, body desecrations, and vicious display of mob cruelty towards its victims.[29] Also, in 1928 Virginia passed a sweeping antilynching law, the first of its kind in the United States; after its passage, no lynchings were officially *reported* in Virginia. While the law was *de facto* never enforced, the lack of *reported* lynchings gave the impression that racialized mob violence in the Commonwealth had been eradicated much earlier than in the rest of the South.[30]

Brundage argues that "lynchings were less likely to occur in Virginia than in Georgia for the simple reason that white Virginians believed that racial boundaries could be maintained without the need to resort to persistent violence."[31] This volume builds on this premise to explore what set Virginia apart from other southern states in displaying a more restrained, if equally effective, system of racial control through terror. As civil rights lawyer and activist Oliver Hill remarked in 1985, "In Virginia, the powers that be were a little more sophisticated than they were in the deeper South, and they'd always apparently been. And as a consequence, you didn't have as much physical violence [against Blacks] in Virginia as you had in the deeper South. [. . . But] Virginia and the whole South were police states. There isn't a question about that."[32] This volume suggests that Virginia's "police state" could count on alternative forms of social control to terrorize the African American population. In addition to the legal machinery of Jim Crow and its punitive criminal justice system against alleged Black criminals, the *threat* of lynching was a powerful means of intimidation.

Lynching scholar E. M. Beck recently identified more than six hundred instances of *lynching threats and averted lynchings* in Virginia between 1866 and 1955, one of the highest numbers in the South.[33] There is little doubt that these threatened and averted lynchings intimidated local Black communities, reaffirming that white supremacist violence could be deployed at any moment against perceived transgressors. As Tolnay and Beck note, "Such threats were a constant reminder of the vulnerability of the black population and, conversely, the power that was concentrated in the dominant white population."[34] While lynching threats did not have lethal outcomes, they could nonetheless have very serious consequences for the targeted persons, their families, and the local community. The story of Haney Garrett, a Black woman accused of setting a house on fire in Lebanon, Russell County, in 1890, is instructive in this regard. Following the arson accusation, Garrett had an altercation with mayor Boswell, during which Boswell knocked Garrett down and ordered her to leave town. After a couple of days, Garrett came back to Lebanon and allegedly tried to burn down another house; a white mob furiously searched for her until she was captured and put in jail. The enraged white mob threatened to lynch her, as newspapers reported that "Judge Lynch awaited nightfall to get his effective work." While the mob ultimately did not lynch Garrett, they banished the members of the local Black community that sided with her, forcing them to leave town. At her trial Garrett pleaded guilty, most likely under the threat of violence, and was sentenced to ten years in the penitentiary.[35] This is just one example of how lynching threats enabled racial oppression and coercion, often with disturbing consequences for the Black community. As threatened or failed lynchings are not registered in lynching inventories, they have been excluded from current analyses and understanding of the extent, trends, and social ramifications of racialized mob violence in the South. In this volume, we strive to bring lynching threats and averted lynchings into our analyses to better capture the dynamics of racialized terrorism.[36]

Content and Structure of the Volume

The essays in this volume share an orientation towards understanding lynching as a form of *racial terrorism with varying degrees of connivance by state and local authorities*.[37] Mob violence against Black people was not simply meant as retribution for their alleged crimes: it was a "terrible warning" for other Black folks, an instrument to intimidate and terrorize the whole community. This violence could have happened only thanks to the explicit or implicit support and complicity of local and state authorities—from sheriffs, coroners, and mayors to judges and governors—in failing to prevent lynchings or to investigate them properly and bring lynchers to justice. Almost every lynching victim in Virginia was already in police custody when a mob captured them and executed them; very few lynchers were ever charged with a crime, and only in two cases were members of a lynch mob convicted and given light sentences. (In one case, the murderers were later pardoned.)[38] However, Virginia officials were *more prone to protect* Black prisoners from would-be lynching mobs than other Southern states, partially explaining the discrepancy between the large volume of *lynching threats* and the low number of actual lynchings.

A key figure in curbing lethal mob violence was Gov. Charles O'Ferrall (1894–98), a staunch white supremacist who also feared the lawlessness of the mobs and their potential to challenge authorities with violence. In 1893 a white mob in Roanoke engaged in a violent confrontation with the local militia protecting the jail where Thomas Smith, a Black man, was awaiting trial, provoking the death of nine people and ultimately the lynching of the prisoner. The Roanoke Riot left a lasting impression on Virginia political elites, as they understood that lynching mobs represented a threat to the authority of the Commonwealth.[39] Elected governor at the peak of anti-Black violence in the South and soon after the Roanoke Riot, O'Ferrall aggressively reined in mob violence by sending state militias to protect Black prisoners and adopting an antilynching stance to preserve law and order in the Old Dominion. As a result of his policies, the number of lynchings in Virginia drastically dropped.[40]

While his successors were not as determined as O'Ferrall in preventing lethal mob violence, with the number of lynchings rising again after the end of his governorship, Virginia remained a state where intervening to prevent a lynching was more common than in other Deep South states. It is worth nothing that state (and sometimes local) officials' propensity to oppose lynching focused almost exclusively on preventing—*but almost never punishing*—lethal mob violence. While mobilizing state militias or moving prisoners for safekeeping was within the acceptable boundaries of the conservative quest to preserve Virginia's order (and reputation), actively punishing lynchers and would-be lynchers would risk upsetting the local white communities that often supported mob violence. Virginia's distinctive effort to protect Black prisoners from lynching was rarely animated by a sincere preoccupation to save Black lives and uphold their basic constitutional rights; it was a way to impose order and neutralize violent challenges to the state as well as to boost its reputation in the New South.

Virginia's partially successful effort to suppress mob violence only confirms that most lynchings *could* have been prevented if local, state, and federal authorities had undertaken a serious effort against them. In 1920 a sheriff in Wise County prevented a lynching by opening fire and killing two members of a white mob that was attempting to break into the local jail and murder a Black man. NAACP investigator Walter White praised the sheriff's actions, writing: "If every community in America, particularly in the South, had officers of the law who would fulfill all their offices [. . .], it would be but a short time before lynching, the greatest blot on American civilization would be entirely wiped out."[41] Antilynching organizations like the NAACP had a role in denouncing lynching and pushing authorities to take an aggressive stance against mob violence in Virginia, but journalists like John Mitchell Jr. at the *Richmond Planet* played an especially important role. The relentless antilynching campaign by the *Richmond Planet* constantly prodded Virginia authorities to embrace a more active responsibility in curtailing mob violence, hastening the apparent demise of Judge Lynch in the Old Dominion.[42]

The emphasis in this volume on racial terror and virtual impunity for mob violence situates lynching as part of a broader campaign of racialized terrorism against minority communities in the South. Documented lynchings, in fact, capture only a fraction of the racial violence and its constant threat in the Jim Crow South; *threatened* and *averted* lynchings must be brought into our analyses of racialized terrorism.[43] There are thousands of episodes in the Jim Crow South in which (mostly white) mobs attempted to capture and kill people accused of committing crimes, or even just violating informal racial norms; while in these cases the mob did not kill someone, they had similar intimidating effects on Black communities. To better appraise the extent of racialized terrorism, threatened lynchings should thus be part of our discussion of completed lynchings too.[44] This more nuanced understanding of racial terror[45] suffuses many essays in this volume, with some contributors pushing their analyses even further by advancing the argument that the death penalty and legal executions of African Americans should also be included in our understanding of racialized terrorism. Virginia is an excellent case to test this argument, as the death penalty was historically used as an instrument of racial control—especially after the end of Reconstruction, when legal executions were overwhelmingly used against African American men. In 1894 Governor O'Ferrall further exacerbated the weaponization of legal executions against Black men by including *attempted rape* as a crime punishable with the death penalty. Show trials were often held under the direct threat of mobs outside of the courtroom, leading to gross miscarriages of justice and the legalized killing of Black defendants.

As much as they differ in perspectives and style, the essays invite us to rethink the role of racialized violence in Virginia, challenging important aspects of the scholarship on southern lynching and Virginia history. Due to its relatively small number of lynchings, Virginia is often deemed an outlier; however, when considering the unusually large number of threatened lynchings and legal lynchings, it becomes apparent that *racialized terror* was a central element of Virginia's formal and informal "police state." As such, this volume aims to foreground the role of racial terror in the history of the Old Dominion, thus challenging the idea that race relations in Jim Crow Virginia were "perhaps the most harmonious in the South."[46]

The eleven essays in this volume are divided into four sections. I introduce each section with a short essay touching on the topics examined in the section. In the concluding essay, I discuss the legacy of lynching today and the importance of remembering our past of racialized violence to better inform contemporary public discussions on race and justice.

The first section, "Newspapers and Lynching Narratives," includes two essays that examine two episodes of lethal mob violence: Jim Hall's "Impossible Love: An Interracial Romance in Post-Reconstruction Virginia" investigates the lynching of Arthur Jordan in 1880 in Fauquier County. Dolores Flamiano explores a triple lynching in her contribution, "'You Shudder at the Picture': The *Richmond Planet* and the Lynching of Three Black Miners in Clifton Forge in 1891." Both essays explore these two violent episodes by focusing on the role (white) Virginia newspapers had in constructing and legitimizing lynching narratives, while Black newspapers like the *Richmond Planet* elaborated antilynching counternarratives. With their portrayals of the events surrounding the lynching, as well as their characterizations of the lynchers and their victims, mainstream newspapers were constitutive of the system of complicity that made racial terrorism in Virginia tolerable.

The second section examines "Lynching in Southwest Virginia." This area of Virginia had at least twenty-six lynchings, the highest concentration of lethal mob violence in the state. Southwest Virginia had a small African American population and never had a plantation economy; these demographic and economic factors are usually associated with very low numbers of lynchings. So how can we explain such a high frequency of lethal mob violence in this area? The two essays in this section examine this puzzle from two different perspectives: James William Hagy provides a comprehensive examination of the area in "Lynchings in Southwest Virginia, 1883–1927," while Tom Costa and Zoe Crihfield look at three lynchings that took place in a single county in "Justice and Injustice in the Coalfields: Lynchings in Wise County."

The third section features four essays examining "The State Response to Lynching." Focusing on different state actors and policies, these essays analyze the interactions between lynch mobs and the legal and political systems that were supposed to curb their lawlessness. In "Faces of O'Ferrall: Virginia's Antilynching Governor in the Jim Crow Era," Charles T. Blair investigates one of the key figures in this section: Charles O'Ferrall, whose interventions to protect prisoners from mobs effectively reduced the number of lynchings. However, O'Ferrall's criminal justice policies, especially the decision to make attempted rape a crime punishable with the death penalty, showed his staunch commitment to summarily execute Black "brutes" threatening white women. Dale Brumfield's "How 'Judge Lynch' Influenced Virginia Courts, Lawmakers, and Journalists" examines how lynching threats informed the legal and political system, as law enforcement and courts often exploited the threat of mob violence to indict and legally execute hundreds of Black people. It is not surprising that the death penalty has often been denounced as "legal lynching," a notion that is extensively discussed in two other essays in this section. In "Uneven Justice: The Origin and Practice of Legalized Lynch Law in Jim Crow Virginia," Kevin Hegg provides an overall examination of the statistical data on legal executions, extralegal executions, and lynching threats, dissecting the complicated relationship between the death penalty and lynching in Virginia. Josh Howard's "Six Sham Trials: Judge George Anderson and Jim Crow in Alleghany and Botetourt County Courts" instead offers an in-depth examination how one Virginia judge meted out the death penalty against Black defendants through show trials. Ultimately, this section suggests how the death penalty was often used as a more palatable alternative to mob violence, while ensuring that the accused were still quickly (and legally) executed, often relying on the flimsiest of evidence.

The fourth section, "Collective Memory and Memorialization of Lynching Victims," looks at contemporary efforts in Virginia to revive the collective memory of lynching victims. Two essays focus on the 1898 lynching of John Henry James in Albemarle County. Brendan Wolfe's "The Train at Wood's Crossing" meticulously reconstructs the lynching and connects it with the modern landscape of Charlottesville; while in "Public History as Activism:

Helping a Community Come to Terms with Racial Violence," Andrea Douglas discusses recent institutional and community efforts to memorialize Black history in Charlottesville, proposing a more inclusive account of its past. The third essay, "Restoring History: Writing the Narratives of Alexandria's Two Documented Lynchings," is a collective work by the Alexandria Community Remembrance Project Research Group detailing the lynchings of Joseph McCoy in 1897 and Benjamin Thomas in 1899 and exposing the complicity of Alexandria's authorities before, during, and after those lynchings.

In the conclusion, I discuss the ramifications and legacy of racial terror in Virginia. Recent events like the deadly Unite the Right rally in Charlottesville in 2017 and the January 6, 2021, attack on Capitol Hill remind us that white mobs are still actively trying to impose white supremacist ideas through intimidation, coercion, and violence. Thus, in the concluding remarks, I indicate how various contemporary issues, from armed white militias to police violence to the death penalty, are deeply rooted in the lynching tradition of racial terror practiced with virtual impunity by white supremacists. The afterword by Fitzhugh Brundage situates these essays within the larger context of how extralegal violence pervaded American society both inside and outside the South, and how the mere threat of lynching impacted Black lives during Jim Crow.

Ultimately, I argue that that the history of racial violence in Virginia (and, more generally, the United States) should be more widely discussed to better understand key contemporary issues of racial injustice. It is time for Virginians to reckon with its often forgotten past of lynching and to build a more inclusive and just Commonwealth.

Notes

1. "A Lynching in Alexandria," *Richmond Planet*, Aug. 12, 1899, 1, 4.
2. "A Negro Lynched," *Evening Star*, Aug. 9, 1899, 2.
3. "Hanged to a Lamppost," *The Times* (Washington, DC), Aug. 9, 1899, 1.
4. Ibid.
5. "Mob Acts Deplored," *Evening Star*, Aug. 10, 1899, 1. For a detailed account of the lynchings of Joseph McCoy and Benjamin Thomas, see the final essay in this volume from the Alexandria Community Remembrance Project Research Group.
6. Patricia Sullivan, "In a Summer of Racial Protests, Alexandria Remembers a Young Lynching Victim," *Washington Post*, Aug. 7, 2020, https://www.washingtonpost.com

/local/virginia-news/alexandria-lynching/2020/08/07/45eead66-d8bb-11ea-930e-d88518c57dcc_story.html. See also here: https://www.alexandriava.gov/cultural-history/basic-page/in-memoriam-2020-benjamin-thomas-august-8-1899.

7. Anthony L. Brown and Keffrelyn D. Brown. "'A Spectacular Secret': Understanding the Cultural Memory of Racial Violence in K–12 Official School Textbooks in the Era of Obama." *Race, Gender & Class* 17, no. 3/4 (2010): 111–25.

8. "Changes Made to History, Social Science SOLs", *Farmville Herald*, Oct. 23, 2020, https://www.farmvilleherald.com/2020/10/changes-made-to-history-social-science-sols/.

9. With colleagues at James Madison University, we have developed several lesson plans to teach about lynching in Virginia in K–12 schools: https://sites.lib.jmu.edu/valynchings/curriculum/. See Gianluca De Fazio, Mary Beth Cancienne, Ashley Taylor Jaffee, Kevin Hegg, Elaine Kaye, and Nicole Wilson, "Critical Digital Pedagogy and Civic Education: The Experience of the Racial Terror: Lynching in Virginia Project." *Scholé: Rivista di Educazione e Studi Culturali* 59, no. 1 (2021): 65–78.

10. Relying on local newspapers, I have revised and updated the lynching database compiled by sociologists Tolnay and Beck for the state of Virginia, identifying 115 lynching victims between 1866 and 1932. For a detailed discussion of the research process, see Gianluca De Fazio, "Improving Lynching Inventories with Local Newspapers: Racial Terror in Virginia, 1877–1927," *Current Research in Digital History* 2 (2019) https://doi.org/10.31835/crdh.2019.04.

11. "Charlotte Harris Historical Marker Unveiled," (Harrisonburg) *Daily News Record*, Sept. 27, 2020.

12. For a similar approach, see Brent Campney, *This Is Not Dixie: Racist Violence in Kansas, 1861–1927* (Urbana: University of Illinois Press, 2015); Brent Campney, *Hostile Heartland: Racism, Repression, and Resistance in the Midwest* (Urbana: University of Illinois Press, 2019).

13. Christopher Waldrep, *The Many Faces of Judge Lynch: Extralegal Violence and Punishment in America* (New York: Palgrave MacMillan, 2002).

14. Manfred Berg, *Popular Justice: A History of Lynching in America* (Chicago: Ivan R Dee, 2015).

15. Richard Maxwell Brown, *Strain of Violence: Historical Studies of American Violence and Vigilantism* (Oxford: Oxford University Press, 1975), 39.

16. Michael Pfeifer, ed., *Lynching beyond Dixie: American Mob Violence outside the South* (Urbana: University of Illinois Press, 2013); William D. Carrigan and Clive Webb, *Forgotten Dead: Mob Violence against Mexicans in the United States, 1848–1928* (Oxford: Oxford University Press, 2013).

17. Racial Terror: Lynching in Virginia, https://sites.lib.jmu.edu/valynchings/victims/. There are no documented lynchings between 1872 and 1876.

18. Campney, *This Is Not Dixie*; George C. Wright, *Racial Violence in Kentucky: Lynchings, Mob Rule, and "Legal Lynchings"* (Baton Rouge: Louisiana State University Press, 1996).

19. See, for instance, Michael Pfeifer, *The Roots of Rough Justice: Origins of American Lynching* (Urbana: University of Illinois Press, 2011).

20. Fitzhugh Brundage, "The Press and Lynching," in *Journalism and Jim Crow: White Supremacy and the Black Struggle for a New America*, eds. Kathy Roberts Forde and Sid Bedingfield (Urbana: University of Illinois Press, 2021).

21. Amy Kate Bailey and Stewart E. Tolnay, *Lynched: The Victims of Southern Mob Violence* (Chapel Hill: University of North Carolina Press, 2015), 3.
22. Bailey and Tolnay, *Lynched*, 4. For a discussion on the issues surrounding the definition of lynching, see Christopher Waldrep, "War of Words: The Controversy over the Definition of Lynching, 1899–1940," *Journal of Southern History* 66, no. 1 (2000): 75–100.
23. See Charles Seguin and David Rigby, "National Crimes: A New National Data Set of Lynchings in the United States, 1883 to 1941," *Socius* 5 (2019), https://doi.org/10.1177/2378023119841780. Stewart Emory Tolnay and E. M. Beck, *A Festival of Violence: An Analysis of Southern Lynchings, 1882–1930* (Urbana: University of Illinois Press, 1995).
24. De Fazio, "Improving Lynching Inventories."
25. Tolnay and Beck, *Festival of Violence*, 261.
26. For instance, Tolnay and Beck's *Festival of Violence* is the most comprehensive sociological study of the social, economic, and political factors that shaped the evolution of lynching in ten southern states; however, Virginia is not included in their analyses. While there are a few studies of individual Virginia lynchings (e.g., Ann Field Alexander, "'Like an Evil Wind': The Roanoke Riot of 1893 and the Lynching of Thomas Smith," *Virginia Magazine of History and Biography* 100, no. 2 [1992]: 173–206), comprehensive analyses of southern lynchings rarely mention Virginia.
27. Fitzhugh Brundage, *Lynching in the New South: Georgia and Virginia, 1880–1930* (Urbana: University of Illinois Press, 1993).
28. Stewart Tolnay and E. M. Beck. "Lynching." *New Georgia Encyclopedia*, last modified Aug. 12, 2020, https://www.georgiaencyclopedia.org/articles/history-archaeology/lynching/.
29. For instance, a lynching spree over two days in February 1893 killed six Black men in Tazewell County, and, in the same year, a white mob's attempt to lynch Thomas Smith provoked the Roanoke Riot, in which at least nine people died. The 1927 spectacle lynching of Leonard Woods in Wise County was the event that precipitated the passing of antilynching legislation in Virginia the following year.
30. In 1932 local and state authorities covered up the lynching of Shedrick Thompson in Fauquier County, classifying his death as a suicide to avoid the embarrassment of admitting that another lynching had occurred in Virginia; see Jim Hall, *The Last Lynching in Northern Virginia: Seeking Truth at Rattlesnake Mountain* (Charleston, SC: History Press, 2016). As historian Douglas Smith has noted, support by state officials for the antilynching law "seemed to be determined more by pride of Virginia's reputation than by concern for the well-being of the commonwealth's black populace." J. Douglas Smith, *Managing White Supremacy: Race, Politics, and Citizenship in Jim Crow Virginia* (Chapel Hill: University of North Carolina Press, 2002), 180.
31. Brundage, *Lynching in the New South*, 141.
32. Smith, *Managing White Supremacy*, 3.
33. In his published research, Beck reported more than three hundred episodes of threatened lynchings in Virginia: E. M. Beck, "Judge Lynch Denied: Combating Mob Violence in the American South, 1877–1950," *Southern Cultures* 21, no. 2 (2015): 117–39; Stewart E. Tolnay and E. M. Beck, "'Racialized Terrorism' in the American South: Do Completed Lynchings Tell an Accurate Story?," *Social Science History* 42, no. 4 (2018): 677–701. Since then, Beck has compiled additional cases, documenting more than six hundred threatened lynchings in Virginia. See also Kevin Hegg's essay in this volume.

34. Tolnay and Beck, *Racialized Terrorism*, 678.
35. *Roanoke Times*, July 10, 1890; *Clinch Valley News*, July 18, 1890; *Alexandria Gazette*, July 10, 1890; *Abingdon Weekly Virginian*, July 31, 1890. As of 2019, only 1 percent of the population in Russell County is Black: https://datausa.io/profile/geo/russell-county-va.
36. Tolnay and Beck, *Racialized Terrorism*; Campney, *This Is Not Dixie*.
37. Tolnay and Beck, *Festival of Violence*.
38. Two white men, Shayler B. Tate and A. L. Napier, were sentenced to two years in prison for their participation in the 1920 lynching of David Hunt, a Black man. After serving about half of their sentences, Virginia governor E. Lee Trinkle pardoned both men; Douglas Smith, *Managing White Supremacy*, 160–61. In 1899 six white men were found guilty of second-degree murder and sentenced to five to six years of prison for the lynching of Lee Puckett, a white man, in Patrick County (*The Times*, Jul. 4, 1899).
39. Alexander, "Like an Evil Wind."
40. Brundage, *Lynching in the New South*, 166–77. For an in-depth examination of Governor O'Ferrall and his complicated and sometimes contradictory campaign against lynching, see the essay by Charles T. Blair in this volume.
41. *Big Stone Gap Post*, Dec. 8, 1920. Walter F. White to A. P. Corden, Dec. 10, 1920, in NAACP Administrative files, lynching, Virginia.
42. Ann Field Alexander, *Race Man: The Rise and Fall of the "Fighting Editor," John Mitchell Jr.* (Charlottesville: University of Virginia Press, 2002). On the *Richmond Planet* antilynching crusade, see the essay by Dolores Flamiano in this volume.
43. Tolnay and Beck, *Racialized Terrorism*.
44. Campney, *This Is Not Dixie*.
45. See also Kidada Williams, *They Left Great Marks on Me* (New York: NYU Press, 2012).
46. Douglas Smith, *Managing White Supremacy*, 4.

PART I
✳
NEWSPAPERS AND LYNCHING NARRATIVES

It is hard to overestimate the importance of historical newspapers for understanding lynching in the Jim Crow South. Almost everything we know about lynching cases comes from news stories published at that time, as official sources of information, such as coroner's reports and death certificates, are only rarely available.[1] Court records are also scant, as in only a handful of cases did lynchers go to trial; newspapers, with all their biases, are thus the primary sources of lynching research. As Susan Jean notes, scholars' reliance on mostly white Southern newspapers "is extraordinarily problematic, for white southern newspapers helped to shape the racist discourse of their time, often through their reports on lynchings."[2] As there are no real alternatives to newspapers to systematically gather information about lethal mob violence, press reports need to be carefully contextualized and examined.[3]

Newspapers are constitutive of what we know about lynching not just because of their reporting of the "facts" (what they say happened) but, perhaps even more importantly, because of the way they framed those facts, the representations of those violent rituals.[4] Newspapers helped construct the meaning of lynching in different ways. At one level, even before a lynching had occurred, newspapers already contributed to the racial ideology that incited and justified white mob violence against Blacks. Anti-Black attitudes were built into newspapers' daily coverage of local and national news, spreading the toxic tropes of Black degeneracy and criminality. The image of the "Black rapist" threatening southern white women, and, by extension, white purity and supremacy, was the cornerstone of lynching apologia in the South. Newspapers reporting an alleged crime by a Black person typically followed a script that included inflammatory language, unsubstantiated accusations, and near-certainty of the accused's guilt, a combination that often led to a lynching. When reporting about a lynching, newspapers often used sensationalistic tones and provided very different representations for Black and white individuals. Black lynching victims were characterized as diabolic, fiendish, brutish ravishers; whites were instead "almost always represented positively: prominent, well-known, highly respected, popular in the city. Even mobs are described as controlled and silent, efficient in their business."[5] The implied "respectability" of the mob, often with the "most prominent citizens" at its helm, lent legitimacy to the mob's actions. When not directly inciting and celebrating mob justice, newspapers were often complicit with the lynchers, as they would fail to condemn their actions, provide their names, or call for a proper investigation and punishment for their extralegal acts.[6]

Not all white newspapers subscribed to these scripts, and some were, at times, vocally opposed to lynching. Especially from the 1920s onward, newspapers across the South had a harder time defending mob violence, as public opinion increasingly deemed lynching as unacceptable. Reporters thus started changing their coverage of lynching, more openly denouncing this barbaric practice.[7] The slow change in public opinion and authorities' willingness to curb mob violence was the result of decades of antilynching campaigning, mostly from Black activists and journalists like Ida B. Wells and organizations like the NAACP. John Mitchell Jr., the editor of the *Richmond Planet*, the leading Black newspaper in Virginia, was one of the staunchest critics of lynching.[8] As historian Fitzhugh Brundage notes, "Mitchell's single-handed [antilynching] campaign 'to howl, yes howl loudly, until the American people hear our cries'"[9] was instrumental in the decline of lynchings in Virginia.

The two essays in this section meticulously inspect the press coverage of two lynchings, highlighting newspapers' roles in creating and challenging lynching narratives. In "Impossible Love: An Interracial Romance in Post-Reconstruction Virginia," journalist and writer Jim Hall reconstructs the events leading to the 1880 lynching of Arthur Jordan in Fauquier County. Jordan, a Black farmhand, fell in love with Elvira Corder, the twenty-four-year-old daughter of his employer. After Elvira became pregnant, the couple fled to Maryland to start a new life together. When Elvira's family was able to locate the couple, they kidnapped Jordan and brought him back to Warrenton, Virginia, where he was put in jail. Two nights later, a mob took Jordan from the jail and hanged him. Newspapers in Virginia and elsewhere extensively covered this affair, as miscegenation stories elicited some of the strongest reactions in the white public. Reporters often described Jordan disparagingly as "large, bull necked and thick lipped, very black and forbidding-looking"; moreover, they did not accuse Jordan of any crime—he was simply assumed to be guilty. After the lynching, a newspaper quipped that Jordan went "where bad darkeys go via hemp." While some newspapers outside of Virginia condemned the lynching and asked for the lynchers to be punished, most Virginia papers were ambivalent at best about the murder, often providing rationalizations to excuse it. In so doing, white newspapers provided cover for mobs, ensuring their virtual impunity when acting against "bad darkeys."

In the second essay, media scholar Dolores Flamiano compares how Black and white newspapers covered a triple lynching in Alleghany County. The chapter "'You Shudder at the Picture': The *Richmond Planet* and the Lynching of Three Black Miners in Clifton Forge in 1891" unveils how white newspapers characterized the three lynched men as outlaws and desperados, while the Black press described them as victims of a vile attack by an angry mob. While white newspapers presented the lynching as a warranted instance of vigilante justice, the *Richmond Planet* depicted it as an unjustifiable murder of Black men who had been acting in self-defense. Notably, newspapers attempted to support their versions of the story with illustrations based on before-and-after photographs of the lynching victims. The *Richmond Planet* used a picture of the three men hanging from a tree as more than evidence of a specific lynching: it became a "symbolic marker of ongoing atrocity." By exposing false claims from the white press and providing additional details about the men who were lynched, the *Richmond Planet* challenged white newspapers' narratives and waged an antilynching campaign to promote state and federal intervention against mob violence.

Notes

1. Michael J. Pfeifer, *Rough Justice: Lynching and American Society 1874–1947* (Urbana: University of Illinois Press, 2004). In collaboration with the Library of Virginia, I have recently created an online repository of available archival records related to lynching in Virginia: Gianluca De Fazio, "Documenting Lynching in Virginia: A Transcription Project at James Madison University," *The UncommonWealth*, https://uncommonwealth.virginiamemory

.com/blog/2023/09/13/documenting-lynching-in-virginia-a-transcription-project-at-james-madison-university/.
2. Susan Jean, "'Warranted' Lynchings: Narratives of Mob Violence in White Southern Newspapers, 1880–1940," *American Nineteenth Century History* 6, no. 3 (2005): 353.
3. Roberto Franzosi, Gianluca De Fazio, and Stefania Vicari, "Ways of Measuring Agency: An Application of Quantitative Narrative Analysis to Lynchings in Georgia (1875–1930)," *Sociological Methodology* 42, no. 1 (2012): 9. Recently scholars have used oral history to provide new insights about lynching and its impact on the families of lynching victims and Black communities. However, this kind of research is very hard to replicate for thousands of lynching events. Karlos K. Hill, *Beyond the Rope: The Impact of Lynching on Black Culture and Memory* (Cambridge: Cambridge University Press, 2016).
4. Fitzhugh Brundage, "The Press and Lynching," in *Journalism and Jim Crow: White Supremacy and the Black Struggle for a New America*, eds. Kathy Robert Forde and Sid Bedingfield (Urbana: University of Illinois Press, 2021).
5. Franzosi, De Fazio and Vicari, "Ways of Measuring Agency," 26.
6. See also the digital project Printing Hate maintained by the Howard Center for Investigative Journalism, University of Maryland Philip Merrill College of Journalism, https://lynching.cnsmaryland.org/.
7. Jean, "'Warranted' Lynchings," 364.
8. Ann Field Alexander, *Race Man: The Rise and Fall of the "Fighting Editor," John Mitchell Jr.* (Charlottesville: University of Virginia Press, 2002).
9. Fitzhugh Brundage, "'To Howl Loudly': John Mitchell Jr. and His Campaign against Lynching in Virginia," *Canadian Review of American Studies* 22, no. 3 (1991): 338.

IMPOSSIBLE LOVE

An Interracial Romance in Post-Reconstruction Virginia

JIM HALL

At the Corder farm in northern Fauquier County, Virginia, the job of caring for the cows fell to Elvira, the daughter of a white couple, Nathan and Elizabeth Corder. Each afternoon she herded the animals into the barn and milked them.

Only later, after Elvira had run away with Arthur Jordan, a Black farmhand, did the family realize that their romance was apparent in how she did these chores. Elvira was later in returning to the house for supper each evening, and Arthur had started carrying the milk pails for her from the barn to the dairy. The Corders, later described as one of the "first families" of the county, thought little of it at the time.

Then, during the Christmas season of 1879, the couple ran away together. Elvira was pregnant, and the pair fled, eventually settling in western Maryland. Nathan Corder followed but could not find them, and a policeman who spoke to him in Alexandria, Virginia, described him as angry and heartbroken. He had promised his wife he would bring Elvira back "dead or alive." As for Arthur, who was already a married man with an infant daughter, "I certainly will kill him," Nathan said.[1]

For all their careful planning and defiance, Elvira and Arthur did not anticipate how her family and neighbors would react to their flight. Or perhaps they did and didn't care. If so, it was a fatal mistake, for theirs was an impossible love.

By January 1880, Arthur was hanging from a tree in the Warrenton Cemetery in Fauquier. Elvira was alone, still in Maryland, never to return home or be heard of again.

Jordan's death came near the beginning of a new, violent era in Virginia and the South, a fifty-year lynching nightmare. The reasons for his murder and the way it occurred were repeated hundreds of times in the coming decades. His death and others in those early years also illustrate a lethal change in Virginia's attitude towards interracial intimacy.

We have no photos of Elvira, only the descriptions that appeared in news stories at the time. She was about twenty-five, the eldest child and only daughter, and big sister to brothers John, Will, and Charles. Her mother, Bettie, died before Elvira was nine. Nathan remarried, this time to a wealthy widow and distant relative, Elizabeth Corley. When Elizabeth joined the household, she brought with her Ann, her fifteen-year-old daughter, and William, her thirteen-year-old son.

Elvira would have shared in the housework, the farm chores, and the care of her younger brothers. Her duties no doubt increased after her mother died and may have changed again with the arrival of Elizabeth and her children. Did the new arrivals share in the chores, or, Cinderella-like, add to them?

Elvira's relationship with her stepmother apparently was not close. Years later, when Elvira began the secret relationship with Arthur and their romance exploded into view, Elizabeth was as surprised and angry as others. Elvira had never confided in her.

As the daughter of a yeoman farmer, Elvira would have been capable and independent, the result of dawn-to-dusk farm work. She probably knew how to hitch a plow and where to find the best pond ice. She had attended school until at least age fourteen and could read and write. But her world appears to have been limited, typical of life in the small farms and villages of rural Virginia. There is no evidence that Elvira had ever married, lived anywhere but Fauquier, or done anything but farmwork.

Reporters described Elvira as pretty, petite, and buxom. Yet each compliment was followed by a condescending assessment of her intellect. She was said to be simple, half-witted, and an unsophisticated maiden.[2]

In press accounts she was a victim rather than a willing participant in the relationship with Arthur. Only then could readers begin to understand why a young white woman would run off with a married Black man.

Later, another explanation for her behavior appeared in news accounts. This scenario held that Arthur had forced himself on her and threatened to kill her if she told anyone. "Desperate, despairing and made wild with grief and shame, the poor girl consented," said one report.[3]

Missing from this narrative of assault is any possibility that their relationship was consensual. Later events would indicate that, despite the taboos, the couple had fallen in love. She had saved money for their elopement, then, like Shakespeare's Jessica, stole money from her father. In addition, the couple boarded a train for Washington, DC, from separate stations. They carried out this plan without anyone becoming suspicious.

A decade later, civil rights advocate Ida Wells-Barnett wrote that southern white men refused to recognize an alliance between a white woman and a Black man—that a relationship was proof of force. Yet, she said, these liaisons were usually "voluntary and clandestine."

"There are white women in the South who love the Afro-American's company, even as there are white men notorious for their preference for Afro-American women," she wrote.[4]

Perhaps most revealing was Elvira's reaction when her father and his friends arrived unexpectedly to kidnap the couple from their new home in Maryland. When Elvira saw what was happening, she did not react as if she were a prisoner being rescued. Instead, she realized that her lover and the father of her unborn child was being forced to return to Fauquier and would probably be killed. She was "very indignant at such proceedings and refused to be comforted, although one of the young gentlemen did all in his power to console her," said one news story.[5]

Instead of returning her to her home in Fauquier County, one of the riders took Elvira to nearby Williamsport, Maryland, and placed her in the Taylor Hotel in the care of the hotelier. Newspapers reported that the family would return to Maryland for her and travel home by train because of her "delicate" condition.

Yet there is no evidence that Elvira ever returned home. Her fate is the most mysterious aspect of her story. After her arrival at the hotel, she all but disappears from the public record. News stories vividly described Arthur's kidnapping and death, but they barely mentioned Elvira. She does not appear in later census records or court records. Her child, presumably born in mid-1880, does not appear in any Washington County, Maryland, records, including adoption records.

The only clue to Elvira's fate is a cryptic mention in her father's will, written in 1890, ten years after her alliance with Arthur. In the first part of the document, he makes an equal division of his holdings among his wife and sons.

He mentions Elvira in paragraph four: "This is to certify that I have not overlooked my daughter Elvira Corder who died in the State of Maryland and to whom and to her issue should she have left any, I give and grant them one cent as their sole interest in my estate."[6]

Nathan does not say how, when, or exactly where she died. It is interesting to consider what he meant by Elvira's "death." It is possible, given her disappearance from the records, that she did die. But it is also possible that Nathan disowned her, that she died a social death because of the dishonor she brought to him and his family.

What seems certain, however, was her father's anger. Ten years after Elvira's flight, Nathan was still upset and again punished her and her child. As Capulet told his daughter in *Romeo and Juliet*, "What is mine shall never do thee good."[7]

In one sentence, he protected himself and his heirs from them. He owned three hundred acres of valuable farmland, yet he left her only a hostile token: a penny.

He Generally Presented a Neat Appearance

In Arthur, Elvira chose a man who was twenty-five, like her, and like her, a native of Fauquier. He was the second of five children, born about 1855 to Henry and Lizzie Jordan. Like his father, he was a laborer. He did not read or write and apparently had little schooling.

The Jordans were probably once enslaved people since there is no mention of them in census records or in any listing of free Negroes in Fauquier. By the 1870 census, however, the records show a scattered family, apparently because of Henry's death. Arthur, then sixteen, was living with the extended Peter King family and other unrelated adults. His two sisters, Polly and Elizabeth, were on their own. His mother, with her two youngest sons, was living in the household of Thomas Diggs, working as the white family's servant.

On the day after Christmas 1878, Arthur married the former Anna Roe, twenty-one, also of Fauquier. The following year Anna gave birth to an infant daughter, Annie. Arthur was working for the Corders at the time. He and his family lived in the Carter's Run Church section of the county, south of the Corder farm.

As with Elvira, the only descriptions we have of Arthur are those that appeared in newspapers after the couple fled. The most detailed of these was in the *Alexandria Gazette,* a regional daily. The *Gazette* correspondent interviewed Jordan as he and his captors were on their way from Maryland to the jail in Warrenton. The riders stopped for a few moments in Orlean, Virginia, a village south of the Corder farm. The reporter described Arthur as about six feet tall, 160 pounds, "black as a crow," and "by no means prepossessing."[8] In another story, Arthur is described as "remarkably well built," with a well-shaped head. "His hands and feet were not as large as the common run of negroes. His hair was always well combed, and he generally presented a neat appearance."[9]

Jordan was said to be reliable and hardworking. He was also confident and independent, qualities that Elvira may have found attractive. However, to others he seemed impudent, even defiant. His bearing was noted in several accounts and seems to have been as galling to his white captors as his alliance with Elvira.

Arthur would have been about ten years old when the Civil War ended. He would have grown up in a new climate, one in which young Black men rejected the rituals of submission. They were "undisciplined by slavery and unschooled in proper racial etiquette," wrote historian Leon Litwack. "This new generation could not be trusted to stay in its place without force."[10]

When the *Gazette* correspondent interviewed Arthur, still bound on horseback, Jordan defended himself, saying he had done nothing wrong. He and Elvira had run away on the one-year anniversary of his marriage to Anna and one month after the birth of their daughter. When told that his departure had thrown his wife into spasms, he replied, "I don't care if it did." The paper added that "he was very indifferent to his fate."[11]

In fact, Jordan was defiant throughout his ordeal, including in the Warrenton jail when mob members entered his cell and asked, "Which one of you is Jordan?" Jordan must have known why the men were there, yet he stood from his blanket and replied, "I am." Later, as the mob dragged him toward the cemetery, he continued to cry for help until one of the men silenced him.

She Was Carrying Nathan's First Grandchild

Arthur and Elvira were adventurous for ignoring the barriers erected by white men to constrain women and Black people. But they also clung to the fanciful notion that in 1880 Virginia they could flee the Corder farm and live happily ever after. As Suzanne Jones has noted, when novelists of the nineteenth and early twentieth centuries tell stories of interracial romance, they usually describe them as "tragic impossibilities" with an "irresolvable conflict" at their core.[12] It is an apt portrayal of Arthur and Elvira.

Elvira's actions, especially her unwed pregnancy, hint at dysfunction within her family. It is possible her relationship with Arthur was in some way a rebellion against her father. Or she may have simply enjoyed his affections. To her family, however, Elvira's pregnancy was dishonorable. She was carrying her father's first grandchild, yet he wanted nothing to do with the baby.

The couple's romance was easily concealed, at least for a while. As historian Martha Hodes has noted, southern white women knew that if they had an affair with a Black man, he wouldn't say anything for fear of being killed. "The woman has only to avoid being impregnated and it is all safe," she writes.[13] Indeed, Elvira's pregnancy changed what was probably a months-long affair. No longer could they meet in private; an alternate plan, in this case flight, was needed.

The two began their journey on a train headed east from Fauquier. They boarded the train from separate stations about ten miles apart and presumably sat in separate cars, given the racial restrictions of the time. They passed through Alexandria and ended the first leg of their journey in Washington, DC.

The couple continued their trip, probably by train, to Washington County, Maryland, a farm region near the Pennsylvania border. There, they lived and worked with the Shupp family, just north of Williamsport. Abraham Shupp and son Charles owned farms in the region. It's not clear why Arthur and Elvira chose western Maryland or if one of them knew the Shupps.

By all accounts, they were happy at the farm, even venturing into nearby Williamsport. But the sight of an interracial couple and pregnant white woman offended at least one Williamsport resident. He sent a letter to the Markham post office near the Corder farm, revealing where the couple was living. The letter found its way to Nathan, who asked his neighbors for help. Four volunteered to ride with him to confront the couple in Maryland.

With this invitation, the romance of Arthur and Elvira changed from a family dilemma to a community affair. The volunteers were leading citizens of the region, including Civil War veterans. They united in retribution, drawn by what sociologist Mattias Smångs has described as the "fellowship of the hunt."[14]

The men rode north for about eighty miles, stopping for the night in Williamsport, where one observer described them as "well dressed, well mounted and heavily armed."[15] After breakfast, they continued to the Shupp farm, where they surprised Arthur as he was cleaning stables. Like antebellum slave-catchers, they shackled him and headed for home. When the party recrossed the Potomac and reached Winchester, Virginia, about forty miles south of Williamsport, Arthur fought back.

It is not clear why the men stopped in Winchester, a Shenandoah Valley town of about five thousand people. As they rode down Loudoun Street, in front of Robinson's Hardware, Arthur, in the words of a Winchester paper, "made a great outcry, shouting 'police' and 'help.'"[16] He refused to go farther, even though two of the men whipped his horse and yelled for him to move on. A crowd gathered, including two policemen. Arthur said he was being abducted and wanted to see a lawyer. Black people in the crowd ran to find an attorney, while the officers took the riders and Arthur to see a local judge.

Judge Crebs heard their stories and sided with the white men. Crebs swore in one of the men as a special constable and instructed the group to deliver their prisoner to the Warrenton jail. Meanwhile, Black residents found an attorney, but when they reached Crebs's office, the party was gone. The Black residents were said to be "greatly excited"[17] and predicted correctly that Jordan would be lynched.

The incident in Winchester, though it probably took less than an hour, illustrates what would become a decades-long reality for Black residents of Virginia. With emancipation, the end of the Civil War, and the passage of the 13th, 14th, and 15th Amendments, Black males at least could hope to become full citizens in a democratic system. But little had changed. If these white men wanted to cross a state line and kidnap a Black man and later hang him, nobody was going to stop them.

They Raised Their Crops and Paid Their Debts

Fauquier County was then and still is an agricultural county, part of Virginia's Piedmont region. It shares the rugged terrain of the Blue Ridge Mountains to the west and the fertile coastal plain to the east.

Nathan Corder moved to Fauquier from adjacent Rappahannock County in the years before the Civil War. He had been farming in Rappahannock and living with his widowed mother and four of his siblings. When his mother died, the family moved to Fauquier, where a younger brother, Butler, had already settled. Nathan was thirty-eight and married to his cousin Bettie Cowgill. They had one child, two-year-old Elvira.

Within two years, Nathan and Butler were joined by their younger brother A. B. Corder. The three families lived next to one another and numbered about eighteen people, including the children.

The Corders' farm, called Wheatfields, covered about five hundred leased acres. It was bigger than the farms of many of their neighbors but still one step below the county's largest farms.

Before emancipation the Corder brothers used slaves to do much of the work. County tax records show Nathan and Butler owned five slaves. They also rented slaves from their neighbors, paying for a year's labor.

After Elvira and Arthur ran away, a newspaper described the Corders as "plain, hard-working, honest people, who asked no favors, tilled the ground, and paid their debts."[18] Yet their reputation suffered when Elvira fled.

Young women were expected to be restrained, abstinent, and, most of all, subordinate. As historian Crystal N. Feimster has noted, "Southern white women were legally subordinated to and economically dependent on their fathers and husbands. They had little choice but to accept paternalistic domination in exchange for male protection and a measure of discrete power within the household."[19]

We have no way of knowing what Elvira was thinking when she chose Arthur and later fled with him. She was twenty-five and may have underestimated the forces she would unleash. She had indulged her desires and now was the unchaste daughter. She had exposed herself and her family to public censure.

As Atticus Finch said of Mayella Ewell, a white woman who made sexual advances towards Tom Robinson, a Black man, in *To Kill a Mockingbird:* "She has broken a rigid and time-honored code of our society, a code so severe that whoever breaks it is hounded from our midst as unfit to live with."[20]

One indication of this disgrace can be seen in the coverage of the local weekly newspaper, the *True Index*. Its editor understood reader interest in the story, so about two weeks after the couple's flight, the paper reported on their disappearance, how she had stolen money from her father, and how Arthur had abandoned his wife and child for "the erring girl." But the paper also decided that the details were just too sordid. It said that Elvira "brought the gray hairs of an old father in sorrow down to the grave. Out of sympathy for his distressed family, we suppress names."[21]

The Mother of American Slavery

Virginia's ban against interracial intimacy was more than two hundred years old when Arthur and Elvira began their relationship. Since colonial times, those who crossed the color line for sex or marriage were told their love was unnatural and illegal. As legal scholars A. Leon Higginbotham and Barbara K. Kopytoff note, "Many people applaud Virginia as the 'mother of presidents' and the 'mother of revolutionaries.' Yet few stress that colonial Virginia was also the 'mother of American slavery' and a leader in the gradual debasement of blacks."[22]

Prohibitions against racial mixing first appeared in the seventeenth century and continued for almost three hundred years. Violators were subject to fines, jail time, banishment, corporal punishment, and, for indentured servants, extended service. Children born to enslaved mothers became enslaved themselves. A white woman who bore a mixed-race child was fined, and if she couldn't pay, church wardens could auction her services for a term of five years. Mixed-race children were bound out until they reached adulthood.

The language used in these miscegenation laws—phrases like "abominable mixture"—reveal how white people felt about their Black neighbors. White residents saw themselves as defenders of their civilization and beneficiaries of a natural order that rated Black people as inferior and subservient. After Arthur's lynching, one account praised the mob's action, calling it the "execution of a solemn duty in thus avenging the violation of one of the most sacred unwritten laws of society."[23]

Virginia and the rest of the southern states were the first to adopt these laws and the last to abandon them. When the US Supreme Court ruled in *Loving v. Virginia* in 1967 that laws banning interracial marriage were unconstitutional, sixteen states still had them on the books.

Whiteness was the preferred identity, and the law protected this "fictional white purity from mixture," writes law professor Sheryll Cashin.[24] Chief Justice Earl Warren, writing for the court in the Loving case, reviewed Virginia's long history of racial discrimination and said it was "designed to maintain White Supremacy."[25]

Ironically, Arthur and Elvira might have found Fauquier to be more tolerant had the year been 1860, rather than 1880. Historians such as Martha Hodes have traced a change in southern attitudes toward interracial romances. Before the Civil War, many communities practiced forbearance, though not approval, when a white woman was intimate with a Black man. "White neighbors judged harshly, gossiped viciously, and could completely ostracize the transgressing white woman," notes Hodes. "As for the black man, it was a lack of sure violence that is historically significant."[26]

Later, without the structure of slavery, white residents sought to rebuild the world they had known. "The early years of Reconstruction marked the beginning of an era of terrorism in the American South," Hodes writes. "Those vanquished patriarchs and their sympathizers replaced slavery with lethal violence in an effort to maintain control."[27]

The Virginia Supreme Court blessed this bias in 1878, two years before Arthur and Elvira ran away. Andrew Kinney, a Black man, and Mahala Miller, a white woman, had been living together, unmarried, with their three sons in Augusta County. They feared being charged with cohabitation, so they went to Washington to be married, knowing they could not be married in Virginia. However, when they returned home, they were charged with "lewdly associating and cohabiting." Local officials believed that their marriage in Washington was no bar to prosecution. Finally, on appeal, the state supreme court ruled against the couple, with Justice Joseph Christian voicing the racism that had been a ruling principle in Virginia since colonial times: "The purity of public morals, the moral and physical development of both races, and the highest advancement of our cherished Southern civilization" require that the races be kept "distinct and separate," he wrote.[28]

To Christian, romance across the color line was unthinkable.

Prisoner from Rectortown

The NAACP would later list community support as one of the defining features of lynching, and this can be seen in Jordan's death. Nathan and his sons did not kill Jordan by themselves in an act of blood revenge. Instead, they sought the help of their friends and neighbors.

The end came four days after Arthur's kidnapping in Maryland, while he was confined in the Fauquier jail in Warrenton, the county seat. That night, a Sunday in January 1880, at least forty men rode together from northern Fauquier. One eyewitness reported being awakened by the rumble of the horsemen as they entered town. Some of the men approached the jail, while others stayed with the horses.

The men were intent on murder, yet their bravado had its limits. They arrived in darkness, abducted Jordan, killed him, and quickly rode away. Said one news account, "The remarkable part of this lynching was the entire absence of excitement."[29] Walter White, executive secretary of the NAACP, would later ridicule lynchers as cowards who were willing to participate in the crime as long as it involved no personal risk.[30]

The self-appointed avengers chose a public place for Jordan's execution, the town cemetery near the jail, rather than a remote site outside town. This aspect of lynching was repeated often in later years as victims were killed at the county courthouse or on city streets, as was the case in downtown Alexandria, where lynchers left the body suspended for all to see, since their goals were intimidation and punishment.

When Jordan's killers seized him at the county jail, they deceived jailer Horace Pattie, using a ruse that would be repeated often in future years. It began when the men blackened the face of one of their own, tied his hands and banged on the jail door.

"What do you want?" Pattie said from an upstairs window after they awakened him.

"Prisoner from Rectortown," they replied.

Pattie opened the door and was immediately overwhelmed by intruders. He tried to hide the keys to the cells, but one of the men saw what he was doing and retrieved them. Some of the men held Pattie at gunpoint in the jail's courtyard, while others went to the cellblock to get Jordan.

The dim light at the cell door made it hard to see, but another inmate, Anthony Smith, counted maybe eight invaders, all armed and all but two masked. Their leader was unmasked, and another inmate, Frank Matthews, described him as stout but not tall, with a full, short beard.

"Keep still and you won't get hurt," the man told Matthews and Smith.[31]

The man tied Jordan's hands behind his back. He also placed an oak stick in Jordan's mouth to serve as a gag. The stick had a piece of leather at each end, which the man tied behind Jordan's head. The man also attached a long rope to Jordan's upper arm and led him from the cell.

The man ordered the other inmates to lie down, which they did. "They frightened me," Smith said later.

The men locked the cell door and marched Jordan back to the courtyard. One of them returned the keys to Pattie and told his guards, "Let the old man go."

Pattie's family also lived at the jail, and when his teenage son, Caldwell, realized what was happening, he ran for the town sergeant.

"How many of them are there?" the sergeant asked.

"About forty," the younger Pattie replied.

"That's too many. I'm going back to bed," the town sergeant said.[32]

Critics such as newspaper editor John Mitchell Jr. would later accuse jailers of cowardice and complicity. Mitchell pointed out that authorities generally did not move their prisoners to distant jails for safety, station extra guards on duty, or ask state authorities for help. One study of Virginia lynchings found that in more than one third of the cases, lynchers met with indifference, even cooperation, from local jailers.[33] Jailers surrendered keys or stood aside and let the lynchers take their prisoners. "Very few peace officers defend their prisoners to the point of endangering themselves," said one report on lynching.[34]

The men left as they had entered, through the front door. When Pattie got there, he could hear their retreat south from the jail on what was then Seventh Street. The mob pushed and pulled Jordan toward Lee Street, then down the hill to their destination a few hundred yards away, the Warrenton Cemetery.

By then, Jordan, bound and gagged, must have realized he was being led to his death. He spit the gag from his mouth and twice cried for help. After the second scream, one of the men struck him just above the eye with his rifle butt. The blow knocked him to the ground, unconscious. Someone took the rope that had been on Jordan's arm and placed it around his neck. From there, "willing hands," said one news story, dragged him to the cemetery. His body left an impression in the muddy lane.

At the cemetery, the mob chose a hanging tree in the rear of the property. Other trees could have served as Jordan's scaffold, but this one offered symbolic sacrifice at the base of the new Confederate Memorial a few yards away. One of the county's most prominent landmarks, the white obelisk had been erected three years earlier to mark the burial of hundreds of Confederate soldiers killed early in the Civil War.

The men departed the cemetery after hanging Jordan, no doubt satisfied with themselves. From their point of view, their plan had worked perfectly. They had ridden into town unchallenged, tricked Pattie, and seized and killed the prisoner without firing a shot.

With their actions the lynchers displayed their distrust of the judicial system in Fauquier, preferring to administer punishment that was certain, speedy, and terrible. For mobs like these, it was not the absence of a criminal justice system that mattered but rather its style. The law was "too capricious, too unpredictable, too formal, too abstract and too concerned with process," writes historian Michael J. Pfeifer.[35]

With their actions, the mob spared the Corders from having to testify in court. Elvira did not have to describe her relationship with Arthur or detail her sexual history. The mob returned to their homes in northern Fauquier, never to be charged with Jordan's murder.

The lynchers sent a message of fear and vulnerability to African Americans in Fauquier. To the white community, their message was one of solidarity and empowerment. It was also a matter of honor. They would long be able to boast of what they had done. It would become a part of how they saw themselves.[36]

From Jordan's point of view, just the opposite was true. The nightmare that began with his abduction in Maryland had ended with his murder in

Virginia. He had tried but failed to save himself. He did not have a chance to defend himself or challenge his accusers in court. His love for a white woman, unremarkable in another time or place, had resulted in his death.

By morning, town residents had gathered at the cemetery to see the man in the tree. One of the spectators was Dr. Gustavus R. B. Horner, a local physician, who made a pencil sketch of what he saw.

Jordan's body, suspended from one of the leafless branches of a tree, dominates Horner's drawing. He is pictured barefoot, wearing a workman's shirt and pants cinched at the waist, with his hands tied behind him. Horner's Jordan is a man of medium height and weight, less than six feet tall, who looks older than his twenty-five years. He has a round face with a mustache and close-cropped hair. The physician added a caption that says, "Arthur Jordan, hung by men unknown at Warrenton, 2 o'clock a.m., Monday, Jan. 19th, 1880."[37]

A coroner's jury assembled after Jordan's body was cut down. It produced a sixteen-page report, describing in detail his seizure and death. The jurors concluded that Jordan died "by unlawful violence, by strangulation with a rope around his neck." The mob that killed him numbered between forty and sixty men, "whose names are unknown to us," the jurors added.[38]

The verdict would become a familiar one, as local officials rarely charged lynchers. As one civil rights group concluded, "It is obvious that in most communities where lynching occurs, it is not considered a crime."[39]

Turn My Back and Shut My Eyes

The Virginia House of Delegates was in session in Richmond when Jordan was murdered, and the members took up the case two days after his death.

A Black delegate from Norfolk, Richard G. L. Paige, pointed out that Jordan died two weeks after the lynching of another Black man, Columbus Miles, in Amherst County. Paige wanted Gov. Frederick Holliday to post a reward for the capture of the persons responsible and to bring them to trial.

"The question is whether an armed mob can take without any signs of justice and hang the citizens of this Commonwealth, be they black or white," he said.[40]

Paige was born a slave in Norfolk. By 1880 he was a successful attorney and one of the early leaders of the college that became Hampton University.[41]

William Henry Fitzhugh Payne, a white legislator and a lawyer from Fauquier, rose to oppose Paige. Payne was a hero of the Confederacy during the Civil War, a brigadier general who was wounded several times in battle.

Both Paige and Payne were natives of the state and men of struggle and achievement. One was young, Black, and unafraid to test the limits of the new freedoms. The other was white, almost fifty, and longing for a lost order. Their standoff in the House that day was brief but serves as a mirror on the state of race relations and a preview of the terror that was to come.

Payne defended the mob's murder of Jordan, describing him as a married man who had seduced a naive young white woman. "He was in the employment of the father, and using his power and position in the house, he seduced this idiotic child and carried her out of the state as his mistress," Payne said.

Payne then spoke for many white southerners when in a single sentence he offered a defense of lynching. His words, spoken from the floor of the state capitol by an elected member of the assembly, may not have surprised the Black legislators seated around him or the Black residents of the state, but they must have been discouraging. If Black people had any hope of equal rights under the law in a new postwar Virginia, they now had to temper that hope.

"When such a thing as this happens," Payne said, "I will turn my back and shut my eyes for a few minutes while the operations are going on."[42]

The assembly applauded, and Payne asked that Paige's motion be sent to committee, effectively killing it. The vote was 69–13: all of the Black delegates opposed it, and all but one of the white delegates supported it.

Seized, Gagged, and Ferociously Murdered

Local officials may have been indifferent about Jordan's death, but newspaper editors were not. At least forty papers published stories about Arthur and Elvira, including publications as far away as Australia and New Zealand. Thanks to the telegraph, readers in Pittsburgh, Minneapolis, Baltimore, New York, Richmond, Norfolk, Washington, DC, and St. Louis learned about the hanging. The regional *Alexandria Gazette* carried seven stories, including stories on four consecutive days. Editors recognized in Arthur and Elvira a timeless tale of forbidden love, a mix of sex, race, and violence.

In these stories Jordan was never *accused* or *alleged* to have done anything wrong. He was always assumed to be guilty. The stories also used racial epithets, the same slurs seen later to describe other lynching victims. In lynching coverage by Virginia newspapers from 1880 to 1900, almost half the stories portrayed Black victims as menacing and animal-like, or, as in Jordan's case, "large, bull necked and thick lipped, very black and forbidding-looking." After death, he was said to have gone "where bad darkeys go via hemp."[43]

In these and other ways, coverage in white-owned papers inspired and excused lynching. Even though it was murder they were commenting on, editorial writers didn't voice full-throated criticism. They wavered, often defending the mob's action as justifiable, citing delays in court procedure or the uncertainty of punishment. What happened to Jordan was terrible but understandable given his crimes, editorials said. One would expect a father to chase after the couple and bring them home, they said, but what happened after that was regrettable.

In this way, newspapers excused felonious behavior and tried to please their communities rather than challenge them. It would be decades before white-owned papers would muster any serious opposition to lynching. According to critic Jesse Ames, "The [papers] find themselves in the difficult position of a rider who must sit two horses at the same time, one facing backward, the other forward."[44]

Later, Black editors and critics, such as Mitchell and Wells-Barnett, began to "howl loudly" at the practice. To them, lynch victims were human souls made in God's image with a right to life. Lynching violated their constitutional guarantees but also hurt the community, they argued, by driving capital and prosperity from the door.

Mitchell waged a relentless campaign against lynching in his weekly newspaper, the *Richmond Planet*. He wrote editorials, ran lists of lynch victims, and printed photos of lynchings. "You Shudder at the Picture! Of Course You Do," said the headline accompanying a picture of three lynch victims hanging from a tree in Clifton Forge in 1891.

"Mitchell filled the *Planet* with eyewitness accounts and reported lynchings that failed to reach the white press," writes historian Ann Field Alexander.[45]

After Jordan's death, there was little published criticism from within Fauquier. One Warrenton resident wrote to the *Richmond Dispatch*, criticizing the hanging, though he was not concerned for Jordan as an innocent man, or as a father, husband, brother, and son. He feared that the lynching made Warrenton look bad.[46]

Criticism came from elsewhere, including Lebanon, Pennsylvania, where the local paper asked Maryland governor William Hamilton to extradite those responsible for Jordan's kidnapping.[47] In Harrisburg, Pennsylvania, the paper said the state legislature's inaction was an endorsement of lynching.[48]

The *Religious Herald*, a weekly in Richmond, Virginia, offered what would become a common type of newspaper editorial, cynically described as the "two-handed" approach. On the one hand, the paper said, nobody opposed the mixing of the races more than it did. On the other hand, Jordan's death was inexcusable: "A public building is entered fraudulently," it said, "the custodian is overpowered, and a man, innocent in the eyes and judgment of the law, is seized, gagged and ferociously murdered."[49]

The *Weekly Louisianian* in New Orleans adopted a similar approach, finding merit and misconduct in the lynching. In a front-page editorial, the paper said it understood how an angry people might resort to lynching when the alleged crime is "particularly odious."

But Elvira was an adult and could do as she pleased, it said. A man was killed even though Elvira was not a minor, it added, and there was no hint of violence on Arthur's part.[50]

The *Alexandria Gazette* flirted with condemnation of the murder, but also stopped short, recognizing that if Elvira was an "imbecile," Jordan's murder was understandable. However, added the paper, "it would have been infinitely better to have allowed the law, which had the culprit in its hands, to have meted out the prescribed punishment."[51]

In Winchester, Virginia, after the riders departed town with a shackled Jordan in tow, residents predicted that he would be hanged. Not so, reported the local paper. This was because two of the riders had served with Col. Turner Ashby's famed cavalry unit in the Confederate Army. "They are bold and daring fellows, some of whom followed the plume of Ashby in the late war, but they are not of the lawless sort," the paper reported.[52]

In truth, the men were lawless in all they had done. If a posse is an armed body of men summoned by a sheriff to pursue a criminal, these men were not a posse. They were terrorists, and what they did was an act of terror, a preview of the violence that would befall Black people for decades to come.

On the morning of his death, Jordan's body was cut down from the tree in the cemetery and taken to the courthouse for the coroner's inquest. His final resting place was in the "colored cemetery," presumably the Black section of the Warrenton Cemetery, in what is today an unmarked grave.

As Wells-Barnett wrote years later of lynching victims, "They had no requiem, save the night wind, no memorial service to bemoan their sad and horrible fate. Their bodies lie in many an unknown and unhonored spot."[53]

Notes

1. "More Miscegenation," *Winchester Times*, Dec. 19, 1879, 2.
2. "Lynched by a Mob: A Negro Fiend in Virginia Hanged to a Tree," *Washington Post*, Jan. 20, 1880, 1; "Lynch Law in Virginia," *South Branch* (WV) *Intelligencer*, Jan. 23, 1880, 2.
3. "The Lynching of Arthur Jordan," *Alexandria Gazette*, Jan. 20, 1880, 2.
4. Ida B. Wells-Barnett, *On Lynchings* (Salem: Ayer Co., 1993), 11.
5. "The Lynching of Arthur Jordan," *Alexandria Gazette*, Jan. 21, 1880, 2.
6. Will Book 40, Page 250, Fauquier County (VA), Circuit Court Clerk's Office, Warrenton.
7. William Shakespeare, *Romeo and Juliet* (New York: Simon & Schuster, 1992), Act 3, Scene 5, Line 206.
8. "Lynching of Jordan," *Alexandria Gazette*, Jan. 21, 1880, 2.
9. "The Lynching of Arthur Jordan," *Alexandria Gazette*, Jan. 22, 1880, 2; "Lynching of Jordan," *Alexandria Gazette*, Jan. 21, 1880, 2.
10. Leon F. Litwack, *Without Sanctuary* (Santa Fe: Twin Palms Publishers, 2000), 11.
11. "Lynching of Jordan," *Alexandria Gazette*, Jan. 21, 1880, 2.
12. Suzanne W. Jones, *Race Mixing: Southern Fiction since the Sixties* (Baltimore: Johns Hopkins University Press, 2004), 149.
13. Martha Hodes, "Illicit Sex across the Color Line: White Women and Black Men in the Civil War South," *Critical Matrix* 5, no. 1 (Dec. 31, 1989): 29.
14. Mattias Smangs, "Doing Violence, Making Race: Southern Violence and White Racial Group Formation," *American Journal of Sociology* 121, no. 5 (March 2016): 1338.
15. "Our Neighbors," *Martinsburg Independent*, Jan. 24, 1880, 1.
16. "An Unnatural Elopement," *Winchester Times*, Jan. 21, 1880, 3.
17. "Excitement at Williamsport: A Raid into Maryland, Seizure of a Negro for Abducting a White Girl," *Virginia Star*, Jan. 21, 1880, 2.
18. "Lynching of Jordan," *Alexandria Gazette*, Jan. 20, 1880, 2.
19. Crystal N. Feimster, *Southern Horrors: Women and the Politics of Rape and Lynching* (Cambridge, MA: Harvard University Press, 2009), 9.
20. Harper Lee, *To Kill a Mockingbird* (New York: Harper Perennial Modern Classics, 1960), 231.
21. (Fredericksburg) *Virginia Star*, Jan. 10, 1880, 3.

22. A. Leon Higginbotham Jr. and Barbara K. Kopytoff, "Racial Purity and Interracial Sex in the Law of Colonial and Antebellum Virginia," *Georgetown Law Journal* 77 (August 1989): 1967–2025.
23. "Virginia Vengeance: Lynching a Negro for Social Indiscretion," *St. Louis Post-Dispatch*, Jan. 22, 1880, 2.
24. Sheryll Cashin, *Loving: Interracial Intimacy in America and the Threat to White Supremacy* (Boston: Beacon Press, 2017), 5.
25. Cashin, *Loving*, 3.
26. Martha Hodes, *White Women, Black Men* (New Haven, CT: Yale University Press, 1997), 3.
27. Hodes, *White Women*, 148.
28. Peter Wallenstein, *Tell the Court I Love My Wife: Race, Marriage, and Law—An American History* (New York: Palgrave Macmillan, 2002), 153.
29. "The Virginia Lynching: The Quiet Mob that Hanged a Negro for Running Away with a White Girl," *Lancaster* (PA) *Daily Intelligencer*, Jan. 21, 1880, 3.
30. Walter White, "I Investigate Lynchings," *American Mercury*, Jan. 1929, 77.
31. "Coroner's Inquest of Arthur Jordan, January 19, 1880," Afro-American Historical Association of Fauquier County, Arch 02329, 4–6, 12–13, https://aaha.pastperfectonline.com/archive/F06DF3B8-140A-419C-A4A9-384843315858.
32. "Coroner's Inquest," AAHA, 13.
33. James E. Hall, "Black and White: A Historical Examination of Lynching Coverage and Editorial Impact in Select Virginia Newspapers" (MA thesis, Virginia Commonwealth University, December 2001), 38.
34. Commission on Interracial Cooperation, *The Mob Still Rides: A Review of the Lynching Record, 1931–1935* (Atlanta: Commission on Interracial Cooperation, 1936), 12.
35. Michael J. Pfeifer, *Rough Justice: Lynching and American Society, 1874–1947* (Urbana: University of Illinois Press, 2004), 67.
36. Smangs, "Doing Violence," 1338.
37. Dr. Gustavus R. B. Horner, *Papers of Horner and Horner Family*, Albert and Shirley Small Special Collections Library, University of Virginia, MSS 379, Box I, Diary 10 (1876–1880), 202–4.
38. "Coroner's Inquest," AAHA, 3.
39. Commission on Interracial Cooperation, *Mob Still Rides*, 11.
40. "Recent Lynchings," *Richmond Daily Dispatch*, Jan. 22, 1880, 2.
41. "The Fauquier Lynching," *Winchester Times*, Jan. 28, 1880, 3.
42. Eric Foner, *Freedom's Lawmakers: A Directory of Black Officeholders During Reconstruction* (New York: Oxford University Press, 1993), 166.
43. "Lynched by a Mob," *Washington Post*, Jan. 20, 1880, 1; "Lynching a Seducer: A Brutal Negro Is Taken from the Jail and Sent Where the Bad Darkeys Go, Via Hemp," *National Police Gazette*, Feb. 7, 1880, 35.
44. Jessie Daniel Ames, *The Changing Character of Lynching* (Atlanta: Commission on Interracial Cooperation, 1942), 51.
45. Ann Field Alexander, *Race Man: The Rise and Fall of the "Fighting Editor," John Mitchell Jr.* (Charlottesville: University of Virginia Press, 2002), 48.
46. Amateur, "A Vindication of the People of Warrenton," *Richmond Dispatch*, Jan. 21, 1880, 3.
47. "The Virginia Outrage," *Lebanon* (PA) *Daily News*, Jan. 23, 1880, 4.
48. *Harrisburg* (PA) *Daily Independent*, Jan. 27, 1880, 2.

49. "A Shameful Outrage," (Richmond) *Religious Herald,* Jan. 29, 1880, 2.
50. "Lynch Law," *Weekly Louisianian,* March 20, 1880, 1.
51. *Alexandria Gazette,* Jan. 20, 1880, 2.
52. "An Unnatural Elopement," *Winchester Times,* Jan. 21, 1880, 3.
53. Paula J. Giddings, *Ida: A Sword among Lions* (New York: Amistad, 2008), 153.

"YOU SHUDDER AT THE PICTURE"

The *Richmond Planet* and the Lynching of Three Black Miners in Clifton Forge in 1891

DOLORES FLAMIANO

On Saturday, October 17, 1891, a group of young Black miners traveled from Iron Gate and Low Moor where they lived and worked to nearby Clifton Forge, a railroad boomtown in western Virginia. Charles Miller, John Scott, and Robert Burton stopped at a downtown photography studio to have their portraits taken, Wild West–style, with pistols and tough-guy bravado (see the top portion of fig. 1).[1] The fact that the Black workers patronized a white-owned photography studio suggests they had money and attitude—two things likely to attract the suspicion and envy of white townspeople. Little did the men imagine that this day would be their last or that their images would grace a souvenir postcard, juxtaposed with a grisly postlynching photograph that showed their corpses hanging from a tree (fig. 1). The card was embossed in flowing script with the name of the town's photography studio: S. S. Griffith & Co. For Black people, lynching postcards inspired fear and served as stark visual reminders of the threat of racial terror. White people used such cards to celebrate white supremacy and share memorable events with family and friends, sometimes with a racist message or joke jotted on the back.[2] As this essay demonstrates, the meaning of the Clifton Forge lynching photograph would be challenged and subverted by Black newspaper editor John Mitchell Jr., who made it part of a decades-long antilynching campaign in the *Richmond Planet*.

That autumn day in Clifton Forge in 1891, the Black miners walked through town, reportedly in high spirits and enjoying themselves, until they attracted the attention of a white man who tried to arrest them. (Local newspaper accounts were vague about their alleged crime.) The miners resisted arrest

FIGURE 1. Cabinet Card, S. S. Griffith & Co., Clifton Forge, Virginia, 1891.

and managed to leave town, but then a self-appointed posse of white men pursued them. The two groups met in a firefight that killed two men (one white and one Black), and injured others. Four Black men were taken to jail, where a white mob kidnapped them. The mob released one member of the group (a teenager), but proceeded to kill Miller, Scott, and Burton by hanging them from a tree and shooting their bodies full of bullets.

Lynching was a fact of life in the southern part of the United States in the decades after the Civil War. Between 1866 and 1932, Virginia documented 115 lynching deaths, with the largest numbers recorded during the 1880s and 1890s (39 and 40, respectively).[3] Led by small groups but including many participants, a lynching was a community event that could draw hundreds of spectators by the time it culminated in the public execution of an alleged criminal, almost always a Black male. Victims were killed by hanging, burning, or shooting—or all three. Lynch mobs committed unspeakable acts of cruelty. They claimed multiple victims and riddled victims' bodies with hundreds of bullets. Some spectators collected trophies (bits of clothing or body parts), while others (including those in Clifton Forge) memorialized the event by creating and selling souvenir postcards. The elements of mob violence, murder as spectacle, and extreme brutality (even after death) demonstrate that lynching was not simply murder; it was an act of racial terror.

The press served a key role in lynching. Studies of lynching coverage in white southern newspapers have identified a stereotypical narrative featuring a desperate, vicious Black murderer and an innocent, respectable white man. Some also featured a blameless white female rape victim, intensifying the outrage of press coverage. The brutal lynching of Sam Hose in Georgia in 1899 would not have been possible without the *Atlanta Constitution*'s reporting, editorializing, and embellishments to activate and spur on the mob. The media cycle began "with headlines breathlessly reporting sensational crimes, to be followed by speculations about the prospects for extralegal actions, and later yet by accounts of any attempted or accomplished lynching."[4] By the end of the cycle, Hose had been transformed into a horrific, larger-than-life murderer and rapist, though he was a reserved farmworker who killed his employer in self-defense. This formulaic reporting was widespread, and because it started with a presumption of Black guilt and white innocence, it predictably presented lynchings as just and warranted.[5]

In the absence of competing narratives like court documents (most cases were never tried), researchers have relied heavily on white newspaper accounts while acknowledging that their bias makes them deeply problematic sources. Black newspapers provide necessary counternarratives. One of the South's leading Black newspapers was the *Richmond Planet*, a weekly founded in 1883 by descendants of enslaved people. By the mid-1890s it had a circulation of five thousand and a growing national reputation as a strong voice against lynching.[6] Editor John Mitchell Jr. was a fierce and fearless advocate for victims of racial violence. His journalism career began with a column in the *New York Globe*, a Black newspaper. Known as a "fighting editor" because of his powerful rhetoric and his calls for Black people to take up arms in self-defense, Mitchell used the *Planet* to expose the scope and brutality of lynching and to challenge prevailing narratives that glorified the practice. Mitchell's protest extended beyond writing on several occasions when he personally intervened to prevent lynching, arranged legal counsel for unjustly convicted people, and raised funds to cover their legal costs.[7]

In addition to reprinting and editorializing about lynching reports published in white newspapers, the *Planet* added to and corrected the historical record by including personal information about Black victims, which the white press generally omitted. It also published eyewitness accounts and criticized distorted and erroneous reporting. It lacked the resources to do original reporting on most lynching incidents. For noteworthy cases, however, such as the triple lynching in Clifton Forge in 1891, the *Planet* would send a reporter to the crime scene and publish its own reports.[8]

The *Richmond Planet*, like other Black newspapers and organizations, mobilized Black audiences (and, to a lesser extent, white allies) to speak out against lynching. It helped to forge among the Black community a racial consciousness, a collective racial identity, and what scholars call an "ethic of protest."[9] Like other Black publications—notably the Indianapolis *Freeman*, the *Chicago Defender*, and Ida B. Wells's antilynching pamphlets and columns—the *Richmond Planet* rejected and sought to correct the intense racial biases that pervaded lynching accounts in white newspapers. The most pervasive biases included the myth of Black male criminality and an implicit assumption that the law would not punish lynchers because it was "not considered a crime to kill a Negro."[10] To the contrary, lynching was seen as a virtuous act, and white journalists "typically heaped praise on lynchers for their decorum."[11] Indeed, for some religious communities in the Jim Crow South, lynching took on a deep religious meaning beyond punishment. In this view, the burning of Sam Hose and others like him was an act of expiation that extinguished guilt and restored balance to a community in moral turmoil.[12]

In the face of deeply entrenched ideologies of white supremacy and Black criminality, the *Planet* demanded equal rights for all Americans and argued that anyone accused of a crime had the right to a hearing, and no one deserved execution by a lynch mob. Editor Mitchell's outspoken activism earned him the respect of fellow Black journalists and activists. For example, Frederick Douglass noted in 1884, when Mitchell assumed editorship of the *Planet* at the age of twenty-one: "I have no fear but young Mitchell will make his way in the world and be a credit to our race."[13]

The *Planet*'s clarion call was "lynch law must go," and Mitchell combined facts, figures, and rhetorical arguments with illustrations (notably pen-and-ink drawings based on photographs), to drive home the message.[14] The *Planet* reappropriated lynching images like souvenir postcards that were created and circulated by white people to celebrate their power and to intimidate Black people. Mitchell wanted to use these images to shock readers and spur them into action. To be sure, he was a businessman who was not averse to showmanship, and he probably saw sensational images as a way to increase circulation. However, he used them not primarily to shock but to support activism.[15]

The *Richmond Planet* combined oppositional narratives (news reports, editorials, and other features) with sensational images to support its antilynching agenda. To better understand the *Planet*'s work, this essay examines written and visual documentation of the Clifton Forge lynching. To provide context for the *Planet*'s coverage, it is necessary to start with white newspaper coverage, which reveals the prevailing narratives of lynching to which the *Planet* responded. Unlike white newspapers, the *Planet* published illustrations of the Clifton Forge lynching victims, both before and after their deaths. Two specific illustrations will be examined closely: "You Shudder at the Picture," an 1891 broadsheet advertisement for the *Richmond Planet* that foregrounded the triple lynching at Clifton Forge as emblematic of a larger problem; and "The Reign of Lawlessness," a recurring graphic feature published in the *Richmond Planet* during the 1890s. Also based on the Clifton Forge lynching, this feature paired an illustration of the lynched men with a tabular report of the week's lynching numbers nationwide. Both illustrations were based on a lynching photograph that originally appeared in a souvenir postcard. When analyzed alongside the secondary literature, this written and visual documentation confirms that Clifton Forge was an act of racial terror.

Photographer S. S. Griffith used the Clifton Forge lynching to promote his photography business. He or one of his workers photographed the men in his studio early in the day and then took camera equipment outdoors to shoot the aftermath of the lynching. He then combined the prelynching portraits of the three men with a postlynching photograph and attached the four images to a heavy card stock to make a picture card or cabinet card (fig. 1). This was a popular format for portraits in the late 1800s; people would share them with family and friends. Unlike many surviving lynching postcards that only show the postlynching scene, the Clifton Forge card told a moralistic "before-and-after" story of crime and punishment. The text "11 a.m." appears above the portraits and "11 p.m." below the lynching scene.

Such cards were sold as keepsakes or souvenirs that "allowed those unable to attend the spectacle the opportunity to be equally inculcated as a member of a larger imagined community."[16] The fact that "S. S. Griffith & Co." appears on the card below an ornate border suggests that Griffith either supported the lynching or felt neutral about it. In any event, he saw the lynching card as a suitable advertisement for the business. For the white citizens of Clifton Forge, the postcard represented business interests and white supremacy. In the years that followed, however, the meaning of these images would change as they became a significant part of the *Richmond Planet*'s antilynching campaign.

In general, lynching narratives in white newspapers celebrated white supremacy. They did this by creating and perpetuating harmful racial stereotypes and by excusing or even glorifying the practice of lynching. Over time, these narratives have obscured the realities of lynching. An analysis of the *Richmond Planet* shows that it deliberately challenged and inverted white newspaper narratives of the Clifton Forge lynching. These counternarratives illuminate truths that were hidden or misrepresented, giving us a more complete and nuanced understanding of racial terror in Virginia. Before turning to Clifton Forge counternarratives in the *Richmond Planet*, it is necessary to consider how the incident was covered in the white press.

Newspaper headlines tell an important part of the story, as they convey facts in a compressed and telegraphic style. The lynching of Miller, Scott, and Burton was front-page news in Clifton Forge, Staunton, Roanoke, and

Terrible Affair at Clifton Forge.

ONE WHITE MAN SHOT AND KILLED AND ANOTHER WOUNDED, AND ONE NEGRO SHOT AND KILLED AND ANOTHER WOUNDED, AND THREE NEGROES LYNCHED AND HANGED—IMMENSE EXCITEMENT TROOPS CALLED FOR IN ANTICIPATION OF AN ATTACK.

FIGURE 2. *Staunton Spectator*, October 14, 1891.

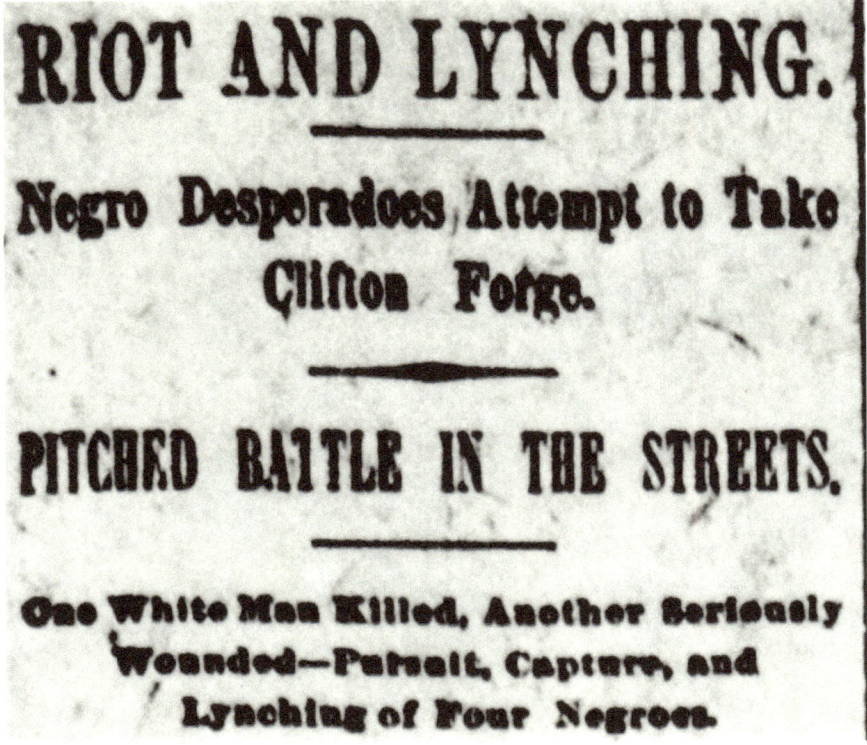

FIGURE 3. *Richmond Dispatch*, October 18, 1891.

Richmond. The details varied from one newspaper to another, but the overall narrative was consistent. The headlines assumed that white lives were valuable and Black lives were expendable. This can be seen in the precedence given in the Staunton and Richmond newspapers to white deaths, which always appeared at the top of the list (see figs. 2 and 3).

Another dominant theme was embedded in a *Richmond Dispatch* headline: "Riot and Lynching: Negro Desperadoes Attempt to Take Clifton Forge." By labeling the men "Negro desperadoes," the headline disparaged them as outlaws without providing any evidence of their alleged crimes. It also falsely suggested that Clifton Forge was a frontier town where vigilantism prevailed over the rule of law. Ultimately, the label implied that the men deserved to die because they were outside the law and did not deserve the same legal protections as law-abiding (white) citizens. In a similar vein, the Clifton

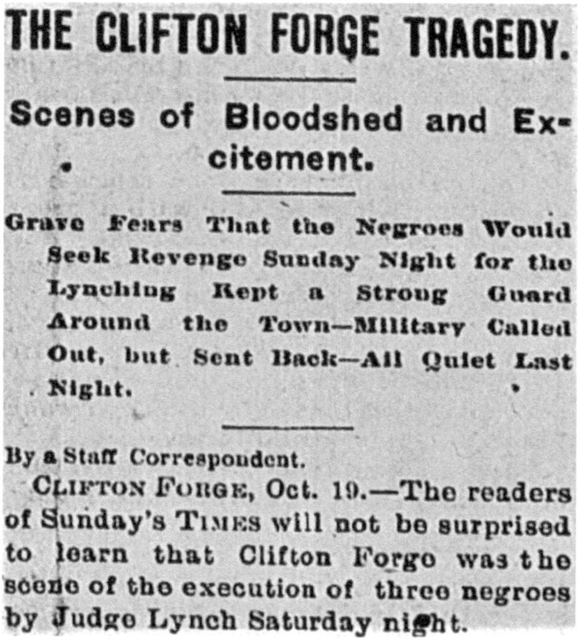

> **THE CLIFTON FORGE TRAGEDY.**
>
> **Scenes of Bloodshed and Excitement.**
>
> Grave Fears That the Negroes Would Seek Revenge Sunday Night for the Lynching Kept a Strong Guard Around the Town—Military Called Out, but Sent Back—All Quiet Last Night.
>
> By a Staff Correspondent.
>
> CLIFTON FORGE, Oct. 19.—The readers of Sunday's TIMES will not be surprised to learn that Clifton Forge was the scene of the execution of three negroes by Judge Lynch Saturday night.

FIGURE 4. *Roanoke Times*, October 20, 1891.

Forge newspaper justified the lynching with a two-word headline: "Swift Vengeance," and the Roanoke newspaper called the killings "executions" by "Judge Lynch" (fig. 4).[17]

It was not unusual for white newspapers to misappropriate the term "desperado," which is defined as a desperate or reckless person, especially a criminal. In 1892 white newspapers used the term to justify the lynching of Thomas Moss and two other Black grocery store owners in Memphis, Tennessee. Journalist and activist Ida B. Wells was Moss's friend and the godmother of his child, and she knew that he was not a desperado. In fact, this lynching inspired her to launch the antilynching crusade that became her life's work. The Moss lynching revealed an ugly truth: lynching was sometimes used against Black men deemed too prosperous and successful by their white rivals.

In Clifton Forge, white newspapers labeled the miners as desperadoes to support the argument that their killing was warranted and even necessary. This confirms Fitzhugh Brundage's observation that white news stories "warped the life histories of mob victims to fit the conventional portraits of black criminals." Moreover, Black men with transient jobs (like railroad workers or miners) "kindled hostility even without committing a crime." The region's growth also fueled racial tension. Between 1880 and 1890, the Black population in Alleghany County (where Clifton Forge is located) grew from 1,132 to 4,013. Lynching thus became "a tool to define boundaries in a region where traditional racial lines were either vague or nonexistent."[18]

In response to the distorted and damaging stories about Clifton Forge's Black miners in white newspapers, the *Richmond Planet* told a very different story on October 24, 1891. With the headline "VIRGINIA'S SHAME!," the *Planet* claimed the moral high ground vis-à-vis the lynchers and pointed to their actions as shameful. This contrasts with white newspaper's headlines that absolved the lynchers of responsibility by characterizing the killing as a "terrible affair" or a "tragedy." "VIRGINIA'S SHAME!" also contrasts with the white newspapers description of a "riot and lynching," which falsely suggests a cause-and-effect scenario in which the Black men ran riot, and lynching followed as an inevitable result. Below the headline, the *Planet* subhead subtly challenged white supremacy by inverting the typical order and listing Black victims first: "Three Colored Men Lynched, Two White Men Killed." In an implicit critique of biased and uninformed white reporting, the *Planet*'s follow-up report promised to reveal the "true facts" behind the "murders." Not surprisingly, white newspapers generally refused to equate lynching with murder.[19]

Opponents of lynching faced an enormous challenge in trying to strip white lynching narratives of their power. To understand these narratives, newspaper headlines are revealing, but they are only the start of the story. To grasp the Clifton Forge lynching narratives, it is necessary to analyze the articles: specifically, their four-part structure of crime, pursuit, lynching, and aftermath. This analysis shows how the *Richmond Planet* challenged racially charged rhetoric, corrected errors and inconsistencies, and gave voice to people in the Black community whose words were omitted from the official white lynching narratives.

The media cycle begins with the alleged crime. When they were lynched on the evening of October 17, 1891, Miller, Scott, and Burton stood accused of murdering one white man and wounding another. However, the Clifton Forge citizens who killed the three men treated them as outlaws even before a single shot was fired—indeed, soon after they entered the town. What was their crime? The *Staunton Spectator* described the men as armed and dangerous outsiders from Low Moor, a predominantly Black mining town, who entered town "avowing it was their purpose to take the place." It called them "boisterous in their boastings and misbehaving generally." In other words, the men were loud braggarts and show-offs. These activities were not crimes (at least not when enacted by white men), but they violated the racial code of acceptable behavior for Black men. According to this code, insolence by Black men was punishable.

The *Roanoke Times* also reported the miners' seemingly offensive behavior but embellished the story with more sensational details: the Black miners reportedly told their friends they were going to Clifton Forge for blood, for a fight, and to paint the town red, and they "filled up on mean whiskey." This article mentions the photography gallery where Miller reportedly had his picture taken "with a revolver in each hand." (Figure 1 shows one of Miller's hands, but not both. Scott and Burton were also holding guns, but they were not mentioned here.) These details raise questions about the picture card. For example, when and where was it sold and to what extent did it inform newspaper reports? If reporters saw the portraits of defiant Black men posing with guns, what would they make of them? These images would have aligned with prevailing fears of dangerous Black men and were consistent with the "desperado" narrative.[20]

The *Richmond Dispatch* told a story similar to the Staunton and Roanoke papers but with more threatening and exaggerated language, reporting that eight Black men came to Clifton Forge from Big Island (a nearby mining town) and that they vowed to "take the town." They got drunk, armed themselves "with a brace of pistols," and "paraded the streets in regular western desperado style, flourishing their weapons and cursing and threatening all who approached them."[21] Lynching stories were frequently embellished and dramatized as the story spread beyond outside the local area. For example, the details of Sam Hose's alleged crimes became more graphic and gruesome as the story unfolded in the *Atlanta Constitution*.

In short, white newspapers reported that the Clifton Forge lynching was the result of armed and hostile outsiders coming to "take the town," a vague threat that suggests the newspapers were stoking white fears about the threat of Black rebellion in which armed Black men would try to kill white men and rape "their" women. In such a climate, even a minor violation of "white space" could spur armed and lethal reactions by whites. The *Richmond Dispatch*'s description of Black men "parading the streets" is worth noting as evidence that sidewalks and other public spaces were contested terrain in the 1890s. The previous decade had seen the area's Black population increase fourfold, and whites had more frequent contact with African American strangers. In this shifting social milieu, Black men who "refused to conform to contemporary white notions of appropriate black subservience" could become an excuse for white attacks, including the deadly Roanoke Riot of 1893, in which Thomas Smith was lynched after being accused of assaulting and robbing a white woman. During an assault on the jail in Roanoke, authorities fired on the mob of four to five thousand people and killed seven white men.[22]

In describing the Black miners, the *Richmond Planet* reported some of the same facts as the white press. For example, it acknowledged that they went to Clifton Forge for a good time and "drank liquor freely." But it eschewed labels like "desperadoes" and provided a different perspective on encounters with white townspeople: "Several white men interfered with the miners" and launched a surprise attack on them after they left town to avoid trouble. When Miller shot and killed a man, he did so in self-defense. The *Richmond Planet* also provided context for the miners' guns: "It is true they carried pistols, a custom for white and colored to carry them where they could be seen."[23]

The *Richmond Planet*'s reporting on Clifton Forge differed from the white press in another important way. While the white newspapers did not include any illustrations, the *Planet* published pen-and-ink drawings of Miller, Scott, and Burton based on their portraits on the picture card. The use of headshots of lynching victims added another dimension to the *Planet*'s antilynching efforts, which included telling readers something about their life stories and showing them as flesh-and-blood individuals, not the stereotyped brutes and outlaws portrayed in white press accounts.

The next stage in the lynching narrative is the pursuit. At Clifton Forge, after the miners left town, white men formed a posse and pursued them. This pursuit led to a shootout, the killing of two people, the wounding of two others, and the jailing of the Black men. The hunting, trapping, and killing of Blacks has been a persistent theme in lynching narratives from the nineteenth century to the 2012 murder of Trayvon Martin. Scholars have noted that "pro-lynching discourse commonly used tropes of the hunt to normalize lynching as a practice of subsistence and survival."[24]

The trope of the hunt was prominent in the white press coverage of Clifton Forge, giving the story drama and urgency while also dehumanizing the

Black men. The *Staunton Spectator* reported that the posse (a word choice that implied endorsement by local law enforcement authorities) commanded the Black men to halt and both parties fired. Philip Bowling, a white brakeman, was shot and instantly killed. Frederick Wilkinson, a white railroad employee, was shot and wounded. The Black victims, however, remain nameless, and we learn nothing about their backgrounds: "One of the negroes was shot and killed and another wounded." Four of the Black men were captured, handcuffed, taken to town, and put in the jail. According to the article, "Great indignation and intense excitement prevailed."[25]

Advances in transportation and technology heightened the newsworthiness of lynching narratives as well as the sensationalism with which they were reported. The *Richmond Dispatch* promised readers that the Clifton Forge report was made possible by "special telegram," a claim supported by the article's breathless, spare, "on the ground" style that mixes present and past tenses and appears to have been written on the fly: "The citizens formed a posse and attempted to disarm them. They resisted and a regular pitched battle occurred. . . . The battle became desperate, resulting in the mortal wounding of Fred Wilkinson and the instant killing of Philip Bowling, citizens of Clifton Forge. . . . Among the rioters, Charles Miller, who killed Bowling, and Robert Burton, who wounded Wilkinson, are both wounded and captured. Robert Scott, another of the rioters, is captured." The captured men were lodged in jail. "At 8:30 p.m. the city is full of excited people, many armed with Winchesters."[26]

For its part, the *Roanoke Times* gave a more detailed and lurid account of what happened after the shootout: Burton suffered a broken leg, Morton was wounded in the head, and Scott fled into the woods, "the blood streaming from his body." Burton, Scott, Miller, and Morton were captured, carried to the city prison, and locked up.[27]

Compared with its white counterparts, the *Richmond Planet* provided a different account of events leading to the shootout. Sources included eyewitnesses who shared a similar perspective to the lynched men and expressed no animosity toward them. For example, the *Planet* reported that Miller and his friends left town because they did not want to have any fuss. They did not expect to be followed. A white man asked police to arrest "the boys," but when he was told there was no arrest warrant and the police could do nothing, the man became angry and started "yelling like a mad-man, attracting many boys and men to join the chase." The group approached Miller and friends from the rear and fired on them. Miller shot in self-defense and killed one of the white men. The Black men were captured around three p.m. and lodged in jail.[28]

The next stage in the narrative is the lynching itself. According to the *Staunton Spectator,* at around ten p.m. a large body of men (many masked) went to the prison, broke in, took two of the Black men, dragged them to Slaughter Hollow, hung them, and riddled their bodies with bullets. They did the same to the wounded Black man who was not at the jail.[29]

The *Richmond Dispatch* reported that a mob attacked the jail and overpowered the guard, took out four Black "rioters and hung them to the railroad bridge," and riddled their bodies with bullets. (This was the only report that mistakenly reported that four men were killed, called the men "rioters," and mentioned the bridge.)[30]

The *Roanoke Times* reported that the white mob "broke down the prison doors with two large sledgehammers" and opined ominously: "Nobody at Clifton Forge needed to be told that Judge Lynch would arraign the prisoners and execute them as soon as the mantle of darkness fell." By invoking the metaphorical "Judge Lynch" the *Times* implied that the outcome was inevitable, and no specific individuals were responsible. Despite the sledgehammer assault, the reporter took pains to portray the mob as orderly and quiet: "Some three hundred men gathered near city hall and in a respectable manner informed the mayor of their intention." The mayor pleaded with them, but seeing that it was futile, "asked the leader to go quietly about his work." The Black men were drawn up to the tree limbs with ropes and then "volley after volley was fired at the bodies . . . over forty finding lodgment in Miller's."[31]

In contrast to the white newspapers, the *Richmond Planet* acknowledged that there were conflicting reports of the lynching and included details apparently obtained from Black townspeople. For example, it reported that "the Mayor made no effort to prevent the lynching" and "the men did not break open the jail but the keys were furnished them." The *Planet* also gave a chilling account of local citizens' preparations for the lynching, which seemed very methodical. For example, stores were ordered not to sell weapons or ammunition to Black men. At the same time, stores not only sold firearms to white men, they gave them to "those who couldn't buy them." Bars and markets closed, and "nearly every white citizen in town" (from three to four hundred people) allegedly "joined the lynching party."[32] These facts illustrate the coordinated complicity of local institutions in the Clifton Forge lynching and thus support the argument that lynching was state-sanctioned terrorism again the Black community, as well as being a community leisure event like a picnic or carnival.

The *Planet* noted the lynching took place at the [animal] slaughter pens near the city limits and that the men who did the lynching wore their usual clothing, with no disguises. This contradicted the *Staunton Spectator*'s report of masked men. The *Planet* also identified some of the people involved (by occupation, not name). For example, a butcher who mostly served the Black community "took a leading part in tying the rope" and "a white doctor took part in the hanging by counting the time."

Most notably, the *Planet* included information that confirmed the lynching was designed to terrorize people in the Black community. For example, the hanging tree was located within fifty yards of Black people's houses, and when men in the mob fired their pistols, they did so "in all directions and dared (people) to poke their heads out of doors." A Black woman defiantly told the lynching party she "would die with the men and stood right by the tree during the awful murder."[33]

The final stage in the lynching narrative is the aftermath. Two themes dominated the Clifton Forge postlynching story in the white press: the restoration of peace in the town and rumors of revenge attacks by Black residents of nearby mining towns. Some reports claimed that after the lynching, the community experienced a kind of redemption. The most dramatic description of the immediate aftermath of lynching appeared in the *Clifton Forge and Iron-Gate Review:* "In less than an hour the streets of Clifton Forge were as quiet as a churchyard. The moon was shining almost as bright as day. It bathed in a silvery light the ghastly faces of the three misguided men who were left hanging on the tree."[34] At first glance such language seems bizarre and unfitting; it only makes sense when lynching is seen as a ritualistic and quasi-religious celebration of white supremacy. In this view, lynching ends with a cathartic expunging of sin and evil.[35] The lynching of Sam Hose provides the most vivid and disturbing example of lynching as an intensely religious experience for white southern Protestants, especially men.[36]

Somewhat less poetically, the *Staunton Spectator* reported that after the lynching the town became quiet, and not a Black man was to be seen. It also reported rumors of a possible attack on the town in retaliation for the lynching, which led the town to ask Gov. Philip McKinney to send troops. The paper also reported a coroner's inquest that returned the following verdict:

"The men were hanged by parties unknown to the jury."[37] These accounts further show the complicity of white institutions that let the mob lynch with impunity. Unfortunately, such verdicts were standard components of the white lynching narrative. The *Roanoke Times* also reported rumors of a counterattack in revenge for the "lynching of the desperadoes." The end of the article (seemingly as an afterthought) listed alleged offenses committed by Miller the previous year, including firing shots on a citizen of Buchanan who attempted to arrest him and the attempted murder of a railroad conductor.[38]

The *Richmond Planet* also reported the rumors that Black people in nearby communities planned to avenge the Clifton Forge lynching, but the newspaper did not give the reports any credence. Unlike the white papers, it provided personal details and background information about the Black victims, notably John Scott of Irwin, Virginia, who was described as a quiet, law-abiding citizen. The *Planet* had little to say about Miller, except to identify his home as Big Island. Mitchell noted that he telegraphed to Clifton Forge and received the photographs from which the pen-and-ink illustrations (headshots of the victims) were made. This suggests that Mitchell or his local contacts received the picture card with the miners' portraits and the lynching photograph (fig. 1). The *Planet* only used the head and shoulders and omitted the portion with the pistols.[39]

In the years after the Clifton Forge lynching, the *Planet* published illustrations based on the lynching photograph shown in figure 1, pairing them with headlines of outrage that spoke directly to a Black audience: "You Shudder at the Picture" and "The Reign of Lawlessness" (figs. 5 and 6). While most white newspapers presented the lynching as a warranted instance of vigilante justice, in the *Planet*'s counternarrative, the Clifton Forge lynching was the unjustifiable murder of Black men acting in self-defense. Framed this way, the image was more than evidence of a specific lynching. It became instead a "symbolic marker of ongoing atrocity."[40] The lynching postcard created a shared identity and sense of community among lynch mob supporters who were not able to participate in the event. Perhaps the same image reprinted in the *Planet* with words of outrage and protest could create a shared identity and sense of community among those who opposed lynching.

The *Richmond Planet*'s broadside advertisement "You Shudder at the Picture" was designed to attract new subscribers and gain support for the newspaper's antilynching campaign. The focal point was an engraving based on

FIGURE 5. Broadside advertisement, the *Richmond Planet*, October 31, 1891.

the Clifton Forge lynching photograph. It is important to note that the *Planet* took some liberties with the original photograph, creating a more minimalist visual by obscuring the white spectators and changing the background. This was probably an attempt to create an iconic symbol of lynching rather than a document of a specific incident.

The headline ("You Shudder at the Picture"; fig. 5) acknowledged the horrific nature of the image, especially for a Black viewer whose first reaction might understandably be a visceral one: a literal shudder or shiver of fear. Upon further reflection, one might reasonably think: "That could be me or my loved ones." In other words, the combination of image and text validated the emotions provoked by the image. The next line ("Of Course You Do") continued in the mode of direct address, affirming a shared humanity and a common

FIGURE 6. Richmond *Planet*, July 31, 1897.

commitment to the antilynching cause. The broadside advertisement also identified the lynching victims and briefly explained the circumstances leading to their murder. They killed two white men, but they did so in self-defense. These actions would have resonated with editor Mitchell, a staunch advocate of taking up arms in self-defense. The best remedy for lynching, he wrote in 1890, was "a 16-shot Winchester rifle in the hands of a dead-shot Negro who has nerve enough to pull the trigger."[41] The rest of the advertisement (about one third of the space) declared the *Planet*'s commitment to justice, human rights, and maintaining the rule of law. Taken together, these seemingly contradictory messages show Mitchell's embrace of multiple strategies.

"The Reign of Lawlessness" was a two-column wide graphic updated weekly and published in the *Planet* (see fig. 6). These statistical tables documented the lives lost to lynching nationally every week for most of the paper's forty-five-year run. Equally important, to quote Jacqueline Goldsby's description of similar efforts by the Black community to comfort and support the loved ones of lynching victims, the *Planet*'s tribute to the victims of lynching can be seen as part of larger community efforts of "restoration and repair" that sought to give comfort to survivors. Other efforts addressed the most basic needs: recover the victims' bodies, plan their funerals and burials, and organize fundraising campaigns to aid suffering families.[42]

"The Reign of Lawlessness" (like "You Shudder at the Picture") was illustrated with an engraving based on a photograph of the Clifton Forge lynching. Beneath the main headline were three smaller ones: "Judge Lynch's Bloody Work," "A Fearful Record," and "The Law Sleeps," followed by a question: "Shall this barbarity continue until the God of retribution marshals his strength against the barbarians?" Note the multipronged appeal to the rule of law, religion, and emotion. Finally, the graphic listed the people lynched that year to date. The information was presented in a table with six columns: year, name, color, alleged crime, place lynched, and number of people. The alleged crimes ran the gamut from "nothing" to "writing insulting letter" to "murder." This exposed the arbitrary nature of lynching and debunked the ideology of Black criminality.

This graphic stood as a grim weekly reminder that lynching claimed the lives of Black people every year, including some who were accused of frivolous crimes or no crime at all. As such, it paid tribute to the victims of mob violence and heaped shame on lawless places where lynching flourished because local authorities allowed the perpetrators to go free. Through repetition, this symbolic marker of ongoing atrocity served as a "eerie, silent statement of outrage" and linked its "traumatic impact on viewers with the importance of a militant black press."[43]

The *Richmond Planet*'s creation of "You Shudder at the Picture" and "The Reign of Lawlessness" in response to the Clifton Forge lynching suggests that it was an early adopter of lynching images as a form of protest. "The Reign of Lawlessness" predates similar and better-known features based on lynching photographs in Ida B. Wells' pamphlet *A Red Record* (1895), the NAACP magazine *The Crisis* (notably 1912 and 1930), and the Black newspaper the *Chicago Defender* (1930). Over time, images became more graphic. When Wells published an article about the 1893 lynching of C. J. Miller in Bardwell, Kentucky, it included a drawing that showed the victim naked except for a cloth covering his genitals. The image was followed by a note apologizing for the graphic image and explaining that it was the only way to "give an adequate idea of the inhumanity of the case." The note called attention to another distressing feature: "There were so many young people among the witnesses of an act of brutality and savagery."[44] There is no evidence that Mitchell ever apologized about the lynching images he published, though he acknowledged that they could cause distress.

The fight against lynching was ultimately a cultural contest about the meaning of American citizenship. As Ersula J. Ore notes, "Lynching was a form of social control that maintained the racial status quo through its denial of due process of law. By denying black victims the right to due process, lynchers were in fact arguing that the protections and privileges of American citizenship were the exclusive rights of the white men and women who lynched them."[45] The fight against lynching was also about the role of the Black press, activists, and organizations like the NAACP to challenge this social control and the dominant white narratives that supported it. As journalists, historians, and media scholars have shown, white newspapers generally condoned racial violence through headlines, editorial commentary, and narratives that presented lynch mobs as peacekeepers. In the worst-case scenarios, newspapers essentially mobilized lynch mobs, as in Oklahoma's Tulsa Massacre of 1921, when the *Tulsa Tribune* published a front-page news story with the headline "Nab Negro for Attacking Girl in Elevator."[46] The *Richmond Planet* and other Black newspapers challenged prevailing lynching narratives as part of a larger campaign to shame whites for lynching and to promote state and federal antilynching laws. More broadly, the Black press created a rhetoric of civic belonging for its readers, affirming their identity as American citizens. It produced a "vibrant black print culture and public sphere in which racial, class, and gender identities, and ideas of racial progress, protest, community and citizenship, were constructed and contested."[47]

The Clifton Forge triple lynching of 1891 was a noteworthy event that produced valuable written and visual evidence, notably a postcard that helped fuel the *Richmond Planet*'s antilynching campaign. A review of Clifton Forge coverage in white newspapers shows consistent narratives of Black criminality (even in the absence of supporting evidence) and official white complicity with the murders. These narratives confirm that lynching was state-sanctioned racial terror designed to intimidate and punish Black people, especially those who dared to step outside their prescribed roles in white society. In contrast, a review of coverage in the *Richmond Planet* finds counternarratives that challenged and subverted white press coverage and its inaccuracies and distortions. The *Planet* affirmed the Black community's right to self-defense, spoke out against state-sanctioned lawlessness, and contributed to an ethic of protest in the Black press.

The Clifton Forge lynching is significant because it left behind unusual pre- and postlynching photographs. Such images have most often been used to preserve white supremacy. In the hands of John Mitchell, however, they became tools to spark outrage and protest and to mobilize people for racial equality. Much work remains to be done to understand these images. For example, how did people in the Black community respond to "You Shudder at the Picture"? How did white journalists and politicians (especially those who were being targeted by Mitchell) react to such features? This graphic and other visual antilynching features in the *Planet* (including editorial cartoons, some drawn by Mitchell himself) almost certainly influenced Ida B. Wells and W. E. B. Du Bois in their later efforts. Over time, the NAACP would amplify the antilynching message and turn it into a data-driven national campaign. Meanwhile, this campaign worked in tandem with the professionalization of journalism to put an end to white newspaper coverage that heaped praise on lynch mobs. By the 1930s, lynching was in retreat, though white supremacy persisted in other forms. Ultimately, the triple lynching in Clifton Forge is part of a much bigger, continuing story about the countless people whose lives were destroyed by lynching and those who have struggled (and continue to struggle) to tell their stories. One important chapter in this story is the passage in March 2022 of the Emmett Till Antilynching Act, a landmark law that makes lynching a federal crime.

Notes

1. "Lynching Victims in Clifton Forge," *Encyclopedia Virginia,* accessed June 1, 2021, https://encyclopediavirginia.org/10405-20daab7dfoef8a3/.

2. *Lynching Postcards: Token of a Great Day,* dir. Christine Turner (MTV Documentary Films, 2021), 00:15:22, accessed April 28, 2023, https://www.firelightfilms.tv/films/lynching-postcards-token-of-a-great-day.
3. Racial Terror: Lynching in Virginia, Department of Justice Studies, James Mason University, accessed Jan. 3, 2021, https://sites.lib.jmu.edu/valynchings/.
4. Fitzhugh Brundage, "The Press and Lynching," in *Journalism and Jim Crow: White Supremacy and the Black Struggle for a New America,* eds. Kathy Roberts Forde and Sid Bedingfield (Urbana: University of Illinois Press, 2021), 86. For a detailed analysis of the lynching of Sam Hose, see Edwin T. Arnold, *"What Virtue There Is in Fire": Cultural Memory and the Lynching of Sam Hose* (Athens: University of Georgia Press, 2009).
5. Susan Jean, "'Warranted' Lynchings: Narratives of Mob Violence in White Southern Newspapers, 1880–1940," *American Nineteenth Century History* 6, no. 3 (August 2006): 351–72.
6. Henry Lewis Suggs, ed., *The Black Press in the South, 1865–1979* (Westport, CT: Greenwood Press, 1983), 16.
7. Ann Field Alexander, *Race Man: The Rise and Fall of the "Fighting Editor," John Mitchell Jr.* (Charlottesville: University of Virginia Press, 2002), 42–59.
8. James E. Hall, *Black and White: A Historical Examination of Lynching Coverage and Editorial Impact in Select Virginia Newspapers* (MA thesis, Virginia Commonwealth University, Richmond, 2001).
9. D'Weston Haywood, *Let Us Make Men: The Twentieth-Century Black Press and a Manly Vision for Racial Advancement* (Chapel Hill: University of North Carolina Press, 2018), 9.
10. Ida B. Wells, quoted in Aleen Ratzlaff, "Ida B. Wells, Crusader against the Lynch Law," in *Seeking a Voice: Images of Race and Gender in the Nineteenth-Century Press,* eds. David B. Sachsman et al. (West Lafayette, IN: Purdue University Press, 2009), 156.
11. Brundage, *The Press and Lynching,* 90.
12. Donald G. Mathews, *At the Altar of Lynching: Burning Sam Hose in the American South* (Cambridge: Cambridge University Press, 2017).
13. Anne McCrery, "Mitchell, John, Jr. (1863–1929)," *Encyclopedia Virginia,* accessed May 28, 2021, https://encyclopediavirginia.org/entries/mitchell-john-jr-1863-1929/.
14. Pen-and-ink drawings based on photographs were widely used in newspaper illustrations until the halftone process made it feasible to reproduce photographs at the turn of the twentieth century.
15. Amanda Frisken, *Graphic News: How Sensational Images Transformed Nineteenth-Century Journalism* (Urbana: University of Illinois Press, 2020).
16. Ersula J. Ore, *Lynching: Violence, Rhetoric, and American Identity* (Jackson: University Press of Mississippi, 2019), 22.
17. *Staunton Spectator,* Oct. 14, 1891; *Richmond Dispatch,* Oct. 18, 1891; *Roanoke Times,* Oct. 20, 1891.
18. Fitzhugh Brundage, *Lynching in the New South: Georgia and Virginia, 1880–1930* (Urbana: University of Illinois Press, 1993), 144.
19. *Richmond Planet,* Oct. 24, 1891, Oct. 31, 1891.
20. *Roanoke Times,* Oct. 20, 1891.
21. *Richmond Dispatch,* Oct. 18, 1891.
22. Rand Dotson, "Race and Violence in Urbanizing Appalachia: The Roanoke Riot of 1893," in *Blood in the Hills: A History of Violence in Appalachia,* ed. Steward E. Bruce (Lexington: University Press of Kentucky, 2012), 237–71.

23. *Richmond Planet*, Oct. 31, 1891.
24. Ore, *Lynching*, 9.
25. *Staunton Spectator*, Oct. 14, 1891.
26. *Richmond Dispatch*, Oct. 18, 1891.
27. *Roanoke Times*, Oct. 20, 1891.
28. *Richmond Planet*, Oct. 31, 1891.
29. *Staunton Spectator*, Oct. 14, 1891.
30. *Richmond Dispatch*, Oct. 18, 1891.
31. *Roanoke Times*, Oct. 20, 1891. Note the use of the word "respectable" to describe the lynch mob, which supports the discourse of middle-class respectability around "warranted" lynching in white press accounts. See Jean, "'Warranted' Lynchings."
32. *Richmond Planet*, Oct. 31, 1891.
33. *Richmond Planet*, Oct. 31, 1891.
34. *Clifton Forge and Iron-Gate Review*, Oct. 23, 1891.
35. Andrew S. Buckser, "Lynching as Ritual in the American South," *Berkeley Journal of Sociology* 37 (1992).
36. Mathews, *At the Altar of Lynching*.
37. *Staunton Spectator*, Oct. 14, 1891.
38. *Roanoke Times*, Oct. 20, 1891.
39. *Richmond Planet*, Oct. 31, 1891.
40. Frisken, *Graphic News*, 154.
41. *Richmond Planet*, Feb. 8, 1890, quoted in Ann Field Alexander, "'Like an Evil Wind': The Roanoke Riot of 1893 and the Lynching of Thomas Smith," *Virginia Magazine of History and Biography* 100, no. 2 (April 1992): 199.
42. Jacqueline Goldsby, *A Spectacular Secret: Lynching in American Life and Literature* (Chicago: University of Chicago Press, 2006).
43. Frisken, *Graphic News*, 146.
44. Ida B. Wells, "The Brutal Truth," *Daily Inter Ocean*, July 19, 1893, 17, quoted in Mia Bay, *To Tell the Truth Freely: The Life of Ida B. Wells* (New York: Hill and Wang, 2009), 174.
45. Ore, *Lynching*, 19.
46. Yuliya Parshina-Kottas, Anjali Singhvi, Audra D. S. Burch, Troy Griggs, Mika Gröndahl, Lingdong Huang, Tim Wallace, Jeremy White, and Josh Williams, "What the Tulsa Race Massacre Destroyed," *New York Times* (May 24, 2021), accessed June 2, 2021, https://www.nytimes.com/interactive/2021/05/24/us/tulsa-race-massacre.html.
47. Haywood, *Let Us Make Men*, 11.

PART II
✶
LYNCHING IN SOUTHWEST VIRGINIA

Southwest Virginia presents an interesting puzzle in the history of lynching in Virginia. While scarcely populated in comparison with the rest of the Old Dominion, this region had the highest concentration of lynching in the state. Referring more generally to the Appalachian South, Brundage summarizes this unusual pattern: "The preconditions for collective racial violence seemingly should have been absent in the region. The large white majority faced little serious threat, economic or otherwise, from the small and vulnerable black population in the region. Plantation agriculture and its attendant traditions of violent and exploitative labor relations remained peripheral to the mountain economy. Yet during the late 1880s and early 1890s mob violence in the mountains reached levels comparable to other regions of the South."[1] In Southwest Virginia, these levels were the highest of the Commonwealth. How can we explain this pattern? This is a complex question, but there is little doubt that the rapid rural industrialization in the mining and timber sectors produced a sudden wave of social change that revolutionized the region. Lumber mills, coal mines, and the expansion of railroads attracted workers from outside the region, including Black laborers and foreign immigrants; these economic and demographic transformations created the conditions for ethnic and racial hostilities to fester. As Brundage notes, "The whites who lived in Appalachia used violence as a tool to define racial boundaries in a region where traditional racial lines were either vague or nonexistent."[2]

The two essays in this section grapple with the puzzle of the origins and extent of racial violence in Southwest Virginia, adopting two different analytical approaches. While the first essay, by James William Hagy, provides a comprehensive overview of lynching in Southwest Virginia, the second essay, by Tom Costa and Zoe Crihfield, offers an in-depth investigation of racialized mob violence in Wise County, highlighting the interplay between completed lynchings and threatened lynchings.

In "Lynchings in Southwest Virginia, 1883–1927," historian James William Hagy identifies the twenty-six men who were lynched in what is usually called Far Southwest Virginia, that is, the counties and cities west of Roanoke. Of the twenty-six victims, twenty-three were Black and three were white; nineteen were accused of murder, and seven were alleged to have assaulted or attempted to assault a white woman. Hagy attempts to explain why this mountainous farming and coal mining area featured so many extralegal killings by looking at its political, economic, and social transformations at the end of the nineteenth century. A tradition of interpersonal violence, sudden industrialization, an influx of migrant workers, and the development of the railroad system are among the reasons he offers to explain the large number of lynchings in Southwest Virginia. Furthermore, this essay examines *threatened* lynchings in the area, adding another layer of analysis to understand racial terror in the region and the role of law enforcement in trying to prevent lethal mob violence under certain circumstances.

Historian Tom Costa and graduate student Zoe Crihfield dissect the three recorded lynchings of African Americans in Wise County in "Justice and Injustice in the Coalfields: Lynchings in Wise County." Wiley Guynn was shot in 1902; David Hurst (or Hunt), was hanged in 1920, and Leonard Woods was hanged, shot, and burned at Pound Gap on the Virginia side of the road leading into Kentucky in 1927. In each of these three incidents, a white mob took extralegal action against a Black man who had allegedly attacked a white person. Early twentieth-century Wise County saw rapid demographic and economic changes, and each of the Wise County incidents had its own unique features, as local officials sought to keep order in changing communities. Wiley Guynn's killing took place as another Black man, Robert Foy, languished in jail for killing a white man in the same locality some six months earlier. Numerous delays in Foy's case may have inflamed local whites to summarily punish Guynn's alleged offense. The lynching of David Hurst took place under the watch of a local sheriff, A. P. Corder, who prevented another attempt to lynch a Black man two weeks after Hunt was killed. Corder was also able to arrest several members of the mob who had hanged Hunt, sending two of them to prison. Leonard Woods's lynching took place as Virginia governor Harry Byrd was becoming increasingly concerned about the negative press lynchings generated. The Woods case prompted Byrd to enact a comprehensive antilynching law in March 1928. In addition to discussing the unique circumstances behind each lynching, this essay also situates them within the larger context of Southwest Virginia.

Notes

1. Fitzhugh Brundage, "Racial Violence, Lynchings, and Modernization in the Mountain South," in *Appalachians and Race, The Mountain South from Slavery to Segregation*, ed. John Inscoe (Lexington: University Press of Kentucky, 2001), 306.
2. Brundage, "Racial Violence," 308.

LYNCHINGS IN SOUTHWEST VIRGINIA, 1883-1927

JAMES WILLIAM HAGY

In his *Lynching in the New South: Georgia and Virginia, 1880–1930* (1993), W. Fitzhugh Brundage analyzed the lynchings that occurred during the Jim Crow era in Virginia. He discovered twenty-nine in the southwestern part of the Old Dominion, which surprised readers because the area had fewer African Americans than other sections of the state. Twenty-four of the victims were Black and five white.[1]

Since there is no standard definition of what comprises Southwest Virginia, this article concentrates on the counties west of Roanoke, a smaller and more cohesive area than that used by Brundage.[2] This region is mostly mountainous and agricultural, but in the late 1880s part of it dramatically changed with the exploitation of coal.

No cities existed in the region before the Civil War, and the only one in the area during the Jim Crow era was Bristol, which dates from 1890. In addition, the state did not create Bland County until 1861, and Dickenson became a county in 1880.

Most of the land is too mountainous to farm: the Appalachian chain dominates the north and the Blue Ridge defines the south, but the valleys have rich farmland. Because of the terrain, land holdings were generally small to moderate in size.

The growing season is too short for cotton and sugarcane, the crops that used the most slave labor prior to the Civil War. Instead, farmers in Southwest Virginia produced grains, animals, and tobacco. These factors and the altitude meant the economy and society differed from Piedmont and Tidewater

Virginia.³ As a result, most of the counties had few enslaved people and free persons of color in 1860.⁴

Most of the information in this essay comes from local and statewide newspapers. Those accounts chosen are hopefully the most accurate; however, it is not possible to know if these reports are true, especially when some newspapers contradict others or have details that cannot be corroborated elsewhere. Indeed, all descriptions may contain errors, especially regarding the character and actions of those lynched. Those "facts" typically came from people involved in the lynchings and should not be trusted. In addition, newspaper editors sometimes printed accounts that later proved to be false. An example is a report of a lynching in Tazewell County. On April 20, 1920, the *Virginia Pilot,* and on April 21, the *Richmond Times,* printed an account that came by telegraph that stated that John Peters, a Black man, had assaulted Kate Ritchie, a sixteen-year-old white girl near Tazewell and that he had been chased by bloodhounds, captured, and put in jail. At midnight, according to the informer, a mob broke down the jail door with axes, put a noose around the accused man's neck, dragged him about two hundred yards down the railroad tracks, and shot him hundreds of times before hanging his dead body on a tree. On April 27, however, the *Shenandoah Herald* reported that "the lynching at Tazewell on Thursday of John Peters is entirely without foundation." The real story appeared in the *Clinch Valley News* in Tazewell on the same day as the one in the *Virginia Pilot.* That paper related that Mrs. D. A. Daugherty awoke to find Peery [or Peters], in her bed. When she screamed, he fled. Afterwards, he was captured and tried twice, but both juries failed to agree on his guilt. The court then released him on the condition that he leave the state in twenty-four hours.⁵ There are other instances of inaccurate accounts.⁶ Unfortunately, many counties did not have local newspapers, or those that did exist have not survived or been made available. In addition, some newspapers that reported on Southwest Virginia were based outside the state: the best example is the *Bristol Herald Courier,* which was then on the Tennessee side of Bristol but is now in Virginia.⁷

Newspapers, however, were not the only sources. Local histories have also been used. Some are well documented and accurate, but others can contain false information. For example, V. N. "Bud" Phillips, in *Pioneers in Paradise: Legends and Stories from Bristol Tennessee/Virginia,* told a tale about African American people in Bristol, Virginia, lynching a Black man, but no record of the lynching or any of the people supposedly involved could be found in newspapers or public records. Such a lynching, had it happened, would certainly have been known because the Black mob was supposed to have suspended the victim from the Mary Street bridge over the railroad tracks so that an oncoming train smashed into his body.[8] Furthermore, the publications of local historical societies, on and offline, were utilized. In addition, county and circuit court records were searched. Some of these have information on lynchers who were indicted and what resulted from their trials—if any were held.

Following is a summary of each documented lynching victim in Southwest Virginia.

Bluford Smith, Tazewell County, 1882

On December 23, 1882, after some sort of dispute, Bluford Smith, a Black man, allegedly murdered a white man, Charles Kinser. Smith was arrested and jailed, but six days later, a mob broke into the building, overcame the guard, took the prisoner out, and shot him. Newspapers reported that no one was tried for the killing.[9]

William M. Crockett, Wythe County, 1883

Sometime in early 1883, William M. Crockett, age twenty-nine, and Joseph Hurt, both white, gambled as they played ten-pins, during which Hurt won a considerable amount of money. Crockett became upset at his loss and killed Hurt. Subsequently, the sheriff arrested Crockett and took him to jail. On April 11 a mob went to the jail, where one of them tricked the jailer into opening the door by telling him he was a deputy with a prisoner to admit. The rest pushed their way in, managed to get the keys, took the man out, put a gag in his mouth, tied his arms and legs, and carried him about fifty yards to Slater's mill. There they put a rope around his neck, pulled him up about thirty feet, and shot at him about twenty times: he was hit by four bullets. A coroner's jury ruled Crockett had died as a result of strangulation and gunshot wounds by "unknown" parties.[10]

Unnamed Black Youth, Russell County, 1884

On June 6, 1884, a mob lynched an unnamed African American boy in the Castlewood area in Russell County. According to one account, two sons of Harvey Osborne, white, were picking strawberries when a fourteen-year-old Black boy joined them. When one of the Osborne boys left the field, the African American shot the other in the stomach and left him in a sinkhole. Later, according to this account, he went to the Osborne home and confessed what he had done. The mother rushed to her son, who lived long enough to tell her what had occurred. Another version of the story related that the boys were hunting and got into a quarrel about a nest of partridge eggs, and, without provocation, the Black boy killed the white boy. This account, furthermore, states that he "described with a fiendish laugh the manner in which the little boy fell when shot." Authorities arrested the youth and put him in a house for safekeeping, but on June 6 or 7, thirty or forty masked men surrounded the house and demanded that the youth be turned over to them. The guard refused and managed to escape with the youth, but after an exchange of gunfire, the mob overpowered the guard, took the teenager, and hanged him on a rail placed between two gateposts. One of these accounts is obviously incorrect, and the other probably is as well. No lynchers were identified.[11]

Alvy Jackson, Bland County, 1885

On January 30, 1885, Alvy Jackson, eighteen years old, an African American also known as Ivy and Ab, was accused of killing a white man believed to be named Terry on the road running from Sharon Springs in Bland County to Burkes Garden in Tazewell County. For this, a mob lynched him on February 4. Newspaper accounts varied as to the facts of the event and even the name of the victim. Some journals obviously embellished the accounts they received, and local lore handed down for several generations provided different descriptions than the newspapers of the time. Basically, the stories relate that Terry (or Jerry) talked to Alvy Jackson when he passed through Sharon Springs on his way to find work at the coal mines in Pocahontas,

Tazewell County. Jackson supposedly trailed and shot him about four miles from Sharon Springs. The following day two men discovered the victim's nude body. For reasons unknown, people suspected that Jackson had killed the traveler. The sheriffs found him on a Saturday night in his father's house where he was "playing a banjo for other negroes to dance." He claimed he was innocent and told conflicting stories, one being he had seen two other Black man kill the stranger, but he, according to the accounts, was wearing the dead man's bloody clothes: the coat showed two bullet holes, and Alvy had blood on his shirtsleeves. They also claimed to have discovered Perry's (or Terry's or Jerry's) pants in the accused man's bed. Jackson was arrested and taken to the county jail. The Bland County Court Order Book, 1884–1891, shows that Jackson was indicted on Wednesday, February 4, but that night a mob of about twenty men broke down the door of the lockup, threatened the jailer with their pistols, and forced him to give up the keys to his cell. They took Jackson from the jail, tied him to a fence, and riddled his body with bullets.[12]

William Henry Jones, Wythe County, 1888

In July 1888 a Black man whose real name was William Jones (he also used the names Walker Jones, Henry Smith, and William Henry Smith) was accused of assaulting a Mrs. Metcalfe, a white woman, near New River Bridge in Pulaski County. According to one newspaper account, which may be untrue, Mrs. Metcalfe later died along with her unborn child. The sheriff arrested Jones in Pulaski County but took him to the jail in Wytheville for his protection. On July 10 the sheriff learned that a mob had formed to lynch the man. The sheriff then took Jones from the jail with the intention of taking him to the more secure jail in Lynchburg; however, when lawmen boarded a train with the prisoner, some twenty-five men were waiting for them. They seized the suspect, placed a rope around his neck, and despite the efforts of the sheriffs to prevent it, took him off the train and dragged him to a nearby tree where they hanged him. An eyewitness claimed that Jones confessed to the crime. The participants in the lynching were "unknown." While under arrest, Jones confessed to having murdered Lizzie Wilson, sixteen, in Roanoke in 1884.[13]

Martin Rollins, Russell County, 1889

Martin Rollins, a Black banjo picker, was accused in March 1889 of murdering Perry Combs by hitting him on the head with a stick. Rollins seems to have been an outsider who came to the area to find work on the railroads. The sheriff arrested Rollins and took him to the jail in Lebanon. After 10:30 p.m. on April 2, 1889, a mob took him from the jail and paraded him through the street. When he began to pray, the mob stopped him and told him that if he prayed any more, they would shoot him through his heart. After that, they took him about one mile east of town and hanged him on an ash tree along the Fincastle Turnpike. They then shot him through his legs, chest, and head. Later, a grand jury began an investigation, but no records of a trial could be found.[14]

Unnamed Black Man, Russell County, 1890

According to a single newspaper, on August 9, 1890, a Black man was accused of "outraging" the young wife of John W. Gibson near the old Russell Courthouse at Dickensonville. The sheriff arrested him that afternoon and took him to a preliminary hearing immediately. But the next morning his body was found with thirty-six bullet holes in it and dangling from a tree. Nothing further could be found in newspapers or court records.[15]

Robert "Bob" Clark, City of Bristol, Virginia, 1891

On June 7, 1891, Bob Clark, a twenty-year-old African American, allegedly committed "a horrible outrage" on Mrs. John Warren, "a respectable white lady," while her husband was working at night. Suspicion fell on Clark because he had reportedly served time in prison in both Tennessee and Virginia (which would have been impossible because of his age). Newspapers described Clark as a drunken brute "whose blood was poisoned by a loathsome disease" (syphilis), a charge sometimes made to poison public opinion against the lynching victim. The evidence against him consisted of some footprints near the house that matched the size of his shoes. The police arrested him on June 12, and the following morning the mayor of Bristol gave him a preliminary hearing and returned him to the jail. By that time, a great crowd had gathered and would not disperse. According to one newspaper account, hundreds of people of all colors, ages, and races reportedly gathered around the jail. A few prominent men begged the crowd to let the law take its course, but the mob hissed them down. Eventually, the rioters crashed the door open, went inside, and brought the prisoner out. They then took him about a mile from town and hanged him on a tree. A Black man in the crowd remarked that if people of his color had stuck together, Clark would not have been lynched. That resulted in four men threatening him with guns, and for a moment it appeared he might be lynched as well. After a week of hearings, on June 19 a grand jury indicted five men for their involvement in the lynching: Charles Davis, Flemming Littrell, Nick Detter, Steve Collins, and Frank Nave. On January 13, 1892, the circuit court in Abingdon, in what was considered a test case, tried Davis, but he was acquitted. Having failed to convict him, the court did not try the others. [16]

Nathan Burgess and Sherman Lucas, Russell County, 1892

In late October 1892 Nathan Burgess and Sherman Lucas, both white, allegedly murdered Oak Sutherland, a white resident of Cleveland, Virginia. The sheriff arrested them and locked them up at Lebanon. Sometime between Saturday, October 29, and Monday, October 31 (the sources are not clear), a mob of "unknown" masked men stormed the jail, overpowered the guard, and took the men to the west end of town. They handcuffed them and hanged them together on a tree and then and riddled their bodies with bullets. The lynchers claimed that they did that because the two prisoners might escape, as they nearly had done a few days earlier.[17]

Jerry Brown, Sam Kirkpatrick, John Johnson, Spencer Branch, Sam Ellerson, Sam Blow, Sam Barns, Tazewell County, 1893

On January 30, 1893, two white merchants, Alexander Ratliff and Benjamin Shortridge, from Buchanan County, travelled to Richlands in Tazewell County where they "showed their money." When they left a saloon, a group of Black men reportedly followed and robbed them of $31. According to the story, the thieves beat the white men on their heads with clubs and a hatchet and left their bodies in a bloody mess on the railroad tracks. Jerry Brown, the first man to be arrested, allegedly confessed to the murder and implicated others. The news quickly spread to Buchanan County by telegraph, which resulted in a mob arriving in Richlands, where, at 11 p.m., January 31, they lynched Brown on a tree near the train depot and left his body hanging there with a guard to prevent its removal. Meanwhile, officers arrested Spencer Branch and John Johnson for involvement in the killing. To protect them from the increasing threat, the lawmen took them three miles through some woods to Cedar Bluff, with the aim of taking them by train to the jail at Tazewell. But when the officers and their prisoners boarded the train, they found it filled with men seeking revenge. In addition, authorities discovered a fourth man, Sam Ellerson, on the train. He had tried to flee to the west but had been arrested in Russell County.[18] The horde forced the engineer to stop and take on other men who had been searching the woods. After that, they marched the three Black men back to Richlands and forced confessions from them in which they stated that they had banded together to rob others. They confessed that the money and hatchet could be found at a certain location, but the sheriff found nothing there. To kill the accused men, the mob put them on a horse, one by one, with nooses around their necks, and gave the animal a strong blow that caused it to lurch forward, breaking their necks. The lynchers then hanged the bodies on the same tree as Jerry Brown. Before that, one of the men stated that Sam Blow, also Black, had killed a white man, Joseph Hunt, under similar circumstances in September 1891. The mob found Blow at Cedar Bluff and hanged him beside Indian Creek, the fifth hanging in twenty-four hours. The informer also stated that Blow had been assisted in the killing of Hunt by two white men, Thomas Lambert and a man whose last name was Harman. These two had been arrested for the murder but were released because of the lack of evidence, whereupon they fled across the border into West Virginia. Lambert was later arrested in that state but escaped through a train window.

In addition, a deputy sheriff, John Peery, reported that a sixth man, Sam Barns, had been hanged at Doran, a mile west of Richlands, for complicity in the murder of Hunt. That murder was similar to the Richlands murders in that the perpetrators hit Hunt on the head, robbed him, and placed his body on the railroad tracks so that it could be mangled by a train. The *Clinch Valley*

News and *Richmond Times* named Sam Kirkpatrick as one of those lynched on the second night of the killings. If true, that made seven men lynched over the course of a few days. The circuit court indicted several men, but the local newspaper indicated only that Thomas Blankenship was tried for murder three years later: he was acquitted. Without naming them, the *Bedford Times* reported that two of the men lynched were from that area. For many years after that people talked of seven men being hanged in 1893.[19]

Charles Morgan, Tazewell County, 1893

Kiz Reed, a Black woman labelled "the wickedest woman in West Virginia," operated "disorderly" houses in Bluefield, West Virginia, and across the border in Graham, Virginia (now also named Bluefield). In February 1893 someone shot a Black police officer, John Chandler, at Reed's business just outside Bluefield. For that, she was jailed temporarily. During that time, a vigilante committee took her out of the jail, conducted a mock hanging, and then gave her a beating. The race or races of the vigilantes is unknown. But troubles were not over. On April 3, Charles Morgan, an African American described as a rough, bad character from the "coal diggings," drew his revolver and shot indiscriminately into a crowd, killing young John Leese, also Black. Morgan fled across the border into Graham, where a Black policeman arrested and confined him, apparently without a guard. At midnight a mob of Black men lynched Morgan on an apple tree on the banks of Bluestone River, after which they shot him through with bullets. No white people apparently took part in the lynching. The mayor of Graham vowed he would get to the bottom of the affair and see that justice was done. Whether he succeeded is unknown. This was one of a few cases in Virginia where African Americans lynched one of their own race.[20]

George Halsey, Smyth County, 1893

On May 11, 1893, George Halsey, a "coal black negro" about twenty years of age, purportedly brutally beat and criminally assaulted Mrs. Ira Adkins in Marion, who was home alone. Her husband, Z. T. Adkins (the county treasurer), and a daughter had gone to Wytheville to attend a parade by the Knights Templar, a fraternal Christian organization. According to the story, Halsey went to the Atkins house and demanded that Mrs. Atkins give him her keys and tell him the whereabouts of the family's money. When she refused to comply, he allegedly struck her on the head with some stove wood, dragged her into the dining room, hit her again, and raped her. After the assault, he hit her again and stomped on her, cut her throat, rolled her into a closet, closed the door, and then searched the house for the keys. When he could not find them, he returned, let her out of the closet, told her that she had lied before, and said if she did not tell him what he wanted to know, he would finish her off. She then told him. Afterwards, he beat her over the head with a chair, knocked her down, and stomped on her chest and neck. Thinking her dead, he locked the door to the dining room and went upstairs. While he was there, she regained consciousness a second time, crawled through a window, and managed to get to the house of her father-in-law, Joseph Atkins. He raised an alarm; shortly, "hundreds of citizens were in pursuit of the fiend." Upon notification, her husband immediately returned home. Meanwhile, Halsey had been captured, and Mrs. Atkins identified him as her attacker. On that same day, a source in Marion reported: "He will be lynched to-night." That, indeed, happened. Officers took him to jail, but at ten p.m., angry citizens of the town, joined by Knights Templars, took Halsey from the jail, hanged him on a tree, and riddled his body with bullets. No one wore masks or any other disguises. The following day A. P. Killinger, the coroner, and A. M. Dickenson, the commonwealth's attorney, directed the sheriff, W. D. Wilmore, to summon a jury for an inquest into how Halsey had met his death. Their verdict was that he "came to his death by being hung by persons to the jury unknown."[21]

Samuel Wood, Scott County, 1894

On May 14, 1894, near Gate City, a band of masked white men calling themselves "Regulators" decided to rid the community of houses of ill repute. The women occupying these places had been forewarned and fled. When they reached the house of Samuel Wood, a Black man aged twenty or twenty-one who was known to be peaceable and not an operator of a house of prostitution, he refused to allow them to enter. The Regulators then fired about thirty bullets through the door and killed Wood, though they missed his wife and children on the bed of the tiny house. Enraged, John Mitchell Jr., editor of the African American newspaper the *Richmond Planet,* wrote that Black people should arm themselves for protection. On June 11 the circuit court indicted twelve men for murder, who then were released on bond. The court dropped charges against two of them. One of these, Charles Wax, had already sold his property, paid his debts, and moved west. Following that, the court tried the rest, but the jury declared them not guilty.[22]

Paris Suits, Wise County, 1898

On April 28, 1894, the *Alexandria Gazette* reported: "A telegram from Coeburn states that at the coal mines near there yesterday Paris Suits, a desperate young fellow, shot and killed a white man and a negro without cause. Suits turned to make his escape, but was shot to death by bystanders, his body being riddled with bullets. Suits' slayers were not arrested." No other information on this killing could be found. Although this usually would not be thought of as a lynching, it was the killing of someone by two or more persons without a hearing or trial upon learning that some wrong had been committed. It is therefore included in this study.

Floyd McP. "Mack" Howlett, Carroll County, 1898

Two white farmers, Floyd McP. "Mack" Howlett and Carr Allen, disputed the use of a road in 1898. Allen had to pass through Howlett's farm to get to his property, but the Allens often left the gate open, which allowed Howlett's cows to wander off. Howlett told Allen that he could no longer use the road and blocked it. When the Allens began to remove the obstacles, Howlett fired his shotgun and killed Allen. Allen's sons fetched the sheriff, who arrested Howlett and his sons and took them to jail on May 28, 1898. Fearing a lynching, the sheriff temporarily hid the Howletts but returned them to jail when he perceived the threat was over. Yet on June 20, 1898, a mob of about twenty men arrived and demanded that the jailer turn over the Howletts. The jailer refused; he was hit on the head and had his keys taken. Another jailer present at the scene did nothing to stop the mob. The attackers grabbed Howlett, who fought "like a tiger" and "knocked his assailants right and left." Finding that they could not control him, the leader of the crowd ordered his men to shoot Howlett, which they did at close range. The group then disbanded. The people of the county felt the lynching was justified, and no one was indicted or prosecuted.[23]

Daniel Long, Wythe County, 1900

On December 6, 1900, Daniel Long, an African American man, age twenty-three, allegedly choked Mrs. Robert Fisher of Ivanhoe until she was unconscious and then raped her. When she revived, she screamed for help, which soon arrived. A search for Long began. The next day a constable found him and a friend, Lewis Hale, also Black, at Shanty Row, a Black section in Ivanhoe. Mrs. Fisher identified Long but said she had never seen Hale. Nevertheless, the officer arrested both men and started to transport them to the jail when nearly a hundred heavily armed and undisguised men suddenly appeared and confronted the authorities. They took Long, allowed him to pray, and then attempted to hang him to the limb of a tree. When the rope or limb broke, the mob tied the victim to the tree and shot him to death. A grand jury released Hale without any charges and did not indict any of the lynchers.[24]

Wiley Gwynn, Wise County, 1902

On June 6, 1902, Wiley Gwynn (or Guynn), an African American man twenty-eight years of age, was accused of attempted assault on Mary Green, a white girl, ten or twelve years old, who was carrying some berries over a hill towards a mine. According to accounts, people heard her screams and came to her rescue. The story is similar to one in Bristol, Tennessee, in 1925, where an eleven-year-old girl claimed a Black man had attempted to assault her. After police searched for six days amid threats of mob action, the girl admitted that she had lied because she was late for school and feared her father would whip her for that. Mary Green may have simply been frightened: at the time some white parents taught their children to fear Black men by telling them that if they misbehaved a "nigger" man would get them. Gwynn was arrested, after which a mob of both races seized him and filled his body with bullets until it "was but a bloody, torn, and mass of flesh." The attorney for the Commonwealth, W. G. G. Dotson, was present at the killing and pled with the angry crowd to let the law take its course, but in their furious state, the lynchers ignored him without consequence.[25]

Henry Pennington, Buchanan County, 1909

In Hurly, on the night of September 21, 1909, someone murdered Elizabeth Baker Justus, her daughter, Lydia Justus Meadows, her son-in-law, George Meadows, and their three children, Will, Noah, and Lafayette, all white. The murderer(s) burned the cabin. The following morning, neighbors found the remains of the women and children in the smoldering embers, while George Meadows lay about thirty feet from the house. A baby appeared to have been burned alive on the doorstep. Evidence quickly pointed to Howard Little, a white man who had received a life sentence for a murder in Kentucky but had been pardoned after he had served five years. At the time of the massacre, he lived in Mohawk, West Virginia, and worked at the Ritter Lumber Co. in Grundy, Virginia. After detectives arrested him, the circuit court tried him and found him guilty of first-degree murder. He was sentenced to death by the electric chair. As Little waited to be executed, Henry Pennington, a white man, shot and killed Sam Baker in the streets of Hurley on Christmas Eve. Baker's wife was a daughter of Elizabeth Justus, and he was a relative of George Meadows, while Pennington was a friend of Howard Little. Some people believed that Pennington had been involved in the massacre. After shooting Baker, Pennington fled, but that night an armed group exchanged gunfire with him, which resulted in his being wounded and captured. The sheriff locked him up in a boarding house and surrounded it with a strong guard, but at midnight, a mob overpowered the guard, seized Pennington, hanged him on a pipe, and riddled his body with bullets. On April 19, 1910, the circuit court indicted Wayne Justus, Lafayette Justus, Richard Lawson, and P. L. Johnson for their participation in the hanging. The commonwealth's attorney charged them even though he had been warned that enough rope was left to use on anyone who tried to bring the guilty parties to justice. No newspapers reported if trials were held, and, regrettably, records from the circuit clerk's office have disappeared. One can assume that they were not tried.[26]

J. H. Hurst, a.k.a. David Hunt, Wise County, 1920

On Friday, November 12, 1920, a Black man, age twenty-five, identified initially as David Hunt but later named as J. H. Hurst, reportedly assaulted a sixty-year-old white woman, Sarah Ball, at her home at Kent Junction. After his arrest, a mob broke into the jail, took him out, and hanged him. The commonwealth's attorney, C. R. McCorkle, indicted fifty of the participants. Two were tried and sentenced for short terms, but Gov. E. Lee Trinkle pardoned them because they were the only ones that had been convicted.[27]

Raymond Arthur Byrd, Wythe County, 1926

Raymond Byrd[28] enlisted in the US Army on August 2, 1918, and served in Company H of the 807th Pioneer Infantry, a Black unit that labored on construction in France during World War I. He received his discharge on July 16, 1919, and soon afterward married Tennessee "Tennie" Hawkins. In 1926 Byrd toiled on a farm near Rural Retreat owned by Grover Cleveland Grubb, a white man who worked away from home six days a week. On July 23, Minnie Grubb, nineteen-year-old daughter of Grover, gave birth to a child that had been fathered by Byrd. This greatly upset Grubb, who tried, without success, to have Byrd arrested for rape. Then the father discovered that another daughter, Essie May, age twenty-two, was also pregnant by Byrd. Unable to prosecute Byrd because the daughters were legally adults, the father next claimed that his twelve-year-old daughter, Mary, had been molested by Byrd, although the charge appears to have been false. The last charge attracted a crowd that intended to lynch the Black veteran; however, the sheriff of Wythe County, W. C. Kincer, and deputies arrived and calmed the mob. They arrested Byrd and put him in jail at Wytheville, but on the night of August 15, disguised lynchers arrived. According to the jailer, they threatened him with their shotguns, so he handed them the keys. Some suspicion arose about the jailer's actions because he did not call the sheriff for about half an hour. He claimed that the telephone line had been cut before the mob invaded, so he had to go to a hotel to summon aid, but the hotel was only a short walking distance from the jail. Meanwhile, one of the mob shot the sleeping man and others beat his head to a pulp with clubs and rifle butts. After that, they tied his body to the running board of a car and dragged it (or dragged it by hand, according to some accounts) to a place near Byrd's house where they hanged him on a tree and fired bullets into his remains. On this occasion, Gov. Harry Byrd and the board of supervisors offered a reward for the arrest and conviction of the participants in the lynching. Next, the commonwealth's attorney, H. M. Heuser, and Judge Horace Sutherland travelled to Richmond to consult with the governor, who appointed two special prosecutors to investigate the matter. The ineptitude of the police can be seen in their investigation: they cut down the tree on which Byrd had been lynched and took it for evidence because it bore the freshly carved initials of "H. H." and "R. B." The sheriff deduced that the initials stood for Howard Huddle, white, who had recently moved to West Virginia, and Raymond Byrd. Police arrested Huddle a few days later, but a special grand jury released him without charges. In early 1927 authorities also arrested Floyd Willard because he had bragged on a hunting trip that he had participated in the lynching, but at his trial he claimed that he was drunk at the time he made the statements and was home asleep when the lynching occurred. The jury, after ten minutes of deliberation, returned a verdict of not guilty. No other arrests were made.[29]

Leonard Woods, Wise County, 1927

On November 17, 1927, Leonard Woods, Black, shot and killed Herschel Deaton, white, as he drove from Wise County into Kentucky. Sheriffs arrested Woods and took him to jail in Kentucky. Following Deaton's funeral, carloads of men drove from Virginia into the Bluegrass State, broke into the jail, and seized Woods. They took him to the state border where they hanged him, filled his body with bullets, and then set it afire with gasoline. The two states wrangled over which side of the border he was on when he was killed. In Kentucky, a grand jury investigated but indicted no one. Even though Virginia governor Harry Byrd declared that the lynching took place in Kentucky, he faced increased pressure to outlaw lynching in the Commonwealth. The following year, the Virginia General Assembly passed a sweeping antilynching law.[30]

After lynchings, local leaders often chose to put the incidents out of their minds. An example is William C. Pendleton (1847–1941), who in 1920 published the *History of Tazewell County and Southwest Virginia*. He barely mentions slaves except to say they loyally took care of their owners' families during the Civil War. He says nothing about the lynchings in that county.[31] This despite his having lived through the Civil War (when he served in the 8th Virginia Cavalry), Reconstruction, and the Jim Crow era.

Ten of the lynching victims were hanged, twelve shot, five hanged and shot, and one hanged, shot, and burned. The cruelest killing was that of the unnamed fourteen-year-old boy in Russell County that a mob strung up between two fence posts—which meant he slowly choked to death. Nineteen lynchings took place in the recently industrialized counties of Tazewell, Wise, Buchanan, and Russell, rather than in agricultural counties (the exception is Wythe). Sixteen of the lynchings occurred in the 1890s, the decade when lynching reached its peak throughout the South. After that, extralegal executions began to be less frequent, and accused men were more likely to be tried by circuit courts.

Nineteen of those lynched had been accused of murder, while seven supposedly assaulted or attempted to assault a white female. Although one newspaper reported that Wiley Gwynn "had committed the foulest crime known to man—the ravishing of a baby girl," she could have simply been frightened by seeing a Black man.[32] In the case of Raymond Byrd, the issue was miscegenation rather than assault. One person, Samuel Wood, was shot simply because he did not open his door to a white mob looking to terrorize houses of prostitution. While the victims were mostly Black males who were summarily executed by white mobs, African American people lynched one Black person and participated in the lynching of another two.

In at least nine instances, perhaps more, lynchers faced some kind of inquiry before an official body, whether an inquest, a coroner's jury, a grand jury, or trial. Indictments, however, did not usually result in trials, and only two men were convicted—only to be soon pardoned by the governor. Interestingly, one man in Tazewell County was indicted and tried three years after a lynching, which would suggest sheriffs did not always give up on prosecuting individuals. In some cases, the lynchers were listed as unknown or masked, which probably meant that no official attempt was made to identify them. In one case, a paper reported that people believed the lynching was justified.

Sometimes accused men facing a lynch mob confessed to having committed offenses. While some of them may have been truthful, the forced confessions in Tazewell County in 1893 proved to be false. In addition, some people confessed to crimes they did not commit. This would be especially true if a man faced certain death by lynching. In that position, he might believe that if he confessed, his life might be spared. An example of this occurred in 1894 in Lebanon, Indiana, when a Black man confessed to having assaulted a woman. After his trial, he said in an interview that he was not guilty of the crime but pled guilty "because he was afraid of being lynched and if he pled guilty, he would be taken away from Lebanon promptly and thus escape mob violence." He received a sentence of twenty-one years in the penitentiary.[33] Even more likely, the confessions may not have happened at all but were reported to newspapers by people who took part in or observed the lynchings to justify the mob's actions.

Some of those lynched may have been outcasts or had committed other crimes; however, newspapers printed gossip about their characters, and those descriptions could have been manufactured after the fact. Some of the lynched men were seen as "floaters," or itinerants, as is evident by their involvement in events in other places. Also, few of those lynched appear in census records of the places where they died. Exceptions to this would be Alvy Jackson, Sam Blow, Spencer Branch, and Raymond Byrd.

In instances where the ages of the lynched men are known, most were in their twenties—"young bucks," as whites called them—at the peak of their physical power and likely unmarried, thus the most feared by whites. The youngest was fourteen and the oldest thirty-one.

For the most part, the lynchings happened before anyone had time to ascertain the facts and prepare a defense. A person could be captured and lynched a few hours later, as happened with an unnamed man in Russell County in 1890.

In Southwest Virginia no evidence was found that showed law enforcement officers encouraged, participated in, or covered up a lynching. Lack of evidence, however, does not mean it did not happen. At the same time, nineteenth- and twentieth-century policing should not be judged by twenty-first-century standards. For example, in the 1890s Tazewell County witnessed several lynchings as well as conflicts between miners and their employers. The sheriff had two deputies: one was the jailer while the other was stationed in the western part of the county.[34] Those three men dealt with a population of 19,899 residents.[35] Furthermore, they did not have training or know modern forensics. Travel around the rural counties was also a problem except where trains ran. For the most part, law enforcement had to ride on horseback: the roads were bad and travel slow and difficult. In 1910 Virginia could boast of only seven miles of macadamized road, none of which served Southwest Virginia.[36] Counties also did not have detectives to investigate. Investigations relied instead on the Baldwin-Felts Detective Agency, which is better known for violently repressing miners when there were conflicts with the owners. That company did not have to observe boundaries of counties or states or be particular about civil rights. Finally, lynchers had kith and kin, likely throughout the county, who would have been very reluctant and afraid to report on them. The *Clinch Valley News*,[37] when reporting on the lynchings in Richlands, stated, "It has always been well nigh impossible to implicate individuals in such cases because of participation or unwillingness of witnesses." The paper also stated that "men who did not wish to carry with them accurate knowledge regarding the lynching at Richlands turned away their heads at the critical moment."[38] In *The Silent Shore,* Charles L. Chavis Jr. noted the same reluctance of people to become involved after a lynching in Maryland. Police faced a "system of silence" after the event. This included not only the people who participated in the event or who had some knowledge of the killings but also people who had only heard of it.[39] People who openly discussed the lynchings could possibly face retribution by the legal system or from those who took part.

In addition, each county had an elected attorney for the commonwealth whose duties included making criminal charges and prosecuting cases. Both the sheriff and the attorney resided in their counties and could face being defeated at the next election or having their or their families' lives threatened. When faced by an angry mob that might kill them, they had little choice but to yield. To do otherwise could be suicidal. Their oath, according to Section 7 of the Virginia Constitution of 1870, which was taken by all state and county officials, did not require them to sacrifice themselves but to uphold the Constitution of the United States. Section 34 of the Virginia Constitution of 1902 required them to uphold the state constitution as well.

If a serious problem arose, the sheriffs could deputize citizens to assist them, which they usually did. There were no state police to help—that organization dates from 1932. The only other option for help would be to ask the governor to send in national guard units, which did happen on occasion. Law enforcement officers, therefore, were not so much unwilling to enforce the laws but limited in their ability to do so. Although most of the people who were lynched were in police custody when mobs took over, police capitulation may have resulted from intimidation, not cooperation. In any case, there is no evidence regarding why law enforcement officers turned over prisoners.

In some instances, local law enforcement officers succeeded in arresting, holding, and trying people despite lynching threats. The incomplete list in the table included here shows twenty-three people who escaped lynchings. Of these, eight were white and fifteen Black. The list also shows that the state put five men to death, two of them white, while twelve received prison sentences that were often shorter than one would expect in the twenty-first century. The governor later pardoned the two white men.[40]

Five individuals in this list, all white, illustrate the extraordinary actions law enforcement took at times to prevent lynchings. The first, Howard Little, was accused of multiple murders of a family in Buchanan County. To protect him, the sheriff took him to the jail in Lebanon in Russell County, but a mob of about fifty men from Buchanan went into Russell County to free him. But the sheriff of Buchanan sent a telegram to the sheriff in Russell, who gathered a posse that turned back the mob. Following that, the sheriff of Russell maintained full-time guards to prevent an attack on the jail. When officers transferred Little back to Buchanan for trial, police closely guarded the jail as well as the courthouse until the trial concluded.

The next two who were protected from a lynch mob were brothers Luther and James Canter, who were accused of brutally murdering a woman in Washington County. Fearful of a lynching, the sheriffs took them by train to the jail in Roanoke until their joint trial began. At Marion, in Smyth County, a posse of twenty-five men boarded their train with shotguns to prevent any mob action. Upon arrival in Abingdon, the train made an unscheduled stop near the courthouse. When the men emerged from the train, a group of about eighty deputized men escorted them to the courthouse. Additional

Persons who escaped lynching, 1883–1922

YEAR	PERSON	COUNTY/ CITY	RACE	CHARGE	RESULT
1883	Ferrall, O. F.	Russell	White	Larceny	Repaid part, fled
1883	Griffin, Evan	Russell	White	Larceny	Repaid part, fled[1]
1890	Akers, Thomas	Montgomery	White	Assault, white girl	Prison, 20 years, later pardoned[2]
1890	Cooper, Robert, Jr.	Montgomery	White	Assault, white girl	Prison, 20 years, later pardoned[3]
1890	Garrett, Haney	Russell	Black female	Arson	Prison, 10 years[4]
1891	Short, James	Tazewell	White	Murder, white man	Prison, 18 years[5]
1891	Nowlin, Henry	Wythe	Black	Murder, white man	Hanged by state[6]
1891	Prince, Jack	Wythe	Black	Shooting, white man	Prison, 9 years[7]
1891	Shucks, John	Wythe	Black	Shooting, white man	Unknown[8]
1903	Woodard, Henry	Tazewell	Black	Murder, white man	Hanged by state[9]
1908	Grice, James	Scott	Black	Murder, white man	Prison, 14 years[10]
1908	Rippey, Walter	Tazewell	Black	Assault, white man	Hanged by state[11]
1908	Smith, Jim	Scott	Black	Murder, white man	Prison, 14 years[12]
1909	Little, Howard	Buchanan	White	Mass murders, whites	Electrocuted by state[13]
1909	Moore, Robert	Washington	Black	Larceny	Prison, 10 years[14]
1909	Smith, Rush	Russell	Black	Shooting, white man	Prison, 5 years[15]
1910	Ross, Jack	Bristol	Black	Letter to white woman	Saved by police[16]
1915	Canter, Luther	Washington	White	Murder, white woman	Electrocuted by state[17]
1915	Canter, James	Washington	White	Murder, white woman	Tried, not convicted[18]
1915	Unknown	Wise	Black	Murder	Unknown[19]
1920	Williams, —	Wise	Black	Murder	Prison, 18 years[20]
1921	Grasper, —	Tazewell	Black	Assault	Prison, 5 years[21]

YEAR	PERSON	COUNTY/ CITY	RACE	CHARGE	RESULT
1922	Harber, Frank	Tazewell	Black	Murder, white policeman	Prison, life[22]

[1] *Richmond Dispatch*, Jan. 26, 1883; *Alexandria Gazette*, Jan. 25, 1883; *Shenandoah Herald*, Jan. 31, 1883.

[2] *Salem Times-Register*, Dec. 27, 1889, Jan. 3, 4, 1890; *Roanoke Daily Times*, Jan. 2, 4, 1890; *Alexandria Gazette*, Jan. 3, 4, 1890; *Richmond Dispatch*, Jan. 5, 7, 8, 1890, March 18, 1890; *Staunton Spectator*, Jan. 8, 1890.

[3] *Salem Times-Register*, Dec. 27, 1889, Jan. 3, 4, 1890; *Roanoke Daily Times*, Jan. 2, 4, 1890; *Alexandria Gazette*, Jan. 3, 4, 1890; *Richmond Dispatch*, Jan. 5, 7, 8, 1890, March 18, 1890; *Staunton Spectator*, Jan. 8, 1890.

[4] *Roanoke Times*, July 10, 1890; *Clinch Valley News*, July 18, 1890; *Alexandria Gazette*, July 10, 1890; Russell County Law Order Book 22, 25–26.

[5] *Clinch Valley News*, Sept. 30, Oct. 7, 20, 1891, Feb. 24, July 21, 1893; *Roanoke Times*, Sept. 23, 27, 1892; *Alexandria Gazette*, Sept. 29, 1892; *Richmond Times*, Nov. 2, 1893.

[6] *Roanoke Daily Times*, Sept. 9, 1891; *Roanoke Times*, Sept. 9, 10, 13, 23, 26, Oct. 14, Dec. 22, 29, 1891; *Richmond Dispatch*, Nov. 21, 1891.

[7] *Roanoke Times*, Aug. 18, 23, 28, 30, Oct. 2, Nov. 21, 1891; *Richmond Times*, Aug. 29, 1891, *Big Stone Gap Post*, Sept. 4, 1891; *Clinch Valley News*, Sept. 4, 1891.

[8] *Roanoke Times*, Aug. 30, 1891.

[9] *Clinch Valley News*, Jan. 8, 1904; *Tazewell Republican*, Feb. 18, April 14, 21, 28, May 12, 1904.

[10] *Clinch Valley News*, April 17, 1908; *Richmond Times-Dispatch*, April 7, Oct. 14, 1908.

[11] *Clinch Valley News*, Feb. 14, 21, 1908, March 20, 1908; *Tazewell Republican*, Feb. 20, March 26, 1908.

[12] *Clinch Valley News*, April 17, 1908; *Richmond Times-Dispatch*, April 7, Oct. 14, 1908.

[13] *Tazewell Republican*, Oct. 21, 1909; *Clinch Valley News*, 19, 26 Nov. 1909; *Richmond Times-Dispatch*, Nov. 15, 26, 1909; *Alexandria Gazette*, Nov. 25, 1909.

[14] *Tazewell Republican*, May 27, 1909; *Richmond Times-Dispatch*, May 25, 1909, Nov. 8, 1909; *Roanoke Times*, May 5, 23, 29, 1909; *Virginia Republican*, July 1, July 22, 1909; *Alexandria Gazette*, May 22, 25, 1909.

[15] *Tazewell Republican*, June 10, 1909; *Clinch Valley News*, April 30, 1909.

[16] *Bristol Herald Courier*, May 3, 1910.

[17] Washington County Law Order Book N, 175, 176, 177, 178, 180, 357; *Abingdon Virginian*, May 7, 1915; *Bristol Herald Courier*, May 5, 6, 7, 8, 9, June 2, 12, 1915; (Roanoke) *World News*, May 6, 7, 8, 10, 14, 15, 17, 18, 25, 26, 28, 29, 1915.

[18] *Abingdon Virginian*, May 7, 1915; *Bristol Herald Courier*, May 5, 6, 7, 8, 9, June 2, 12, 1915; (Roanoke) *World News*, May 6, 7, 8, 10, 14, 15, 17, 18, 25, 26, 28, 29, 1915; Washington County Law Order Book O, 249–50; *Richmond Times-Dispatch*, April 25, Oct. 4, 1918; (Roanoke) *World News*, April 24, 25, June 10, 1918; *Bristol Herald Courier*, April 29, 1918, June 21, Oct. 1, 1918; *Canter v. Commonwealth, Southeastern Reporter*, vol. 87, 327.

[19] *Clinch Valley News*, Dec. 3, 1920; *Big Stone Gap Post*, Dec. 8, 1920; Smith, *Managing White Supremacy*, 161. The last newspaper report said the governor had sent in a militia force in a train to rescue him and he had been taken to Roanoke for safekeeping.

[20] *Richmond Times-Dispatch*, Dec. 6, 1920.

[21] *Clinch Valley News*, Sept. 16, 1921.

[22] *Clinch Valley News*, Feb. 24, March 3, 1922; (Roanoke) *World News*, Feb. 25, 1922.

guards stood on alert in the courtroom. The jury quickly found both men guilty and sentenced them to death; however, on appeal James's sentence was overturned. Then followed five more inconclusive trials for James. Finally, the prosecutors gave up trying to convict him.

Another example of the police taking extraordinary precautions occurred in January 1890 when Thomas Akers and Robert Cooper Jr., both white, were charged with "committing outrages upon two respectable white girls," ages fourteen and twelve, in Montgomery County. The sheriff temporarily jailed them in Salem but returned them to Christiansburg for trial. The circuit court first tried Akers and sentenced him to twenty years in prison. The sheriff planned to send them to Lynchburg for safekeeping, but before he could do that, men planned to lynch the pair. To elude the lynchers, the sheriff took the men into the woods for the first night and then transferred them in private vehicles through two counties to Rockbridge in Botetourt County. From there they travelled by train to Lynchburg. Cooper was left in that city until he could be tried, while Akers was taken to the penitentiary in Richmond. When Cooper was tried in April 1890, the court also sentenced him to twenty years in the penitentiary. In March 1893 the governor pardoned both after many prominent citizens petitioned the governor, "because the alleged victim now swears that the crimes charged was not as first stated."[41]

The number of lynchings in Virginia pales in comparison to those in the Deep South. But why did so many occur in the southwestern portion of the state? There is no easy answer to the question because lynchers, lawyers, and law enforcement officers did not write autobiographies. What follows, therefore, is informed speculation based on half a century of residence, research, and writing by the author.[42]

One possible explanation is that Southwest Virginia has always differed from the distant eastern parts of the state. Richmond is over 430 miles from the southwestern corner in Lee County. The legislature, dominated by the older sections of the state, often neglected the area, which was underrepresented for much of the state's history. Also, the Blue Ridge Mountains impeded travel to the Piedmont and Tidewater area. That resulted in trade routes going up the Valley of Virginia to Philadelphia, not to Richmond or Norfolk. These factors led Arthur Campbell in the 1780s to promote the formation of a new western state known as Frankland, which failed when the General Assembly made it treason to promote the alienation of some of its territory. Residents of what was then western North Carolina and is now East Tennessee took up the movement and renamed the erstwhile state Franklin, which eventually became Tennessee. Some feelings of alienation still exist, especially as a result of the increasing population and diversity of the eastern part of Virginia and the declining numbers, economy, and power of the Southwest. Census records for Buchanan County, for instance, show that its total population has declined 47.8 percent since 1980, while the Black population has had a small increase. A common expression is that most Virginians think the state ends at Roanoke—although the distance from there to the Kentucky border at Cumberland Gap is 263 miles.

In addition, the mountains of the Southwest divided the people into small settlements, and the altitude and topography dictated a different type of economy than the plantations of old Virginia. Most farms were relatively small, and many produced little more than enough to barter for goods at country stores. Small farmers did not need slaves, and Blacks faced a hostile environment. Interestingly, the percentage of African Americans in the Southwest has steadily declined since the Civil War.[43] It is not known why or where they went, but it does not seem to be part of the Great Migration to the North.

The white population in the Jim Crow era also differed from the older regions of the state. People who settled there were mostly of Scots-Irish and German descent. Few were English or other nationalities. Their religion was different: they were largely Presbyterians and Lutherans until Methodism became dominant. Episcopalians were few, and Roman Catholics hardly existed except in mining districts.

Their politics were also different. Republicans, as committed to white supremacy as Democrats, often were the dominant party, while the rest of the state voted solidly Democratic. And many residents had little education.

In addition, the lack of modern transportation kept people isolated. Main highways were not macadamized until well into the twentieth century, and the owners of turnpikes charged tolls. But with the advent of railroads, travel became easier—at least where the roads existed. The first, the Virginia and Tennessee, ran from Lynchburg to the border of Tennessee in 1856. No other railroad penetrated the Far Southwest, the area drained by the Holston and Clinch Rivers, until 1883, when Norfolk and Western began to export coal. Interestingly, the railroads played a role in a number of the lynchings.

Perhaps the most salient reason for the hostility to Blacks is that the rural and isolated white people had little interaction with African Americans. Blacks were oddities that they could ignore, or treat with disdain, hostility, or violence. Thus, the low percentage of African Americans worked to their disadvantage because whites did not have to be accommodating to them or fear an uprising. In addition, the isolation of the people in the area, common to mountainous areas, made them distrustful of all outsiders, white or Black.

Also pertinent to the question of lynching was that violence was not unusual in the highland region. People armed themselves for protection and hunting and often turned their weapons on others. Newspapers and court records chronicled numerous shootings, both accidental and intentional. For example, the *Clinch Valley News,* August 14, 1891, laconically reported in one sentence: "There are ten murder cases on the docket of Scott Circuit Court." Although that was an unusual number, the newspaper said nothing further on the subject. Another brief article in the same paper on December 14, 1900, showed that in Russell County the preceding week Sam Hughes accidently shot Clarence Brown (both were Black) while they were hunting; Ike Smithers, sixteen, accidently shot and killed Buck Rankin while hunting; Will Harding shot Bill Williams at a dance; Harve Puckett shot Ed McCloud while they were drunk; and a Mrs. Malcomb knocked a gun off a table, which discharged and shot her in the hip and resulted in a limb being amputated. Also, on April 6, 1921, the *Big Stone Gap Post* reported that the April term of the Wise County Court had about eight hundred criminal and civil cases on its docket. That helps to illustrate the number of crimes and disputes in the southwest. In addition, the Hatfield-McCoy feud extended into the area.

Finally, there were white outlaw gangs that roamed, robbed, and killed in the borderlands of West Virginia and Kentucky. Perhaps the most notorious one was led by Rush Morgan, who terrorized Lee County. Morgan was convicted of murder in 1891, but his gang broke into the jail and released him. In 1892 the gang continued their crime spree by robbing some miners on payday and trying to take over Daisy Iron Mines at Hogan Station, but the manager of the mine killed two of them and shot three fingers off Morgan. In February 1893 the gang invaded the village of Hubbard Springs looking for detectives that were searching for them. While they were in a house of prostitution, someone killed Morgan. Despite that, the rest of the gang paraded through the street "defyingly and threatingly."[44]

The rural, often isolated, life in the area dramatically changed with the exploitation of the vast coal resources in Tazewell, Buchanan, Russell, and Scott Counties. That brought more violence, including lynchings. The prospect of jobs attracted all sorts of people, including railroad workers, storekeepers, miners, merchants, lawyers, saloon keepers, prostitutes, and single Black and white men looking to make money either legally or outside the law. The *Lebanon News* (as copied in the *Abingdon Weekly Virginian*) on April 11, 1889, stated: "It must be remembered that all along the line of the Clinch Valley Division there have congregated ex-convicts, robbers, cut-throats and outlaws, the very off scouring of the earth, until life and property are not safe." The severe economic depression of the 1890s, known as the Panic of 1893, propelled even more men to migrate to the area looking for work. In addition, the coal companies recruited African Americans, mostly from the South, with other outsiders from Pennsylvania, Italy, Austria, and Hungary. Thus, the coal counties saw rapid increases in population, as shown by census reports. In 1900 Buchanan showed a 65.1 percent increase in population over the 1890 census; Dickenson, 52.6 percent; and Wise 110.3 percent. A lot of people competed for the dangerous work in and around mines, jobs that in 1888 averaged sixty-eight hours per week and paid $1.05 per day.[45]

Brundage wrote that economic problems contributed to lynchings, stating, "The frequency of lynching, in short, was a barometer of the economic frustration of white southerners."[46] In addition, Stewart E. Tolnay and E. M. Beck examined lynchings in five Deep South and five Border States—but excluded Virginia. They wrote, "Lethal mob violence against blacks became more acute during years of economic stagnation when the value of cotton was depressed."[47] While a bad economy can result in friction and violence, including lynching, between races, the value of cotton was not a factor in Southwest Virginia because cotton did not grow there. Still, problems in one part of the country affected other areas, and the economy in the 1890s caused hardship for many people in Southwest Virginia. But not all people suffered. The investors in the coal mines and railroads made fortunes. At the local level, the mines and railroads provided income for numerous employees. The possibility of work for Blacks, whites, and foreigners attracted people despite the low pay and harsh working conditions.

The hardships of the 1890s and the racial animosity after the lynchings of 1893 resulted in some unknown person or people in Buchanan County erecting signs telling Blacks that they should leave or risk the same fate as those already killed.[48] A hundred years later, some white people in Buchanan County would boast that, "No 'nigger' ever spent the night in Buchanan County."

Had Buchanan kept out all African Americans, it could have been classified as one of the "sunset towns" or counties that excluded Blacks after sundown. But Black people have lived there since the county was formed in 1858—although the number has been small. According to census reports, the percentage of the population that was Black in 1860 was 1.1 percent. In 2020, it was 3.5 percent.[49] No evidence could be found of any other county or town in the region that would possibly fit into the "sunset town" category. Yet James W. Loewen, in his *Sundown Towns,* labels the Far Southwest as an area where "many sundown counties and towns existed." He offered no proof and did not name any county.[50]

In conclusion, the lynchings in Southwest Virginia generally followed the pattern as in other places in the country. Yet the causes differed because the area differed from much of the state. The injustices suffered by these victims of lynching cannot be rectified, but remembering their names keeps their stories alive and the details of their agony, one can hope, will prevent such tragedies from occurring again.

Notes

1. The numbers used here come from W. Fitzhugh Brundage, *Lynching in the New South: Georgia and Virginia, 1880–1930* (Urbana: University of Illinois Press, 1993), figure 7, "Lynchings in Virginia, 1880–1930," 142. On page 143 he gives the total as twenty-eight.
2. The counties included in this study are Bland, Carroll, Dickenson, Floyd, Giles, Grayson, Lee, Montgomery, Pulaski, Russell, Scott, Smyth, Tazewell, Washington, Wise, and Wythe. It omits the counties of Craig, Botetourt, Alleghany, Bath, Highland, and the city and county of Roanoke, which Brundage included in his study.
3. All county seats in this area are above 1,000 feet in altitude and nine are more than 2,000 feet. The lowest is Grundy at 1,060 feet, and the highest Lebanon at 2,808 feet. The highest peaks are Mt. Rogers in Grayson County at 5,729 feet and Beartown Mountain in Russell County at 4,688 feet. For comparison, the altitude at Richmond is 167 feet.
4. Following are the percentages of Black people in each county in 1860, including free Blacks, who were few in number: Buchanan, 1 percent; Carroll, 3.7; Floyd, 5.9; Giles, 10.9; Grayson, 6.8; Lee 7.6; Montgomery, 22.3; Pulaski, 29.5; Russell, 11.2; Scott, 4.5; Smyth, 13.6; Tazewell, 13.8; Washington, 16.5; Wise, 2.7; Wythe, 18.8. Bureau of Census, *Population of the United States in 1860; Compiled from the Original Returns of the Eighth Census* (Washington, DC: GPO, 1864), 516–18.

5. *Clinch Valley News*, Apr. 20, 1900; *Shenandoah Herald*, Apr. 27, June 10, 1900; *Richmond Times*, May 21, 1900; *Tazewell Republican*, May 21, July 5, 9, Sept. 27, Oct. 25, Nov. 22, 1900.
6. The *Richmond Planet*, July 23, 1894, reported, "One colored man was lynched near Lebanon, Virginia." However, no other source could be found for this. The editor seems to have this confused with a trial in Lebanon, Indiana, where a man was tried but received a prison sentence. See *Weekly Register*, Point Pleasant, VA, Feb. 7, 1894. In addition, the *Salem Times-Register* reported on July 6, 1888, that "a most horrible outrage was committed by a negro fiend upon a white lady in the upper end of Montgomery County, and the rumor has reached this place that he was caught at Christiansburg Wednesday morning and lynched." Nothing further could be found on that. It seems to have been only a rumor.
7. Even the *Richmond Planet*, an African American newspaper that reported on and fought against lynching, does not have information on most of the lynchings in this study. Newspapers used here can be found on the virginiachronicle website at the Library of Virginia, accessed Oct. 17, 2023, https://virginiachronicle.com; and at Newspapers (Ancestry), accessed Oct. 17, 2023, http://www.newspapers.com.
8. V. N. "Bud" Phillips, *Pioneers in Paradise: Legends and Stories from Bristol Tennessee/Virginia* (Johnson City, TN: Overmountain Press, 2002).
9. *Alexandria Gazette*, Jan. 2, 1883; (Washington, DC) *Evening Star*, Jan. 2, 1883; (Pittston, PA) *Evening Gazette*, Jan. 2, 1883.
10. *Staunton Spectator*, April 17, 1883; (Richmond) *Daily Dispatch*, April 13, 1883.
11. *Staunton Spectator*, June 17, 1884; *Alexandria Gazette*, June 12, 1884.
12. *Richmond Dispatch*, Feb. 6 and 10, 1920; *Staunton Spectator*, Feb. 22, 1885; Ann Hardy Beardsall, *The Lynching of Ivy Jackson: Bland County Court House, Virginia, Feb. 5, 1885* (Bland, VA: Bland County Historical Society, 2011). This pamphlet of a few pages provides some information on the murder and lynching but has contradictions: at one point the author says that Jackson's burial place was unknown but at another point says that he was interred in Red Oak Union Church Cemetery. The author also included some details that were taken from the jailbreak in the William Crockett case in Wytheville in 1883.
13. *Richmond Dispatch*, July 12, 1888; *Salem Times-Register*, July 6 and 13, Aug. 31, 1888; *Alexandria Gazette*, July 12, 1888.
14. *Abingdon Weekly Virginian*, April 11, 1889; *Alexandria Gazette*, April 4, 1889; *Richmond Dispatch*, April 5, 1889.
15. *Staunton Spectator*, Aug. 13, 1890; *Daily Dispatch*, June 11, 1889.
16. *Roanoke Times*, June 14 and 20, 1891, Jan. 14, 1892; Phillips's *Pioneers in Paradise* quotes the indictment and states that all these individuals were tried and found innocent. That history also states that the lynching took place on December 15, 1891, but the newspapers showed it happened in June.
17. *Clinch Valley News*, Nov. 4, 1892; *Alexandria Gazette*, Nov. 1, 1892; *Richmond Dispatch*, Nov. 1, 1892; *Roanoke Times*, Nov. 2, 1892; Russell County, Law Order Book 22, 112, 323.
18. Newspaper accounts offer confusing variations regarding who exactly was lynched. Some papers do not mention Ellerson, and only the *Clinch Valley News* gives information on Sam Barns. Although the evidence is quite slim on these individuals, they are included.
19. *Clinch Valley News*, Sept. 11, 1891, Feb. 3, 10, 17, 1893, Aug. 7, 1896, Aug. 14, 1914, June 30, 1922; *Big Stone Gap Post*, Feb. 2, 1893; *Richmond Dispatch*, Feb. 2, 1893, Aug. 2, 1896; *Roanoke Times*, Feb. 2, 3, 4, 14, 1893; *Richmond Times*, Feb. 2 and 3, 1893; *Shenandoah Herald*, Feb. 10, 1883; *Alexandria Gazette*, Feb. 2 and 4, 1893; *Bedford Times*, Feb. 9, 1893.

Neighbors informed authorities that Blow had bought land, built a house, and owned four oxen and other property without any known source of income.
20. *Clinch Valley News,* Feb. 24, April 7, 1893; *Richmond Dispatch,* April 2 and 4, 1893; *Alexandria Gazette,* April 5, 1893; (Maysville, KY) *Public Ledger,* April 5, 1893; (Stanford, KY) *Evening Bulletin,* April 5, 1893. Some sources state that the shooting took place at her Graham business, which may be true.
21. (Marion, VA) *Southwestern News,* Extra, May 12, 1803; *Roanoke Times,* May 12, 13, 21, 1893; *Staunton Spectator and Vindicator,* May 17, 1893; *Alexandria Gazette,* May 13, 1893; *Richmond Dispatch,* May 14, 1893.
22. *Big Stone Gap Post,* June 6, 1894; *Richmond Planet,* May 19, 1894; Scott County, Minute Book 26, 163, 234, 237, 240; George Wood, Findagrave.com, accessed Jan. 3, 2021, http://www.findagrave.com.
23. *Richmond Times,* June 1, 1898; *Richmond Planet,* July 2, 1898; *Richmond Dispatch,* June 23, 1898; *Alexandria Gazette,* June 23, 1898; *Salem Sentinel,* June 28, 1898; Ron Hall, "Local History: The Killing of Mack Howlett," *Galax Gazette,* accessed Nov. 25, 2020, http://www.GalaxGazette.com; "The Murder of Mack Howlett," Genealogy.com, accessed Nov. 25, 2020, http://www.genealogy.com; "Courthouse Tragedy," http://carrollvamuseum.org, accessed Nov. 25, 2020.
24. *Alexandria Gazette,* Dec. 8, 1900; *Clinch Valley News,* Dec. 14, 1900; *Richmond Times,* Dec. 8, 1900.
25. *Alexandria Gazette,* June 7, 1902; *Richmond Times,* June 7, 1902; *Richmond Dispatch,* June 6 and 7, 1902; *Tazewell Republican,* June 12, 1902; *Bristol News,* April 13, 14, 15, 16, 20, 1925.
26. (Louisville) *Courier-Journal,* Aug. 30, 1891, March 26, 1893; *Owensboro* (KY) *Messenger,* Oct. 6, 1892, Oct. 7, 1909, Feb. 12, 1910; Papers of the Governors of Kentucky, 1792–1899: William O. Bradley, 1895–99, Executive Journal, 1897–99, II, 300; *Tazewell Republican,* Sept. 30, Oct. 7, 21, Dec. 28, 1909, Jan. 6, Feb. 3 and 24, April 28, 1910; *Big Stone Gap Post,* Sept. 29, Oct. 5, 1909; *Big Sandy News,* Oct. 8, 1909, May 19, 1910; *Fairmont West Virginian,* Oct. 6, 1909; (Louisville) *Courier-Journal,* Oct. 1, 2, 6, Nov. 27, 1909, Feb. 12, 1910; (Newport News) *Daily Press,* Nov. 26, 1909; *Daily Press,* Oct. 3, 1909; *Evening News,* Sept. 24, Oct. 5, 8, 19, Nov. 17 and 18, Dec. 3 and 21,1909; *Times Dispatch,* Nov. 27, Dec. 2, 3, 7, 14, 1909, Feb. 11, 1910; *Staunton Dispatch-Times,* Nov. 28, 1909; *Clinch Valley News,* Jan. 7, 14, 28, April 29, Dec. 9, 1910, Feb. 11, April 29, 1911; *Bristol Herald Courier,* Dec. 28, 1909; *Evening News,* Dec. 28, 1909, Jan. 6, April 30, 1910; *Alexandria Gazette,* Dec. 17, 1898; *Winchester Evening Star,* Dec. 27, 1909; *Richmond Planet,* Jan. 1, 1910.
27. *Clinch Valley News,* Dec. 19, 1920; *Richmond Times-Dispatch,* Nov. 15, 1920; *Alexandria Gazette,* Nov. 16, 1920; *Big Stone Gap Post,* Aug. 17 and 24, 1921; *Richmond Planet,* Nov. 20, 1920; *Roanoke World News,* Aug. 19, 1921, Jan. 22, 1923; *The* (Danville) *Bee,* Jan. 23, 1923; J. Douglas Smith, *Managing White Supremacy: Race, Politics, and Citizenship in Jim Crow Virginia* (Chapel Hill: University of North Carolina Press, 2002) 159–61.
28. Some sources give his family name as Bird, but official records such as his induction and discharge from the army as well as his government-issued tombstone show it to be Byrd.
29. Application for Headstone for Raymond Byrd, Feb. 28, 1936, accessed Nov. 25, 2020, https://ancestry.com; *Bristol Herald Courier,* Aug. 16, 17, 18, 1926; *The* (Danville) *Bee,* Aug. 31, 1926, Jan. 13, Sept. 12, 1927; *Bluefield Daily Telegraph,* Sept. 1 and 11, 1926; (Staunton, VA) *News Leader,* Sept. 2, 1926, April 12, July 20, 1927; (Newport News, VA) *Daily Press,* Sept. 3, 17, 19, 1926, July 21, 1927; *Harrisonburg Daily News,* Sept. 7, 10, 1926;

Smith, *Managing White Supremacy,* 167–70; Paul G. Beers, "The Wythe County Lynching of Raymond Bird: Progressivism vs. Mob Violence in the '20s," *Appalachian Journal,* 22 (1994): 34–59.

30. Report of the Lynching by the County Attorney of Fletcher County to the Governor, "Long Ago in Eastern Kentucky" blog entry, May 26, 2011, accessed Nov. 25, 2020, http://ekyhistory.blogspot.com/2011/05/detailed-story-of-lynching.html,; *Bristol Herald Courier,* Nov. 29, 30, Dec. 1, 2, 4, 1927; (Louisville) *Courier-Journal,* Dec. 1, 2, 3, 1927; (Owensboro, KY) *Messenger Inquirer,* Nov. 30, 1927, Dec. 2, 1927; *News Leader,* Jan. 30, 1928; *Daily Press,* Jan. 17, 1928; *Owensburg Messenger,* Jan. 7, 1928; *Kingsport* (TN) *Times,* Nov. 30, 1927; Beers, "Wythe County Lynching of Raymond Bird;" Smith, *Managing White Supremacy,* 170–73; Roy L. Sturgill, "The Murder of Hershel Deaton," *Historical Sketches of Southwest Virginia,* Publication 12 (1978), accessed Oct. 17, 2023, /https://sites.rootsweb.com/~vahsswv/historicalsketches/murder%20deatonh.html.
31. William C. Pendleton, *History of Tazewell County and Southwest Virginia, 1748–1920* (Richmond: W. C. Hill, 1920).
32. In some families, children were told that if they misbehaved a "nigger" man in the woods would come and get them. The author heard this as late as 2017.
33. *Weekly Register,* Feb. 7, 1894.
34. *Clinch Valley News,* April 19, 1895. Other counties seem to have had the same number of law enforcement officers.
35. Population figures in this study come from http://census-online.com/.
36. Virginia State Police, accessed April 2, 2021, https:///www.vsp.virginia.gov.
37. *Clinch Valley News,* Feb. 17, 1893.
38. *Clinch Valley News,* Feb. 24, 1893.
39. Charles L. Chavis Jr., *The Silent Shore: The Lynching of Mathew William and the Politics of Racism in the Free State* (Baltimore: Johns Hopkins Press, 2021), 6–10.
40. Newspapers probably did not report all pardons. One would have to research the papers of the governors to find that information.
41. *Richmond Dispatch,* Jan. 5 and 7, 1890, March 18, 1893; *Staunton Spectator,* Jan. 1 and 8, 1890; *Alexandria Gazette,* Jan. 3 and 4, 1890; *Salem Times-Register,* Dec. 27, 1889, Jan. 3, 1890; *Roanoke Daily News,* Jan. 2, 4, 1890.
42. The author was born and raised in Southwest Virginia, spent a majority of his life there, and retired there. He has published articles regarding the area in the *Virginia Magazine of History and Biography, Tennessee Historical Quarterly, Publications of the East Tennessee Historical Society, Bulletin of the Historical Society of Washington County, Virginia, Filson Club Historic Quarterly,* and *Register of the Kentucky State Historical Society.* He is also the author of *Castle's Woods and Early Russell County, 1769–1799, History of Washington County, Virginia, to 1865,* and *After the War Was Over: Reconstruction in Washington County, Virginia, 1865–1870.*
43. As examples, Pulaski County, which had a Black population of 29.5 percent in 1860, had only 5.05 percent in 2019; Montgomery declined from 22.3 percent in 1860 to 13.4 percent; Wythe from 18.8 percent to 3.0 percent; and Washington from 16.7 percent to 1.5 percent.
44. *Richmond Times,* Feb. 3, 1893; *Big Stone Gap Post,* Dec. 15 and 22, 1892, Feb. 2 and 9, 1893; (Lexington, KY) *Weekly Leader,* Feb. 2, 1893. People especially feared Morgan because it was rumored that he had killed seventeen people.

45. *History of Wages in the United States from Colonial Times to 1928* (Washington, DC: Government Printing Office, 1934), 334.
46. Brundage, *Lynching in the New South,* 10.
47. Tolnay and Beck, *Festival of Violence,* 121.
48. Brundage, *Lynching in the New South,* 146.
49. USA Facts, accessed Oct. 17, 2023, https://usafacts.org/data/topics/people-society/population-and-demographics/our-changing-population/state/virginia/county/buchanan-county/.
50. James W. Loewen, *Sundown Towns: A Hidden Dimension of American Racism* (New York: New Press, 2005), 57, 73. In table I the author does not list any counties in Virginia that had no or few Blacks.

JUSTICE AND INJUSTICE IN THE COALFIELDS

Lynchings in Wise County

TOM COSTA AND ZOE CRIHFIELD

On June 5, 1902, Wiley Guynn (or Gwynn, or Gynn), a twenty-eight-year-old Black boarding house proprietor and miner, was arrested for assaulting the twelve-year-old daughter of Franklin Green, a white farmer living near Tom's Creek, just outside Coeburn in Wise County, Virginia. Guynn allegedly grabbed the young girl, who screamed, attracting a group of white men who apprehended Guynn. He was taken before a justice at Bondtown and given a hearing; as he was about to be locked up in a nearby primitive cell, a mob of close to five hundred men, including the girl's father, descended on the jail demanding the prisoner. As the white men conveyed him away from the lockup, Guynn broke free and was shot to death trying to escape.

There were two more documented cases of lynchings of Black men in Wise County. Eighteen years after Guynn's death, David Hurst (or Hunt) was lynched by a white mob after being accused of assaulting an elderly white woman. The final documented lynching of a Black man in Wise County occurred in 1927, when Leonard Woods, a Black miner originally from Pittsburgh, was lynched. Woods, who lived in Jenkins, Kentucky, had been jailed in Whitesburg, Kentucky, for allegedly shooting to death a white man from Coeburn named Herschel Deaton. A mob of Kentucky and Virginia whites took Woods from the Whitesburg jail, carried him just across the border into Virginia, hanged and shot him, and burned his body.

Each of the three Wise County lynchings had characteristics of lynchings elsewhere in the South. In each lynching, a Black man was accused of a violent crime against a white person; in each incident, a white mob seized its victim from legal custody, exacting community "justice" by returning the victim to someplace near the scene of the crime. The 1902 lynching of Wiley Guynn seems to have been a spontaneous occurrence; the other two lynchings exhibited evidence of more careful planning. Each of the lynchings featured torture or more extreme cruelty as a common characteristic, and the victims' bodies were left on display. In Wiley Guynn's case, the victim's "mutilated" body was left by the railroad tracks for passersby to view. David Hurst's body was dragged by an automobile and deposited for viewing on the side of the main road from Norton to Appalachia. Woods was hanged and shot, and then his body was burned and left on the platform.

Another feature common to the three lynchings was the newspaper coverage each received. Early coverage of each incident contained numerous errors and provided few details, but within a week or so, reports became more detailed and contained more horrific descriptions of the victims' alleged crimes, demonizing them further. Finally, with one important exception, the white perpetrators were not prosecuted.

Recent scholarship on violence in the mountain South has served to correct older assertions of a propensity for lawlessness among the rough Scots-Irish population, explaining lynching as part of an overall pattern "rooted in a peculiar mountain culture."[1] Rather, it was the changes wrought by the rapid industrialization and the accompanying demographic transformation that created conditions for racial violence. According to Fitzhugh Brundage, violence against Blacks in Appalachia "fit seamlessly along the continuum of orthodox race relations in the Jim Crow South. . . . The mountain South was neither blessed by exceptionally benign race relations, nor cursed by implacable race hatred."[2]

Yet the Wise County lynchings do not necessarily fit the pattern described by Brundage and others. The rapid changes during the decades of the 1880s and 1890s help explain a propensity to violence during that period, but all three Wise County lynchings took place after 1900, when, according to Brundage, violence against Blacks in Appalachia subsided, as "racial etiquette in the region was codified in law and practice."[3] It was when special circumstances caused this "codification of racial etiquette" to break down that mob violence against Blacks exploded in Wise County. In each incident, Wise County officials attempted to intervene to prevent violence. They failed to prevent extralegal justice in the cases of Guynn, Hurst, and Woods, but in other attempts by mobs to exact racial vengeance, Wise officials succeeded in preventing lynchings. Official reactions before and after the lynchings illustrate the fine line between justice and injustice in a region where local officials exhibited a great sense of responsibility to enforce the rule of law, in partnership with the corporate interests of the coal companies, but on at least three occasions, they failed, leaving Blacks vulnerable to extralegal violence.

The Victims

Little is known about the three lynching victims. During the late nineteenth and early twentieth centuries, Wise County, like much of the central Appalachian South, became the scene of tremendous demographic changes. Timber and coal companies moved in to transform the landscape, and workers from outside the county, Blacks from the South, as well as southern and eastern European whites, moved in to work in the mines. "Between 1880 and 1900, the Black population of Wise County grew from 101 to 1,965."[4]

None of the three victims was an original inhabitant of Wise County; they all migrated into the county seeking work. Wiley Guynn came from North Carolina, while his wife Laura and son Willie were born in Virginia. In 1900 he had been married for four years; Willie was six years old. Guynn could read and write, and although described in some accounts as a miner, he operated a boarding house in Bondtown, a neighborhood just north of Coeburn where many Black miners lived. Along with Guynn, Laura, and Willie, seven of the eight Black laborers living in the house in 1900 were from outside Virginia. Guynn was shot to death trying to escape from a white mob bent on vengeance for his alleged assault of a young white girl.

David Hurst hailed from Alabama. His death certificate lists him as an employee of Blackwood Coal and Coke Co., but he "had been working in the coal mines at Blackwood and had been in that section only a short time."[5] His death seems to fit the pattern of earlier violence in the coalfields: actions by whites designed "to communicate codes of black behavior rather than to purge the region of blacks."[6] Targets of such violence, as may have been the case with Hurst, were often "young, itinerant, black workers whose raucous and sometimes violent lifestyles provoked considerable concern among whites." The mob targeted Hurst because he had allegedly assaulted a white woman.[7]

Leonard Woods, the final documented victim, who was lynched in 1927, was also not an original inhabitant of Wise but migrated from Pittsburgh, Pennsylvania, to southeastern Kentucky seeking work in the coalfields. Letcher County, Kentucky, like neighboring Wise County, Virginia, saw tremendous demographic changes as the region experienced the coal boom, although the Eastern Kentucky boom came two decades after that of Wise. Spurred by recruiters working for the Consolidated Coal Company, described as "the nation's largest extractor of bituminous coal," Letcher County's population more than doubled between 1910 and 1920, and many of the new inhabitants were African Americans who had migrated north seeking work. Woods was an exception in that he came south from Pennsylvania.[8] As is the case of the two earlier victims, details of Woods's life before his lynching are few. After his death, inquiries went out asking after a brother "somewhere in the world." Rev. C. E. Woods of Kansas City, Missouri, wrote to the NAACP, which responded that it had no way of knowing whether Reverend Woods was related to Leonard Woods. They suggested he write to Harry Moore, county attorney of Whitesburg, whom the Kentucky governor had asked to report on the incident.[9]

The Lynchings

The circumstances leading to Wiley Guynn's death in 1902 began with his alleged assault of a twelve-year-old Alice Green, near Tom's Creek, a neighboring community of Coeburn, Virginia. Early reports of the assault varied: the *Alexandria Gazette* simply reported that Guynn "attempted to commit an assault." The *Roanoke Times* said that "Guynn tried to muffle the girl's mouth with a handkerchief, and in her desperate struggle with the Negro her face was seriously lacerated," while the *Richmond Dispatch* alleged that Guynn "had seriously torn the child's face with his fingernails during her struggle to get out of his clutches." But it was the local *Big Stone Gap Post* that went the farthest in demonizing Guynn, headlining its account of his lynching, "For Attempted Rape on a Twelve Year Old White Girl."[10]

Regardless of what really happened, the girl's cries attracted a group of white men, who apprehended Guynn and took him to a nearby lockup in Guynn's own neighborhood of Bondtown. As the mob continued to grow,

Wise County's commonwealth's attorney, W. G. G. Dotson, came to plead with them. Nonetheless, the mob, now perhaps numbering almost five hundred, took Guynn from the jail with the intention to hang him from a tree nearby. Realizing what the mob was planning, Guynn broke, ran, and was "riddled with bullets," according to numerous accounts. Guynn's body was left by the side of the railroad tracks: "Late in the afternoon those passing on the railway trains saw lying beside the track the mutilated body of a man who had committed the foulest crime known to man—the ravishing of a baby girl."[11]

Guynn was a married man, father of a child at the time he was killed. He and his wife operated a boarding house for Black laborers in Bondtown.

The incident remains shrouded in mystery. What really happened in the encounter between Guynn and Alice? We may never know, but we can speculate based on similar stories of Black men who confessed to rape, or to the rape and murder, of white women. In 1934 Philip Jones was arrested for killing two white sisters in Clifton Forge while trying to prevent them from running to tell that he had scared them. Jones narrowly escaped being lynched and was transported to the Richmond penitentiary where, after several false starts, he eventually confessed. According to Jones, "I scared the children and they said they were going home to tell their father and I begged them not to." He tied them up and brought them to his home. When they jumped out of a second story window, Jones chased them down and struck and killed both with the stock of his gun. "I didn't know what to do with them," he confessed. "I was scared to let them go back home. . . . I knew if I had let them went on they would have gotten to their house before I could have gotten away. I knew they would have mobbed me or shot me or killed me."[12]

Jones's confession offers a plausible scenario to explain what transpired when Wiley Guynn happened upon and frightened Alice Green. He then tried to prevent her from telling, and, in the process, she scratched his face and began screaming, attracting nearby whites. The fact that Guynn broke and ran as the mob was conveying him from the lockup is another indication that he was fully aware of the fate that awaited him. The Jones case offers an example of how lynching worked: Black men in the South were so terrorized that a relatively innocent encounter with two white girls turned into a murder because Jones feared the retribution of the mob. This may have been what happened to Wiley Guynn.

Guynn's alleged attack represented a clear violation of the racial code, and the white mob reacted quickly to exact revenge. But their spontaneous reaction in killing Guynn may also be explained by another local case, in which the "codification of racial etiquette" withstood a test. In December 1901, six months before Guynn's death, a Black miner named Robert Foy shot and killed Dayton Miller and wounded Charles Williams, two white men who worked for the Crane's Nest Coal and Coke Co., also located near Tom's Creek. Foy had rented a room from the company but insisted he never occupied it. When he found out that the company had deducted the rent from his pay, Foy went to see company treasurer Miller, in his words, "with pistols ready to do the shooting." In the ensuing argument, Foy killed Miller and wounded Williams.[13]

Arrested and lodged in the Wise jail, Foy awaited what promised to be a speedy trial and execution, as called for in the code. "Chances are he will be hung, provided a mob which is expected any time, does not lynch him." The local *Big Stone Gap Post* assumed that county officials would do their duty but assessed Foy's chances to escape lynching as slim. "The negro is in jail at this place, and the officers would doubtless make a stubborn resistance should a mob attack the jail, but we doubt if any guard could save him should a determined mob appear."[14]

But the expected mob never materialized. Perhaps the fact that his victim Miller was a high-ranking official with the coal company and not a local made the whites less zealous to go after Foy, who was tried quickly. On January 30, 1902, the *Post* reported that he had been found guilty and sentenced to hang in March. There was some confusion as to what happened next. Most accounts indicate that Foy's initial trial resulted in a hung jury, with a lone juror advocating life rather than hanging. A new jury was empaneled, and Foy was again found guilty and sentenced to hang. His lawyers appealed the verdict all the way to the Virginia Supreme Court, and Gov. Andrew Jackson Montague granted a stay of thirty days while the case was under review, although he refused to pardon Foy.

The story does not end there. In May 1902 Foy was among seven prisoners who escaped from the Wise jail in a "Bold Break for Liberty," as the local headline put it.[15] While most of the escapees were quickly caught, Foy remained at large for a week. Eventually captured, it was then discovered that he had contracted smallpox, causing further delays in his execution. In August 1902, nine months after the death of Dayton Miller, Foy was finally hanged. The long delay in executing a man whom many thought should have been lynched right away for a murder one paper called "fiendishly malicious"[16] undoubtedly heightened racial tensions throughout Wise County, but especially in and around Coeburn, locus of Miller's death as well as Guynn's alleged attack. Thus, when Guynn was accused of attacking Alice Green, local whites acted quickly to enforce extralegally the dominant racial code. The Robert Foy case, in which local officials did their duty and prevented a lynching, may have caused Guynn's death at the hands of a white mob frustrated over the relatively long delay in Foy's case. Foy was legally executed for the murder of a white man, but the code dictated extrajudicial punishment for a seemingly lesser crime against a white girl. Despite the attempt by Commonwealth's Attorney Dotson to stop the mob, there is no record of anyone being charged with Guynn's death, possibly because he was killed in the act of trying to escape. Together, the two examples of racial violence in 1902 provide ample evidence of how lynching acted to terrorize the Black population of Wise County into obedience. The fact that the white community did not lynch Foy does not mean that justice for Blacks was the norm; rather the delay in executing Foy was itself a violation of whites' expectations and may have enabled the extrajudicial killing of Wiley Guynn.

The next lynching in Wise County occurred in 1920, eighteen years after that of Wiley Guynn. The period immediately following World War I saw a rise in racial tensions throughout the country, as Black soldiers who had served overseas returned to encounter the same racial prejudice they thought they had left behind. According to John Hope Franklin, "Whites had steeled themselves against the day when Black soldiers would return and make demands for first-class citizenship," and Franklin has called the year 1919 "the greatest period of interracial strife the nation has ever witnessed." Anti-Black violence swept across the entire country, as racism combined with exaggerated fears of Bolshevism inflamed whites. The secretary of the NAACP, James Weldon Johnson, termed the middle of 1919 "Red Summer."[17] The heightened racial tension manifested itself in Wise County the following year with David Hurst's lynching and the near lynching of another Black man named Sydney Williams.

The lynching of David Hurst occurred between Norton and Appalachia, Virginia, near the coal town of Dunbar. On November 12, 1920, Hurst allegedly broke into a home at Cane Patch and assaulted an elderly white woman, "choking her until she was unconscious."[18] She recovered and managed to scare Hurst off, then flagged down a passenger train near her home. Several railroad workers followed Hurst down the tracks, captured him, and took him to the Wise County Jail. Hurst's time in the jail was short, however. In the early hours of the morning of November 14, a mob broke Hurst from the jail, transported him to the environs of the crime he was alleged to have committed, and hanged him from a trestle bridge, according to some accounts—others assert he was hanged from a coal tipple near Cane Patch. According to the local *Post*, "While the body was hanging it was riddled with shots and later tied, it is supposed, to an automobile and dragged to a point near Blackwood where it was found Sunday morning lying by the roadside. All of the negro's clothes were torn off and his body was terribly cut up by bullets."[19]

As in the cases of Wiley Guynn and Robert Foy, local officials had seen Hurst apprehended and locked up in jail, and they remained determined to see justice done. But the white mob apparently planned their action carefully, taking Sheriff A. P. Corder and other officials by surprise. Between three and four in the morning, "entrance was gained to the jail by breaking down the doors."[20]

Angered by Hurst's lynching, Sheriff Corder later stated he would have prevented it had he received earlier warning. Several members of the mob were prosecuted, after the commonwealth's attorney got one of the men to admit they were present. Two of the mob were convicted: Shayler Tate and A. L. Napier were sentenced to two years each for "incitement to riot." Gov. Elbert Lee Trinkle at first refused to pardon the two white men, earning praise from New York journal the *Nation*, whose editor wrote: "Governor Trinkle rightly declares that to grant clemency to this lightly punished man would be to 'lend my sanction to mob violence.'"[21] Commonwealth's Attorney C. R. McCorkle's insistence and Sheriff Corder's assistance in the prosecution of the men who lynched Hurst were rare instances of authorities arresting any member of a lynch mob, much less prosecuting and convicting them. On the other hand, in October 1923, Governor Trinkle quietly issued a pardon for the two men convicted in the Hurst lynching.[22]

Two weeks after Hurst's death, Sheriff Corder got a second chance to see justice affirmed. In early December, a Black man named Sydney Williams was arrested for assaulting a white merchant named Creed Robinette in

Appalachia. As Corder housed Williams in the Wise County jail, he got wind of a plan to break him out and lynch him. The sheriff hired extra guards, and on the morning of December 5, a group of whites approached the jail "and demanded the prisoner." Corder "flatly refused and warned them to leave," stating, "he would defend the prisoner and uphold the law no matter how great the sacrifice." The mob refused to leave, and gunfire broke out. Two white members of the mob were killed, and Corder put Williams on a train to Roanoke later that day.[23]

The *Roanoke Times* praised Corder as a "courageous official bent upon discharging [his] sworn duty." Furthermore, "Wise County has been spared the disgrace of a second lynching in less than a fortnight." The NAACP went even further in its praise of the intrepid sheriff: "We wish to express to you its commendation in the highest terms," as Investigator Walter White wrote, "for the manly stand taken by you in preventing the lynching of a colored man named Williams. . . . If every community in America, particularly in the South, had officers of the law who would fulfill all their offices as you have done, it would be but a short time before lynching, the greatest blot on American civilization would be entirely wiped out."[24]

The two cases, so close together, illustrate another key factor in understanding lynching. Lynching was almost always state-sanctioned racial terror: sometimes officials simply refused to protect Blacks jailed for alleged crimes; more often local authorities actively abetted lynch mobs. The fact that Sheriff Corder's action in protecting Sydney Williams was so unprecedented implies that lynching could have been prevented if officials had been serious about protecting prisoners in their care.

Leonard Woods

It would take seven more years for Virginia finally to outlaw lynching, at least in the legal code. Following the lynching of Leonard Woods in 1927 in Wise County, the state, led by Gov. Harry Byrd, passed Virginia's first antilynching law, indeed the first of its kind in the South.[25] Leonard Woods's lynching quickly gained national coverage and is arguably the most significant story associated with Wise County's racial history. Woods's case saw the complete breakdown of whatever "racial etiquette" had existed.[26]

In 1926, the year before Woods was lynched, Virginia was rocked with the news of the lynching of Raymond Byrd in Wythe County, about a hundred miles from Wise County. Raymond Byrd was a laborer on the farm of Grover Grubb, where he became romantically involved with two of Grubb's daughters. When the younger gave birth to his child, then refused to say Byrd had raped her, he was jailed for miscegenation. On the evening of August 6, a mob of whites broke Byrd out of Wythe jail, drove him to Rural Retreat, and hanged him from a tree near the Grubb farm. In stories published about the case, Byrd's name was spelled "Bird" to prevent embarrassing the governor.

Governor Byrd's opposition to lynching, at least on paper, was well established. The lurid details surrounding the case, and the fact that the victim shared the governor's last name and was a veteran of World War I, created an embarrassing situation for the governor, whose attempts to send state officials to help local authorities investigate were rebuffed. The frustrated governor finally acted to make lynching a state crime after Leonard Woods was lynched the following year.[27]

The sensationalism surrounding Byrd's lynching in 1926 can be considered a prelude to Woods's lynching in November the following year. But the extrajudicial murder of Woods featured a host of issues and represents the complete breakdown of any real or imagined system of "racial etiquette" for a variety of reasons: a dispute between Kentucky and Virginia, including correspondence between governors of the respective states; conflicting stories about what happened the night before Woods's arrest; the well-publicized accounts that many members of the white mob were known to officials; and the high social standing of the white man Woods was alleged to have killed, all combined to make Woods's lynching as sensational as Byrd's. Above all, perhaps, there were questions about the "official" account of the incident (the alleged murder of a white man) that led to Woods's death.

Woods's victim, Herschel Deaton, a young white man from Coeburn/Tom's Creek, was a newly married twenty-seven-year-old graduate of Coeburn High School and Virginia Tech. Deaton was a Mason, a man of some repute in his community. On Sunday, November 27, 1927, he and two friends, Bill Townsend (or Townsley) and Ernest Jordan, of Coeburn, Virginia, were returning to work in Fleming, Kentucky. According to the report by Kentucky attorney Harry Moore, Deaton's companions were Kentuckians from

Fleming, but a *Coalfield Progress* article dated November 30 claimed that the two friends, like Deaton, hailed from Coeburn. This is just one example of discrepancies in accounts of the affair. Late that night, driving into Slick Rock, the Black community near Jenkins, the three white men encountered Woods, who was in the company of two Black women, Susan Armister and Anna Mae Emery. According to the account published in the *Coalfield Progress* and accepted by the authorities, Woods, Armister, and Emery jumped onto Deaton's car, thinking it was a taxi. Deaton ordered them off, whereupon Woods, given a gun by one of the women, shot and killed Deaton, threatened the other two men, and ran off.[28]

Kentucky officials acted quickly, targeting the area's Black inhabitants. They blocked the roads in and out of Jenkins and Fleming and "immediately started a sweeping drive to round up all negroes who could not give a clear account of their movements during the previous few hours." The two women, Armister and Emery, questioned at their boarding house, identified Woods as the shooter, and he was captured soon after. The three were taken first to the jail in Jenkins, then moved to nearby Whitesburg to avoid the angry whites who were gathering in Jenkins.[29]

On the Virginia side, there was outrage over the shooting. Herschel Deaton was a pillar of the Coeburn/Tom's Creek community. His father, J. A. Deaton, was chief engineer of the Virginia Iron Coke and Coal Company, and Herschel was "widely and popularly known" in Coeburn and Norton. He had recently married Virgie Counts, a former nurse at the Norton Hospital. Norton had been home to an active chapter of the KKK, which openly advertised its meetings, although by 1925 the organization seemed to have flamed out.[30] Deaton's funeral on the morning of Tuesday, November 29, attracted a large crowd of people "from all over Wise County." Described as "the largest gathering of people seen in Coeburn in recent years," the service at the Methodist Church was arranged by Deaton's brother Masons, members of the Knights Templar and Blue Lodge, and his expensive stone was carved with the Masonic symbol and the epitaph, "Death Loves a Shining Star," all indicative of Deaton's standing in the community. It would have embarrassed his family and friends had Woods been tried for killing Deaton and testimony revealed an alternative story about what the three white men were doing in Slick Rock at 11:30 p.m. the previous Sunday. This may help explain why, after the funeral, a mob, according to some accounts numbering five hundred whites, in a parade of cars drove across the Kentucky line in search of their own, swift justice and to prevent the real story from coming out.[31]

The assault on the jail in Whitesburg to break Woods out seems to have been a coordinated plan between Virginia and Kentucky whites. Accounts differ about whether the Virginia group actually participated in removing Woods from the jail. According to one report, car trouble delayed them so that it was the Kentucky men who stormed the lockup, conveyed Woods to Jenkins, and met the Coeburn contingent there. Another story, however, identifies a man from Tom's Creek named Frank Richmond as "one of the first of the Virginia friends to go to Kentucky after receiving news of the shooting," presumably to help plan the lynching.[32]

The *Coalfield Progress* published its version the afternoon of the day of the lynching. "The mob commenced gathering early Tuesday afternoon, when 200 [Kentucky] men rode down on the railroad from McRoberts to Whitesburg, where Woods was in jail." Ignoring Sheriff Reynolds of Whitesburg, who "said" he begged them to leave Woods alone, "promising quick trial," the group attacked the jail "with hack-saws, crowbars and other weapons," finally breaking in through the roof.[33]

After breaking Woods out of jail in Whitesburg, the mob returned him to Slick Rock, where they were joined by the waiting Virginians. As they prepared to hang Woods near the scene of the crime, as was common in lynchings, Jenkins sheriff Sam Privitt, acting in accordance with the wishes of the Consolidated Coal Company, told them to take Woods elsewhere. Initial accounts claimed Privitt accompanied the mob to the Gap, "for protection," an assertion that Privitt later vehemently denied, even driving to Norton to the offices of the paper to correct the story.[34] Sheriff Privitt's action—telling the mob to go elsewhere rather than actively attempting to stop the lynching—as well as Sheriff Reynolds's ineffective remonstrations represent examples of the typical behavior of white southern officials when they faced a mob of angry white men. Kentucky officials zealously pursued Woods after Deaton's death yet were less diligent in their protection of him after his arrest.

Prevented from lynching him in Jenkins, the mob carried Woods across the state line through Pound Gap. There they found a wooden platform that had been erected only two weeks earlier to host a group of dignitaries from both states to celebrate the opening of the road through the Gap. The mob hanged Woods from two supports of the platform, shot him multiple times, with some accounts relating that Herschel Deaton's father was given the honor of firing the first shot. Woods's body was "riddled with more than a hundred bullets from pistols and high-powered rifles," and when it fell from the rope, the mob poured gasoline over it and set it afire. They left his body on the platform for public viewing. There exists a photo of Woods's lifeless body, partially burned, and school children were among the visitors to the site to view his body on the following day. He was hastily buried that evening, and friends from Jenkins soon after removed the body and reburied him in an unknown location.[35]

That Woods was murdered on the platform, constructed by Kiwanians, that had hosted dignitaries just weeks earlier, underscores the sensational and deliberate nature of the crime against him. While asserting that Woods had committed "a dastardly crime," and "should pay his life for the one he took away," the editorial writer of the Norton *Coalfield Progress* also wrote "that he should be jerked from the jail, yanked to the mountain top and there, without trial, be shot and burned by the mob, not apparently as infuriated as it was deliberately planned, is not a lawful act, neither it is a just act."[36]

The *Coalfield Progress*'s rival newspaper in Norton, the *Crawford's Weekly*, edited and published by progressive Bruce Crawford, hinted at an alternate story of what may have happened that night at Slick Rock. Crawford was a tireless crusader for social justice, opposing mining companies' stranglehold on local miners, taking on the KKK, whom he referred to as "an intolerant confederacy of dark-minded cowards hiding under sheets," and fulminating against racism and lynching. Crawford had published pieces decrying the lynching of Raymond Byrd the previous year, and in the wake of Woods's killing, he put his money where his mouth was, starting a fund for the prosecution of the perpetrators and challenging other newspapers to do the same. When asked why a fund, Crawford wrote, "To those who do not believe in mob law, the question answered itself. It is just because we do not think the governors of Virginia and Kentucky will do anything definite about the lynching. . . . Virginia newspapers have always been quick to deplore lynchings, but most of such deplorings have seemed perfunctory and hypocritical."[37]

In an article titled "The Mob," published on December 3, Crawford created a narrative of Deaton's shooting that gave free reign to the speculations surrounding the incident, inventing dialogue between Woods, Deaton, and the others. While not openly diverging from the official story, Crawford questioned it in a preface to the article: "Since the following story was put in type, rumors have been heard to the effect that there may have been more provocation for the shooting than was originally reported." Crawford's inventive account ended with a description of the ghastly scene of souvenir-pickers viewing Woods's body: "Bullets that protruded from the blistered skin of the Negro were picked out by curiosity seekers. Blood-stained scantlings were carried away. Many had carved red shavings from the timbers and taken them for trophies. Cartridges were scooped up by many hands from the ground."[38]

The NAACP version of the story, based on their own investigation, presented a different account of the confrontation between Woods and Deaton. Relying on the evidence of Lawrence Kellis, an African American teacher and social worker who lived in Blackey, Kentucky, the NAACP argued that Woods shot Deaton in self-defense after trying to stop the two women from going along with the white men from Coeburn. This version of the story was soon picked up by several prominent African American newspapers, including the *Baltimore Afro-American,* and the Norfolk, Virginia, *Journal and Guide*. Kellis wrote to the NAACP headquarters asserting that the identities of at least six of the mob were known and urging them to send an investigator: "I have rumors of several persons but being colored myself I cannot talk to the whites and get their names conclusive. All you would have to do is to send some real fair, light complexioned person of Mr. Walter White['s] type or some interested white person." Kellis himself was fed up: "I am leaving Xmas. I cannot stand the KKK conditions in Letcher County any longer."[39]

Kellis's frustration over the failure to prosecute any of Woods's killers was understandable given the jurisdictional questions surrounding the case and the reluctance of Kentucky and Virginia officials to shoulder the responsibility. There was initial confusion about exactly where the lynching took place. Once it became accepted that it happened on the Virginia side, Gov. William J. Fields of Kentucky signaled an interest in investigating the incident by appointing Harry Moore, prosecuting attorney for Letcher County, to look into the matter. But it is apparent from Moore's report, published in full in the Louisville *Courier-Journal,* that his primary objective was to establish that it was men from the Virginia side who initiated the killing of Woods, although Kentuckians participated. Moore wrote that "the idea of lynching Wood [sic] seems to have originated at the burial of Deaton at Coeburn, Va., on Tuesday morning as the crowd left Coeburn in Tom's Creek Tuesday night to carry out the plan and were reinforced by others joining in at Borton [sic] and Pound Gap." The mob then "came to Whitesburg in motors bearing Virginia license tags, crossing 'the state line at Pound Gap at intervals of five, ten and fifteen minutes' and 'passing through Jenkins, Fleming and Neon and on in the direction of Whitesburg.'"[40]

Both governors vowed publicly to prosecute members of the mob. Byrd, in particular, made the strongest, albeit empty, pledge: "If the lynching occurred on Virginia territory every resource of the state will be extended to the local authorities to apprehend and punish the perpetrators of this outrage. . . . The lynching was a dastardly and cold-blooded crime without the slightest justification." But Byrd's words were meaningless if local authorities failed to pursue mob members vigorously. For his part, Governor Fields of Kentucky also announced his intention to prosecute. But as the lynching took place in Virginia, Kentucky officials could only charge the men with breaking into the jail at Whitesburg.[41]

Any impetus to prosecute members of the mob was thus stifled by the special circumstances surrounding the crime. In the Woods case, as in the other two Wise County lynchings, it appeared at first that local officials, while unable to prevent the lynching, might have taken steps to prosecute the offenders. But in the Woods case, the jurisdictional issue and the fact that Virginia members of the mob included many well-connected members of the community meant that there would be little interest in seeing justice done. Despite the pledges of officials, including governors of both Kentucky and Virginia, and the fact that many of its members were reported to have been unmasked, no member of the white mob that lynched Leonard Woods was ever prosecuted. In yet another example of the state-sanctioned nature of lynching, reinforced by the special circumstances of the Woods case, local officials' inclination was to ignore extralegal violence against Blacks.

In March 1928 Governor Byrd signed the state's antilynching law, the first of its kind in the nation. Undoubtedly, the 1926 lynching of Raymond Byrd contributed to Byrd's interest in a state law, but it was Leonard Woods's death in Wise County, as well as the editorial writings of Louis Jaffé of the Norfolk *Virginian-Pilot* and Bruce Crawford of the Norton *Crawford's Weekly* that spurred Governor Byrd finally to act. After 1928 there were no further documented cases of lynching in the state, at least according to state officials, although the NAACP, which preferred a federal law, would continue to investigate suspicious deaths of Blacks until at least 1937.[42]

In September 1932, for example, the decomposed body of a Black man named Shedrick Thompson was found hanging from a tree near Linden, in Fauquier County. Members of the community had sought Thompson for breaking into the home of a white couple, Henry and Mamie Baxley, and allegedly raping the wife after beating them both. After a month of searching the local mountains, officials gave up, and when Thompson's body was found, only a few miles from the Baxley home, a mob gathered, cut him down, and burned his body. The local coroner ruled his death a suicide. The NAACP protested that it was a lynching, listing it as such. Former Governor Byrd himself responded, reminding them that he was responsible for the antilynching law: "As you probably know, it was upon my recommendation as Governor of Virginia that the General Assembly of Virginia passed the most drastic antilynching law ever passed by any southern state," he insisted. "I investigated the alleged lynching in Fauquier and I am convinced as is everyone else that made a similar investigation that this was not a lynching. . . . I trust very much that you will correct this erroneous record."[43] Recent scholarship has validated the NAACP view that Thompson's death was indeed a lynching.[44]

As sweeping as it seemed, Virginia's antilynching law, prompted by the Wise County lynching of Leonard Woods, proved largely symbolic, more a result of white Virginians' desire for the appearance of law and order than it was a step towards racial justice. No white person was ever convicted of lynching after the law was passed.[45] And violence toward Blacks certainly did not cease. As the case of Shedrick Thompson shows, the impetus for mob revenge on Blacks had not died; rather, the public spectacle of white men openly participating abated. Thompson's lynching occurred secretly; only after the body was found did the ritual defiling of his corpse take place.

The three Wise County lynchings show, above all, the persistence of local conditions determining how suspected Blacks were treated.[46] The cases of Guynn, Hurst, and Woods each had its compelling backstory. Wiley Guynn, the boarding house operator, met his death at the hands of a mob frustrated with the delays in the execution of another Black man. Dave Hurst, the single Alabama miner whose crime of house breaking was exaggerated to assault and rape, might have escaped death if quicker action had been taken by the local sheriff. And Leonard Woods's lynching created such a firestorm that Governor Byrd, however reluctantly, acceded to a state law against lynching.

The three lynchings in Wise County show how at least some local authorities tried to uphold justice for both Blacks and whites. But the nature of the county's segregated society and the belief that its Black inhabitants were inherently prone to criminal activity made it impossible to adhere absolutely to a single standard. Even when successful in seeing a measure of justice done to a Black offender, as in Robert Foy's case, the relatively lengthy delay in carrying out the sentence may have led to the unjust killing of Wiley Guynn. Guynn's alleged offense was perhaps less than that of Foy, but its character (an attack on a young white girl) resulted in a spontaneous lynching by a mob, even as Commonwealth's Attorney Dotson pleaded with them.

David Hurst was accused of a clear violation of the racial code. His offense of breaking and entering turned into an assault on a white woman that local media exaggerated into an attempted rape. Hurst's lynching was a poignant reminder that young Black men must act according to a strict code of behavior, or they could face quick extralegal retribution despite the authorities' determination to uphold justice, as Sheriff Corder's actions made clear. Corder might have been able to prevent Hurst's murder; he kept Sydney Williams from being lynched and succeeded in bringing several of the perpetrators of Hurst's murder to justice, unprecedented acts that were praised by the national media and the NAACP alike.

The 1927 killing of Leonard Woods represented the total breakdown of whatever tenuous commitment to justice for Blacks existed in Wise County. The jurisdictional issue, conflicting accounts of what happened to Herschel Deaton, and, above all, the status of Deaton in the community and corresponding standing of the mob that set out to avenge him, made justice for Woods impossible to achieve. Woods's lynching, which only happened in Wise by the vagaries of circumstance, proved such an embarrassment to Byrd that the governor, prodded by public reaction to the editorial comments of Jaffé, Crawford, and other editors, and committed to avoiding federal intervention, finally agreed to a state antilynching law. But the Virginia law lacked the teeth that a federal statute, which southern filibuster repeatedly killed, would have supplied. In March 2022 the long-awaited federal law became a reality when President Joe Biden signed the Emmett Till Antilynching Act, finally recognizing lynching as a federal hate crime.[47]

Notes

1. Fitzhugh Brundage, "Racial Violence, Lynchings, and Modernization in the Mountain South," in *Appalachians and Race: The Mountain South from Slavery to Segregation*, ed. John Inscoe (Lexington: University Press of Kentucky, 2001), 312.
2. Brundage, "Racial Violence," 302.
3. Brundage, "Racial Violence," 313.
4. Ron Eller, *Miners, Millhands, and Mountaineers: Industrialization of the Mountain South, 1880–1930* (Knoxville: University of Tennessee Press, 1985), 161–65; Brundage, "Racial Violence," 307.
5. *Roanoke Times*, Nov. 16, 1920.
6. Brundage, "Racial Violence," 310.
7. Brundage, "Racial Violence," 310. Hurst's death certificate lists him as coal miner. The medical examiner who signed off on Hurst's death was named Hunt, thus the confusion about the victim's name.
8. Alexander S. Leidholdt, "'Never Thot This Could Happen in the South!': The Anti-Lynching Advocacy of Appalachian Newspaper Editor Bruce Crawford," *Appalachian Journal* (Winter/Spring 2011): 199–200.
9. James Weldon Johnson to Rev. C. E. Woods, Dec. 5, 1927, NAACP Administrative Files, Lynching, Virginia-Kentucky.
10. *Alexandria Gazette*, June 7, 1902; *Roanoke Times*, June 8, 1902; *Richmond Dispatch*, June 8, 1902; *Big Stone Gap Post*, June 12, 1902.
11. *Roanoke Times*, June 7, 1902; *Tazewell Republican*, June 12, 1902; *Richmond Dispatch*, June 6 and 7, 1902.
12. "Confession of Philip Jones," Nov. 22, 1934, NAACP Administrative Files, Lynching, Virginia.
13. *Big Stone Gap Post*, Sept. 4, 1902.
14. *Big Stone Gap Post*, Dec. 26, 1901.
15. *Big Stone Gap Post*, May 15, 1902.
16. *Roanoke Times*, Feb. 12, 1902.
17. John Hope Franklin, *From Slavery to Freedom: A History of Negro America*, 4th ed. (New York: Knopf, 1974), 355, 356, 357; Cameron McWhirter, *Red Summer: The Summer of 1919 and the Awakening of Black America* (New York: Henry Holt, 2001), 15. See also Equal Justice Initiative, "Lynching in America: Targeting Black Veterans," accessed Oct. 17, 2023, https://eji.org/wp-content/uploads/2019/10/lynching-in-america-targeting-black-veterans-web.pdf.
18. *Big Stone Gap Post*, Nov. 17, 1920.
19. *Big Stone Gap Post*, Nov. 17, 1920.
20. *Roanoke Times*, Nov. 16, 1920.
21. *Nation*, March 28, 1923.
22. See Douglas Smith, *Managing White Supremacy: Race, Politics, and Citizenship in Jim Crow Virginia* (Chapel Hill: University of North Carolina Press, 2002), 159–61.
23. *Big Stone Gap Post*, Dec. 8, 1920.
24. *Roanoke Times*, Dec. 7, 1920; Walter F. White to A. P. Corden [sic], Dec. 10, 1920, in NAACP Administrative files, lynching, Virginia. Sheriff Corder had a rather colorful career. He spent some time in Oklahoma City, working for the railroad, then returned to Wise to

manage the family mercantile business. He also worked in the coal and timber business and served as Norton postmaster. A lifelong Republican, he resigned on principle when Franklin Roosevelt was elected president, then ran an unsuccessful campaign for Wise County clerk.

25. Douglas Smith, "Anti-Lynching Law of 1928," *Encyclopedia Virginia*, accessed Oct. 17, 2023, https://encyclopediavirginia.org/entries/anti-lynching-law-of-1928/.
26. Brundage, "Racial Violence," 311–12. Brundage asserts that in some cases lynching was averted when local Black leaders met with whites to work out a compromise. There is no evidence that this occurred in Wise County, but the pervasive influence of the coal companies may have operated to produce similar results.
27. See Leidholdt, "Never Thot," 206–8.
28. This is the version published in the *Coalfield Progress*, Nov. 30, 1927.
29. *Coalfield Progress*, Nov. 30, 1927.
30. Leidholdt, "Never Thot," 203.
31. *Crawford's Weekly*, Dec. 3, 1927; *Coalfield Progress*, Nov. 30, 1927.
32. *Coalfield Progress*, Nov. 30, 1927.
33. *Coalfield Progress*, Nov. 30, 1927.
34. *Coalfield Progress*, Dec. 7, 1927.
35. *Coalfield Progress*, Nov. 30, 1927; D. B. Hollyfield, "Stories True and Real in the Life of D. B. Hollyfield," oral account, recorded July 6, audio CD issued 2005.
36. *Coalfield Progress*, Nov. 30, 1927.
37. *Crawford's Weekly*, Dec. 3, 10, 1927; Leidholdt, "Never Thot," 203.
38. *Crawford's Weekly*, Dec. 3, 1927.
39. See NAACP Administrative files, Lynching, folder "Whitesburg," which contains material presenting an alternative story of Woods's lynching. See, in particular, Lawrence Kellis to James Weldon Johnson, Dec. 7 and 14, 1927.
40. (Louisville) *Courier-Journal*, Dec. 3, 1927.
41. *New York World*, Dec. 1, 1927; (Whitesburg) *Mountain Eagle*, Dec. 8, 1927.
42. See Smith, "Anti-Lynching Law of 1928"; Leidholdt, "Never Thot," 222–23. Jaffé won the Pulitzer Prize for his editorials against lynching.
43. Harry Byrd to Walter White, Jan. 23, 1933, in NAACP Administrative files, Lynching, folder "Virginia—Warrenton."
44. See Jim Hall, *The Last Lynching in Northern Virginia: Seeking Truth at Rattlesnake Mountain* (Charleston, SC: The History Press, 2016).
45. Smith, "Anti-Lynching Law of 1928."
46. This is precisely the point Douglas Smith makes in *Managing White Supremacy:* In Virginia "mob violence remained essentially a local affair, virtually unexplainable by larger models of behavior" (156).
47. See Emmett Till Antilynching Act, H.R.55, 117th Congress (2021–22), accessed Oct. 17, 2023, https://www.congress.gov/bill/117th-congress/house-bill/55/text.

PART III

✸

THE STATE RESPONSE TO LYNCHING

Lynching, and more generally racialized violence and coercion, could thrive throughout the South only because white mobs enjoyed a certain level of support, or at the very least tolerance, from local and state officials and the courts. Sheriffs, mayors, coroners, judges, governors, and other officials in the political, legal, and criminal justice systems had, in theory, the power and tools to prevent and punish lynching in myriad ways, *if they chose to*. The following are just some of the courses of action authorities could have engaged to stop lynching: protect Black prisoners threatened to be lynched, appeal to mobs to abide by the courts, identify lynchers, thoroughly investigate the perpetrators of mob violence, charge and bring lynchers to trial, and testify during trials as witnesses or protect other witnesses from retaliation. Furthermore, state officials could have authorized state militias to protect jails and inmates, passed effective legislation to punish participants in mob violence, or investigated local authorities that had failed to protect lynching victims. To their credit, several officials *did choose* at times to intervene to thwart lynchings, as the high number of threatened and averted lynchings in Virginia can attest (see the table in the Hagy essay in part II). Often animated by disdain for mob lawlessness and disorder rather than genuine concern about defending Black lives and basic human rights, some white officials thus demonstrated active opposition to lynching.[1] Nonetheless, a system of tacit complicity, which extended also to most of the (white) press and local communities, propped up lynching as an instrument of racial terror and control for several decades.[2]

As Black activists, journalists, and organizations like the NAACP engaged in a national antilynching campaign, mob violence became increasingly difficult to tolerate, especially as Virginia state officials were fixated with the preservation of the Commonwealth's reputation.[3] By the 1920s, the systematic complicity behind lynching became more and more untenable, and lethal mob violence was openly reproved by state officials and the press. After the spectacle lynching of Leonard Woods in 1927, Louis Jaffé, the editor of the *Norfolk-Virginian Pilot,* mounted a campaign against mob violence that finally led to the passage of the 1928 antilynching law in Virginia.[4] While this law was never really applied, it did send a strong signal to white Virginians that mob violence, especially of the openly defiant type, would not be further tolerated; and, at any rate, courts would be making sure that alleged Black criminals would be swiftly (and often lethally) dealt with.

This section contains four essays that examine how the state of Virginia responded to lynching by focusing on different state actors (governors, courts, judges, and the General Assembly). Most essays pay particular attention to the role the death penalty played in the system of racial terror in Virginia, establishing a strong connection between lynching and the use of legal executions against the Black community. Virginia courts and officials relentlessly used quick show trials to convict Black defendants accused of murder or sexual assault against white women as a powerful weapon to stymie mob violence and the official embarrassment associated with it. As the essays in this section indicate, the extensive use of the death penalty could thus satisfy white Virginians' hunger for swift and lethal "justice" against the threat of "Black criminals" without having to resort to the lawless barbarism of mob violence.

In "Faces of O'Ferrall: Virginia's Antilynching Governor in the Jim Crow Era," lawyer and writer Charles T. Blair analyzes the complex, and sometimes contradictory, positions on lynching taken by Charles O'Ferrall, a stalwart champion of white supremacy, during his term in office from 1894 to 1898. O'Ferrall is now mainly remembered for his opposition to lynching and willingness to use the state militia to prevent vigilante violence against African American citizens. However, as a county judge in Rockingham County in the 1870s, O'Ferrall played a very ambiguous role in the 1878 lynching of Charlotte Harris, the only documented case of an African American woman killed by a mob in Virginia. Judge O'Ferrall conducted the grand jury inquiry that failed to identify any of the lynchers. This case might have shaped some aspects of O'Ferrall's future crusade against lynching. However, he failed to learn the key lessons of Charlotte Harris's murder, as he often depicted lynching victims as undoubtedly guilty rapists and cynically opposed Ida B. Wells's activism against lynching.

In the second essay in the section, journalist and anti–death penalty activist Dale Brumfield investigates "How 'Judge Lynch' Influenced Virginia Courts, Lawmakers, and Journalists." Brumfield argues that courts, journalists, and even Virginia legislators sometimes exploited the threat of lynch mobs to increase the use of death sentences against Black defendants. For example, in 1894 the General Assembly authorized the death penalty for Blacks charged with *attempted rape* "because of fears that failure to do so would risk the lynching of persons accused of that crime." Records show that law enforcement routinely used lynching threats to extract confessions, and lynch mobs even influenced juries.[5] Newspapers often praised these hastily assembled trials that led to rapid, harsh sentences because they "prevented a threatened lynching." The result was that the coordinated goal of law enforcement and courts shifted: arrests and trials for Blacks accused of serious crimes against whites were not solely designed to determine guilt or innocence but often to appease the lynch mobs, real or threatened, with a speedy sentence of death.

In the following essay, "Uneven Justice: The Origin and Practice of Legalized Lynch Law in Jim Crow Virginia," Kevin Hegg systematically dissects the relationship between lynching and the death penalty in Virginia. According to Hegg, the dramatic shift from extralegal to legal lynchings (death sentences against Black defendants) can be traced to Governor O'Ferrall. As lynchings in Virginia peaked in the early 1890s, in his first address to the General Assembly, Governor O'Ferrall urged white citizens not to resort to mob violence and promised them that justice for the "crime too horrible to mention" will be "certain and will never miscarry if the law is allowed to take its course." Extending the death penalty to apply to the crime of attempted rape, O'Ferrall reassured white Virginians that, rather than killed by mobs, "Black rapists" could now be executed legally—and swiftly. This essay thus argues that the definition of *racialized terrorism*[6] should be expanded to include the death penalty as a form of legalized lynching, offering a broader understanding of how terror was used to control African Americans during Jim Crow.

Public historian Josh Howard reviews "Six Sham Trials: Judge George Anderson and Jim Crow in Alleghany and Botetourt County Courts" in the last essay in the section. O'Ferrall's strategy to deploy the state militia and order state inquiries to prevent lynchings led to a significant reduction of lethal mob violence in the Commonwealth, and other southern states started to adopt similar measures. However, O'Ferrall's actions also led directly to an increase in state-sanctioned executions of Black men, the vast majority of whom were convicted at expedited and corrupt capital murder trials. Judge George K. Anderson, who presided over western Virginia county and circuit courts from 1895 to 1930, provides perhaps the most illuminating case study. Anderson was a young local lawyer when a white mob lynched three Black men in Clifton Forge in 1891; he would later become an antilynching advocate who used the death penalty as a substitute for mob violence. As a judge, he presided over at least six trials resulting in death sentences for Black defendants. Each trial was marked by poor defense counsel, sketchy witness testimony, and—at least in one case—exonerating evidence that was outright ignored. Judge Anderson personally made the greater Clifton Forge area a more dangerous place for Black men, both the innocent and guilty; even though he technically stamped out lynching violence, he embraced the death penalty as a more palatable instrument to terrorize the Black community.

Notes

1. Fitzhugh Brundage, *Lynching in the New South: Georgia and Virginia, 1880–1930* (Urbana: University of Illinois Press, 1993), 187.
2. Sherrilyn A. Ifill, *On the Courthouse Lawn: Confronting the Legacy of Lynching in the Twenty-First Century* (Boston: Beacon Press, 2018).
3. J. Douglas Smith, *Managing White Supremacy: Race, Politics, and Citizenship in Jim Crow Virginia* (Chapel Hill: University of North Carolina Press, 2002).
4. Brundage, *Lynching in the New South*, 189–90.
5. In 1899 sentencing deliberations had dragged on for fifteen hours for Noah Finley, a Black man accused of robbery. When "a party of citizens notified [the jury] that if a verdict was not rendered by 10:00 a.m., the negro [Finley] would be lynched," the jury quickly imposed a death sentence; see "Would Be Judicial Murder," *Richmond Planet*, Aug. 12, 1899, 4.
6. Stewart E. Tolnay and E. M. Beck, "'Racialized Terrorism' in the American South: Do Completed Lynchings Tell an Accurate Story?," *Social Science History* 42, no. 4 (2018): 677–701.

FACES OF O'FERRALL
Virginia's Antilynching Governor in the Jim Crow Era

CHARLES T. BLAIR

Among Virginia's governors of the Jim Crow era, the posthumous reputation of Charles Triplett O'Ferrall has fared better than most. Such an outcome would have seemed unlikely when O'Ferrall left the Governor's Mansion in 1898. His popularity was at a low ebb. O'Ferrall had been disowned by his own political party as an arch-traitor because of his refusal to support the Democratic nominee in the 1896 presidential election. He had served out his term as a lame duck and political pariah.

O'Ferrall's departure from office did not soften the bitter feelings against him. His efforts to comment on public issues were met with scorn. "What Governor O'Ferrall says or does is of little or no interest now, anywhere, and least of all to the people of his own State," declared the *Alexandria Gazette*. In April 1898, when the Spanish-American conflict was developing, O'Ferrall let it be known that he was prepared to offer his services to the military. The *Gazette* acidly remarked that O'Ferrall's services "will hardly be required, as the governor is old and weak now."[1]

O'Ferrall was only fifty-eight years old. Consigned to involuntary political retirement, he took up the practice of law in Richmond. He completed a long autobiography and reportedly wrote a romantic novel (never published) featuring a dashing Confederate hero who bore more than a passing resemblance to himself. In 1905, after losing most of his money in a market downturn, O'Ferrall died from what the press described as a "complete nervous collapse."[2]

During his term of office and in later years, some of the most enthusiastic praise for O'Ferrall—a staunch defender of white supremacy who proudly carried a cane made of wood from the birthplace of Jefferson Davis—came from the state's most important African American newspaper. The *Richmond Planet*, under the editorship of the antilynching activist John Mitchell Jr., frequently commended O'Ferrall for his opposition to lynching and willingness to use armed force to prevent vigilante violence against Black citizens. O'Ferrall was hailed as an iron-willed defender of the rule of law. In 1895 the *Planet* declared: "The rule of Judge Lynch is broken in Virginia. Gov. O'Ferrall did it."[3]

Mitchell's reference to the end of lynching proved premature, but his praise for O'Ferrall's stance has echoed over the years. Indeed, O'Ferrall's reputation has risen in recent decades. In 1993 Fitzhugh Brundage credited "O'Ferrall's legacy" with having fostered "the widespread conviction among all Virginians that governors had a personal responsibility to prevent lynchings." In 2002, Ann Field Alexander's biography of Mitchell described O'Ferrall as "the nation's leading antilynching governor" who "was offended by the notion that anyone—white or Black, rich or poor—would receive less than a fair hearing in a court of law." O'Ferrall's reputation was further boosted in 2003 by Suzanne Lebsock's *A Murder in Virginia*, which led readers to view O'Ferrall as a "real-life hero."[4]

Lebsock's work contained a passage in which she brought her readers face-to-face with O'Ferrall. Memorably describing his gray hair "swept straight back from his face and flared full behind his ears" as giving the impression of "perpetual forward motion," she called attention to O'Ferrall's "dark and mournful eyes." This, Lebsock wrote, was the face of a man who "meant to end lynching in Virginia."[5]

O'Ferrall thus presents a puzzle. How did a racially prejudiced, battle-scarred Confederate become an antilynching champion? This essay will attempt to provide answers by tracing O'Ferrall's career as it intersected with issues of racial violence. In so doing, it will examine a number of events that have not been discussed in previously published accounts of his life. The facts that emerge from this examination do not tell a simple story. Rather, they suggest that on matters of racial violence, O'Ferrall was a man of many faces.

"Courtly" is the word often used by those who met O'Ferrall. With a gray moustache, erect military bearing, and aristocratic cane, he presented the picture of "the highest type of the Virginia gentleman of the old school."[6] O'Ferrall worked to cultivate this genteel image. In at least one respect, though, he departed from it. Politicians of his era were expected to at least pretend to follow the precept of "let the office seek the man, not the man the office." O'Ferrall, in contrast, did not hide his raw ambition. In his autobiography, he wrote that he could not "see why I should quietly fold my arms and lie supinely upon my back and pray for the coming of the office in search of me; my ambition was laudable, and I could discover no reason why I should conceal it from my friends."[7] Others saw this trait in a less positive light. His "great fault," a fellow Democrat once said, is that "O'Ferrall wants everything."[8]

Colonel O'Ferrall: Early Life to 1874

O'Ferrall's ambition was apparent from his early days in Morgan County, Virginia (now part of West Virginia), where he was born in 1840. His father, the clerk of the county court, died in 1855. When O'Ferrall was just seventeen, he successfully ran for his father's old position, undeterred by the fact that his opponent was fifty years older.

When Virginia seceded in 1861, O'Ferrall made a decision that defined the rest of his life. Morgan County was strongly Unionist, but O'Ferrall joined the Confederate cavalry. He was an enthusiastic soldier who capitalized on opportunities to advance through the ranks. He was wounded on eight occasions, sustaining five bullet wounds and three sabre wounds. Most famously, O'Ferrall as an acting colonel attacked federal forces in Shenandoah County on April 12, 1865—several days after Lee's surrender at Appomattox. O'Ferrall maintained for the rest of his life that this engagement was a signal moment in Confederate history. He boasted that "my little command held the last Confederate line, made the last fight, and captured the last prisoner . . . upon the soil of old Virginia."[9] Even after learning that Lee had surrendered, O'Ferrall resolved to keep fighting. Only after hearing that Joseph Johnson's army had capitulated did O'Ferrall reluctantly disband his men.

The end of the war did not bring peace for O'Ferrall, who found himself in legal trouble stemming from a controversial incident in 1864. O'Ferrall had led a raid against his home county. His troopers stole horses, arrested citizens who supported the new state of West Virginia, and marched several elderly prisoners (one of whom had been a friend of O'Ferrall's father) to be imprisoned in Richmond. For these deeds, West Virginia's governor proclaimed O'Ferrall an "enemy of the State." Morgan County residents, angrily recalling their support of the young candidate a few years earlier, complained that O'Ferrall had repaid their kindness with treachery.[10] A criminal indictment was issued after the war, and O'Ferrall escaped only through appeals to Governor Pierpont of Virginia and President Andrew Johnson.

By September 1865 O'Ferrall had moved to Staunton, Virginia, to operate a hotel. The American Hotel, situated next to the train depot, was a resting place for travelers on their way to the fashionable mineral springs to the west. O'Ferrall ran the hotel for about two years with his younger brother, Plunkett.[11] O'Ferrall gained local prominence by delivering speeches at Confederate memorial events and other civic occasions. Then, and for the rest of his life, he was generally regarded as a skillful and entertaining speaker. His lengthy orations were described as "gemmed with radiant thought," while a few complained that "O'Ferrall, as a rule, is a gallon of words and a spoonful of ideas."[12]

In Staunton, O'Ferrall had confrontations with federal authorities and African American citizens. The *Staunton Spectator*, in O'Ferrall's first month as proprietor of the hotel, reported the following:

> On Friday evening last, two colored persons, a man and woman, got out of the stage at the American Hotel, and, presuming upon social equality, went into the sitting room of the Hotel and seated themselves upon one of the sofas, whilst another was occupied by white ladies who had just arrived. As soon as the Proprietor discovered the unwarranted liberties taken by this "gemmen ob color," he showed him in a *striking* and *forcible* manner that he had wholly mistaken his social status. The negro sought redress by reporting the case to the Provost Marshal, who after hearing the facts, told the negro that he had received the kind of treatment he deserved, but not to the degree to which his improper conduct justly entitled him. We suppose the negro doubts whether "de bottom rail be on de top now."[13]

A few months later, in 1866, O'Ferrall's brother Plunkett was summoned before the provost, Capt. W. Storer How of the 83rd New York Infantry, for assaulting a former federal soldier who uttered insulting words at the hotel. O'Ferrall appeared at the hearing and listened as Plunkett's violent behavior was rebuked by How, who commented that "where I came from—we let the law take its course." According to the *Spectator*, the following exchange took place between Colonel O'Ferrall and Captain How: "Ah! Says the Colonel, I understand you then to say, if a scoundrel . . . insults me or those in charge of my house . . . I must tamely swallow it and content myself with hunting up some limb of the law, and institute a suit against him for slander. That is your idea, Capt. H., is it not? Yes, sir, you must not under any circumstances take the law into your own hands. But sir, says the Colonel, we of the South are accustomed to a different code of honor, of conduct, or morals."[14] A few months later, O'Ferrall may have acted on his claim of being subject to a "different code" beyond the law. The records of the Freedmen's Bureau contain an entry dated August 1, 1866, that states as follows: "John Hill v. Col. O'Ferrall, assault—[illegible] bound over in sum of $200 to answer to Grand Jury."[15] No evidence of further proceedings on this charge has been located.

In 1868 O'Ferrall enrolled in Washington College (now Washington and Lee University) in Lexington, Virginia, and studied law during Robert E. Lee's tenure as president of the school. In his autobiography, O'Ferrall recalled an incident that occurred while he was a student: "For several years after the peace the young men of the South could not look upon the negroes as their equals under the law, or as possessing the same legal rights as themselves. Many of the negroes about Lexington, as well as everywhere else, were greatly puffed up with the idea of freemanship, and were self-assertive, presuming, and irritating. The students of Washington College could not tolerate the disrespect and impudence which was frequently shown them by these people, and they resented it, and in some instances carried their resentment too far." According to O'Ferrall's account, a group of students decided to break up a political meeting "of the colored people." The planned assault was prevented only when Lee directed the students to stay away. O'Ferrall's role in this incident is unclear, but his sympathetic tone toward these "young men of the South" is unmistakable.[16]

In August 1869 O'Ferrall moved about fifty miles north to Harrisonburg and began practicing law. He quickly turned to politics, winning a seat in the House of Delegates as a Conservative in 1871. For the next twenty-five years, O'Ferrall displayed relentless energy and political ambition; scarcely a year passed in which he did not either occupy or run for some public office. When he entered the General Assembly, O'Ferrall sought to make a name for himself as a maverick "independent Conservative." He boldly ran for the US

House of Representatives in 1872 and was soundly defeated. O'Ferrall soon rethought his position; he is said to have decided to "stop [. . .] his campaign against the party organization" out of concern that "a split in the party might give control to the Republicans and the Negroes."[17]

Judge O'Ferrall: 1874-1880

O'Ferrall's embrace of the Conservative party orthodoxy was followed by his appointment as judge of the Rockingham County Court in 1874. In his autobiography, O'Ferrall recalled that being a judge was hard work and caused him "constant anxiety and perplexity."[18] Local sources offered mixed assessments of O'Ferrall's performance as a judge, praising his diligence while remarking that "one could scarcely have called him a brilliant man" and that he was not "great or profound" in matters of law.[19]

During his fifth year on the bench in March 1878, word reached Harrisonburg of the sadistic lynching of an African American woman named Charlotte Harris in eastern Rockingham County. The lynching stemmed from the burning of a barn a few days earlier. The fire was said to have been set by James Ergenbright, a seventeen-year-old African American working for the prosperous white farmer who owned the property. Ergenbright apparently had confessed and implicated Harris, claiming he had committed the crime at her instigation. Finding that Harris had left the area, the local constable gathered a group of men to capture her. They arrested her in Albemarle County and brought her back to Rockingham.

At a preliminary hearing, held at the home of the aggrieved farmer, the magistrates decided that sufficient evidence existed against Harris to take her to the county jail. The authorities, however, decided to wait until the next morning to transport Harris, reputedly because the hour was late, and the jail was about fifteen miles away. Harris was confined in an outbuilding on the farm and was guarded by four men. That night, at around eleven p.m., men with their faces darkened appeared. They entered the building with pistols drawn and were joined by a larger group of people who were also disguised "as colored people." The guards, when verbally threatened by the armed men, offered no resistance. The mob took violent hold of Harris and dragged her outside. They carried her up the road until they reached a blackjack oak tree.

According to multiple accounts, the tree was a large sapling that was particularly tough. Five men applied their strength to bend the tree over. After tying a rope to the tree and looping the other end around the neck of Harris, they suddenly let go of the tree. Harris was pulled upwards as the sapling sprang back, and she landed on the other side of the tree, which the mob propped up with a fence rail. Harris hung there, struggling in agony, until she was dead.

From the time of her death, Harris's partly clothed body was allowed to remain dangling at this spot, in prominent view on the roadside, for nearly two days before it was cut down. News of the event spread across the country. Stories appeared within days—in Richmond; Washington, DC; Wheeling, West Virginia; Philadelphia; New York; Indianapolis; Chicago; and Kansas City—telling of "The Lynching of a Woman," "A Virginia Atrocity," and the "Disgusting Details of the Affair." Under a headline reading "What Is the Matter in Virginia?," the *New York Herald* asked, "How could it be possible that there is any excuse for the practice of this kind of barbarity in Virginia?"[20]

According to contemporary accounts, O'Ferrall's reaction upon hearing of the lynching was to become so "very indignant" that he immediately summoned a grand jury to investigate.[21] Court records, however, show that the grand jury was not convened until more than two weeks after the lynching. When deliberations began, the jurors quickly returned an indictment against Ergenbright for arson.[22] They met for several more days and presented indictments for unrelated matters involving liquor-law violations, lewd and lascivious cohabitation, and no fewer than seven charges of keeping a house of ill fame, but took no action on the lynching. No charges were brought, against anyone, for the death of Charlotte Harris.

Judge O'Ferrall then discharged the grand jury. He also considered requests from the four men who had helped to arrest and confine Harris. This posse, which included a son of the farmer who owned the damaged barn, asked to be paid 75 cents per day for their services. O'Ferrall approved these payments, without any reduction or censure for the fact that the "guards" had abandoned their prisoner.[23]

At this point in his career, O'Ferrall was a political judge whose stature was intertwined with Confederate nostalgia. He had shown little regard for legal constraints when it came to Black citizens. There was every reason to believe that he would support the accepted narrative justifying the community's "righteous indignation" against alleged criminality.

But O'Ferrall did not follow the script. Shortly thereafter, James Ergenbright was brought to trial on the felony charge in O'Ferrall's court. Court records reveal little about the trial other than its unexpected outcome: a verdict of "not guilty."[24] The local press said almost nothing about the matter. Outside of Rockingham County, however, this verdict ignited a new round of coverage as the acquittal of Ergenbright was immediately linked to Charlotte Harris. Headlines of "Lynched, Yet Innocent" appeared in many papers. "Alas, for Virginia" declared the *Chicago Tribune*, "It turns out that the negro woman who was hanged by a mob of chivalrous Virginians . . . had actually nothing to do with the crime." The *Cincinnati Commercial* drew the same conclusion. It angrily wrote that "[a] few weeks ago the chivalrous Virginian Judge Lynch hung a negro woman for the alleged crime of setting fire to a barn. . . . The sequel is a little uncomfortable. It now comes out that the negro woman was wholly innocent of the crime; but that will hardly bring Charlotte Harris back to life. Maybe it will be a consolation to her family and friends."[25]

This negative publicity provoked consternation in the local press. Hoping to change the storyline, one editor wrote O'Ferrall asking for information that might put things in a better light. The judge responded with a remarkable and deeply ambiguous letter.[26]

On one hand, O'Ferrall's response gave answers that the editor did not want. Instead of endorsing the view that Charlotte Harris was a bad woman who deserved what she got, the judge forthrightly said, "I have very grave doubts as to the guilt of the woman." O'Ferrall indicated that he was familiar with the evidence and had reached the conclusion that "I do not think the woman could have been convicted" upon the testimony. O'Ferrall then revealed facts that could not have pleased the editor. He said that Ergenbright had been acquitted because the young man's confession and implication of Harris had been coerced. According to O'Ferrall, Ergenbright was subjected to extended questioning and, after initially denying guilt, changed his story only when the constable told him that the farmer would have to pay his wages (which apparently were in arrears) if he did so. Ergenbright's confession had been excluded from evidence because of this improper inducement. Although not stated in the letter, such a ruling would have been made by O'Ferrall as the presiding judge.

By making these facts public, O'Ferrall did something significant. He transformed the case of Charlotte Harris into a rarity in the annals of lynching; a judgment in favor of the victim was pronounced by the judge who would have presided over the case. For once, the lynchers did not have the last word on the guilt of their victim. O'Ferrall could have dodged the inquiry. Instead, he answered and said things he knew would be unpopular with many.

On the other hand, O'Ferrall's letter also included elements that are indefensible. Despite the acquittal in Ergenbright's case, O'Ferrall announced that he personally considered the young man guilty. This reckless statement violated basic principles of judicial behavior and could have endangered Ergenbright in a climate in which one person had already been lynched. O'Ferrall also played up his own role in the investigation, stating that his grand jury had "summoned and examined" about 150 witnesses. He claimed that "no clue had yet been discovered as to the lynchers," while maintaining that "this unfortunate affair, a most disgraceful act upon the part of a few lawless men, is condemned by all the right thinking people in the county." O'Ferrall ignored the glaring contradiction in his words: if the lynching was condemned by all "right thinking people in the county," why had 150 citizens under oath refused to identify the lynchers? He never acknowledged that the legal system had failed twice—once by failing to protect a prisoner in custody and again by failing to punish her killers.

Perhaps the most revealing aspect of O'Ferrall's letter was what it did not say. Other than paying lip service to the "unfortunate affair," he offered not a word of compassion or any recognition of the suffering of Charlotte Harris. He did not even say her name, referring to her only as "the woman." O'Ferrall, well-known for his long flowery speeches, could not find a syllable of sympathy for a woman who was dragged off into the darkness to die an unimaginable death.

Congressman O'Ferrall: 1884-1893

O'Ferrall's term as judge expired the following year and, with the Readjusters in control of the legislature, he was not reappointed. O'Ferrall briefly returned to the practice of law before launching a bid in 1882 to unseat the incumbent Readjuster congressman, John Paul. Paul initially prevailed on election day with a narrow plurality, but O'Ferrall challenged the results; he filed an election contest in the House of Representatives, claiming that there had been fraud "mostly among the colored, who were all against me."[27] O'Ferrall ultimately was seated in 1884 and went on to serve five more terms. As a congressman, O'Ferrall was chiefly known for his service on the committee that judged contested elections and for his opposition to federal legislation protecting Black voting rights. He became popular among his Democratic colleagues, and a fellow congressman presented him with a cane carved out of a log taken from the old house in Todd County, Kentucky, where Jefferson Davis had been born in 1803.[28]

Governor O'Ferrall: 1894-1898

O'Ferrall achieved one of his fondest ambitions in November 1893 when he was elected as Virginia's governor. During the campaign, and indeed since the death of Charlotte Harris fifteen years earlier, O'Ferrall had said little about the lynching of African Americans, even though such incidents were occurring with increasing frequency. But by the time O'Ferrall took office, the issue had become unavoidable in Virginia politics due to violent events in Roanoke.

On the morning of September 20, 1893, a white woman selling produce in Market Square was robbed and beaten. An unemployed Black laborer named Thomas Smith was arrested and held in the city jail. Soon, the streets filled with crowds clamoring for Smith to be hung. Henry Trout, Roanoke's mayor and a Confederate veteran, tried to protect the prisoner. After he and other officials unsuccessfully pleaded with the crowd to disperse, Trout called out the city's militia—the Roanoke Light Infantry—to reinforce the police.

Tensions grew throughout the day until, around eight p.m., the mob rushed the jailhouse doors. The militia opened fire. Over the next two minutes, a roar of gunfire left eight dead and thirty-one wounded. An eyewitness described the street in front of the jail as "a shambles, blood in forty places, the street car rails slippery with it."[29] Another account has portrayed the scene as resembling a battlefield, where "windowpanes were shattered, buildings were pockmarked with bullet holes, and there were fallen bodies, fragments of flesh, and pools of blood everywhere."[30] In a nearby church, attendees at a prayer service reportedly hid beneath the pews as bullets ricocheted inside the sanctuary.

FIGURE 1. "Governor Charles T. O'Ferrall and His Well-Earned Honors," *Richmond Dispatch*, January 2, 1894.

As the mob temporarily fell back, the authorities evacuated the jail. Smith was taken to a spot outside of the city; the militia was sent home. Mayor Trout, who had been wounded in the foot, sought refuge in a nearby hotel. The mob soon reassembled and, finding the jail empty, went on a rampage. Around three a.m., with armed, liquor-fueled rioters roaming the streets, the police decided to turn their prisoner over to the mob. Smith was carried off and, as he maintained his innocence, was hung from a hickory tree and riddled with bullets. In the morning thousands came to view the corpse, which had been decorated with a sign reading "Mayor Trout's Friend." A local studio took photographs showing a crowd of smiling men and women standing around the body of Smith, who was hanging "like a prize buck or bear . . . dressed in a shabby suit and wearing pants with patches over the knees, dangl[ing] only a few feet off the ground, his white socks hanging off his feet, his eyes and tongue protruding out of his badly swollen head, and his ears bleeding from spots where hunks had been cut off as souvenirs."[31]

The crowd carried the body to the banks of the Roanoke River, where a pyre was built and thousands watched as Smith's oil-doused body was consumed by the flames. Following this savage spectacle, members of the mob renewed their efforts to find Mayor Trout and militiamen. They expressed outrage that deadly force had been used in an effort to prevent a lynching.

Just a few days later, on September 25, 1893, O'Ferrall passed through Roanoke on the gubernatorial campaign trail. He met with political allies at the Hotel Roanoke and made a statement to the press attacking his Populist opponents. O'Ferrall's statement said nothing whatsoever about recent events in the city.[32]

By the time O'Ferrall took office in early 1894, opinion had solidified against the Roanoke mob. Lynching now appeared as more than a threat to African Americans; it had endangered white public officials, white homes and businesses, and the state's economic interests among northern investors. Under these circumstances, O'Ferrall struck a strong note in his inaugural address. He pledged that if disorder occurred, "whether in crowded city or rural district," he would lose no time in acting "to restore the supremacy of the law, let it cost what it may, in blood or money."[33]

John Mitchell's *Richmond Planet* greeted O'Ferrall's remarks with enthusiasm. "This is notice to the lynchers that their days of bloodshed and revelry are at an end," the paper said. Mitchell was pleased when O'Ferrall acted swiftly in 1894 to prevent lynchings by ordering troops to Manassas and Staunton. He was further encouraged when the governor met with him and the mother of a young African American who had been sentenced to death. Mitchell was impressed that O'Ferrall grasped his hand and said, "Oh yes, I read your paper every week."[34]

Yet O'Ferrall proved to be an unpredictable ally. In February 1894 he reduced the jail sentence of James Richardson, one of the few participants in the Roanoke Riot to have been convicted of a felony, to just twenty-four hours. That same year, O'Ferrall delivered a personal affront to Mitchell when the Afro-American Press Association held its annual meeting of journalists from across the country in Richmond. Mitchell was president of the organization and called on O'Ferrall to invite him to address the convention. Mitchell and several colleagues were "courteously received" in the governor's office. O'Ferrall told his visitors that he could not immediately answer their invitation but would shortly let them know. The next day, a letter arrived that surprised the Black editors. "I would not think of accepting an invitation," O'Ferrall wrote, "to address any convention or assembly that endorsed, as your convention did last evening, the course of Ida Wells in her slander of the people and civil authorities of the South." Wells, a member of the association, was already well known for her activism against lynching. O'Ferrall criticized her for sympathizing with "brutes" who committed "a certain crime." He chastised the convention for having "struck the South a blow that she did not deserve" and insultingly added that "if your convention would condemn the crime which has caused all the lynchings in the South, with rare exceptions, and the leaders of the colored people would frown down upon it, and not exert their energies and devote their time to a denunciation of the lynchings, there would be fewer outrages and, if so, fewer instances of mob violence."[35]

O'Ferrall's letter was not written in an impulsive fit of pique. Rather, the day before he had received Mitchell and his associates with a courtly show, he had already dispatched an equally virulent message. On September 10, 1894, he telegraphed the *New York World* to respond to news that a group of eminent British supporters of Wells planned to visit the South to learn more about the lynching problem. O'Ferrall's telegram was harshly aggressive:

> Things have come to a pretty pass in this country when we are to have a lot of English moralists sticking their noses into our internal affairs....
>
> Do they want to know that the white people in the South have lynched negroes whose miserable lusts led them to the Black crime of rape upon white women? If so, they need not investigate for such is the fact. Do they desire to know that this has been done by infuriated communities for the protection of white women and to save victims of these fiends from the humiliation of testifying in courts? If so, this is the fact. Do they want to know whether there was any doubt as to the guilt of the men lynched? If so, for the satisfaction of their yearning souls, they could have ascertained without encountering the perils of a sea trip that their guilt was clear in every instance. If they had a desire to learn whether these lynchings were permitted or countenanced by the civil authorities, they could have learned through the regular channels of correspondence that in every case the civil authorities were either without knowledge or were overpowered....

> Lynching will surely cease when the crime of rape ceases. These sympathetic Englishmen might find missionary work among the negroes of the South in warning them against the consequence of the forcible gratification of their devilish lusts.[36]

By equating lynching victims with rapists whose guilt was a foregone conclusion, O'Ferrall ignored not only one of Wells's primary points but also his own experience. Had he forgotten about Charlotte Harris, a victim whose death had nothing to do with rape and whose guilt could not have been proven, according to O'Ferrall himself?

Nevertheless, O'Ferrall's management of events was politically successful. A letter to the *Richmond Dispatch* reported approval for his "manly" actions in rebuking "an assemblage of negro ingrates and enemies" that had endorsed the views of a "unscrupulous, designing female with the fires of hate burning fiercely in her bosom." O'Ferrall, the writer said, had earned the esteem of "all white men in the South who are opposed to negro domination, negro impudence, and negro ingratitude . . . his popularity knows no bounds."[37]

O'Ferrall displayed a different face in 1895. After a murder of a white woman in rural Lunenburg County, he acted to prevent the lynching of three African American women who were accused of complicity in the crime. O'Ferrall sent two companies of militia to provide security during the trial. The women, with no lawyers to defend them, were found guilty by a local jury and sent to the Richmond jail to await their executions. When irregularities in the trial were later exposed, the county judge who had presided announced his intention to "correct" the record and ordered that the prisoners be returned to Lunenburg. It was widely believed that once the women were back on county soil, local citizens would administer "justice" before the judicial process ran its course.

When O'Ferrall was asked to intervene, he rose to the occasion. His normal day of official duties was leisurely, running from nine a.m. to three p.m.[38] But the night of Saturday, November 9, 1895, found the governor in his office with a host of advisors. This group could not provide a sound legal basis for action. O'Ferrall acted anyway. He directed an aide to pick up the telephone and convey his order: "The prisoners will not be taken back to Lunenburg."[39]

The *Richmond Planet* printed a dramatic account of what happened when Lunenburg's sheriff attempted on Monday morning to take the women into custody. As the jailer read O'Ferrall's order, the sheriff and his deputies became angry and muttered ugly threats; the condemned women watched with relief and allowed "smiles to beam upon their countenances."[40] Some newspapers around the state criticized O'Ferrall's action.[41] Virginia's court of appeals ultimately held that O'Ferrall had acted beyond his authority but found other grounds to rule that the prisoners deserved new trials. Ultimately, charges against two of the women were dropped. O'Ferrall himself pardoned the third.

Soon afterwards, O'Ferrall included the subject of lynching in his message to the General Assembly. O'Ferrall began as follows: "With pain and mortification I bring to your attention the frequent taking of human life without due process of law within the borders of our State. . . . In Virginia lynching cannot be defended; it must be reprobated." His message challenged the linkage of lynching with the crime of rape, even though O'Ferrall himself had done so just one year earlier: "I know there is a crime too horrible to mention. . . . But lynching has not been confined by any means to such cases; for in the last fifteen years only about one-third of those lynched has met their deaths upon charges of actual and attempted commission of this shocking crime." In his address O'Ferrall urged the legislators to use their power to stamp out lynching: "Christianity demands it; public morality requires it; popular sentiment exacts it," he said. He proposed laws to require cities and counties to pay a tax of up to $10,000 for each lynching that occurred in their jurisdiction and to repay the state for each instance where the military needed to be called out. He proposed remedies directly against law enforcement officers. "If any sheriff, jailor, sergeant, constable or other officer having in custody a prisoner, shall permit said prisoner to be taken from his custody without exhausting all means in his power to prevent it," O'Ferrall suggested, "he shall be summarily suspended from office by the court in which he qualified, until a motion to remove him shall be heard and determined by a jury." He further recommended that a "right of action for damages be given to the prisoner taken from custody as aforesaid, if living—if dead, to his widow, if he leaves one, if not, to his heirs—against the officer from whom the prisoner was taken . . . and that upon trial of the motion to remove said officer, or of the suit for damages, the burden shall be upon said officer to prove that he exhausted all means in his power to prevent the taking of the prisoner from his custody."[42]

O'Ferrall returned to these themes in an address to the legislature in 1897. He presented a statistical table of all lynchings in Virginia during the last seventeen years. This table showed sixty-one lynchings in that period, only three of which had occurred during O'Ferrall's term. He pointedly criticized the public officials and police of Alexandria for allowing one of the recent lynchings, as well as condemning the role played by newspapers in encouraging such behavior. O'Ferrall said that the press had persistently asserted "that the lynchings have been almost exclusively for criminal assaults, or attempted assaults, or for 'the usual crime,' as they term it, which is far from being correct." He urged the legislature to enact his statutory proposals to make lynchings "dangerous to the participants, and expensive to the communities in which they occur." He expressed the hope that Virginians would back up the law with a "warm, living, sustaining public sentiment" against lynching.[43]

O'Ferrall's antilynching message continued for the rest of his term but was never free from confusing contradictions. He repeatedly warned against equating lynching with the crime of rape but did exactly that in some of his proposals. He proposed, for instance, a mandatory death penalty for both rape and attempted rape convictions and recommended that trials for these crimes be scheduled more quicky than all other matters. "If an act embodying such provisions is passed," O'Ferrall stated, "lynchings will no longer occur in Virginia."[44]

O'Ferrall's popularity remained strong into 1896. His political downfall came that year not because of his position on lynching, but because he decided to oppose those in the Democratic party who favored an expansionary monetary policy involving the coinage of silver. O'Ferrall believed this position would enhance his prospects for a US Senate seat, but he badly miscalculated. He was instead ostracized as a "Traitor to True Democracy" for bolting the party.[45] In retirement, seeking to repair his reputation, O'Ferrall cast himself as a man of principle who had suffered for his beliefs. His autobiography discussed those principles at length, spending hundreds of pages on his devotion to the Confederate cause and his views on the state debt, coinage, and many other topics. To the issue of lynching, however, he devoted little more than one page out of nearly four hundred.

How then to explain the puzzle of a white supremacist unleashing a vigorous antilynching campaign in Virginia? And what to make of the ambiguities, and often contradictions (only partially cataloged here) that permeated his efforts? Because O'Ferrall chose to say little in public about his motivations, these questions remain the subject of speculation.

Part of the explanation may lie with what Fitzhugh Brundage has termed "the peculiar tenor of Virginia politics."[46] By the 1890s the state's conservative Democratic party was not seriously threatened by its political rivals. In comparison to other southern states, it was less dependent on appeals to overt racial aggression to sustain power. After the Roanoke Riot, Virginia's establishment came to regard mob violence as an imminent threat to social order and economic progress. Opposition to lynching, rooted in law-and-order principles, was socially acceptable. The antilynching views expressed by Virginians were, however, rarely accompanied by humanitarian compassion for the victim and almost never led to inquiry into other racial injustices. O'Ferrall, in embodying this collection of traits that would be contradictory and inconsistent in the twenty-first century, was a man of his era.

But if part of the explanation lies in O'Ferrall's times, part also rests with the man himself—especially in what O'Ferrall called his "laudable" ambition. He proved willing to embrace jarring contradictions to achieve his goals. He was, after all, a man who started his career by leading a cavalry raid on his own home county (plundering the citizens who had elected him to office just a few years earlier) and ended it by bolting from the political party he had championed for decades (severing ties with longtime friends over a now-obscure issue of monetary policy). Likewise, on matters of racial violence, O'Ferrall's inconsistent positions often had the common denominator of serving his near-term interests. His battles in the 1860s with the Freedmen's Bureau and his support for violence against African Americans got his name in the newspapers at a time when he was seeking a foothold on the political ladder. O'Ferrall had little to say about racial violence during the ensuing decades, even as the number of lynchings increased in the early 1890s. Only when Virginia's establishment became concerned about mob violence after the Roanoke Riot did O'Ferrall voice loud antilynching sentiments. During his term as governor, he used military force in an aggressive way that discomfited his conservative allies, but that too aligned well with his political brand, which portrayed O'Ferrall as a gallant warrior.

These explanations go far but are not completely satisfying. O'Ferrall, in his best moments, went beyond actions that can be characterized as adherence to social norms or pure political opportunism. His actions in the Lunenburg case and other incidents were aggressive and politically risky. Contemporaries such as John Mitchell, who observed O'Ferrall at close quarters while they themselves were living in the shadow of racial terror, viewed him as a genuine ally with real convictions. They credited O'Ferrall with having saved lives.

Nevertheless, if O'Ferrall shares in the credit for Virginia's relative success in reducing lynching, he also has responsibility for a problematic legacy. He maintained the pretense that Virginia's judicial system—if allowed to run its traditional course—would deliver impartial justice. The insidious consequences of this falsehood during the ensuing decades are ably examined by Kevin Hegg elsewhere in this volume. Between 1900 and 1963, sixty-eight men were legally executed in Virginia for the crime of rape or attempted rape. Not one of those men was white.

While my research has found no evidence that O'Ferrall consciously entered into a Faustian pact with Virginia's lynchers to bring about this result, his antilynching vision was undeniably limited. He acted to ensure that criminal defendants were delivered safely to the courthouse but turned a blind eye to the injustice that awaited them in the courtroom. Hasty trials of African Americans, often without the assistance of counsel and under circumstances that discouraged witnesses from testifying in favor of the accused, made a mockery of the principles that O'Ferrall professed to hold. With his background as a judge, O'Ferrall knew better than anyone exactly how this system worked. Yet there is no evidence that he focused his acclaimed rhetorical skills on those abuses. To the contrary, O'Ferrall argued that such trials should be expedited.

O'Ferrall's long public career has left behind a daunting amount of documentation that can be sifted for insights. This information, however, is often like a double-sided jigsaw puzzle; the same pieces can be put together to form two different pictures. It has led some to join John Mitchell in viewing O'Ferrall as a force for good, regarding his better actions as moments of light in a dark era in Virginia's history. It has led others to view O'Ferrall as an early architect of "legal lynching," simply replacing mob hangings with judicial executions as a tool of racial terror. With his multiple faces and ambiguous legacy, O'Ferrall is not easily defined. The true man remains elusive. He seems likely to continue as an enduring subject of interest—and debate—for those who seek to confront the history of lynching in Virginia.

Notes

1. *Alexandria Gazette,* Sept. 10, 1897, 2.
2. "Ex-Gov. O'Ferrall Breathes His Last," *Harrisonburg Daily News,* Sept. 23, 1905, 1.
3. *Richmond Planet,* July 20, 1895, 2.
4. W. Fitzhugh Brundage, *Lynching in the New South: Georgia and Virginia, 1880–1930* (Urbana: University of Illinois Press, 1993), 180; Ann Field Alexander, *Race Man: The Rise and Fall of the "Fighting Editor," John Mitchell Jr.* (Charlottesville: University of Virginia Press, 2002), 51, 63; James C. Foster, review of *A Murder in Virginia,* by Suzanne Lebsock, *Law and Politics Book Review* 13, no. 4 (April 2003).
5. Suzanne Lebsock, *A Murder in Virginia: Southern Justice on Trial* (New York: Norton, 2003), 62.
6. *Richmond Times-Dispatch,* Sept. 23, 1905, 2.
7. Charles T. O'Ferrall, *Forty Years of Active Service* (New York: Neale Publishing Co., 1904), 228.
8. "The Campaign in Virginia," *New York Times,* Sept. 12, 1893, 9.
9. O'Ferrall, *Forty Years,* 132.
10. "A Proclamation," *Wheeling Daily Intelligencer,* May 23, 1864, 2; "From Morgan County," *Wheeling Daily Intelligencer,* July 14, 1864, 2.
11. Reviews of the hotel often focused on the proprietor's war record. See, e.g., "American Hotel," *Staunton Spectator,* Oct. 31, 1865, 3: "The gallant Colonel, with his half-dozen wounds, Roman-like, all in front, is very popular and succeeding admirably in his new capacity"; and "Col. C.T. O'Ferrall," *Valley Virginian,* Aug. 1, 1866, 3: "[A] Prince among hotel keepers, and the same zeal, energy, and ability which characterized him as a soldier."
12. "Celebration at New Market," *Staunton Spectator,* May 28, 1867, 3; "Daniel and O'Ferrall," *Salem Times-Register,* Sept. 17, 1897, 2.
13. "In The Wrong Place," *Staunton Spectator,* Oct. 3, 1865, 3 (emphasis in original).
14. *Staunton Spectator,* March 20, 1866, 3. O'Ferrall also was reportedly involved in an altercation with a Freedmen's Bureau official in a Richmond hotel. "Local News," *Staunton Spectator,* June 19, 1866, 3.
15. Virginia, Freedmen's Bureau Office Field Records, 1865–72, Register of Complaints, v. 1–2 [NARA M1913 roll 175], 48, https://familysearch.org/ark:/61903/3:1:S3HT-DRQL-Y6?cc=1596147&wc=9LMK-923.
16. O'Ferrall, *Forty Years,* 188. In 1870 Plunkett O'Ferrall was indicted for shooting an African American man who allegedly showed "gross impudence to the ladies of the family." He was acquitted by a jury in Rockbridge County. "Shooting Affair," *Richmond Dispatch,* April 25, 1870, 2; "Letter from Lexington," *Richmond Dispatch,* June 15, 1870, 2.
17. Allen W. Moger, *Virginia: Bourbonism to Byrd* (Charlottesville: University Press of Virginia, 1968), 19.

18. O'Ferrall, *Forty Years*, 199.
19. Charles E. Wynes, "Charles T. O'Ferrall and the Virginia Gubernatorial Election of 1893," *Virginia Magazine of History and Biography* 64, no. 4 (Oct. 1956): 437–53; John W. Wayland, *A History of Rockingham County* (Dayton, VA: Ruebush-Elkins Co., 1912), 358–59.
20. For contemporary accounts of the lynching, see "What Is the Matter in Virginia?," *New York Herald*, March 10, 1878, 10; "A Woman Lynched," *Philadelphia Times*, March 11, 1878, 1; "Crimes and Casualties," *Richmond Daily Dispatch*, March 12, 1878, 10; *Staunton Spectator*, March 12, 1878, 3; "The Female Lynchers," *Kansas City Daily Journal of Commerce*, March 13, 1878, 3; "Lynch Law In East Rockingham," *Rockingham Register*, March 14, 1878, 3; "Lynching Case in East Rockingham," *Old Commonwealth*, March 14, 1878, 3.
21. *Rockingham Register*, March 21, 1878, 2.
22. Rockingham County Circuit Court Minute Book No. 5, 1876–78, 415.
23. Minute Book No. 5, 423–24, 436.
24. Minute Book No. 5, 452–54.
25. *Atlanta Daily Constitution*, April 21, 1878, 2; *Cincinnati Commercial*, April 19, 1878, 4.
26. "The Rockingham Lynching," *Rockingham Register*, May 23, 1878, 2; "A Leaf of County History," *Old Commonwealth*, June 6, 1878, 2.
27. O'Ferrall, *Forty Years*, 216.
28. "O'Ferrall Caned," *Rockingham Register*, April 4, 1890, 3.
29. Paul R. Dotson Jr., "Magic City: Class, Community, and Reform in Roanoke, Virginia, 1882–1912" (PhD diss., Louisiana State University, Baton Rouge, 2003), 214.
30. Ann Field Alexander, "Like an Evil Wind: The Roanoke Riot of 1893 and the Lynching of Thomas Smith," *Virginia Magazine of History and Biography* 100, no. 2 (April 1992): 189.
31. Dotson, "Magic City," 217.
32. "Col. O'Ferrall Here," *Roanoke Times*, Sept. 26, 1893, 2.
33. "O'Ferrall Our Chief," *Richmond Dispatch*, Jan. 2, 1894, 1.
34. "Gov. O'Ferrall's Inaugural," *Richmond Planet*, Jan. 6, 1894, 4; "Ben White's Mother," *Richmond Planet*, April 21, 1894, 1.
35. "The Gov. Refuses," *Washington Bee*, Sept. 22, 1894, 2.
36. "Get Out, Englishmen!," *New York World*, Sept. 11, 1894, 5.
37. "O'Ferrall and the Negro Editors," *Richmond Dispatch*, Sept. 23, 1894, 12; "O'Ferrall Endorsed," *Richmond Dispatch*, Sept. 12, 1894, 4; "English Meddlers," *Richmond Dispatch*, Sept. 11, 1894, 6; "Gov. O'Ferrall's Plain Talk," *Roanoke Times*, Sept. 13, 1894, 1.
38. Minor T. Weisiger, "Charles T. O'Ferrall," in *The Governors of Virginia: 1860–1978*, ed. Edward Younger (Charlottesville: University of Virginia Press, 1982), 142.
39. "Gov. O'Ferrall Says 'No,'" *Richmond Times*, Nov. 10, 1895, 1.
40. "Have Not Returned to Lunenburg County," *Richmond Planet*, Nov. 16, 1895, 1.
41. "Have We a Dictator," *Bedford Democrat*, Nov. 14, 1895, 2; "Taken from His Bed," *Norfolk Virginian*, Nov. 15, 1895, 3; *Alexandria Gazette*, Nov. 25, 1895, 2; "News and Comments," *Shenandoah Herald*, Nov. 29, 1895, 3.
42. *1895 Journal of the Senate of the Commonwealth of Virginia*, 32–34, https://catalog.hathitrust.org/Record/009787857.
43. *1897 Journal of the Senate of the Commonwealth of Virginia*, 15–17.
44. *1895 Journal of the Senate of the Commonwealth of Virginia*, 34.
45. The criticism of O'Ferrall was intense, ranging from Shakespearean mockery to attacks on his previously sacrosanct war record. Examples may be found at "O'Ferrall

and Chesterman," *Roanoke Times,* Oct. 8, 1896, 8; *Clinch Valley News,* Oct. 2, 1896, 2; "Charles T. O'Ferrall," *Roanoke Times,* Oct. 1, 1896, 1; "A Mean Attack," *Richmond Times,* Oct. 18, 1896, 4. It was said that O'Ferrall "could not now be elected to mind chickens any where in the State." "From Washington," *Alexandria Gazette,* Oct. 17, 1896, 2.

46. Brundage, *Lynching in the New South,* 183.

HOW "JUDGE LYNCH" INFLUENCED VIRGINIA COURTS, LAWMAKERS, AND JOURNALISTS

DALE BRUMFIELD

> Justice is often painted with bandaged eyes. She is described in forensic eloquence, as utterly blind to wealth or poverty, high or low, white or black, but a mask of iron, however thick, could never blind American justice, when a black man happens to be on trial.
> —Frederick Douglass

On February 18, 1909, Virginia executed a twenty-four-year-old Black man named Charles Gillespie for attacking nineteen-year-old Marie Louise Stumpf, daughter of E. A. Stumpf, a prominent Richmond brewer.

The January 10 crime and the trial six days later were a perfect storm of racial antagonism, creating a fertile environment for a lynching. It featured a muscular, "vicious-looking" Black man, "brutally" attacking the defenseless nineteen-year-old white daughter of a well-liked business owner on her way to morning mass "in the most fashionable section of Richmond."[1]

The news coverage of the assault relentlessly painted Gillespie as a savage brute who "sprang at" the defendant early on the morning of Sunday, January 10. Stumpf in turn was considered the vulnerable yet courageous hero, who despite being knocked down, got up and "fought for her life" "with superb courage" while trying to escape. When she screamed, Gillespie reportedly pulled a knife and threatened to cut her throat.

A passing man heard Stumpf's scream, thwarting the attack and scaring Gillespie away.

The *Newport News Daily Press* reported that Stumpf "bore every mark of a most fiendish assault." Another report claimed she had been "bitten numerous times about the face," in an attempt perhaps to make Gillespie appear even more ruthless and animalistic.

Police captured Gillespie two hours after the attack, and as news of the assault spread throughout the neighborhood, a lynch mob numbering in the dozens gathered outside the Richmond police station clamoring for those inside to release Gillespie to them. A circuit court judge named Witte arrived in person at the station, however, and pleaded to let the law take its course. He assured the mob that Gillespie would receive a speedy trial and that he would summon a special grand jury to indict him as soon as physicians allowed Miss Stumpf to testify.

For Witte and other authorities like him, there was nothing improper about explicitly promising a "speedy trial" and suggesting state-sponsored electrocution to mollify a mob. Judges were more concerned with preserving their versions of the sanctity of the courts and legal authority than with protecting the prisoner, and local sheriffs and mayors were mindful of potential bloodshed and property damage if a mob got out of control. In Gillespie's case, terms such as "let the law take its course" and "speedy trial" may be interpreted by the angry lynch mob as dog-whistles for "we will do what you want, only legally."

Fearing that mob violence was probably imminent if they found Gillespie not guilty, the court judicially bulldozed him, calling a parade of forty witnesses for the prosecution and none for the defense. The judge characterized the offense from the bench as a "crime against the very womanhood of the city" and said that it was of "vast importance" that justice was served (or more truthfully, that a legal execution take place so an extralegal lynching would not). Finally, the victim Stumpf took the stand, and the courtroom "was cleared meanwhile to spare the feelings of the young lady and her relatives." Her "recital" reportedly "moved all present to tears."

During the trial, the *Richmond Daily Press* reported that Gillespie "seems absolutely callous and indifferent as to whether he is electrocuted or not." The article also anticipated not that the court would find Gillespie guilty or innocent but that he would be executed on February 17.

The jury was out less than five minutes, and Gillespie was executed thirty-six days after the crime. The paper missed the execution date by a single day.

The example of Charles Gillespie illustrates that, in Jim Crow era Virginia, the ever-present threat of lynching in Black-on-white criminal cases influenced laws, manipulated courtroom procedures, guided (and intimidated) juries, streamlined executions, and even drove and affected news coverage.

While lynching is frequently stereotyped solely as the actions of an enraged mob, we see in the Gillespie case and in many others that the act had intimate connections to the criminal justice system, not just in Virginia but in many southern states. Lynchings and post–Jim Crow legal executions both aimed to send a strong message to the Black communities that their lives were ultimately managed by the white power structure.

Most Virginia politicians for decades decried lynching violence yet never directly acted legislatively to stop it, highlighting the Commonwealth's contradictory relationship with the practice. While they declared publicly that the act of lynching was unacceptable, a different story frequently unfolded in the courtroom, in the General Assembly, in the field, and especially in the press, where the looming threat of "Judge Lynch" functioned in the background as a confession-extractor and verdict influencer. Judge Lynch embodied a general fear tactic used against the Black population, taking convenient advantage of its insidious authority before and long after the 1928 passage of Virginia's antilynching law.

In this essay, I will explain the seemingly contradictory impact of lynching's looming presence in Virginia, examining its influence on law enforcement practices; its effect on courtroom proceedings; how the specter of lynching impacted legislation considered and passed by the General Assembly; and how the Virginia press covered lynching and the threat of lynching. In conclusion, I question if the legacy of lynching continued to influence capital punishment procedures in Virginia until it, too, was abolished in 2021.

Lynching Influence on Law Enforcement Practices

The following description of Silas Rogers, a Black man beaten into confessing to murdering a white Petersburg police officer, Robert Hatchell, was chronicled in Hustings Court record 2855, *Silas Rogers v. Commonwealth of Virginia* (1943):

[Rogers] was there severely beaten by the members of the Petersburg Police Force. He was struck over his head by a blackjack which inflicted a severe gash and a knot on his head. He was also hit with hard fist blows about the body and face, which caused him to bleed profusely from the head and nose. Three glasses of water were poured up his nose as he was pinned to the floor on his back by several police officers. A police officer pointed a gun in his face and threatened to kill him. His hair was pulled, he was slapped down, and his hands were bent backwards to the near-breaking point.

The haphazard, mob-driven, racially prejudiced law enforcement procedures of late-nineteenth and early-twentieth-century Jim Crow would be unrecognizable to most Virginians today. After a serious (i.e., Black-on-white) crime was committed (or alleged to have been committed), suspects were frequently caught not by law enforcement but by hastily thrown-together posses of angry, armed white men consumed with finding someone, anyone. Suspects such as Silas Rogers were routinely bullied, beaten, and threatened into confessions. They were sometimes (mis)identified by traumatized children. Many suspects were unable to read or write, yet frequently had no legal counsel. They cowered in jail cells, sometimes under intense interrogations, while lynch mobs outside howled for their heads. Bogus trials sometimes lasted only twenty or thirty minutes, and jury deliberations were mere formalities, sometimes, as in the Gillespie case, taking less than five minutes. Defense attorneys, at least those with a modicum of concern for their clients, frequently had to prioritize keeping the defendant off the gallows or out of the electric chair rather than proving their innocence. There were few if any appeal procedures, and, like lynching, an execution was practically guaranteed.

After capturing a suspect, overwhelmingly white law enforcement officers frequently placed these clueless culprits in inherently coercive situations, with the disturbingly routine procedure of surrounding them, then giving the choice of confessing or declaring their innocence, if they dare—both options most likely resulting in a sham trial followed by certain execution.

After Silas Rogers was beaten, waterboarded, and coerced into confessing, the court sentenced him to death based on purely circumstantial evidence. He was at one point only days away from electrocution when his sentence was commuted to life in prison. He was subsequently exonerated in 1951 after

Richmond News-Leader editor and Massive Resistance advocate James J. Kilpatrick championed his case.

A third—and possibly worse—option included the suggestion that exoneration by the court would result in being released to the (real or imagined) fury of a lynch mob.

That fear was palpable. In *Lynching in the New South,* Fitzhugh Brundage writes of the threatened lynching of Glen Wilton in 1909, in which he cites an unnamed prominent proprietor telling Wilton and the mob that "it will be the greatest shame on the county and the greatest setback to law and order . . . if we let this fellow be lynched. . . . I'll give you my word of honor, that if a shyster lawyer gets him off . . . I'll lead the lynching party, and we'll hang the negro and the shyster to the same branch of one tree."[2]

Since journalists were never allowed into interrogations, this interrogation-confession Catch-22 was rarely honestly reported. Researchers may deduce this progression, however, which followed a familiar pattern: the fervor of the populace and the police to find and punish a perpetrator; the relative ease of accusing and getting a conviction of a powerless, marginalized Black person; and the omnipresent influence of lynch law. As a result, law enforcement officers found themselves in the duplicitous position of being expected to uphold the law by stopping lynch mobs yet using those very mobs' menace to their advantage in the first steps to securing a conviction.

Like Rogers's "admission of guilt," confessions obtained by police for those charged with Black-on-white crimes were prevalent but should be highly suspect. In 1909 Alexandria police chief R. Goods, under intense public pressure, arrested Henry Smith for the murder of a white man named Walter Schultz. As a Black former penitentiary inmate, Smith was an easy mark, and according to the January 12, 1910, *Evening Star,* he admitted he had been detained in an Alexandria jail cell on a spurious robbery charge for four days—given no food or water and apparently bound in some manner—to force a confession.[3]

And he indeed confessed, implicating three others. Smith, however, withdrew that confession throughout his trial and appeals process, telling Alexandria commonwealth's attorney Crandal Mackey that he had lied under extreme police coercion. Nonetheless, on June 3, 1910, he was executed for the murder on hearsay evidence.

While those coercive methods, including lynching threats by Chief Goods, were never exposed in court procedures, Smith later revealed them in a poem he composed before his death in the electric chair. Published in the January 14, 1910, edition of the *Alexandria Gazette,* it is one of Virginia's earliest examples of death row poetry:

> People of this city, will you listen to what is true?
> And I will tell you with all my heart,
> What the chief made me do.
> He locked me close in a cell,
> Where I was bound and compelled to do just like he says,
> But if I did but only refuse I should go through a terrible spell.
> I wrung my hands together,
> And wondered what I must do.
> He then gave me a little Bible,
> And told me to read,
> For the lynchers may be coming after you.
> Then the tears were streaming down my cheeks,
> As I did holler and cry,
> "Chief, let me see my wife and child once more.
> Be fair, for I die, for no more liberty shall I see.
> Chief, please take out your gun and kill me."
> But God is still looking and sees all over the land.
> I wish he would point down his finger and show who murdered that man.[4]

After Alfred Wright was sentenced to die for the alleged rape of a white Appomattox County woman in 1912, he attempted during his appeal to retract a confession given while an actual mob screamed for him outside of the Appomattox County jail. Since Wright was tried and sentenced only forty-eight hours after the alleged crime, his attorney Duncan Drysdale claimed that the speed showed "great prejudice in the county against him," leading to the withdrawal of his confession. However, Circuit Court Judge Hundley, a former officer in the Confederate Army, ruled that the prisoner's fear that he will not get a fair trial was insufficient and that specific proof was necessary before a verdict rendered under such circumstances could be set aside.[5]

Not all lynching attempts resulted in a death. Margaret Vandiver's *Lethal Punishment* describes how intended lynchings across the South were sometimes prevented in four ways. First, the mob stopped a killing on its own initiative; second, quick action by law enforcement stopped the lynching;

third, it was stopped by whites acting in nonofficial capacities (at great personal risk); and, finally, the lynching was stopped by the resistance of Blacks, sometimes including the victim (also at great personal risk).[6]

While there are instances in Virginia where law enforcement made no efforts to protect prisoners from lynch mobs, there are examples in which law enforcement did their duty and stepped in, sometimes at the nick of time and with considerable creativity, to prevent lynching, underscoring the incongruity they worked under. In October 1908 a mentally disabled man named William Finney—called "an idiot" in the October 8, 1908, *Roanoke Evening News*—was convicted and sentenced to die for assaulting a young white girl in Franklin County. The crime triggered so much public anger that Finney had to be transferred to the Roanoke jail to avoid lynching. Gov. Claude Swanson later commuted his death sentence to life in the penitentiary.[7]

On November 4, 1909, a mob of about fifty men traveled to the Bedford city jail with the intention of lynching Thurman Spinner, who was charged with the murder of Charles Noell, a white resident of Bedford County. Deputy Sheriff McGhee received warning of an approaching mob and took Spinner out of his cell into some nearby woods, where the two hid all night. The mob angrily searched the jail, then reportedly left in disgust. Spinner was later executed for the murder.[8]

Albert Barrett endured an unusually horrifying situation with a lynch mob in Charlotte County in July 1917 after being accused of killing a white farmer, W. T. Roach. After the discovery of Roach's body, a mob captured Albert and his son Aubrey near Mt. Zion. A small group of vigilantes took Aubrey in one car, while the larger mob took Albert; they all headed to the town of Red House, intending to lynch the entire Barrett family, including his wife and daughter.

Local law enforcement, Lynchburg militia, and even Roanoke-based Baldwin-Felts detectives rushed to the area. At three a.m. Campbell County sheriff R. L. Perrow and Charlotte County sheriff J. C. Priddy first reached Red House, where they found Albert Barrett standing manacled in a field near the town, while a mob numbering over five hundred argued among themselves whether to shoot Albert, hang him, or soak him and his entire family in gasoline and burn them alive.

Perrow and Priddy were miraculously able to calm the situation, perhaps with a wink and a nod and that familiar press-reported adage, "Let the law take its course." The sheriffs took charge of Albert while another deputy rescued Aubrey, and soon both Barretts were in the Lynchburg jail. The law took its breakneck course, and Albert Barrett was electrocuted on August 31, 1917. The court spared Aubrey the electric chair when it was revealed, after his trial, that he may have been under the age of seventeen.[9]

The Martinsville Seven case in 1950, at the dawn of the civil rights movement, remains not only a stain on Virginia's penological history but also a candid and more recent acknowledgment of how law enforcement would use the threat of lynch mobs to intimidate suspects and extract confessions. On the evening of January 8, 1949, a white woman named Ruby Floyd accused seven Black men of raping her while she walked through a Black neighborhood in Martinsville to collect six dollars owed by a woman for some clothing. Floyd did not know the area, so she stopped at the home of Dan Gilmer to ask directions to the house. In *Race, Rape, and Radicalism: The Case of the Martinsville Seven, 1949–1951*, Eric Rise notes that on May 31, 1949, the *Daily Worker* had reported that Gilmer cautioned her to return home, since on Saturday nights the locals "like to celebrate and have a nice time."[10]

After the attack, police arrested and charged Booker T. Millner, Frank Hairston Jr., John Taylor, James L. Hairston, Howard Lee Hairston, Francis D. Grayson, and James Henry Hampton. According to Rise, while the seven men sat in the Henry County Jail, the jailor admitted that he was so incensed by the crime that if a lynch mob showed up and demanded the key, he would freely relinquish it.

The Rev. Robert Anderson, the pastor of Fifth Baptist Church and spiritual minister to John Taylor, told the *Richmond Afro-American* newspaper that at least two of the defendants informed him of improper conduct by the Martinsville police during questioning. The Martinsville Seven were allegedly threatened with being beaten to death if they did not admit guilt and were told (falsely) that their companions had already confessed and implicated them. If they did not confess, they would be handed over to a "mob of a thousand men waiting outside." Anderson was unsuccessful in getting this information to Gov. John S. Battle during the appeals process.[11]

All seven Black men were executed at the penitentiary over the course of two days for rape and aiding and abetting rape, both capital crimes at the time dispensed only against Black men.

Startling contrasts emphasize the weaponization of rape law against Black men, a practice that began in the 1890s under Gov. Charles O'Ferrall. Around the same time as the Martinsville case, a white farmer in Amherst County named Witt was convicted of raping a pregnant nineteen-year-old Black woman. He was not executed but was found guilty and fined $350. A white man named Dudley raped a "feeble-minded" Black woman near Glasgow, Virginia, in October 1948. The October 16 *Norfolk Journal and Guide* reported that Dudley was found guilty and fined $20.[12]

Lynching Influence on Courtroom Procedures

It was common in Jim Crow era social and cultural environments to paint a dehumanizing picture of people of color, rendering them unworthy of humane treatment and convincing whites it was socially acceptable to brutalize, execute, and even lynch them. A carnival game called "The African Dodger" was even hawked by vendors who invited white men to throw three baseballs at a Black man hired to stick his head through a hole in a canvas sign with the intent of causing serious injury. "Kill the coon! Kill him I say!" an operator in a Nebraska fair barked in 1888.[13]

In that atmosphere, few places exceeded Virginia's criminal justice system and its Jim Crow courtrooms in giving wretched life to the spectacle of menacing, bestial, subhuman Black assailants who confessed when faced by the peril of lynching orchestrated by supremacist whites.

On November 15, 1909, Staunton jail inmate and trusty Clifton Breckenridge abruptly confessed to Staunton chief of police Liscomb that two weeks earlier he had assaulted the six-year-old daughter of the jailer. The system sprang into action, rivaling the speed and ruthless efficiency of any lynch mob. A special grand jury was called the next day, November 16, at 11:00 a.m., and forty-five minutes later it returned an indictment. The trial began two hours later, at 2:00 p.m., and by 3:37—after only twelve minutes of deliberation—the jury sentenced Breckenridge to death.

Breckenridge's court-appointed lawyer pronounced out loud that he was representing the defendant "unwillingly."[14] During this sham trial, infuriated citizens repeatedly interrupted proceedings by demanding that Breckenridge be lynched, not realizing a legal lynching was occurring before their very eyes. And the more they howled, the faster the proceedings progressed. The protestations eventually got so intense that prosecutor Carter Braxton requested that the courtroom be cleared of everyone but the attorneys, officers, jurors, and reporters.

After the trial and sentencing, with anger at Breckenridge still boiling over, the Staunton fire bell sounded at midnight to again summon a lynch mob. Several dozen men and boys surrounded the jail and attempted to break Breckenridge out, but they were driven back by the sheriff and several officers. Breckenridge was electrocuted thirty-one days later, on December 17, 1909.

Lynching fears continuously threatened and influenced the 1912 Norfolk-area trial and sentencing of Virginia Christian, the only female sent to Virginia's electric chair between 1896 and 2010. Charged and ultimately convicted for the murder of her white employer, Ida Belote, Christian never took the stand on her own behalf; her attorneys, Joseph Thomas Newsome and George Washington Fields, feared her "uncouth appearance and her insolent way of describing the deed" could incite mob violence being threatened against Norfolk's entire Black community.[15]

Despite vigorous claims of self-defense, and with these mobs lurking in the background, the Elizabeth City County prosecutor used the case to remind the local Black community that the consequences of killing a white person, especially a woman as prominent and beloved as Mrs. Belote, was *always* going to be death—an unsubtle warning that the sentence could be carried out legally or, if necessary, otherwise. Worse, there was fear that any verdict less than death would trigger mass lynchings in Christian's neighborhood, again placing Christian and her counsel in a no-win situation.

Virginia Christian was found guilty and electrocuted in the basement of the Virginia State Penitentiary on August 16, 1912, the day after her seventeenth birthday.

In February 1909 police arrested Aurelius "Felix" Christian (no relation to Virginia Christian), a seventeen-year-old Black male, and charged him with assaulting and then stabbing to death a fourteen-year-old white schoolgirl in Botetourt County. His trial, which took a breathless twenty-one minutes, became merely an excuse to stop an infuriated mob that was shrieking for his lynching. The *Virginia Citizen* newspaper on February 26 reported that "this was the swiftest meeting [sic] out of justice in the history of the criminal courts of Virginia" because "it prevented a threatened lynching."[16]

Sometimes the threat of lynch mobs infiltrated jury deliberations. In 1899 Noah Finley was tried for robbing and shooting at (and missing) a respected white business owner in Pulaski named Major Darst. Finley was found guilty, but the *Richmond Planet* reported that when the jury was unable to decide on sentencing after fifteen hours of deliberation, "a party of citizens notified them that if a verdict was not rendered by 10 o'clock this morning the Negro would be lynched."[17]

The *Planet* then reported, "The verdict was brought in promptly at the specified time." The jury of course sentenced Finley to death, and he hanged on September 15, 1899.

Lynching Influence on Legislation

A Virginia statute enacted in 1765 stated: "It shall not be lawful for any county or corporation court, to order and direct castration of any slave, except such slave shall be convicted of an attempt to ravish a white woman, in which case they may inflict such punishment."[18] (Prior to the Civil War, death sentences for Black-on-white crime were rarely used because the accused was valuable property.) Following the Civil War and the emancipation of slaves, in 1894 the Virginia General Assembly finally, yet somewhat indirectly, responded to the lynching problem. Since Black-on-white rape was already a capital crime, they threw out the unused castration statute for attempted rape of a white woman by a Black man and elevated this offense to a capital crime because of fears that failure to do so would encourage lynch mobs.

According to the amended Section 3888 of the Virginia code, whites could also be punished with death for rape and attempted rape (of a white woman), but juries had the discretion of sentencing them to a minimum of five years for rape and three years for attempted rape, which they almost always did. (Yet, as mentioned above, a white man who raped a Black woman could be let off with a fine.) According to the Death Penalty Information Center, fewer than ten white men were sentenced to death for rape in Virginia[19] (and only of white women, never Black women), but all had their sentences commuted to prison terms.

The last man to receive a death sentence in Virginia for rape was Cecil Wood, a Black man, sentenced in 1972. His sentence was commuted later that year to life in prison due to the *Furman v. Georgia* Supreme Court decision, which found the application of capital punishment cruel and unusual. In 1979 a federal court fully exonerated him due to incompetent defense.

As early as 1848 a Black Virginian (enslaved or free) could receive the death penalty for any offense for which a white man could be sentenced to three or more years in prison. In perspective, it also should be noted that Virginia did not execute any white person for a crime against a Black person until 1997, when Thomas Beavers was executed for the murder of Marguerite Lowery.

The 1921 Augusta County case *Hart v. Commonwealth,* which sentenced a Black man named Harry Hart to death for the attempted rape of a seventeen-year-old white woman, upheld the 1894 law while affirming the risk of lynching for attempted rape. The written decision seems to suggest a return to antebellum legislative paternalism over the chaste white female citizenry, while railroading Black rape suspects into the high-speed, bogus trials of that period: "It is a matter of history of the State, and of common knowledge among its people, that the crime of attempted rape is well nigh, if not altogether, as heinous as the consummated offense of rape. . . . The likelihood of the resort to lynch law, unless there is a prompt conviction and a severe penalty imposed, and thus a resultant grave shock to the peace and dignity of the Commonwealth, is well known to exist, almost, if not quite equally, in the case of an attempted as of a consummated rape."[20] Harry Hart was electrocuted on January 23, 1922, at the Virginia State Penitentiary.

In 1895 Gov. Charles O'Ferrall recommended several other somewhat modest measures to the General Assembly to reduce lynchings, but he stopped short of calling for an outright ban. Those included a $200-per-thousand-citizens fine within the city or county where a lynching occurred, payable into a public school fund, and also required that the locality refund the costs of any militia action required to protect a prisoner from lynching. O'Ferrall also reaffirmed that not only should the penalty for rape and attempted rape always be punishable by death, with no noted exceptions, but that an indictment for either take precedence over every other case on the docket.

"In my opinion," O'Ferrall wrote, "if an act embodying such provisions is passed, lynchings will no longer occur in Virginia." O'Ferrall's recommendations went to the senate's Courts of Justice Committee but did not progress to a floor vote.

Still, Fitzhugh Brundage notes that lynchings dropped precipitously during O'Ferrall's term: his predecessor clocked an alarming twenty-seven, while O'Ferrall saw only four. This could be attributed to his outspoken opposition to the practice and his more aggressive efforts as governor to stop it. His success was only temporary, however. During J. Hoge Tyler's term, seven Blacks and three whites were lynched, leading Hoge to lament in 1898, "The lynch spirit is so strong again."[21]

Coincidentally, it was Governor Tyler who convened the 1901–2 constitutional convention to rewrite Virginia's 1870 constitution, with the goal of disfranchising the African American population without violating the federal Constitution's 14th and 15th Amendments. The convention considered these federal amendments as serious but resolvable barriers towards building a "more pure" electorate and system of government. That convention was a literal scheme by white Virginians to legitimize their claims to racial superiority and accomplish what Lynchburg delegate Carter Glass called "a new emancipation, not now of the black man, but of the white man, whom the black man has enslaved in turn."[22]

While the new constitution did create new enforcement apparatus for Jim Crow, with devastating impacts on the legal rights of Blacks, it is not clear if it had any effect on lynchings, which steadily decreased after its ratification.

In 1928 one of Virginia's first female legislators, Sarah Lee Fain, introduced a death penalty abolition bill revised from a similar bill introduced two years earlier that had preserved the death penalty only for assault (rape)—crimes overwhelmingly charged to Black men. Hopes were high among fellow House members that the bill would gain traction the second time around, but it died in committee under fears it would lead to an increase in lynching—which, ironically, was outlawed the same session by a bill signed by Gov. Harry F. Byrd Sr. This antilynching legislation was groundbreaking in that it was the first in the nation to specifically define lynching as a state crime.

Byrd admitted in his opening address to the General Assembly that year that the rigid enforcement of merciless capital punishment laws negated the need for lynching. "There is no excuse for lynching in a State where the enforcement of the law in cases likely to provoke mob violence has been prompt and rigorous. Attempted rape in Virginia may be punished by death, and juries are quick to punish crimes that once incited men to take the law in their own hands."[23]

Byrd obviously needed those "prompt and rigorous" capital punishment laws to remain in effect to get his antilynching bill passed, thus Fain's abolition bill quietly died in committee.

Lynching Influence on Press Coverage

In *Practical Journalism: A Complete Manual of the Best Newspaper Methods* (1894), Edwin L. Shuman explained the obligations of professional journalists thus: "Truth in essentials, imagination in non-essentials, is considered a legitimate rule of action in every office. The paramount objective is to make an interesting story." White-owned newspapers often avoided even "truth in essentials" when covering alleged Black-on-white crimes.

Most Virginia-based Black-owned newspapers, which proliferated after the 1866 publication of the *True Southerner*, were very short-lived, and by the first decade of the twentieth century, only three remained: the *Norfolk and Guide*, the *Charlottesville Messenger*, and the *Richmond Planet*.

The *Richmond Planet* was considered the leader and reported lynchings and other extralegal crimes against Blacks with aggressive, factual coverage and editorial comments that "howled loudly, until the American people hear our cries." The *Planet*—self-described by editor John L. Mitchell Jr. as a "safety-valve for the boiling black protest"—was unsparing in its outrage to these crimes, keeping a running tally of lynchings that occurred not just in Virginia but across the entire American Southeast.

Mitchell was fearless, even considered foolhardy, in confronting racism and lynching, especially in southern Virginia's "Black belt."[24] He was not afraid to take on the governors and their lukewarm responses to threatened and even actual lynchings that occurred in Emporia, Danville, and especially Lunenburg County, where William Marable murdered Lucy Pollard in 1895. Marable in turn implicated three innocent women, Mary Abernathy, Pokey Barnes, and Mary Barnes, leading to sham trials and sentences to hang.[25]

Mitchell was unrelenting in his support for the three women and worked closely with Governor O'Ferrall to stop the lynchings of the defendants while openly declaring their innocence in the pages of the *Planet*. O'Ferrall even delayed the execution of Marable, a man he considered guilty, so he could testify at the women's retrial, and he refused to let Lunenburg County's commonwealth's attorney take the three women from Richmond to Lunenburg due to the threat of mob violence against them. In the end, the courts fully exonerated Mary Abernathy and Pokey Barnes. Mary Barnes received a sentence of ten years as an accessory to murder in June 1895, and, according to the January 2, 1897, *Richmond Planet*, was released Christmas morning 1896 after serving less than two years. Mitchell generously praised O'Ferrall for his work ensuring a fair trial for the women and, especially, stopping mob violence against them.[26]

Unlike the Black media, white-owned newspapers frequently took lurid, biased, and hyperbolic approaches to race issues and lynching. White media's hyper-exaggerated, factually dubious reporting styles grew originally from such pre–Civil War news magazines as *Frank Leslie's Illustrated Newspaper* and *Harper's Weekly*. And while many readers felt these publications routinely crossed lines of propriety, their methods nonetheless made good copy and certainly sold well. These papers were the start of what became known as "yellow journalism," the practice of melodramatically sensationalizing or even altering news stories with "imagination in non-essentials" so that newsboys could hawk more of them.

Therefore, with few objective safeguards in place and with reporters granted creative latitude, the specter of lynching provided ample opportunities for less than scrupulous reporters and editors to embellish the story and incite their readership.

Black-on-white crimes received heavy news coverage, frequently on the front pages of publications based in the localities where the crimes occurred, and most of it was gratuitously lurid and often openly malicious towards the accused. Lynchings frequently drew salacious headlines: "Hanged to a Tree: A Lynching in Patrick," trumpeted the February 9, 1886, *Richmond Dispatch*. "Hanged to a Horse-Rack," claimed the same paper in 1884 of the lynching of Peter Bland. "Four Negroes Swing from the Same Limb" reported a *Big Stone Gap Post* headline in 1893.

Frequently the papers took a prognostic approach, going so far as to anticipate or predict guilt or innocence, even expressing relief when a lynching occurred. A front-page *Richmond Dispatch* headline from February 3, 1880, avowed "Page Wallace's Crime: A Virginia Negro Who Will Be Lynched If Captured." "Excitement at Poca[hontas]," declared the February 14, 1908, *Clinch*

Valley News. "Walter Ripply, Believed to Have Committed Criminal Assault, May Be Lynched."

"Judge Lynch!" proclaimed the February 12, 1892, *Roanoke Times*. "Little Alice Perry has been Avenged . . . Roanoke's First Execution . . . Will Lavender Hanged to a Tree."

After a mob lynched five Black men in Tazewell in February 1893, a *Clinch Valley News* reporter stated that "the crime for which the men were hung was such as to deserve any punishment, and the act of the lynchers has rid the country of a gang of fiends and saved the public the disagreeable duty of trial and execution."[27]

Sometimes the press proclaimed with pride that a reckless, spurious trial successfully prevented a lynching. "Virginia Shows How to Prevent Rule of Mob" declared the July 2, 1912, edition of the *Staunton Leader* of the speedy conviction and sentencing of Alfred Wright, without commenting on how wretchedly unfair that trial had been.

"Lynching was in the air," the *Alexandria Gazette* reported of the Petersburg jailing of John Williams for his assault at gunpoint of a white Nottoway woman, "and the presence of a determined leader might have resulted in violence."[28] Williams's arrest prompted the first declaration of martial law in Petersburg since 1862.

Despite repeatedly speaking out against lynching and mob violence, the February 13, 1894, *Alexandria Gazette* disingenuously reiterated the convenience of lynching's threat in response to terrorist "bomb-throwers" in France: "Probably a resort to the simple and rude, less public, but more speedy Southern custom of lynching, would be a more effective deterrent."[29]

The gruesome hanging, shooting, and burning of James Jordan after he was accused of attacking a white woman in Sussex County prompted the *Waverly Dispatch* to complain on March 27, 1925, that "an enormous amount of unfavorable publicity for the county and the town of Waverly in particular" resulted from the barbarism. "Although it is likely that the same thing would have taken place in any other town or county in Virginia under similar provocation and circumstances." The article went on to say that despite the negativity, some good would possibly come from it. "Now that the lynching has taken place and cannot be recalled, it should, and perhaps will, serve as an object lesson to the colored men of the 'black belt.'"

Treating lynching as an "object lesson" for Blacks while ignoring the culpability of the guilty white mobs emphasizes the use of the practice not as punishment for an individual for an alleged crime but as a way to victimize an entire community to maintain racial dominance. Many Virginia lynchings were not for an alleged criminal act but for social transgressions, some of them minor. A mob hanged Fred Tinsley in 1902 near Newport News for simply paying attention to a married white woman.[30]

Virginia media often downplayed lynchings as being orderly and polite, possibly in an attempt to mitigate their brutality and justify their use, drawing a stark contrast between the savagery of the "Black brute" and the polite white retribution. "The whole thing was conducted in a very business-like manner," reported the *Shenandoah Herald* of an 1890 lynching of eight Black men in Charleston, South Carolina, describing an episode that sounded more like a general store transaction. It was so orderly that "the citizens of the town" did not know "anything about it."

Susan Jean writes in "'Warranted' Lynchings: Narratives of Mob Violence in White Southern Newspapers, 1880–1940," that the most conspicuous feature of reporting of "warranted" or "respectable" lynching was the salacious language used to describe the alleged crime and the lynch mob's actions.[31] Reporters hiding behind their anonymity often contrasted the bestiality of the accused Black men with the innocent purity of the alleged white victim and the quiet determination of the mob, encouraging readers to identify with the lynchers and justifying the revenge taken.

The April 11, 1902, *Virginia Citizen* reported that the lynching of seventeen-year-old James Carter by almost three hundred masked men was "a quiet one." Of Peter Bland's 1884 lynching in King William County, the *Richmond Daily-Dispatch* dryly noted, "The Lynchers very Polite but very Determined."[32]

Finally, in classic cases of victim-blaming, some papers attributed lynching to Blacks and their uncivilized, disrespectful behavior. The February 8, 1893, *Danville Register* stated: "Time and again the colored people throughout the North have denounced lynching in the South and they are even now asking Congress to investigate the matter. But we have yet to hear of a meeting of colored people to denounce the brutal outrages which provoke lynching bees in the South."

"Negroes can contribute much to the eradication of lynching, by demonstrating the ability, character, and good citizenship of the race," Franklin

Raper paternalistically advised Blacks in the 1933 *Southern Commission on the Study of Lynching*. They could accomplish this "by seeking individually and through their churches, lodges, schools and newspapers to allay interracial fear and hostility; by consistently disavowing all disposition to condone crime and to shelter criminals; by reporting to officials and influential white friends when mob danger threatens; and by using their political influence wherever possible in the interest of honest and competent local government."

There is most likely no better example of the press's willingness to manipulate public opinion for or against a lynching than in their egregiously biased coverage of a lynched white woman, Peb Falls, who was found hanging from a tree in September 1897 in a remote section of Rockingham County.[33]

The press set the stage by describing Falls's life as "hideously depraved from her early youth," and depicted her as "the worst white woman in the Virginia Mountains." These and other equally cruel descriptions suggest to modern-day readers a woman who was most likely mentally ill or substance-abusing, who was unjustly labeled as disgraceful because of her propensity for socializing "with the low negroes." These venomous descriptions of Falls's fraternization with Black men separated her from the chaste, revered status white Virginia women traditionally received in the press, while giving her downfall and murder the provocation the reporters actively sought.

After news of the discovery of Falls's hanged body began circulating, several northern press reporters arrived in Rockingham County, seemingly intent on ginning up a race war by openly speculating that the Blacks she lived with had lynched her under some phony pretense that she stole their savings. "Some of her negro friends, inspired by the lynching example of the whites, may have decided it was their duty to . . . murder the woman outright," hypothesized an *Allentown* (Pennsylvania) *Morning Call* reporter.

Rumors of more lynchings emanated excitedly from unscrupulous journalists, as Rockingham sheriff's deputies and detectives questioned locals about the murder while trying to maintain calm. One reporter with the *Buffalo* (New York) *Evening News* warned with no documentation that "citizens there will not wait for the law, but will as soon as the perpetrators of this outrage are discovered, lynch those immediately concerned."

Locals speculated that the same whites who had months earlier tarred and feathered Falls as a warning to stop consorting with Blacks had lynched her. The reporter, however, added that her lynching, if performed by local Blacks, "must never be forgiven or forgotten, even if the woman did sink down to the negro level. Universal horror is expressed at the lawless murder, and the community declares its intention to round up the negro killers and lynch them without delay."

He had no comment on the consequences for potential white lynchers.

The October 1, 1897, *Stanford* (Kentucky) *Interior Journal* ultimately placed a condescending coda on the entire affair, lamenting that "Virginians must be deteriorating when they get to lynching women."

Soon, Rockingham County became so embarrassed by the entire affair that the *Rockingham Register* took the absurd step of claiming that no lynching occurred at all, asserting falsely that "neither the Commonwealth's Attorney nor the Sheriff of Rockingham has received any information of the alleged hanging and they discredit the whole story absolutely."

Epilogue: "Well Calculated to Inspire Terror"

In *Rough Justice: Lynching and American Society, 1847–1947*, Michael Pfeifer writes: "To dismiss the relationship between lynching, law and the death penalty is to ignore a debate that constantly ignited fin-de-siècle midwesterners, westerners, and southerners as well as lynching's first historians."[34]

Virginia's 1928 antilynching legislation raises dual questions: Did lynchings continue in the twenty-first century under the pretext of capital punishment? Is capital punishment a direct legacy of lynching? Contemporary research appears to agree—in an article published in 2021 Charles Seguin and David Rigby established that both victims of lynching and those executed by the state were disproportionately Black and male.[35] In support of this, they quote Carol Steiker and Jordan Steiker's 2020 report on how lynching and capital punishment were seen as substitutes for one another and that some states, such as Virginia, preserved capital punishment laws out of concern of a revival of lynching.[36]

Hugo Bedau, in *The Death Penalty in America* (1964), concurs. He outlines seven links between the historical practice of lynching and capital punishment, and almost sixty years later, they are still salient. To paraphrase: 1) both lynching and the death penalty involve a similar mentality that tolerates lethal punishment; 2) lynchings and modern executions occur in the same states, mostly in the South; 3) both lynching and the death penalty show a disregard for due process; 4) both involve community-approved white violence against Blacks; 5) those who opposed lynching often urged executions as an acceptable substitute; 6) killings by posses fell into an area between lynching and quasi-legal execution; and 7) defenders of lynching relied heavily on states' rights arguments, as do contemporary defenders of capital punishment.

Virginians were for years led to believe that to get rid of one necessitated the use of the other. Gov. Harry Byrd declared that lynching was not needed with a robust capital punishment system in place. And some newspapers, such as the *Newport News Daily Press,* declared that eliminating the death penalty would unleash a wave of rapes by Blacks against white women, leading to another wave of lynching: "But, after capital punishment is abolished and the negro criminal begins his attacks, there will prevail a mob violence in Virginia such as no state has ever known, for Virginia men would never allow the punishment for such crimes to be mere incarceration of the guilty ones in the penitentiary, which is no punishment at all for them. . . . For the negro fears death, and death alone."[37]

It was not just about death but how fast it could be accomplished. For years lynching was justified by the mobs because of the slowness of capital punishment procedures. In *Rough Justice* Michael Pfeifer writes that "[lynch] mobs were impatient with the inevitable delays of legal process and disdainful of the alleged leniency of legal solutions."[38] Similar arguments circulate today among death penalty supporters who, while unwilling to return to the lynching of the past, loudly denounce the extended capital appeals process and consider opposition to the death penalty as a stance that is soft on crime. During the 1930s, when lynching stopped directly threatening Virginia's capital punishment practices, the Commonwealth's "rocket docket" appellate process—while a far cry from the truncated minimum thirty-day timeline of the early twentieth century—still became the fastest in the nation. Even as late as 1999, lynching's dogged legacy streamlined the interval from sentencing to execution in Virginia to just under five years—more than twice as fast as runner-up Delaware, at eleven years.[39]

"In Virginia, we've fixed it!" Gov. Jim Gilmore responded to a group of pastors in 2000 who told him Virginia needed to fix the death penalty. "It's moving faster than ever!"[40]

In conclusion, an editorial in the October 14, 1908, *Richmond Times-Dispatch* unwittingly made the ultimate comparison between the use of Virginia's electric chair in executions as being almost identical to lynching: the chair was "well calculated to inspire terror in the heart of the superstitious African." But just as lynching stopped inspiring terror in the hearts of Blacks with the stroke of a governor's pen in 1928, Gov. Ralph Northam's pen on March 24, 2021, ended a similar terror biased toward Blacks—the death penalty.

"The practice is fundamentally inequitable," Northam explained (using terminology that also could be used to describe lynching one hundred years earlier) at the ceremonial signing in front of Virginia's death chamber at Greensville Correctional Center in Jarratt. "It is inhumane. It is ineffective."

Notes

1. All quotations from the Gillespie case are from "Brutally Beaten in Heart of City," *Lexington Dispatch,* Jan. 13, 1909; "Young Woman Attacked by Burly Negro in Richmond, Va," *Salt Lake Herald,* Jan. 11, 1909, 1; "Fiendish Assault in City of Richmond," *Newport News Daily Press,* Jan. 12, 1909, 1; "Miss Stumpf's Assailant Sure of Death Sentence," *Newport News Daily Press,* Jan. 12, 1909, 1; and "Death Sentence Comes Quickly to Gillespie," *Newport News Daily Press,* Jan, 17, 1909, 1.
2. Fitzhugh Brundage, *Lynching in the New South: Georgia and Virginia, 1880–1930* (Urbana: University of Illinois Press, 1993), 181.
3. "Didn't Kill Schultz!," *Washington Star,* Jan. 12, 1910. 1.
4. "Smith Sentenced," *Alexandria Gazette,* Jan. 14, 1910, 1.
5. "Death Sentence for Alfred Wright," *Richmond Times-Dispatch,* April 13, 1913, 1.
6. Margaret Vandiver, *Lethal Punishment: Lynchings and Legal Executions in the South* (New Brunswick, NJ: Rutgers University Press, 2006), 142.
7. "Finney's Sentence Has Been Commuted," *Roanoke Evening News,* Oct. 10, 1908, 1.
8. "Spinner Escapes Lynching," *Lynchburg News Advance,* Nov. 11, 1909, 1.
9. "Two Negroes Rescued from Infuriated Mob," *Roanoke World News,* July 20, 1917, 1.
10. Eric W. Rise, "Race, Rape, and Radicalism: The Case of the Martinsville Seven, 1949–1951," *Journal of Southern History* 58, no. 3 (Aug. 1992): 451–90, quote on 465.
11. *Richmond Afro-American,* Feb. 10, 1951, 1.
12. "White Man Charged with Rape on Feebleminded Woman Gets Fine of $20," *Norfolk Journal and Guide,* Oct. 16, 1948, 1.
13. Untitled news short, *Nebraska State-Journal,* Sept. 7, 1888, 5. The Museum of Jim Crow Memorabilia at Ferris State University in Big Rapids, Michigan, states: "With everyday objects, forms of entertainment, advertising and public policies confirming this [supremacist] hierarchy, it is possible to see how whites came to believe they were superior, and

how some blacks could internalize these images, practices, attitudes and policies and come to see themselves as inferior and to accept the role of target."
14. "Quick Justice for Negro Who Assaulted Child," *Staunton Dispatch*, Nov. 16, 1909.
15. All information regarding the Christian case is from the following: "Murder Confessed by Negress, Slayer of Mrs. Ida Belote," *Newport News Daily Press*, April 11, 1912, 1; "Murder of Mrs. Belote Is Deplored by Negroes," *Newport News Daily Press*, March 20, 1912, 1; "Gov. Mann Grants Respite to Negress," *Newport News Daily Press*, June 14, 1912, 1; "Virginia Christian Murderess, Pays Penalty of Awful Crime," *Hampton Monitor*, August 22, 1912, 1. Also, "Christian Virginia vs. Virginia Christian," *Crisis Magazine*, Sept. 1912; LaShawn Harris, "The 'Commonwealth of Virginia vs. Virginia Christian': Southern Black Women, Crime, and Punishment in Progressive Era Virginia," *Journal of Social History* 47, no. 4 (Summer 2014): 922–42.
16. "Felix Christian," *Virginia Citizen*, Feb. 26, 1909.
17. "Would Be Judicial Murder," *Richmond Planet*, Aug. 12, 1899, 4.
18. Published in *Virginia Statutes at Large*, vol. 1, no. 3, 1835.
19. "Enduring Justice: The Persistence of Racial Discrimination in the U.S. Death Penalty," Death Penalty Information Center, Sept. 15, 2020, 19, https://dpic-cdn.org/production/documents/pdf/Enduring-Injustice-Race-and-the-Death-Penalty-2020.pdf?dm=1683576585.
20. *Hart v. Commonwealth*, 109 S.E. 582, Nov. 17, 1921, https://case-law.vlex.com/vid/hart-v-commonwealth-895706014.
21. Brundage, *Lynching in the New South*, 178.
22. Proceedings of the Constitutional Convention, *Richmond Times-Dispatch*, April 2, 1902, 9–11.
23. Senate Document #6, "An Address by Harry Flood Byrd," Jan. 16, 1928, 9.
24. Allen Tullos, "The Black Belt," *Southern Spaces*, April 19, 2004, https://southernspaces.org/2004/black-belt/.
25. Robert Wilhelm, "False Witness: The Lucy Pollard Murder," Murder by Gaslight (blog), June 19, 2010, http://www.murderbygaslight.com/2010/06/false-witness-lucy-pollard-murder.html.
26. "She Is Free," *Richmond Planet*, Jan. 2, 1897, 1.
27. "Richlands' Lynching," *Clinch Valley News*, Feb. 3, 1893, 1.
28. "Lynchers Invade Courts," *Alexandria Gazette*, April 4, 1916, 3.
29. *Alexandria Gazette and Virginia Advertiser*, Feb. 13, 1894, 2.
30. "Fred Tinsley in Warwick," Racial Terror: Lynching in Virginia, accessed Oct. 20, 2023, https://sites.lib.jmu.edu/valynchings/VA1902060901/.
31. Susan Jean, "'Warranted' Lynchings: Narratives of Mob Violence in White Southern Newspapers, 1880–1940," *American Nineteenth Century History* 6, no. 3 (2005).
32. "Hanged to a Horse-Rack," *Richmond Daily Dispatch*, Feb. 6, 1884, 3.
33. All information on the lynching of Peb Falls comes from "Negroes Lynched a White Woman," *Buffalo Evening News*, Sept. 30, 1897, 1; "A Ghastly Find," *Alexandria Gazette*, Sept. 29, 1897, 1; "The Dead Body of Peb Falls . . ." *Stanford (KY) Interior Journal*, Oct. 1, 1897, 1; "Virginia's Lynching: Excitement over the Hanging of a White Woman by Negroes," (Allentown, PA) *Morning Call*, Oct. 1, 1897, 1; "Looks Like a Hoax," *Rockingham Register*, Oct. 1, 1897, 1.

34. Michael Pfeifer, *Rough Justice: Lynching and American Society, 1847–1947* (Urbana: University of Illinois Press, 2004). 8.
35. Charles Seguin and David Rigby, "Capital Punishment and the Legacies of Slavery and Lynching in the United States," *Annals of the American Academy of Political and Social Science* 694, no. 1 (2021): 206, https://doi.org/10.1177/00027162211016277.
36. Carol S. Steiker and Jordan M. Steiker, "The Rise, Fall, and Afterlife of the Death Penalty in the United States," *Annual Review of Criminology* 3 (Jan. 2020): 299–315, quote on 305.
37. "The Allens and 'Mobs' and 'Fanatics'," *Newport News Daily Press,* March 30, 1913, 4.
38. Pfeifer, *Rough Justice,* 3.
39. Stephen C. Fehr, "Virginia's Efficient System of Death," *Washington Post,* April 4, 1999, C4.
40. Dale M. Brumfield, *Closing the Slaughterhouse: The Inside Story of Death Penalty Abolition in Virginia* (Abolition Press, 2022), 242.

UNEVEN JUSTICE

The Origin and Practice of Legalized Lynch Law in Jim Crow Virginia

KEVIN HEGG

> Gentlemen it was a license to hang Negroes.
> —*Richmond Planet,* May 11, 1895

Thornton Parker woke early on April 19, 1895, to a breakfast of "fried ham and eggs, French rolls, cold veal, butter, coffee and milk, pickles, cheese and crackers, prunes, custard pie, lemon and jelly cake."[1] A few hours later, wearing a new suit of clothes, young Parker's body was lowered into a coffin. This "colored man, convicted of attempted criminal assault on Mrs. Milton, a white woman," was legally hanged in Winchester, Virginia.[2] Both the *Richmond Planet* and the *Richmond Times* reported that Parker was the first victim of a new law that turned *attempted* criminal assault into a crime punishable by death.[3] Criminal assault in the Jim Crow South was a common euphemism for "rape." Linwood Bunch, a young African American, would be the last man executed for rape in Virginia in 1961.

Thirteen formerly enslaved men established The *Richmond Planet* in 1883. Its most famous founder, John Mitchell Jr., served as its editor for forty-five years. The newspaper was a vocal and tireless advocate for African Americans in Virginia and throughout the South until it closed its doors in 1938. The *Times* was one of the dozens of white newspapers published in Richmond in the 1890s. It was a conservative advocate for industry and traditional southern values.

Three weeks after Parker's hanging, the *Richmond Planet* would describe the execution as legalized lynch law: "Then why was the law enacted under the provisions of which Thornton Parker was hanged? Is'nt [sic] it as plain as the nose in your face that it was done in order to an extent, legalize lynch-law, and hang Americans of African descent indiscriminately. It was done too to save the alleged victims the necessity of being ever careful in their testimony. Gentlemen it was a license to hang Negroes. Mark the prediction, some white man will yet fall victim to this trap set for members of the despised race" (May 11, 1895). Mitchell likely wrote this editorial. He traveled across Virginia documenting the injustices of a southern state reestablishing the racial caste system that the Civil War and emancipation broke apart. This editorial was published eighteen years after federal troops left the South under the Compromise of 1877 and almost exactly a year before the US Supreme Court legitimized racial segregation and the doctrine of "separate but equal" through *Plessy v. Ferguson*.

Parker's unfortunate encounter with Virginia's criminal justice system began in Middletown near Winchester on Tuesday, March 5, 1895. He was accused of *attempting* to criminally assault Mrs. Milton. He was arrested and imprisoned three days later. In the middle of the following week, Sheriff Gore called for military troops from Harrisonburg and Tom's Brook to guard the prisoner against a growing and excited mob of would-be lynchers. On Friday, March 15, a heavy military guard led Parker into the Winchester courthouse. The *Shenandoah Herald* reported that a large force of troops stood guard around the courthouse to quell an "immense crowd."[4] Parker was tried, convicted, and sentenced to death by hanging without delay. Pleased with the trial's speed and the sentence's severity, the mob dispersed, and the troops went home. A month and four days later, Parker was hanged in front of a crowd that probably included his parents, who were born enslaved in Culpeper, Virginia.[5]

Figure 1 shows that mob violence increased dramatically as federal troops evacuated Virginia at the end of Reconstruction and peaked around 1890.[6] As the figure demonstrates, Blacks were almost three times more likely than whites to be the target of mob violence. Vigilante mobs across the South used violence and threats of violence as an instrument of racial terror to reestablish and maintain the racial hierarchy disrupted by the Civil War. At the end of the nineteenth century, Charles Triplett O'Ferrall, the 42nd governor of Virginia, initiated a vigorous campaign to pacify and subdue Virginia's vigilante mobs. The governor was not acting out of support or sympathy for the mostly Black victims. He wanted to bring law and order back under the auspices of the ruling white elite.

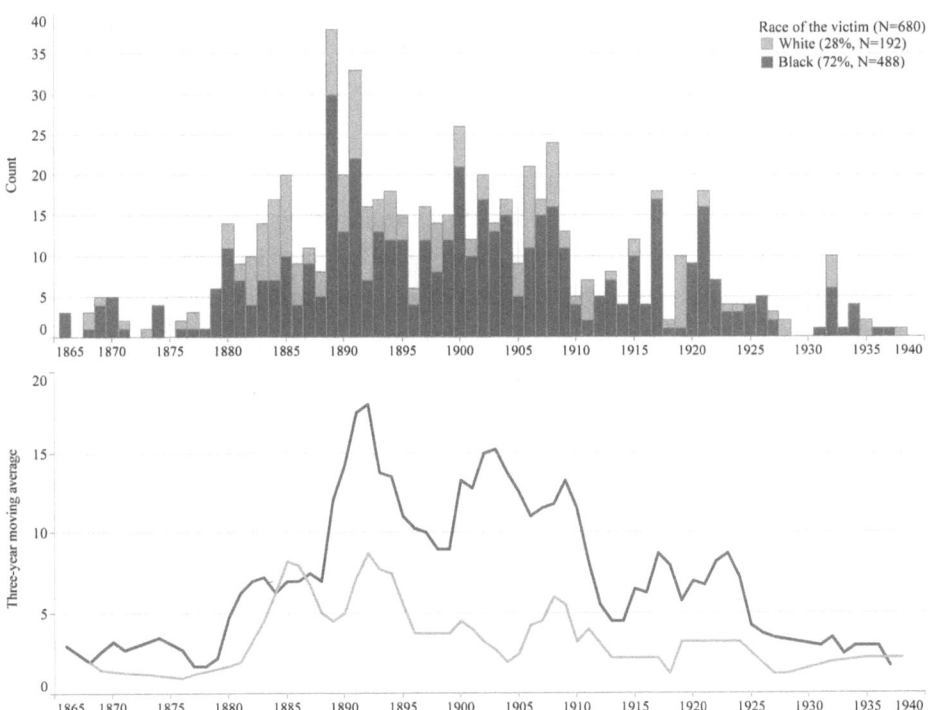

FIGURE 1. Incidents of actual and threatened mob violence in Virginia by race of victim, 1865–1940

This essay examines Governor O'Ferrall's relentless war on mob violence and Mitchell's contention that changes to Virginia's legal code provided a means for legally executing African Americans accused of raping or attempting to rape a white woman. Along with Mitchell, who praised O'Ferrall in the pages of the *Richmond Planet* for his tireless attack on mob violence, historians generally agree that O'Ferrall was a due-process governor staunchly opposed to mob violence. What is less known is that Governor O'Ferrall made a bargain with the white polity as mob lynching peaked in the 1890s: Stop hanging people in the public square; in return, the judiciary will hang them legally in the courtyard. O'Ferrall ignited the dramatic shift from extralegal mob lynchings to state-sanctioned legal lynchings. As part of his strategy to stop mob lynchings, the governor weaponized Virginia's legal code. Virginia would continue to wield the criminal justice system as an instrument of racial terror long after the mobs dispersed and the lynching era came to an end. Justice was not colorblind. Predominantly white judges and juries hanged and electrocuted Black males for rape crimes into the 1960s.

Working as a historian during the lynching era, Arthur F. Raper wrote that "in the efforts to prevent a lynching, or to prevent further mob outbreaks after a lynching has occurred, peace offices and leading citizens often make to mob leaders promises which virtually preclude impartial court procedure" and that it was not "incorrect to call a death sentence secured under such circumstances a 'legal lynching.'"[7] Expanding on this definition in his groundbreaking study of racial violence in Kentucky, George C. Wright wrote that "white authorities and community leaders pleaded with the mob to allow the law to take its course, and in cases wherein a black was accused of rape or murder, 'justice' was swift, sure, and painful."[8] For these authors, a legal lynching begins with a quick indictment and trial and ends in an almost certain execution. The trial unfolds under pressure from a threatening white mob embedded in the courtroom or surrounding the courthouse.

The data presented in this essay demonstrates that Virginia continued to summarily execute Black men long after the lynching era had ended and white mobs had stopped openly menacing Black citizens. For our purposes, a legal lynching does not require the presence of a mob. Subsequent legal lynchings possess all of the hallmarks of the legal lynchings that occurred during the heyday of mob vigilantism. They were swift, certain, and severe. The lethal outcome was rarely in doubt. Overwhelmingly white actors performed the trial in a highly racialized environment. Lip service was paid to due process to placate due process advocates and to prevent convictions from being overturned on appeal.

Crimes of rape by Black men against white women held a special place among white supremacists during Jim Crow. In his nationwide study of vigilante justice in postbellum America, Michael J. Pfeifer states that "punitive, localized, white supremacist justice enjoyed a white consensus in the South, but white southerners attempted to defend lynching from northern criticism by asserting, spuriously, that the law was not a reliable instrument for the punishment of the rape of white women by black men."[9] Many legal and extralegal lynchings were carried out in the South under the pretext of protecting white women from Black men accused of rape or attempted rape. In postbellum Virginia, only one white man was executed for a rape crime. This study confines itself to an analysis of legal lynchings performed under allegations of rape and attempted rape. Further study will undoubtedly reveal that many Black men were legally lynched for other crimes, especially murder, and at least in one case, highway robbery. Murder accusations require more evidence, such as a dead body, than rape crimes. The bar for attempted rape was particularly low. Accusations could result from lesser incidents such as purse snatching or from a consensual relationship gone bad.

Sociologists Stewart E. Tolnay and E. M. Beck recently proposed a redefinition of "racialized terrorism" that not only includes mob lynchings but also threats of lynchings that did not end in murder. They note that historically, research into mob violence in the American South focused "almost exclusively on the record of completed lynchings." They argue that including incomplete lynching threats "nearly doubles" the "total quantum" or measure of "racialized terrorism" in the South between 1880 and 1929.[10] To gain a more complete understanding of how terror was used to control and subjugate African Americans in Virginia during Jim Crow, their definition of racialized terrorism can be further extended to include legalized lynchings.

The essay will also examine the *practice* of legalized lynch law. The Black-on-white rape trials of the Jim Crow era were often little more than show trials performed for a menacing mob gathered around the proceedings. Outcomes were often predetermined. Black defendants did not have access to adequate counsel. Evidence was mostly circumstantial. Some white juries deliberated for less than five minutes. Judges were patronizing and severe. White newspapers represented Black defendants as savage brutes, and, at the same time, as fearfully ignorant. Executions were violent and until the early 1900s very public. Virginia introduced the electric chair in 1908 and used the same chair to electrocute fifty-seven Black men convicted of rape-related crimes between 1908 and 1961.

Charles Triplett O'Ferrall (1840–1905) was born in what was then Berkeley Springs, Virginia. His career in law and order began at the early age of fifteen when he replaced his recently deceased father as clerk of the circuit court of Morgan County. Two years later, he was elected to the position. At the outset of the Civil War, O'Ferrall enlisted in the Confederate Army as a private. He rose quickly through the ranks. By the end of the war, Colonel O'Ferrall commanded the Confederate cavalry in the Shenandoah Valley, where he sustained eight wounds. After the war, he earned a law degree from Washington College (now Washington and Lee University) and settled in Harrisonburg, Virginia, to practice law. He gave up his law practice when he was elected judge of the Rockingham County Circuit Court, a position he occupied from 1874 to 1880.

Judge O'Ferrall was a law-and-order judge unafraid to send criminals to the gallows. His judicial temperament was informed by his unabashed racism and rigid devotion to the southern honor code. The two most infamous cases occurring on his watch were the cold-blooded and botched murder of Mr. Lawson, a white man, and the brutal lynching of Charlotte Harris, a Black woman. Both cases were widely reported beyond Virginia's borders.

The lynching of Charlotte Harris took place late at night on March 6, 1878, in Rockingham County. No member of the mob that lynched Charlotte Harris was ever convicted of, or even indicted for, the crime, even though they were probably well known to the community and Judge O'Ferrall. Newspaper reports noted that Charlotte Harris's body remained suspended from the hanging tree for at least two days. The message to the local Black community was loud and clear.

In contrast, Judge O'Ferrall's court expended considerable energy and money in the prosecution of the murder of Mr. Lawson (white) in 1875. Judge O'Ferrall sentenced two white men and a white woman (Mrs. Lawson) to death for the murder. News that a woman would be executed in Virginia's backcountry quickly spread beyond the Shenandoah Valley and was thoroughly condemned. Female executions were rare in Virginia. Gov. James L. Kemper ordered a temporary respite for Mrs. Lawson. He wrote to Judge O'Ferrall asking for the facts in the case with an eye towards commuting Mrs. Lawson's sentence: "Can't something be done to save the neck of Mrs. Lawson? She is a woman. I do not want her hung if there is any reasonable ground to prevent it."[11] O'Ferrall wrote in his autobiography that it looked like the hand of God delivered to him "two strange young men to come forward and tell their story."[12] The two strange men contradicted testimony given under oath in the trial of Mrs. Lawson. At the judge's behest, the commonwealth's attorney investigated the two young men and reported forthwith that they were of "good character and fair repute."[13] The providential testimony saved Mrs. Lawson from the scaffold. While O'Ferrall devoted seven pages to the famous Lawson murder, he does not mention Charlotte Harris once in his 367-page autobiography.

O'Ferrall gave up his judgeship in 1880 and returned to his law practice. He was elected to the US House of Representatives from Virginia's 7th District in 1884. He ran as a Democrat and was reelected five times.[14] O'Ferrall resigned from his final term in Congress to assume Virginia's governorship on January 1, 1894.

Governor O'Ferrall became famed for his tireless fight to stamp out mob lynchings. In his first message to the Virginia General Assembly, O'Ferrall asserted that "lynching cannot be defended; it must be reprobated."[15] Indeed, by the end of his term, mob lynchings had slowed significantly. Public historian Josh Howard argued that Governor O'Ferrall's war on mob lynching was motivated not by a desire to end the race conflict but "by a desire to create a law-and-order environment attractive to outside investors."[16] As a former congressman who had served on the Committee on Commerce and the Committee on Mines and Mining, O'Ferrall would have been keenly familiar with outside investors and the flow of capital. Governor O'Ferrall's own words to the General Assembly suggest that he was motivated not by a sense of judicial fairness and equality but by a desire to restore law and order: "I know there is a crime too horrible to mention, so black as to cry for vengeance; but even the commission of that crime cannot warrant a resort to mob violence, for justice with us is certain and will never miscarry if the law is allowed to take its course."[17] The black act "too horrible to mention" and crying for "vengeance" is rape. Specifically, it is the rape of a white woman by a Black man. The governor made an ominous pact with Virginia's white citizens: stop lynching colored men in the public square; in return, the criminal justice system will convict and execute them.

Governor O'Ferrall made good on his promise to prosecute the crime too horrible to mention. Under his leadership, Virginia's General Assembly amended Section 3888 of Virginia's code to make attempted rape punishable by death. The short amendment to Section 3888 was enacted by the General Assembly two weeks after O'Ferrall took office.[18] It marked the turn to legalized lynch law in Virginia. It gave local courts a "license to hang Negroes."

The language added to Section 3888 is instructive. The "attempt to commit rape" is added as an exception to more reasonable sentencing guidelines for attempted offenses. The writers of the amendment were careful to add an exception: "punishable by death, or *in the discretion of the jury, by confinement in the penitentiary* [emphasis added]." The jury would decide whom to execute.

In this way, the legal code did not explicitly refer to the defendant's race. After this amendment, no white man was executed for rape or attempted rape in Virginia.

John Mitchell Jr. complained that the "law enacted under the provisions of which Thornton Parker was hanged" was done "in order to an extent, *legalize lynch-law,* and hang Americans of African descent indiscriminately" (emphasis added).[19] These words may hold the first reference to legal lynching in the popular press. Mitchell ended the editorial with the prediction that "some white man will yet fall a victim to this trap set for the despised race." It turns out that Mitchell was wrong. No white man was subsequently executed for a rape crime in Virginia. According to the Espy database, only three white men were executed for rape in the entire history of recorded Virginia jurisprudence.[20] Conversely, 177 Black Virginians were executed between 1626 and 1961 for the crimes of rape and attempted rape.

Mitchell's other prediction, that the enacted law was a "license to hang Negroes," proved true repeatedly over the next six decades. Overwhelmingly white juries and judges summarily executed 93 Black men between the end of Reconstruction and 1961 for accusations of rape and attempted rape. By contrast, Virginia mobs lynched 94 Black men between the end of the Civil War and the last documented lynching in Virginia in 1932.[21] With few exceptions, the trials of Black men accused of raping or trying to rape white women were show trials with a predetermined outcome unfolding swiftly and predictably.

The application of the death penalty in Virginia has been highly racialized and grossly disproportionate. The data in figure 2 confirms that Virginia juries and judges were reliably racist.[22] Throughout the Jim Crow era, Black men were more than four times as likely to face execution than white men. That the number of African Americans executed rose sharply during the lynching era is not surprising. Southern states subverted the legal code to disenfranchise and segregate African Americans between the 1880s and 1960s. Jim Crow laws impacted almost every facet of work and life, from baseball, barber shops, and drinking fountains to transportation, education, and housing.

In Virginia, 72 Black males were sentenced to death and executed for the crime of rape or attempted rape during the era of mob lynching (1877–1932).[23] All but two of the purported victims were white females. During the same period, Virginia courts did not execute a single white male for a rape-related

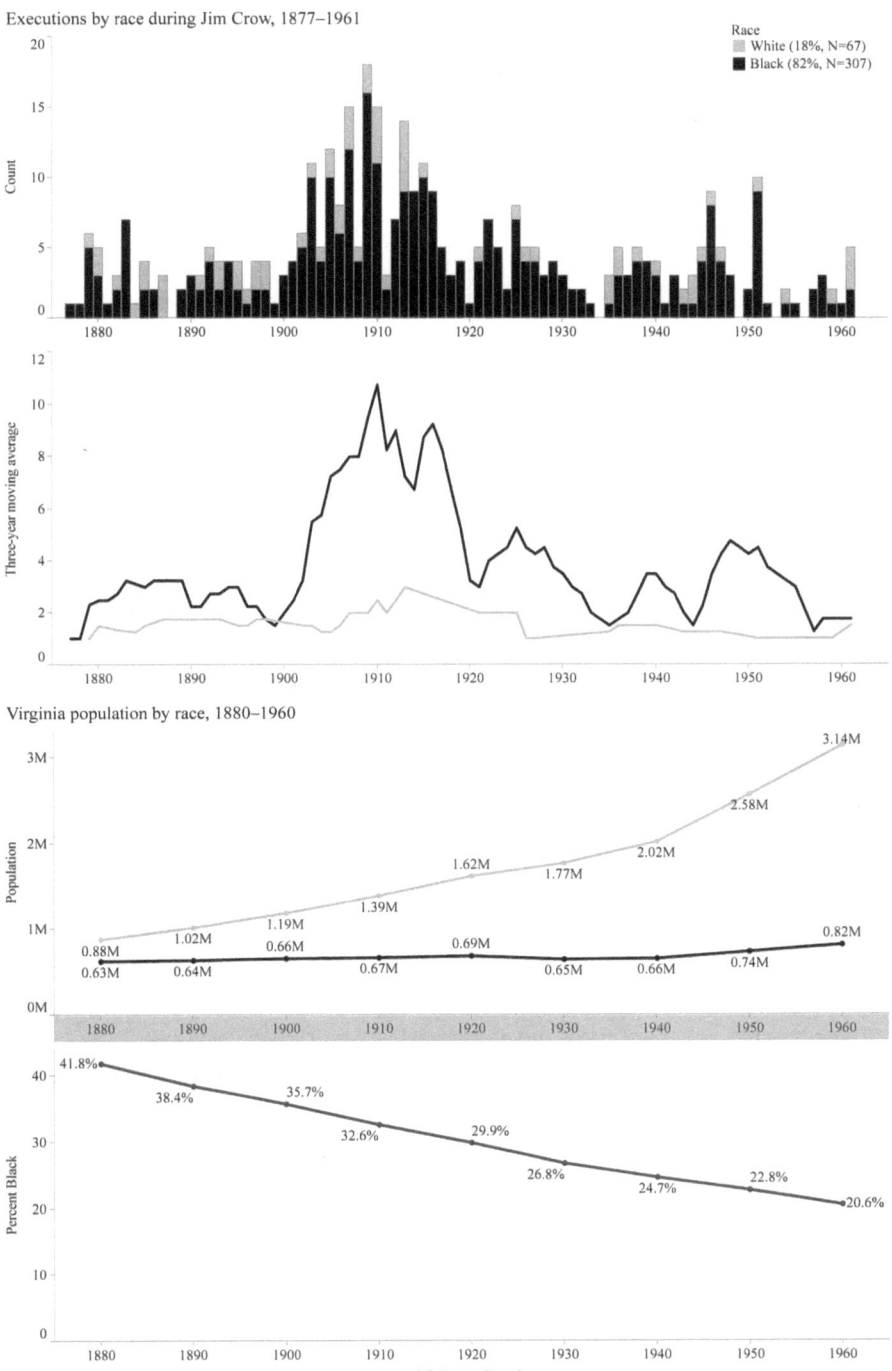

FIGURE 2. Legal executions in Virginia by race, 1877–1961, versus population by race, 1880–1960

crime, regardless of the race of the victim. The top chart in figure 2 shows the highly racialized distribution of the death penalty across all offenses, including murder, arson, rape, robbery, horse stealing, piracy, and espionage. The execution of Black men rose significantly during the lynching era. While mobs were illegally lynching Black males, Virginia's criminal justice system was executing Black males.[24] Conversely, the execution of white men rose only slightly during the lynching era. The number of white executions in Virginia remained relatively flat through the Jim Crow era even though the white population more than tripled between 1880 and 1960.

The two charts in figure 3 reveal the shocking effectiveness of Governor O'Ferrall's crusade to defeat mob lynchings in Virginia. Mob lynching data in this essay comes primarily from the Racial Terror: Lynching in Virginia website inventory, which builds on the CSDE Lynching Database.[25] The Racial Terror inventory was used to construct the "Mob Lynchings" chart at the top of figure 3. The legal lynchings data is an updated version of the Espy database, based on additional research I conducted using digitized newspaper articles. The updated inventory documents 93 legal lynchings between 1877 and 1961.[26] The vertical bands between 1894 and 1898 demarcate the governorship of Charles O'Ferrall. Three-year moving averages create smoother lines that surface general trends across time.

Mob lynchings in the South peaked in 1893, the year before O'Ferrall assumed the governor's office. The top chart in figure 3 illustrates how quickly O'Ferrall's efforts suppressed mob lynchings in Virginia. A slight spike in mob lynchings occurred shortly after O'Ferrall left office in 1898. They declined gradually over the next three decades. The seventeen mob lynchings that occurred between 1903 and 1932 mark a significant decrease.

Not coincidentally, as depicted in the bottom half of figure 3, legal lynchings began in earnest during O'Ferrall's governorship and continued with a few notable gaps and peaks until 1961. There is a striking inverse correlation between legal and extralegal lynchings in Virginia. In return for law and order on the streets of Virginia, O'Ferrall promised white mobs that the criminal justice system would swiftly prosecute and execute those (Black) men accused of the crime too horrible to mention. O'Ferrall quickly and effectively displaced mob lynchings with legal lynchings. He often disrupted the mobs by bolstering local law enforcement with local militia or state troops. Prisoners were frequently moved discreetly and under heavy guard to a prison in a

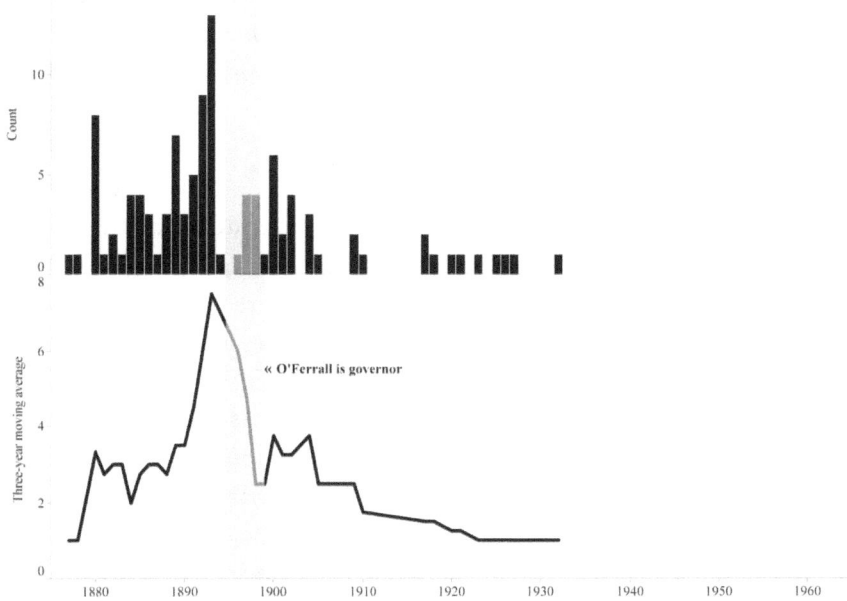
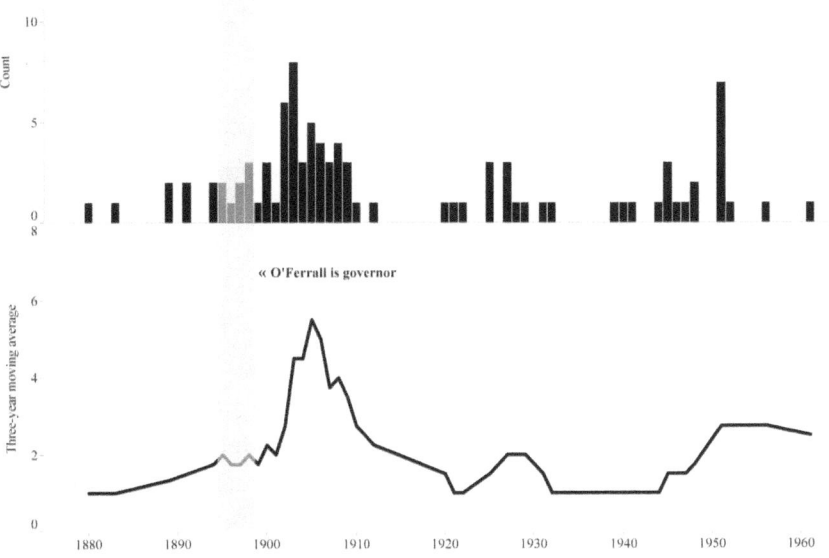

FIGURE 3. Mob versus legal lynchings in Virginia, 1877–1961

nearby community. O'Ferrall also threatened would-be lynchers with prosecution. This Faustian bargain was a losing proposition for Black men across Virginia: Even when the state brought threatening mobs to heel, the lives of 93 Black men accused of rape crimes against white women ended violently on the gallows or in the electric chair.

Sociologist E. M. Beck assembled an inventory of "threatened, foiled, averted, and failed lynchings," recording 3,246 incidents of threatened lynchings occurring in the South between 1880 and 1929.[27] Using this inventory—which is in progress as more cases are constantly added—Tolnay and Beck argue that the "total quantum of racialized terrorism nearly doubles when completed lynchings and lynching threats are combined."[28] The authors, while recognizing that a completed lynching is the "most extreme form of repressive social control exercised over the Southern black populations," suggested that the "very act of publicly threatening lethal violence can be a powerful tool of intimidation" and must be factored into the total "quantum" of racialized terrorism.[29] A weaponized and discriminatory criminal justice system, at times itself under threat, can also be a powerful tool of intimidation. Indeed, Michelle Alexander argued in *The New Jim Crow* that the war on drugs and mass incarceration is a "stunningly comprehensive and well-disguised system of social control that functions in a manner strikingly similar to Jim Crow."[30]

In this section, I extend the conceptual boundaries of racialized terrorism to include legal executions of African Americans. Combining my research with Beck's inventory of threatened lynchings reveals that 52 of the 72 Black males executed for rape-related crimes during the lynching era were targets of violent white mobs before their arrest or during their incarceration.

When a white mob caught its intended victim, one of three outcomes was possible. The mob killed the victim. The victim escaped with his or her life. Or the victim was arrested and accused of the crime that had inflamed the mob's violent passions. O'Ferrall and his successors significantly reduced the likelihood that the mob would have its pound of flesh in the public square. However, as Dale M. Brumfield demonstrates graphically in his essay in this volume, lynch mobs frequently used threats of violence to pressure juries to return guilty verdicts and amplify the severity of sentencing for Black defendants on trial for crimes against whites, especially against white females.

Whether the outcome of an encounter with a lynch mob resulted in an extralegal lynching or in a legal execution played out in Virginia's criminal justice system, the distinction made little difference to the target of the lynch mob. Either way, the victim died violently, and his family and community were left terrified. For example, in "Judge Lynch Denied," Beck described the encounter between a young Black man and a white mob. Local authorities moved Henry Williams, accused of "murderous assault and outrage" of a mother and her three-year-old daughter near Roanoke, to the state penitentiary in Richmond for safekeeping from the mob.[31] Williams was escorted back to Roanoke for trial by three hundred Richmond militia. Details of the trial are found in local newspaper accounts. The *Clinch Valley News* reported on November 18, 1904, that two hundred people witnessed the legal hanging of Henry Williams, carrying away "bits of the rope as souvenirs."

Stories like Williams's encounter with a mob and the criminal justice system were common in Virginia during the lynching era. Brumfield provides several examples in his essay. My research documents additional stories of African Americans executed for crimes against whites. The tragic case of Henry Hart, a twenty-one-year-old Black man charged with attempting to assault a white woman, is another illustration of the hopeless challenge Black defendants faced in a courtroom run by whites and surrounded by a white mob. The *Richmond Planet* reported on February 12, 1921, that "when a white jury sitting in judgment on a colored man, charged with criminally assaulting or attempted to criminally assault a white woman[,] becomes hopelessly deadlocked and fails to agree, it is a 'safe bet' that the colored man is innocent." Regardless, a new jury was quickly empaneled to replace the hung jury and sentenced Hart to die in the electric chair. In the same article, the reporter complained about the mob outside the courthouse that "threatened to take him from the officers of the law unless he was convicted."[32] The *Richmond Planet* reporter was hopeful that the Virginia Supreme Court would overturn the conviction. It did not. Hart went to the electric chair on August 4, 1921.

Recently, Beck has updated his inventory of threatened lynchings with an additional six hundred threats that occurred in Virginia between 1866 and 1955.[33] Figure 4 shows that threatened lynchings follow the same general trend as mob lynchings: they peaked around 1890 and from there gradually declined towards zero by the early 1930s. The top half of the same figure shows that Virginian mobs directed most of their violence against African

Americans throughout the Jim Crow era. Over two thirds of the victims of threatened lynchings were African American. The bottom half shows that Virginian mobs were five times more likely to level accusations of rape-related offenses at Black men than at white men. The gray bands in figure 4 demarcate the lynching era (1877–1932). According to Beck's inventory, Virginia mobs threatened 120 Black males under the pretext of rape-related crimes during the lynching era. Thirty-six of these 120 men appear in my updated inventory of legal lynchings over the same fifty-year period. In other words, 36 of the 120 men threatened with lynching were subsequently executed by the state for a rape crime. I have identified 14 cases of Black males threatened by a mob and subsequently convicted of and executed for rape-related crimes that do not appear in the Beck inventory. The robust correspondence between Black men executed by the state and Black males targeted by lynch mobs during the lynching era in Virginia may in part be explained by Governor O'Ferrall's determined efforts to stop mob lynchings.

In summary, figure 5 provides an aggregation of all documented violence directed at Black males during the lynching era in Virginia. The underlying data includes the 79 legal lynchings compiled through my research, the extralegal mob lynchings collected in the De Fazio inventory, and the threatened lynchings appearing in Beck's inventory. The top chart lists the three major outcomes of mob violence directed at Black males. One in five Black males caught by a mob was lynched by that mob. The majority (61 percent) of threatened lynchings did not end in the death of the targeted victim. Local law enforcement, state troopers, or military troops often disrupted a mob gathering before a lynching could be completed. Such disruptions became more common as the state initiative to stop lynch mobs intensified. The top chart in figure 5 shows that 19 percent of Black males who did survive mob violence were subsequently tried and executed in Virginia courts.

The middle chart in figure 5 combines legal and extralegal lynchings into a single category. White mobs in Virginia led directly or indirectly to the extralegal and legal lynching of 164 Black males during the lynching era. Two out of five encounters between a white mob and a Black male ended in death. The bottom chart filters the data by accusations of rape and attempted rape. A Black man accused by a mob of a rape crime against a white woman was more likely than not to end up dead. Fifty-two percent of Black males targeted by a threatening mob under the pretext of rape or attempted rape were hanged

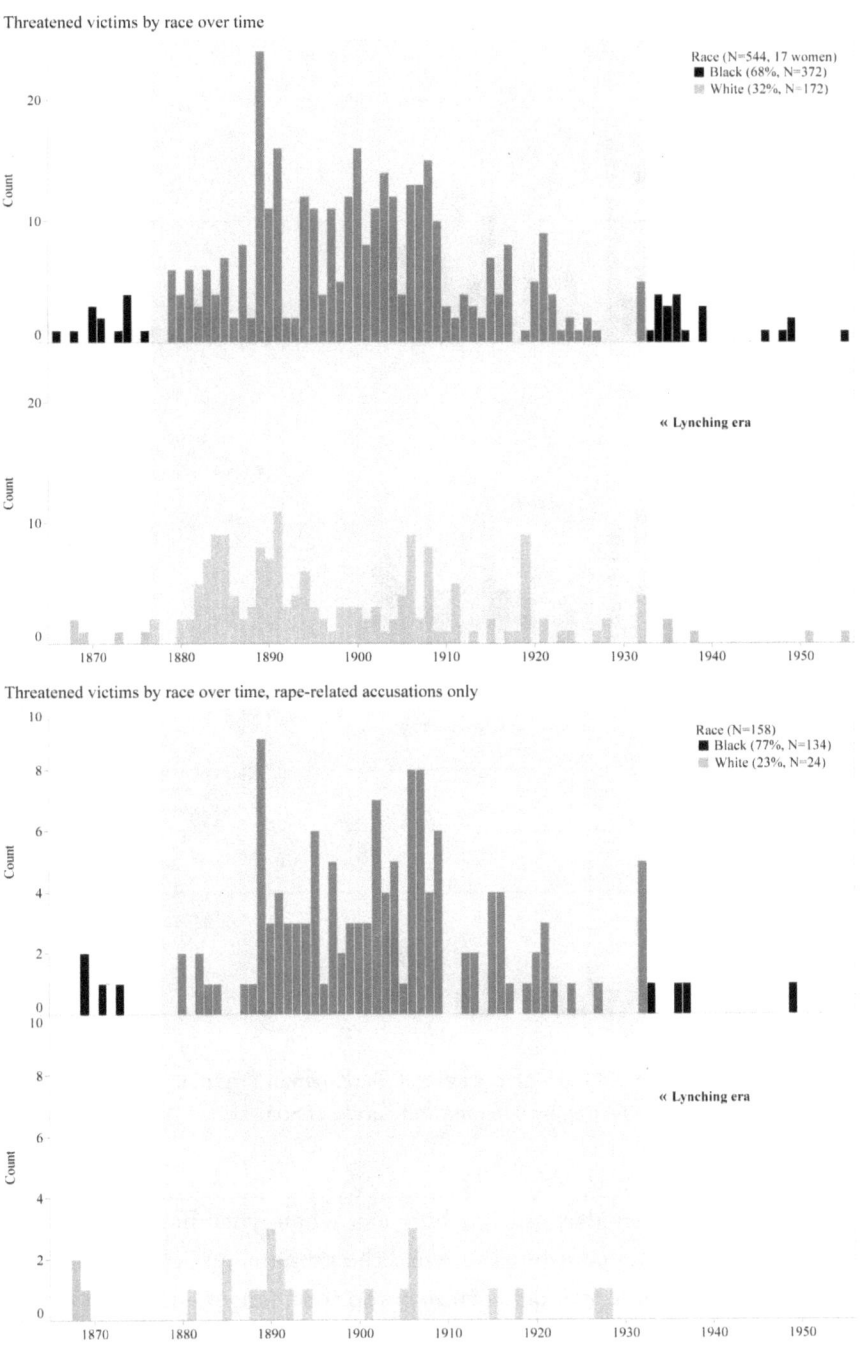

FIGURE 4. Threatened lynchings in Virginia, 1866–1955, all threats and rape-related accusations only

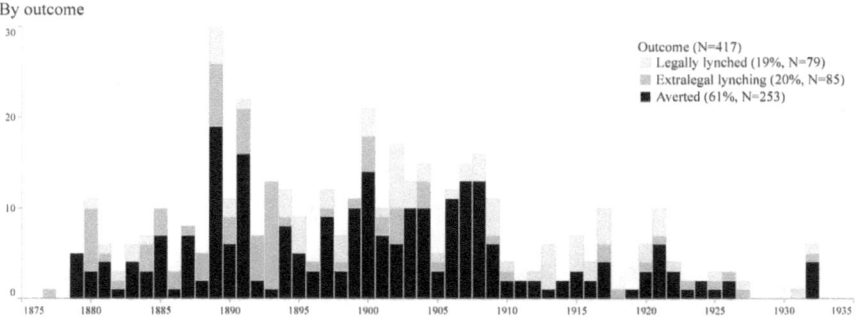
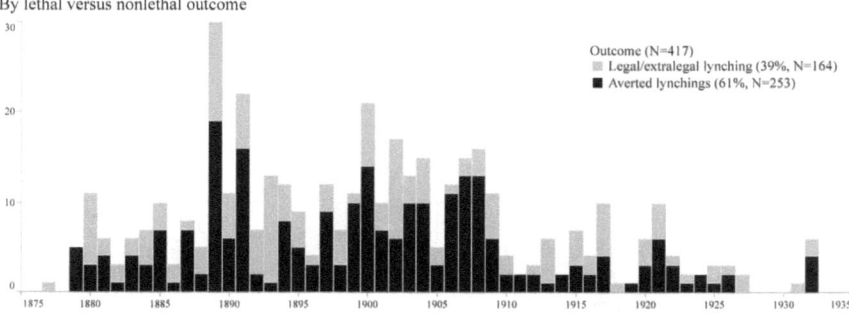
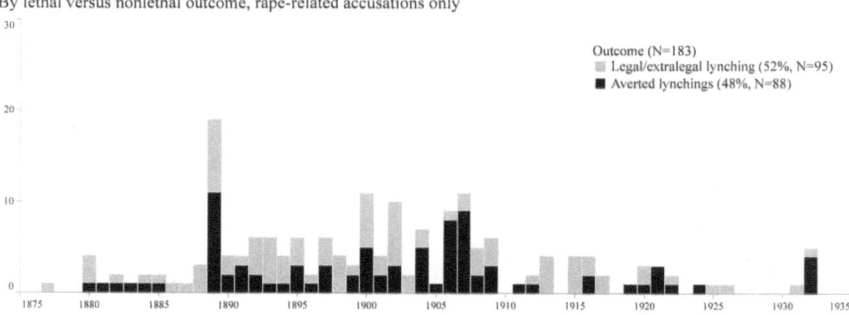

FIGURE 5. Mob violence against Black men in Virginia, 1877–1932, by outcome and nature of accusation

or electrocuted. Even after the lynching era, when lynch mobs had all but disappeared, Virginia continued to wield the criminal justice system as an instrument of racial terror. Between 1933 and 1961, judges and juries sent 21 African Americans to the electric chair in Richmond for rape-related crimes against white women. During all of Jim Crow, not a single white man was executed for a rape crime.

Tolnay and Beck argue that adding threatened lynchings as a measure of racialized terrorism almost doubles the "quantum of such behavior in the 11 Southern states" during the lynching era.[34] The average sum of mob and threatened lynchings per Southern state is 432.[35] According to their research, Virginia's total quantum of racialized terrorism is 312, the sum of 77 mob and 235 threatened lynchings. As demonstrated in this essay, the quantum during the lynching era goes up significantly when other factors and more recent research is considered. Beck's inventory of threatened lynchings has raised the quantum to 553. The number rises to 645 when legal lynchings and more recent counts of mob lynchings are factored into the calculation.[36]

Scholars have generally agreed that the level and intensity of mob lynchings were considerably lower in Virginia and other border states than in the Black belt states. Indeed, Tolnay and Beck's comprehensive analysis of southern lynching outlined in their groundbreaking book *A Festival of Violence* did not include Virginia.[37] Furthermore, when Tolnay revisited the subject of southern mob violence ten years later, in 2015, with a new coauthor, Amy Kate Bailey, Virginia is still missing from the analysis.[38] Research that takes into account threatened lynchings and legal lynchings as part of the racialized terrorism continuum challenges the notion of Virginia as an outlier. Racialized terrorism was much more pervasive in Virginia than previously recognized.

The Jim Crow trials in which 93 Black men were legally lynched were performed to mollify white mobs and reassert the racial caste system. Agents in these show trials cared less about discovering facts and applying the law equitably. Verdicts were for the most part determined in advance. Mostly white juries reached their verdicts with little deliberation, in the absence of robust evidence, and without the benefit of basic due process guarantees. In some cases, the defense attorney and the prosecutor colluded on the trial specifics. In other cases, trials proceeded without a defense attorney. The near certainty of the verdict (guilty) and the severity of the sentence (often death) effectively demonstrated the power of the white officials over their Black citizens. Defense lawyers were reluctant to defend Black defendants. Evidence was often sparse and mostly circumstantial. Cuts and bruises sometimes served as evidence of a capital offense. Witness testimony was vague and inconsistent. White newspapers often reported erroneously that the defendant had confessed. The same papers described defendants as poor, shiftless, ignorant, uneducated, or mentally incapacitated. White newspapers often reported the alleged crimes with sweeping outrage and disgust.

The *Richmond Times-Dispatch* recounted details of the case of Burrell Johnson, a Black teenager: "The charge against Johnson was attempted criminal assault. Justice was meted out speedily. Court convened at 11:30 o'clock this morning. At 3:24 the negro had been indicted, tried, convicted and sentenced to be hanged" (August 23, 1902). In less than four hours, a grand jury was convened, a jury tried Johnson, and Johnson was sentenced to death. Jury deliberations often took less than an hour. Walter Rippey was accused of criminally assaulting a white woman near Pocahontas, Virginia. The front page of the *Clinch Valley News* reported that the jury deliberated his case for fifteen minutes, returning a guilty verdict.[39] They forgot to fix the punishment and were sent back to the jury room. Four minutes later, they returned with a death sentence, which "was well received." Rippey was hanged on March 28, 1908. According to the *Shenandoah Herald,* Charlie Gillespie was tried for attempted criminal assault. In this case, "the jury was out for less than five minutes."[40] Gillespie was electrocuted on February 18, 1909. On August 20, 1915, the *Richmond Times-Dispatch* wrote that George Matthews and John Lewis Rollins were tried and executed together and that their jury was "out less than five minutes." Matthews and Rollins were convicted of criminal assault.

White newspapers took solace and pride in the swiftness and severity with which local courts convicted and sentenced Black men for crimes against white women. Slow justice agitated local mobs. The front page of the *Alexandria Gazette* bragged on May 30, 1913, that the trial of Benjamin Bailey "is said to have never been equaled in the state of Virginia for quickness for so serious an offense, lasting less than two hours."[41] Bailey was sent to the electric chair for criminal assault on August 8, 1913. As with many legal lynchings performed during the lynching era, a threatening mob had formed around Bailey's arrest and was visible at his trial.

The principle of mental irresponsibility sometimes formed the basis of appeals for Black men convicted of rape-related crimes. The *Danville Bee* reported on February 20, 1925, that Governor Trinkle granted Percy Lee a reprieve so that "alienists may examine the negro to determine his sanity." Lee was accused of several crimes and convicted of an "attempted criminal attack on a Westhampton College Student."[42] The *Times-Dispatch* described Lee as the "most dangerous negro that ever menaced the community." Virginia electrocuted Lee on May 1, 1925. Governor Mann granted Benjamin Bailey a reprieve so that he could "make further investigation into the mental condition of the prisoner."[43] The *Alexandria Gazette* noted that Bailey had written to his mother saying that he was well and would be "electrocuted, whatever that is." He expressed hope that "they would 'make haste and do it,' as he wants to get back home." The twenty-one-year-old Bailey was convicted of criminally assaulting a white girl and executed on August 8, 1913.

Most victims of legalized lynch law either had no attorney or were poorly represented. White attorneys did not want to be seen successfully defending Black criminals. Retired judges were often tapped to act as defense counsel. Burrell Johnson unwittingly served as his own attorney. The *Times-Dispatch* of Richmond reported that Johnson sat bewildered and silent when asked "if he wished to strike out any particular four" men from the jury pool.[44] When he did not answer, four were "eliminated by lot." When asked if he wished to question any witnesses for the prosecution, he replied, "No, sur."

According to the *Times-Dispatch,* the court appointed two white lawyers to defend Henry Williams, who was charged with robbery and attempted criminal assault. The lawyers did not introduce any witnesses or interrogate any of the prosecution's witnesses. The *Times-Dispatch* reported with sarcasm that during the closing remarks, "Mr. Bryan spoke with exceeding brevity and came about as near saying nothing as a man could without absolutely dispensing with his humanity and appearing at bar as an oyster." Williams was convicted based on a confession he was not given a chance to deny and was hanged on March 18, 1904. The defense attorney for John Lomax did not call any witnesses, advised Lomax not to testify, and did not make closing arguments.[45] A juror interrupted the trial to ask if the accused had identified Lomax. The sixteen-year-old was hanged on September 9, 1902. In the case of Gabriel Battaile, also sixteen years old and also charged with criminal assault, the appointed defense attorney and the prosecutor agreed to submit the case to the jury without argument.[46] The jury returned a guilty verdict after deliberating for about twenty minutes. Battaile was hanged on June 8, 1906.

Walter Johnson was convicted and sentenced to hang on evidence that consisted of a coerced testimony and mutable testimony. The *Richmond Dispatch* reported that Johnson, acting as his own defense counsel, claimed that he confessed when "a rope had been placed around his neck and pistols were drawn upon him by a dozen men who had taken him to the woods in Nottoway county and threatened him with death if he did not confess." Having narrowly escaped the mob's noose, Johnson was convicted of criminal assault and hanged less than two months later, on May 23, 1891.

In some cases, even an accuser's recantation of her first-person testimony was insufficient to free the accused. The *Times-Dispatch* reported that "William H. Wilson, the negro charged with criminal assault upon Mrs. W. T. Watkins, was found guilty this afternoon, and his punishment fixed at 18 years in the penitentiary."[47] The Richmond military was on high alert and guarded the jailhouse all night. Wilson maintained his innocence, and a credible defense was mounted by Hugh Gordon Miller (white). The court instructed the jury with these words: "The attempt to commit the offense with the use of any force is sufficient to establish his guilt, provided this was against the will and consent of the prosecutrix [sic]." This is a low bar, indeed. The same paper a day earlier described Mrs. Watkins's (the "prosecutrix") statement under cross-examination. She denied that "Wilson used any violence towards her or attempted to throw her to the floor, and further stated that Wilson had been working on the farm off and on for two years, was always respectful and had never treated her amiss before."[48] Despite this testimony, Wilson was sentenced to eighteen years imprisonment. Judge Goodwin reminded Wilson that the "verdict might have been death" and "spoke at considerable length about the enormity of the crime."[49] The *Richmond Planet* called the case "a travesty upon justice" and noted that Wilson withdrew his appeal and accepted the eighteen years to save himself from the "fury of the mob."[50]

The research presented in this essay extends Michael J. Pfeifer's comprehensive exploration of transformation from mob justice to state-sanctioned executions in postbellum America. Pfeifer's research focused on seven states in the American Northeast, South, Midwest, and West. In the South, he turned his attention to Louisiana. This essay is centered on Virginia, a border state. It aligns very closely with Pfeifer's argument that the death penalty replaced lynching as due process advocates sought to end mob violence. My research also mirrors George C. Wright's detailed analysis of the transformation from community-based vigilantism to state-sanctioned legal lynchings in neighboring Kentucky. The excessive and relentless prosecution and punishment of young Black men for rape crimes in Virginia was a successful effort by state officials to stem incidents of mob violence that had gotten out of hand at the end of the nineteenth century. At the same time, legal lynchings, like the mob lynchings they displaced, contributed significantly to Virginia's quantum of racialized terrorism during Jim Crow. Black-on-white rape occupied a special status in the mythology of white supremacists. Rape accusations were a common pretext for mob lynchings and legal lynchings. White newspapers described Black-on-white rape as a supreme menace to local communities and the alleged Black rapists as savage brutes deserving the ultimate punishment.

Governor O'Ferrall's successful efforts to subdue the mob intent on killing Parker only delayed his hanging before a large crowd for several weeks. Parker's case exhibits many of the attributes of a legal lynching. A crowd assembled at the jail where Parker was held yelling, "Lynch him." Deputies moved him to a jail in another town to safeguard him from would-be lynchers. The governor positioned military troops around the jailhouse and the courtroom throughout the judicial proceedings. The trial lasted about four hours, and the jury deliberated for forty minutes. The guilty verdict was greeted in the courtroom with loud applause. Newspapers reported that the swift verdict was justified because the defendant confessed shortly after the trial ended. After the judge sentenced Parker to death, the mob dispersed and the military presence withdrew from the city. Execution day was a highly ritualized spectacle. Parker met with a spiritual advisor. An affectionate deputy helped Parker dress. Parker's last meal may have been one of the best meals of his short life. Parker reportedly stood on the scaffold with "wonderful nerve" and again confessed his guilt.[51]

Even after his execution, Parker's harrowing journey through Jim Crow Virginia was not over. The State Anatomical Board sent his corpse, probably over objections from his parents, to a medical school in Richmond or Charlottesville. My research shows that over 43 percent of the bodies of the 93 Black men executed for rape crimes during Jim Crow were sent to Virginia's medical schools, where white students dissected them in anatomy classes.

Virginia courts wielded the criminal justice system as an instrument of racial terror and oppression throughout the Jim Crow era. Echoes of these practices still blight state and local agencies and institutions in various forms, including brutal police forces targeting young Black men, the war on drugs, mandatory sentencing, and mass incarceration. There is progress on one front: on March 23, 2019, Gov. Ralph Northam signed House Bill 2263, making Virginia the first southern state to ban the death penalty. Upon signing the bill, Governor Northam noted that "Virginia has come within days of executing innocent people, and Black defendants have been disproportionately sentenced to death."[52] Six months later, Governor Northam posthumously pardoned the Martinsville Seven, a group of Black men, mostly teenagers, executed for the rape of a white woman in 1951.

Notes

1. "Parker Hanged," *Richmond Planet*, April 27, 1895.
2. "Parker Hanged," *Richmond Planet*, April 27, 1895.
3. "Parker Hanged," *Richmond Planet*, April 27, 1895; "First Victim of the Law," *Richmond Times*, April 20, 1895.
4. "Military Returned Home," *Shenandoah Herald*, March 22, 1895.
5. These events were reported in various local and state papers, including "Military Returned Home," *Shenandoah Herald*, March 22, 1895; "The Negro Parker Hanged," *Roanoke Times*, April 20, 1895; untitled, *Highland Recorder*, March 22, 1895.
6. Data for the chart in Figure 1 is aggregated from three sources: E. M. Beck, "Virginia Threatened Victims" ([personal communication], 2020); Gianluca De Fazio, Racial Terror: Lynching in Virginia, 2021, http://sites.lib.jmu.edu/valynchings/; Kevin Hegg, Legal Lynchings in Jim Crow Virginia ([unpublished database], 2021). I am indebted to Dr. Beck for sharing his database with me.
7. Arthur F. Raper, *The Tragedy of Lynching* (Chapel Hill: University of North Carolina Press, 1933), 19.
8. George C. Wright, *Racial Violence in Kentucky, 1865–1940: Lynchings, Mob Rule, and "Legal Lynchings"* (Baton Rouge: Louisiana State University Press, 1990), 12.
9. Michael J. Pfeifer, *Rough Justice: Lynching and American Society, 1874–1947* (Urbana: University of Illinois Press, 2004), 94.
10. Stewart E. Tolnay and E. M. Beck, "'Racialized Terrorism' in the American South: Do Completed Lynchings Tell an Accurate Story?," *Social Science History* 42, no. 4 (2018): 677, https://doi.org/10.1017/ssh.2018.22.
11. O'Ferrall, *Forty Years of Active Service*, 202.
12. O'Ferrall, *Forty Years of Active Service*, 204.
13. O'Ferrall, *Forty Years of Active Service*, 203.
14. O'Ferrall, *Forty Years of Active Service*, 250.
15. O'Ferrall, *Forty Years of Active Service*, 235.
16. Josh Howard, "Defending Person and Reputation: Efforts to End Extralegal Violence in Western Virginia, 1890–1900," *American Journal of Legal History* 58, no. 2 (June 2018): 169.
17. O'Ferrall, *Forty Years of Active Service*, 235.
18. Virginia, *Acts and Joint Resolutions*, 1894, 29, 30.

19. "The Negro Parker Hanged," *Richmond Planet,* April 27, 1895.
20. Military courts hanged one in 1626 and another in 1775. The third was John Perkins, a veteran of the Union Army, who was hanged in 1868. The Espy file is the most comprehensive record of legal executions performed in the United States between 1608 and 2002. See M. Watt Espy and John Ortiz Smykla, *Executions in the United States, 1608–2002: The Espy File* [Computer File], 4th ICPSR (Ann Arbor, MI: Inter-university Consortium for Political and Social Research, 2004), https://deathpenalty.procon.org/view.resource.php?resourceID=004087.
21. De Fazio, Racial Terror: Lynching in Virginia, http://sites.lib.jmu.edu/valynchings/.
22. Data for these charts come from US Census and the Espy file. See "1790–1960 United States Census, Virginia" (US Census Bureau), accessed Feb. 6, 2019, https://www.socialexplorer.com/explore-maps; Espy and Smykla, *The Espy File.*
23. For purposes of this essay, I will follow De Fazio in defining the lynching era in Virginia as ranging from 1877, the end of Reconstruction, to 1932, five years after Virginia passed its first antilynching law in 1928 and the year of the last documented lynching in Virginia (see De Fazio, Racial Terror: Lynching in Virginia website).
24. During Virginia's lynching era, two women were illegally lynched and five women were legally executed.
25. De Fazio, Racial Terror: Lynching in Virginia website, http://sites.lib.jmu.edu/valynchings/. The De Fazio inventory builds on and extends the Tolnay-Beck inventory, which is available upon request here: Amy Kate Bailey and Stewart E. Tolnay, "CSDE Lynching Database," accessed Feb. 8, 2019, https://sites.uw.edu/lynching/#/home.
26. In addition to the 82 executions listed in the Espy database, I have identified 10 other victims of legal lynch law.
27. E. M. Beck, "Judge Lynch Denied: Combating Mob Violence in the American South, 1877–1950," *Southern Cultures* 21, no. 2 (2015): 117–39.
28. Tolnay and Beck, "'Racialized Terrorism' in the American South," 677.
29. Tolnay and Beck, "'Racialized Terrorism' in the American South," 677.
30. Michelle Alexander, *The New Jim Crow: Mass Incarceration in the Age of Colorblindness* (New York: New Press, 2012), 4.
31. Beck, "Judge Lynch Denied," 120.
32. "Supreme Court Grants Writ," *Richmond Planet,* Feb. 12, 1921.
33. Beck, "Virginia Threatened Victims Tables and Charts."
34. Tolnay and Beck, "'Racialized Terrorism' in the American South," 696.
35. Tolnay and Beck, "'Racialized Terrorism' in the American South," 691.
36. As indicated in figure 5, 680 incidents of mob violence occurred between the end of the Civil War and 1940. The number drops to 645 when limited to the lynching era.
37. Tolnay and Beck, *Festival of Violence,* 260.
38. Amy Kate Bailey and Stewart Emory Tolnay, *Lynched: The Victims of Southern Mob Violence* (Chapel Hill: University of North Carolina Press, 2015).
39. "Rippey Must Die March 27," *Clinch Valley News,* Feb. 21, 1908.
40. "Convicted in Short Time," *Shenandoah Herald,* Jan. 22, 1909.
41. "Benjamin Bailey to Pay Death Penalty for Crime against Child," *Alexandria Gazette,* May 20, 1913.
42. "Negro Is Electrocuted for Series of Attacks," *Richmond Times-Dispatch,* May 2, 1925.
43. "Resigned to His Fate," *Alexandria Gazette,* July 25, 1913.

44. "Swift Justice for Burrell Johnson," *Richmond Times-Dispatch,* Aug. 23, 1902.
45. "Lomax Found Guilty," *Richmond Dispatch,* Aug. 6, 1902.
46. "Negro Battaile Hanged for Terrible Crime," *Daily Press,* June 9, 1906.
47. "The Nottoway Assault Case," *Richmond Times-Dispatch,* Feb. 9, 1901.
48. "Nottoway Assault Case," *Richmond Times-Dispatch,* Feb. 8, 1901.
49. "Nottoway Assault Case," *Richmond Times-Dispatch,* Feb. 9, 1901.
50. "A Travesty upon Justice," *Richmond Planet,* Feb. 16, 1901.
51. "Thornton Parker Executed," *Highland Recorder,* April 26, 1895.
52. Virginia Governor Ralph Northam, press release, March 24, 2021, accessed March 23, 2023, https://www.governor.virginia.gov/newsroom/all-releases/2021/march/headline-894006-en.html.

SIX SHAM TRIALS

Judge George Anderson and Jim Crow in Alleghany and Botetourt County Courts

JOSH HOWARD

This is the story of Black men murdered by lynch mobs and Black men murdered by the state. Near Clifton Forge, a small city in Alleghany County, at least three Black men died at the hands of white lynch mobs and another five were charged, convicted, and executed between 1890 and 1930. The year 1891 was critical in this story when hundreds of white men chased, shot, and brutally executed three Black men during a single October night. Shortly thereafter, up-and-coming lawyer George Anderson ascended to the regional circuit court judgeship and everything changed, or so it seemed on the surface. Under Judge Anderson's watchful eye, Black men accused of crimes were arrested, held in prison, and given a jury trial as required under state and federal law. On one hand, Judge Anderson supervised professionalization of the police and judiciary in Alleghany County, while on the other, he contributed to the pain and suffering of hundreds of Black Virginians for decades.

Henry Magruder, Robert Bowles, Ben Hubbard, Edmund Thompson, and Aurelius "Felix" Christian were the five Black men who died because of Judge Anderson's court rulings. Each one was charged with similar violent crimes, but the likelihood of their actual guilt ranged dramatically. Robert Bowles defended himself from a racist white man and was likely innocent by reason of self-defense, and Henry Magruder was almost assuredly guilty of at least one capital crime. Truth mattered little in Alleghany County, and this is not the place to readjudicate charges. The aim instead is to place Judge Anderson within the frame. He was the one man who made certain lynch mobs, though many still roamed the area, would no longer succeed in their goals by providing those bloodthirsty men with another form of unjust justice. By the turn

{197}

of the century, Judge Anderson's gavel replaced the noose and everyone in the region, white and Black alike, knew it.

Over the past thirty years, historians have produced extensive writings about lynching, but this was hardly the beginning of lynching scholarship or antilynching activism. Beginning with activists like Ida B. Wells and John Mitchell Jr., most focused on horrific violence committed by white mobs upon Black bodies, a trend that included academic scholarship on lynching. Such lynching narratives include a mob, accusations without evidence, gruesome murders, and the lingering threat of violence.[1] Action transpired in public and in newspapers, only rarely moving into courtrooms. A prime example in Virginia was the Roanoke Riot of 1893, an event that centered on a white mob's murder of Thomas Smith for a crime he likely did not commit. The Roanoke violence—perhaps the most politically impactful lynching in Virginia—spiraled out of control as white mobs poured through town burning buildings, terrorizing Black residents, and taking potshots at law enforcement forcing the mayor, who was himself shot, to flee town. Courtrooms played little role in the Roanoke events; actions were almost entirely found on the city's streets and in its homes and places of business.[2]

During the intervening 130 years, local historians and politicians worked to essentially erase lynching narratives from public memory. Writing in the early 1970s, the author of the only comprehensive history of Clifton Forge, Elizabeth Corron, described historical race relations as "a good cooperative spirit . . . which is attributed to the spiritual heritage of both races."[3] She continued: "Law and order in the early 1890s were handled by private citizens who were summoned by the chief of police and deputized. . . . Railroad men offered the main support to the law enforcement officers, and they served their community well and faithfully," perhaps a tongue-in-cheek reference to lynching without mentioning a few key details.[4] Local newspapers, too, continued this ruse as Roy C. Long's regular "Railroad Recollections" column in the *Hinton News* similarly noted in 1989: "We know of no murders in Alleghany County by Judge Lynch."[5] As recently as 2020, local political leaders professed ignorance of the 1891 lynching, though local Black communities have not forgotten.[6] Compounding such matters was a long-standing local journalistic practice to vilify African Americans. Tracing back over a century to the 1890s, Clifton Forge newspapers depicted local African Americans— roughly 30 percent of the local population—as a dichotomy. Black men were either "industrious and law-abiding" or nothing more than arsonists, highwaymen, and murderers. To drive home the point in such stories, newspapers identified all African Americans appearing in print with "col." or "colored" after their name, a journalistic practice common in white Virginian newspapers through the mid-twentieth century.[7]

Several stories, each horrible in a unique way, follow; each is connected by Judge George Anderson, a white community's desire to see Black men punished, and the fear that must have been felt by local Black communities. Judge Anderson terrorized Black residents of the greater Alleghany County area, but the scope of the damage he caused cannot be contained by a single essay. Regardless, this essay offers a starting point in assessing one man's impact by outlining each individual case to learn their stories and remember the victims' humanity. Henry Magruder, Robert Bowles, Aurelius Christian, Ben Hubbard, Robert Lewis, and Edmund Thompson—six men whose lives met ruin when they met Judge Anderson for the first time.

A Judge and a Lynching

George Kimbrough Anderson, born in Louisa County in 1860, claimed an old Virginia ancestry dating to English and Welsh colonists arriving in the 1640s. Though Anderson's father was a physician and court official, Anderson attended public schools and read law rather than attend any law school.[8] Louisa County voters selected Anderson to be commonwealth's attorney in 1887, but he resigned after three years to open a private law practice in the small but rapidly growing railroad town of Clifton Forge. During the early 1890s his status rapidly grew as he became one of the area's most prominent and wealthy white residents. In 1895 Anderson was elected by the residents of Alleghany and Bath Counties to be the area's next circuit court judge. Anderson immediately leveraged his newfound leadership role to become president of Clifton Forge Mining and Development Co. and First National Bank, and he purchased one of the largest homes in the small city. The next thirty-five years saw Anderson as one of the community's top leaders. He would hold the circuit court judgeship until his death in 1930.[9]

Clifton Forge was a town with two reputations—as an economically promising railroad hub and as a town with a population quick to kill Black men and excuse the bad behavior of whites. The first documented post–Civil War murder of a Black man in the area came in 1881. A white bar owner, J. Andrew Pugh, shot and killed Taylor B. Barwell, a local African American barber, just outside of Pugh's business. Newspapers published Pugh's version of events near verbatim as he claimed self-defense in the absence of other witnesses. With only Pugh's testimony, an all-white jury acquitted him of all charges to the celebration of newspapers and the white public. No record has yet been found detailing how Barwell's family or other Black locals reacted.[10]

A defining event in local history began on the morning of October 17, 1891, when John Scott, Robert Burton, C. W. Miller, Miller Morton, and about four other Black men walked from their workplace in Big Hill, through Iron Gate, and into Clifton Forge. The men had a good time, at first, drinking at a few bars and stopping at a photographer's office for some snaps posing with their guns. Fun ended quickly when a police officer approached and, according to him, the men immediately drew guns and fled back towards Big Hill. The cop spread the news and rallied white men to leave their jobs to form a mob. About one hundred white men answered the call. Chief of Police Paul Gleason deputized them all in a mass action, and within a few minutes they all took off down the railroad tracks in pursuit of the Black men.

About halfway between Iron Gate and Clifton Forge, no more than a mile outside of town, the two groups met. Gunshots reverberated across Iron Gate Gorge as both parties fired away. At least a half dozen men in total were struck by bullets, though nobody could say for sure who shot whom or who fired first. Robert Burton sustained a debilitating leg injury, and both John Scott and Miller Morton received glancing shots. One white mob member, Philip Bowling, was killed and another injured severely. The white mob eventually captured Burton, Scott, Morton, and the uninjured C. W. Miller and escorted all four to the Clifton Forge jail. John Scott's brother Robert was supposedly shot too and died later that day of gunshot wounds, but reporters were never able to verify.[11]

A larger mob formed after sundown. About three hundred white men gathered to demand Mayor Thomas Bowles release all Black prisoners to the mob. The mayor assented, only requesting the mob "go quietly about the work in hand and not to allow [the] men to yell or fire off their pistols, as ladies and children in the immediate vicinity were screaming from fright." Scott, Morton, and Miller were then forced to nearby Slaughterpen Hollow. The white men murdered Scott and Miller, then hung them from a large tree. Unsatisfied by this bloodshed, the mob returned to the jail, carried the injured Burton on a cart to the same location, taunted him with the dead bodies of his friends, and summarily murdered him in the same manner.[12] The fourth Black man, Miller Morton, was not killed that night. His survival was meant by the white mob to "prove" they demonstrated fairness by sparing the youngest captive, though Morton was ordered never to return to the area lest he too be killed. Local African Americans gathered the mutilated bodies the next day for a burial not recorded in local records.[13]

White newspaper narratives the next day claimed the Black men aimed to "take the town" and "intended to paint the town red." Articles also noted local white residents feared African American reprisals that would "raid Clifton Forge and take revenge for the lynching of the desperadoes."[14] The reverend of the largest white church in town canceled services and encouraged the men of the congregation to stand guard throughout town with weapons drawn. Mayor Thomas Bowles called on the governor to send the militia, to which the Monticello Guard responded within the matter of hours. However, seeing there was no actual threat, the guard left town on the first train the next morning.[15] With the departure of twenty-two militiamen and no pending "raid," the Clifton Forge lynching was over, but white mob violence kept threatening African Americans for decades.

The *Clifton Forge Review* reported "almost another lynching" took place later that same year. White men tied a noose, intending to kill a Black man unnamed by newspapers, but the Clifton Forge mayor shipped the man to the Covington jail about ten miles away and the mob dissipated.[16] In response to these events, hundreds of Black men left the area over the next five years as Pittsburgh-based labor recruiters promised better jobs away from southern violence.[17] Threats of violence continued as evidenced by an incident in 1903 when authorities transferred William and Otto Green, two Black men accused of shooting a white man, from the Covington jail to Lynchburg. At least 150 men gathered at the depot in Clifton Forge to stop the train as it passed, remove the Greens, and murder them. Virginia militia volunteers failed to stop the mob from forming. The train continued through town unabated as shots rang out. Passengers and crew hit the floor as dozens of bullets pierced the train. Journalists later reported that Conductor Jack Hall found three bullet holes in his clothes later that day.[18]

Elsewhere in Virginia during the 1890s, lynching violence further escalated and finally resulted in action from elected officials. The 1893 Roanoke Riot especially drew attention and was the main reason for governors Philip McKinney and Charles O'Ferrall to denounce extralegal violence and call for a recommitment to legal processes. In theory, white Virginians listened to these governors (especially O'Ferrall and his aggressive demands made of local mayors and sheriffs), as there officially were no lynchings in the Commonwealth for two years after the Roanoke Riot. However, no antilynching legislative support followed, which meant white mobs could freely continue their gruesome acts with little fear of criminal charges. The judicial branch of government, perhaps sensing that O'Ferrall was motivated by economics and social decorum rather than human rights, instead took up the charge. Racial terror would continue in places like Clifton Forge—it would just take a slightly different form.[19]

Colonel Parsons and George Downey (1894)

When he ascended to a position of local leadership, Judge Anderson both inherited and sought to further develop a lynching community. A careful reading of the 1901–2 Virginia Constitutional Convention and a few prejudgeship perspectives provide insight into Anderson's racial sensibilities beyond his harsh rulings against Black men. Perhaps Anderson's greatest career honor was to represent Alleghany, Bath, and Highland Counties at the 1901–2 Virginia Constitutional Convention, a meeting explicitly called to rewrite the state constitution to disenfranchise Black Virginians. A defining moment of the convention came, for instance, with Carter Glass's loud proclamation: "Discrimination! Why that is exactly what we propose." George Anderson was in the room for such statements, though he spent more time quietly drafting anti-Black legal frameworks and presenting his arguments. For example, Anderson argued against compulsory poll taxes, which many other delegates favored, because they would be ineffective in achieving Black disenfranchisement:

The negro you are trying to reach is not the married negro with a horse and wagon and a cow and household property, but he is the single negro who floats about from one part of the Commonwealth to another, upon whom you cannot lay your hand, whose name you do not know, and all of them are alike. The people who you will hit with this amendment will be the poor white people of the Commonwealth. The treasurer will go to their homes and collect upon their personal property, and every time he cannot collect the capitation tax, the common schools of the Commonwealth will suffer.[20]

In other words, the Commonwealth needed to be more direct in targeting a specific class of Black men first while not harming equally impoverished whites.

Judge Anderson's sensibilities similarly reveal themselves in comparing highly similar cases where the only differences are the defendant's race. One morning in Clifton Forge in 1894, Thomas Goodman, a white railroad conductor, shot and killed former railroad magnate Col. Henry Parsons. Goodman then immediately walked to the police department, handed over his gun, and admitted guilt. Given that Colonel Parsons was in the process of opening Natural Bridge as a tourist destination, the crime and case became a Virginia media sensation. Anderson was hired to be Goodman's local lawyer and served on an expensive murder defense team likely funded by railroad workers. However, the trial did not go according to plan. An Alleghany County jury convicted Goodman of murder and Judge C. F. Moore handed down an eighteen-year sentence.

Also in 1894, the *Richmond Planet* reported that George Downey—a white forty-year-old mason from Clifton Forge—committed the heinous crime of raping his daughter. *Richmond Planet* editors encouraged Black readers to follow the Downey case as it would surely be a bellwether. If Downey were acquitted or if charges were dismissed, it would be a telling sign of social and judicial inequality: Black men had been lynched for far less. Local authorities arrested Downey and charged him with crimes that could potentially carry the death penalty, yet no lynch mob formed. The *Clifton Forge Review* assured its readership that while the accusations against Downey were "grave" and a "shocking outrage," there were "palliating circumstances connected with the affair," so residents should restrain from judgment. The crime itself took place in neighboring Rockbridge County, so jurisdictional confusions clouded prosecution and delayed court action for several weeks.[21]

By the end of the following year, both Downey and Goodman walked free despite each man's obvious guilt. In Downey's case the commonwealth's attorney coerced the young victim to sign statements disavowing earlier accusations, then the Rockbridge County judge forced her to testify in open court. With the daughter's accusations removed from evidence, Downey was ultimately acquitted. No lynch mobs chased after Downey either, further displaying the hypocrisy of mob justice. Anderson himself made no public comment on the case. As for the Goodman murder, Anderson and the defense team secured a retrial with a change of venue due to a few incorrect jury instructions. A new trial with a Charlottesville jury returned a not guilty verdict by reason of self-defense of reputation, a highly unusual and not entirely legal defense. Nonetheless, the acquittal stuck, and Goodman was a free man. Local railroad workers overwhelmingly supported Goodman throughout the trials, so the successful defense made Anderson a folk hero to many. Later accounts of the trial specifically cited Anderson delivering "one of the ablest speeches ever made before that court" as key to Goodman's freedom and Anderson's local stardom. The judge in the first trial, C. F. Moore, quit his position less than a year later to become a minister, possibly out of disgust for the Goodman appeal result. With that, the Alleghany County judgeship was suddenly open for Anderson's taking.[22]

Henry Magruder (1896)

When Anderson described the rootless, "single negro" as being one of a distinct type at the 1901–2 constitutional convention, he was certainly remembering Henry Magruder—the only man as of 1902 that Anderson had sentenced to death. Magruder's case was a test, both for Anderson as his first capital trial as a judge and of Alleghany County as a supposed "postlynching" society. Early in the morning of April 14, 1896, most men in Longdale Station departed for their jobs at local iron mines and furnaces. Not thirty minutes after their group departure, two separate incidents took place at nearly the same time—a Black man gathering firewood found his thirteen-year-old daughter dead, obviously murdered, and a white woman yelled from her porch that she had just been sexually assaulted in her own home. Witnesses reported a young Black man fleeing the scene at both locations. A mob gathered within a few minutes composed of both white and Black locals intent on finding the culprits. Men from as far away as Staunton also traveled to Clifton Forge hoping to find and kill whoever committed these horrors.

The mob soon homed in on Henry Magruder, an eighteen-year-old Black man who had recently arrived in Longdale Station looking for work.[23] Having found no job prospects, Magruder slept at a rail-side camp for two months and loitered in a nearby barroom. At Magruder's eventual trial, several white and Black witnesses positively identified Magruder as the man seen fleeing both scenes. The Longdale Station mob never found Magruder on April 14 as he fled along the railroad tracks towards Clifton Forge. Later that evening a railroad employee spotted Magruder hiding in an abandoned shack; he wore neither shoes nor hat and was acting "suspicious." The railroad employee called the police, who then arrested Magruder and quietly escorted him to the Covington jail. About fifty men gathered in Clifton Forge to lynch Magruder that evening, thinking he was in jail there, but gave up when they realized their error.[24]

Magruder's trial began in Judge Anderson's courtroom about four weeks later. The Commonwealth charged Magruder with the assault of the white woman, a capital offense, and chose not to file murder charges related to the death of Ellen Wheeler, the young Black girl.[25] Judge Anderson instructed the jury that no rape charges had been filed, but a conviction could be delivered if the jury believed such a crime had been proven throughout trial proceedings.[26] Despite the possibility of a death sentence, Magruder's court-appointed lawyer was assigned so late in the process he had less than one day to prepare while the prosecution had a month.[27] Regardless, Magruder's lawyer outlined a competent defense, the strongest component being that the perpetrator was initially believed to be a light-skinned, heavyset African American man, while Magruder was of a darker complexion and was slightly built at 5 foot 3 inches and 131 pounds. When speaking to journalists or through his lawyer, Magruder consistently denied any direct involvement in either incident.[28]

In less than an hour, the jury returned a guilty verdict for assault and attempted rape (a new charge) and recommended the death penalty. Judge Anderson agreed and set an execution date of June 19, 1896. Magruder's last recorded words again proclaimed his innocence and tragically pointed to potential mental health issues: "I would rather be hung this morning than in ten days. I would rather be hung than go to the penitentiary for two years. My head is affected when the moon changes. Good bye." During and after the trial, local African Americans distanced themselves from Magruder. Local Black churches did not allow Magruder to be buried in their cemeteries; he was afforded a final resting place only when an anonymous local farmer volunteered a remote, unused corner of his farmland. With Magruder now legally killed by the state rather than a mob, Judge Anderson must have been pleased.[29]

Robert Bowles (1904)

Robert Bowles, a twenty-two-year-old African American man, was on his third day of work as a yard brakeman with the C&O in Clifton Forge.[30] In the early hours of March 21, 1904, John Ruff, a veteran C&O fireman, incorrectly parked a locomotive such that it would be sideswiped by any passing train, so it needed to be moved quickly. Yard Conductor Albert White suspected there may be a problem with Ruff's parking, so he sent Bowles to check on the situation. Bowles recognized the problem and, per his job, instructed Ruff to shut down his engine. According to later reports, he yelled to Ruff over the roaring engines: "Move that engine quick; if you don't we are going to hit it."[31]

Fireman Ruff, upon hearing Bowles's instructions, dismounted his locomotive. Ruff and Bowles exchanged words. Nobody was close enough to hear specifically what was said, but several witnesses saw what Bowles did next—he drew a pistol and fired five shots. Ruff died of his wounds later that night. Within minutes, Bowles skipped town, fearing a lynching, and rightly so. Several newspapers reported that "men are scouring the country with rifles, and if the negro is captured, he will be lynched." Bowles made it as far as Huttonsville, West Virginia, where he was identified and taken into custody by the police. After his West Virginia arrest, he was quietly transported to Lynchburg to avoid Alleghany County mobs.[32]

In the following weeks, Bowles insisted that he was defending himself from Ruff. By his account the white man swung a pick handle and knocked Bowles to the ground, something unreported by white witnesses. Bruises were still visible on Bowles' body nearly two weeks later according to journalists, though these never formally documented or entered into evidence.

The other narrative, created by Ruff's white coworkers, was based on Ruff's supposed last words spoken to yard conductor Albert White: "I just asked him what he meant by it, and that is all the words I ever had with him." A doctor who tended Ruff's wounds claimed that six hours after the shooting, Ruff said Bowles "gave him a lot of sass" but denied assaulting or threatening Bowles. This was all the evidence the state had upon which to base its case—the word of a Black man versus that of a few whites.[33]

Judge Anderson's court moved swiftly and erroneously. An all-white jury convicted Bowles after eleven minutes of deliberation based on the testimony of Albert White and a cynical interpretation of Bowles's decision to flee town. Judge Anderson sentenced Bowles to death by hanging with an execution date set for June 24, 1904.[34] Bowles's lawyers appealed and won on the grounds of improper jury instructions by Judge Anderson. Such instructions reveal one of few glimpses into the inner workings of Judge Anderson's Jim Crow court. In short, Judge Anderson instructed jurors that they must find Bowles guilty of first-degree murder if they believed he "drew a pistol from his pocket and shot the deceased, giving to him a mortal wound." However, the rest of the instructions outlined the prosecution's series of events, forcing the jury to attribute truth to the prosecution's timeline (as opposed to an alternate timeline forwarded by the defense). For instance, Judge Anderson asserted that Bowles sat down his tools and shot Ruff, a statement at odds with Bowles's defense, and instructions did not allow the jury to consider Ruff's demeanor as a cause of self-defense. Anderson also instructed that first-degree murder was a valid charge despite premeditation never having been proven by the prosecution. The Virginia Supreme Court appeal granted a new trial, a huge victory for Bowles, but the appeal did not grant a change of venue that would have allowed escape from Judge Anderson.[35]

A new murder trial began in Judge Anderson's court in January 1905.[36] The second trial was much like the first; the only significant change was Judge Anderson's jury instructions, which were less specific and without legal error. An all-white jury again found Bowles guilty, and Judge Anderson issued a death sentence. Bowles's lawyers appealed, but the state supreme court did not grant a retrial this time. Local African Americans sympathetic to Bowles's plight petitioned the governor to stay the execution, but they were unsuccessful.[37]

On March 17, 1905, the state carried out Judge Anderson's sentence and killed Bowles. He died at 6:41 a.m. before a small crowd just outside of the county courthouse in Covington.[38] Bowles penned a written statement on the day of his death in which he yet again stated the shooting was in self-defense. Local Black clergymen led the predominantly African American crowd in hymn singing and recitations of the Lord's Prayer. Displaying "remarkable nerve" according to local newspapers, Bowles thanked the crowd, asked that his possessions be delivered to his mother, and stated that he hoped to meet everyone again in Heaven.[39]

Ben Hubbard and Robert Lewis (1906)

Only a year after Bowles's execution, Judge Anderson presided over near simultaneous trials that convicted two Black men—Ben Hubbard and Robert Lewis—of two unrelated capital crimes committed in separate iron mining communities on opposite sides of Clifton Forge. Hubbard was accused of murdering Robert Brown in Low Moor, and Lewis was accused of murdering Gilmer White in Longdale. As in the case of Henry Magruder, both Hubbard and Lewis were rushed through court, convicted, and set to be executed by hanging. Judge Anderson sentenced both to hang on the same day, June 28, 1906, to make the state-sanctioned killings even more efficient.[40]

Immediately after the trials, according to the *Evening News*, a broad movement began to petition the governor to intervene. Hopes were that Lewis would receive a retrial or at least have his sentence commuted to life imprisonment. The reason for this was because a large group of local African Americans believed Lewis acted in self-defense and did not intend to kill. In addition, new eyewitnesses came forward willing to testify as such. Though details were scant in newspaper reports, Lewis's support must have reached high political offices. Judge Anderson and the commonwealth's attorney office both recommended commutation to the governor's office within a matter of weeks. Gov. Claude Swanson heard these pleas and agreed. He first stayed the execution five days before its set date, giving Lewis a thirty-day respite, then commuted the sentence to life imprisonment after a short deliberation. Lewis spent the rest of his life confined in the state penitentiary.[41]

Ben Hubbard did not have such community support and was not so lucky. There was no mass movement to secure a governor's pardon, and so his execution date arrived unimpeded. The Commonwealth executed Hubbard in Covington on June 28, 1906. Newspapers reported "no excitement" at the event. Hubbard supposedly confessed the details of the murder to spiritual advisors, but he chose not to speak at all on the scaffold or leave a written account. No known record exists detailing whether Judge Anderson attended the event or not.[42]

Aurelius Christian (1909)

In the late winter of 1909, Aurelius Christian was a seventeen-year-old Black youth living in Glen Wilton, a rural community in neighboring Botetourt County a few miles outside of Clifton Forge. His life came under threat when a lynch mob accused Christian of two crimes: assaulting an "Italian woman" and murdering Mary Dobbs, a fourteen-year-old white girl found dead in the woods earlier that day. Christian, knowing what fate would befall him if the mob found him, took off out of town towards Clifton Forge, probably trying to escape into West Virginia. He did not make it that far. A different group captured Christian near Clifton Forge and turned him over to authorities. Judge Anderson appeared to personally escort Christian from the Clifton Forge area to Fincastle, the location of the jail and courthouse in Botetourt County. Even though Anderson and Christian had to pass near Glen Wilton along their path, no mob appeared to interrupt the judge's task. The editor of the *Staunton Dispatch and News* took the opportunity to applaud the supposed restraint of mobs in Glen Wilton and Clifton Forge: "The highest praise that can be bestowed on any community is to say that under the greatest provocation to act otherwise, it insists that the law shall take its course. Plausible arguments are frequently advanced by taking the law into one's own hands under certain circumstances, but they are only plausible. There can be no sound argument on behalf of any course outside the law and outside the moral code. Liberty under law is the only genuine liberty. When we break over, it takes years of penance to make amends."[43] In court, Judge Anderson presided over what was now a standard procedure for Black defendants.

Aurelius Christian had three public defenders assigned to him by Judge Anderson with none granted more than a few minutes to prepare a defense. The public defenders then waived Christian's right to a jury trial because Christian supposedly confessed his crime in the lawyers' presence. According to them, Christian admitted to stealing a knife from the Glen Wilton iron furnaces, running into the woods to hide, then killing Mary Dobbs because she discovered his hiding place. No other details explaining Christian's plot were provided to make this story coherent. The state called three witnesses, each of whom identified Christian as the perpetrator, and Judge Anderson delivered a guilty verdict and a death sentence. The total elapsed time from the first accusation in Glen Wilton to Judge Anderson's final courtroom gavel was less than twenty-four hours. A few weeks later, on March 22, 1909, the Commonwealth carried out Aurelius Christian's sentence in Fincastle by electric chair. He had not yet turned eighteen.[44]

Edmund Thompson (1922)

In Fincastle on the morning of December 17, 1920, a group of white teenagers threw some firecrackers at Edmund Thompson, a Black man in his late twenties. Thompson responded by shooting several bullets into a crowd, killing one boy and severely injuring three other people. Police arrested Thompson later that night, but not until after a lengthy chase by a white mob and multiple attempts to wrest Thompson from authorities for a lynching. As police led Thompson to jail, someone in the mob fired a gun and Thompson fell, apparently gravely wounded. The crowd cheered, then slowly dispersed, believing Thompson dead or dying. Suddenly, Thompson leapt to his feet and bolted into the woods—his game of possum clearly worked. Despite such cleverness, a farmer spotted Thompson a few days later, and he was caught by a mob for a second time. Newspapers reported Thompson had trouble speaking and could not properly move his limbs for several weeks after this second mob severely beat him.[45]

Thompson then found himself on trial in Judge Anderson's court. The defense presented a weak case; Thompson himself testified that he believed he had fired his gun over the teenagers' heads to scare them. A jury returned a first-degree murder guilty verdict within an hour. Anderson sentenced

Thompson to the electric chair to be carried out at the state penitentiary on May 6, 1921. The *Richmond Planet* denounced the verdict and sentence, stating simply that premeditation was impossible when Thompson was responding to an assault on himself.

To the surprise of many newspaper editors, the state supreme court granted a stay hours before the execution with the approval of Gov. Westmoreland Davis. Governor Davis did not grant a pardon or commutation and instead chose to delay, thus forcing a potential pardon decision for his successor.[46] That successor, Elbert Trinkle, entered the governor's office February 1, 1922. One of his first actions was to deny Thompson's pardon and commutation. With no reprieve granted, the execution was rescheduled, so the Commonwealth killed Edmund Thompson on February 7, 1922.[47]

To understand lynching—a group action by definition—one must also understand the role of the individual. It is largely impossible to tease out the role of any individual in a typical lynching story. Mobs act almost like a single organism. Surely there were ringleaders in every mob, but historians rarely have any ability to interpret this historical phenomenon. It simply never entered the historic record. Instead, we look to civic leadership. Mayors, sheriffs, police officers, jailors, judges—these social roles have often been dissected by excellent historians seeking insight. The deep dive presented here has illustrated the power held by a single man—George Anderson—who could have ended racial injustice, including lynching, at any point. He simply chose to perpetuate injustice at every turn.

There was no question that Judge Anderson shaped the judicial process in Alleghany, Bath, Botetourt, Craig, and Highland Counties for thirty-five years. Some white defendants were exonerated based on their own testimony, while Black defendants were put to death on minimal evidence. Anderson used a similar bag of legal tricks in all six capital trials with Black defendants: a hurried timeline, no time granted to defense counsel, sketchy jury instructions, and executions scheduled as quickly as possible. All was done in the name of stamping out lynching. Judge Anderson clearly fit within sociologist E. M. Beck's definition of white southerners who prevented lynchings to "assert the state's right to monopolize and arbitrate the administration of justice and to deny legitimacy of the mob as an agent of social control." Lynch law was simply incorporated into Judge Anderson's criminal justice system, as was rapidly becoming the reality throughout the South during the early twentieth century.⁴⁸

Anderson's white lawyering peers did not see his flaws and likely viewed them as assets rather than flaws. F. W. King, who eulogized Anderson after his sudden illness and death in 1930, described him as "the soul of sympathy," "kind and considerate," and "a Christian gentleman and useful citizen." King further noted, "The rare intervals at which the judgement of Judge Anderson was reversed by the Supreme Court of Appeals constitutes a greater compliment to his judicial capacity and to his keen legal judgement and intuition than any words of mine could possibly convey."⁴⁹ The same newspaper issue that printed F. W. King's fond memories, the *Covington Virginian,* ran an editorial similarly praising Judge Anderson and linking his legacy to that of Virginia's earlier Great White Men, especially those of the Civil War generation:

> We of this generation probably have been too prone to believe that all great Virginians passed with the close of the Civil War. It has been so markedly the habit of older folks to stress the great deeds of the giants of that trying period in the history of our beloved State, when the tented field was the scene of their achievements, that we are forgetful of that old adage that "peace hath her victories no less than war." Furthermore, the maintenance of that peace during the trying decades between 1870 and 1900 demanded, in some respects, an even greater courage, certainly a greater moral courage, than the four epochal years of war. Distinctly a product of this trying period to which we have just alluded, was Hon. Judge George K. Anderson.⁵⁰

The "moral courage" referenced was Anderson's efforts to roll back civil rights in Virginia as much as possible while also asserting state control over African Americans. Judge Anderson executed Black men, helped draft the discriminatory state constitution, and helped along the local Lost Cause.

In 1911 Alleghany County built a new courthouse. Local newspaper reports often referred to Anderson as the new courthouse "boss," as he was the highest-ranking court official in the area. A courthouse dedication ceremony was planned with Judge Anderson likely in full control over its contents. The ceremony itself was a full celebration of white supremacy and Lost Cause sensibilities. If one were to stand on stage next to Anderson, off to the crowd's side was a grandstand of three hundred white school children dressed in red, white, and blue arranged to depict the Confederate flag stars and bars.⁵¹

A second ceremony immediately followed the courthouse dedication with Anderson as the official master of ceremonies. The United Daughters of the Confederacy donated a Confederate monument to Alleghany County, received formally by Judge Anderson, that was then placed immediately adjacent to the new courthouse entrance. Children led the crowd in song, primarily Confederate nostalgia tunes such as "Tenting To-night" and "Bonnie Blue Flag." Speakers included several Confederate veterans, local lawyers, and Col. R. E. Lee, grandson of the Confederate general. According to several newspapers, also in attendance were the Covington Band, the Staunton Stonewall Brigade Band, even more Confederate veterans, financial sponsors, local officials, and unnamed "secret orders."[52]

As of 2024, the Confederate monument still stands atop a granite pillar in front of a new jail-courthouse complex in downtown Covington. In the fall of 2020 Alleghany County, with the support of the City of Covington and Town of Clifton Forge, organized the Alleghany Commission on Racial Equality (CORE) to address inequalities and inequities in employment, policing, education, housing, and other areas of concern. One of CORE's first tasks was to address the Confederate monument, though no definitive actions had been taken as of early 2024. Judge Anderson's legacy still quite literally stands in front of and above the county courthouse, just as his photograph hangs on the walls of the courtroom itself.

Episodes like the courthouse dedication clearly broadcasted to the white public that Judge Anderson was on their side. He leveraged his power by bringing lynchings out of the streets and into the courtroom. Shortly after Judge Anderson sentenced Aurelius Christian to death, mobs gathered in Clifton Forge intent to lynch, but ultimately called it off "while he was at that place," meaning the Fincastle jail under Anderson's watch. The judge had it all under control.[53] With the Edmund Thompson case, two separate white mobs had ample opportunity to kill Thompson. One white man obviously tried, but this attempt was more assassination than mob lynching. Thompson was held in local jails for over a year with no further reported lynching attempts. The white community decision not to try to lynch Thompson was more likely deference to their judicial ally Anderson than any change of heart. In effect, Judge Anderson legalized lynching, so long as the mobs allowed the process to play out in county courthouse over a few weeks.[54]

When Anderson distinguished between the "single negro" and "married negro" at the 1901–2 constitutional convention, he implied most Black men fell within the latter category. Henry Magruder and Aurelius Christian were, without question, examples of the "single negro" Anderson believed were harming white Virginia. Anderson spoke with frustration in 1902 when he opined the "single negro" was a character "upon whom you cannot lay your hand." This supposed class featured Black men who were elusive and lived at the fringe of society, in Anderson's view—so he deployed the Commonwealth's power to "lay his hand" whenever a chance arose. Anderson's courtroom was hardly a unique place in early twentieth century Jim Crow Virginia, thanks to the growing influence of eugenicists in law and psychology and a sudden increase in execution rates (including juvenile Black boys like Aurelius Christian).[55]

Anderson's career is also a reminder of how Jim Crow laws, lynch mobs, sham executions, and eugenics all existed in support of one another to create a society that benefited white men at the expense of African Americans. More specifically, a deep look at Judge Anderson's capital cases reveals a local culture of racialized terrorism where Black men were under constant threat of legal execution.[56] As articulated in Michael Pfeifer's *Rough Justice*, the lynch mob still had power in practice if not on paper as "real justice was lodged in the community." White communities consented to systematically administered capital punishment, so long as the community approved of those determining targets that would perpetuate a white social order.[57] In other words, capital punishment replaced lynching in Alleghany County because residents approved of Judge Anderson's jurisprudence.

Similarly, Judge Anderson's capital cases also demonstrate the utter futility of the death penalty. Six Black men were sentenced to death in his court. All six cases still have unanswered questions, but fully half—the cases of Bowles, Lewis, and Thompson—were indefensible wrongs given the fact that each mounted both successful and nearly successful legal challenges during the height of Jim Crow Virginia. For example, Robert Bowles won a retrial, which was a remarkable damning of Judge Anderson's jurisprudence, even though Bowles ultimately died by Anderson's ruling in the end. The dark irony in all of this was that there were glimpses of hope through walls erected by Jim Crow. Robert Lewis's life was spared, though his freedom taken, and Thompson nearly so, but for an incoming governor wanted to appear tough on crime by taking a Black life.

The final takeaway is that George Kimbrough Anderson personally made the greater Clifton Forge area a more dangerous place for Black men, both the innocent and guilty, even though he technically eliminated lynching violence. Judge Anderson was hardly unique to the Commonwealth—surely dozens more racist judges also had blood on their hands—but he was unique to the Alleghany Highlands area in that he definitively took racial terror from the unsavory hands of the lynch mobs into the solemn walls of his courtroom. The new tool of white supremacy was the cruel, arbitrary commination of the death penalty towards the "negro(es) you are trying to reach . . . the single negro who floats about from one part of the Commonwealth to another, upon whom you cannot lay your hand, whose name you do not know, and all of them are alike," to reuse Judge Anderson's parlance. Any Black man conforming to this narrow view was targeted, and Judge Anderson made sure they had no judicial recourse for decades to come.

Notes

1. W. Fitzhugh Brundage, *Lynching in the New South: Georgia and Virginia: 1880–1930* (Urbana: University of Illinois Press, 1993); Amy Louise Wood, *Lynching and Spectacle* (Chapel Hill: University of North Carolina Press, 2011); Crystal Feimster, *Southern Horrors: Woman and the Politics of Race and Lynching* (Cambridge, MA: Harvard University Press, 2009); Stewart Tolnay and E. M. Beck, *A Festival of Violence: An Analysis of Southern Lynchings, 1882–1930* (Urbana: University of Illinois Press, 1995).
2. "Mob at Roanoke," *Clifton Forge Review* (hereafter cited as *CFR*), Sept. 23, 1893; "The Roanoke Riot," *CFR*, Sept. 29, 1893; Rand Dotson, *Roanoke, Virginia, 1882–1912: Magic City in the New South* (Knoxville: University of Tennessee Press, 2008); Ann Field Alexander, "'Like an Evil Wind': The Roanoke Riot of 1893 and the Lynching of Thomas Smith," *Virginia Magazine of History and Biography* 100, no. 2 (Apr. 1992): 173–206.
3. Elizabeth Hicks Corron, *Clifton Forge, Virginia* (Roanoke, VA: Stone Print, 1971), 19.
4. Corron, *Clifton Forge*, 55.
5. Roy C. Long, "Railroad Recollections," *Hinton News*, Dec. 5, 1989.
6. A strong community memory of the 1891 lynching exists with many African American residents of Clifton Forge, especially those whose ancestors were from the area. Evidence of this memory is apparent through community public history projects, such as the "What's Your Story?" oral history initiative and the successful grassroots effort to save Green Pastures, the nation's only historically segregated recreation area within the US Forest Service. For more on "What's Your Story?," see the official Facebook page, accessed Mar. 23, 2021, https://www.facebook.com/WhatsYourStoryVirginiasAlleghanyHighlands/.
7. From census records, Alleghany County reported an overall population of 5,586 with 1,132 Blacks (20.2 percent) in 1880; 9,283 with 2,328 Blacks (25.1 percent) in 1890; and 16,330

with 4,015 Blacks (24.6 percent) in 1900. Roanoke reported 4,929 (30.5 percent) Black residents out of 16,159 overall in 1890 and 5,834 out of 21,495 (27.1 percent) in 1900. Just 1,829 (8.8 percent) Blacks lived in Alleghany's West Virginia neighbor, Greenbrier County, out of 20,683 residents in 1900. The Virginia counties of Augusta (17.6 percent), Bath (18 percent), Botetourt (22.6 percent), Craig (6.1 percent), Highland (6.7 percent), and Rockbridge (18.7 percent) as well as the cities of Staunton (25.1 percent) and Buena Vista (17.1 percent) all had statistically less or equal proportionally Black demography compared to Alleghany. Census records of the 1880–1900 period did not draw borders for the Clifton Forge district that clearly matched the town borders, but estimates can be made from school populations. In 1891 there were 992 white schoolchildren (and sixteen schools) versus 487 enrolled in the five Black schools in the Clifton Forge district; the Covington district population ratio was slightly lower with 676 white and 288 Black, while the more rural Boiling Springs district had 747 white schoolchildren and just 17 African Americans with zero Black schools. Campbell Gibson and Kay Jung, "Historical Census Statistics on Population Totals by Race, 1790 to 1990, and by Hispanic Origin, 1970 to 1990, for Large Cities and Other Urban Places in the United States," US Census Bureau, Population Working Paper No. 76 (Washington, DC, Feb. 2005), University of Virginia, Geospatial and Statistical Data Center, Historical Census Browser (2004), retrieved 2016, http://mapserver.lib.virginia.edu/collections/; US Census, vol. 3, *Population, Reports by State (Virginia)*, 1890, 1900, 1910; Oren Frederic Morton, *A Centennial History of Alleghany County, Virginia* (Dayton, VA: J. K. Ruebush Co., 1923), 80; from *CFR*: "Sent to Jail," Nov. 20, 1891; "Highway Robbery," Oct. 27, 1893; "Attempted Robbery," Nov. 3, 1893; "The Thieves in Jail," Jan. 26, 1894.

8. Reading law was commonplace during this era, especially in a rural Virginia County like Louisa. Anderson studied under Capt. H. W. Murray and was admitted to the bar in 1881. He and Murray formed a partnership soon after.

9. "George K. Anderson," *1930 Annual Reports of the Virginia Bar Association*, 1–4; Louisa County Order Book, 1887–92, 429; *Men of Mark in Virginia: Ideals of American Life; a Collection of Biographies of the Leading Men in the State* (Richmond, VA: Men of Mark Publishing Co., 1908).

10. A little over a year later, Pugh was convicted of embezzlement, having stolen postal funds in his new role as postmaster at Clifton Forge. *Shenandoah Herald*, Mar. 30, 1881; *Staunton Spectator*, Mar. 22, 1881, May 3, 1881, May 20, 1881, Oct. 3, 1882.

11. Bowling's life insurance company refused to pay out to the widow on the grounds that the policy did not cover death due to riot. A compromise was eventually reached where the company paid out $250, which was half of the policy. "Compromise Effected," *CFR*, May 20, 1892.

12. "The Clifton Forge Tragedy," *Roanoke Times*, Oct. 20, 1891; *Public Opinion: A Comprehensive Survey of the Press throughout the World on All Important Topics*, vol. 12 (1892), 72.

13. The bodies of C. W. Miller and John Scott were sent to Big Hill for burial. Robert Burton was buried on a nearby hill in an unmarked grave. (Clifton Forge) *Valley Virginian*, Oct. 22, 1891; unknown author, "An Account of the Clifton Forge Lynching" (Covington, VA: Alleghany Genealogical Society, undated [ca. 1940]); "The Clifton Forge Tragedy," *Roanoke Times*, Oct. 20, 1891; *Richmond Times-Dispatch*, Oct. 17. 1891; *Richmond Planet*, Oct. 31, 1891; Brundage, *Lynching in the New South*, 146–48.

14. "The Clifton Forge Tragedy," *Roanoke Times*, Oct. 20, 1891.

15. T. P. Bowles to Governor McKinney, Oct. 18, 1891, *Annual Report of Officers, Boards, and Institutions of the Commonwealth of Virginia for the Year Ending September 30, 1891: Report of the Adjutant General* (Richmond: J. H. O'Bannon, 1891), 8, 67–68.
16. White mobs and political leaders generally excluded Black residents from society and left them alone so long as their actions did not infringe upon white society, such as with the "Colored People's Fourth" hosted by the Black Baptist church in town. "The Colored People's Fourth," *CFR*, July 15, 1892; "Almost Another Lynching!," *CFR*, Nov. 13, 1891.
17. *CFR*, July 20, 1894.
18. "To Prosecute Mob Men," *Norfolk Landmark*, Aug. 4, 1903; *Independent Herald*, Aug. 6, 1903; "Negroes in Jail at Bedford City," *Evening News*, Aug. 4, 1903; *Richmond Planet*, Aug. 8, 1903.
19. *CFR*, May 9, 1894; "The Staunton Post," *CFR*, May 11, 1894; Ann Field Alexander, *Race Man: The Rise and Fall of the "Fighting Editor" John Mitchell Jr.* (Charlottesville: University of Virginia Press, 2002), 53–54.
20. *Report of the Proceedings and Debates of the Constitutional Convention, State of Virginia Held in the City of Richmond June 12, 1901, to June 26, 1902*, vol. 2 (1906), 2866.
21. "Shocking Outrage," *CFR*, June 1, 1894; "A White Man's Crime," *Richmond Planet*, June 9, 1894; "A White Brute Indicted," *Richmond Planet*, June 16, 1894; "Downey Indicted for Rape," *Staunton Spectator*, June 13, 1894; "Assaulted His Daughter," *Roanoke Times*, May 31, 1894; "Downey Jailed in Lexington," *Richmond Times-Dispatch*, June 1, 1894; "Not Guilty," *Staunton Spectator*, June 20, 1894; "Downey Indicted for Rape," *Staunton Spectator*, June 13, 1894.
22. "Death of Judge Anderson," newspaper clipping, Louisa County Historical Society (Acc. 2012.08.072).
23. Henry Magruder provided several different names to police, including Henry Thompson, Henry Armistead, Henry Shephard, and George Armistead, and his identity was never publicly confirmed. Since he was referred to as "Henry Magruder" in his murder trial, that is the name used here.
24. "Lust and Murder," *CFR*, Apr. 17, 1896; *Commonwealth v. Henry Magruder*, Alleghany County, VA (1896).
25. No clear reason was provided as to why the Commonwealth declined to charge Magruder with the murder of Ellen Wheeler. A possible reason was because evidence of the sexual assault was clear with several witnesses, including the victim, while the only witness in the Wheeler murder was Wheeler's father, who only saw Magruder fleeing the general area. Magruder also claimed he had witnessed another man kill Wheeler, so the murder was a more difficult case to prosecute.
26. No other cases from any other secondary source parallel the instructions given by Judge Anderson in the Magruder case. Sources consulted include: Diane Miller Sommerville, *Rape and Race in the Nineteenth Century South* (Chapel Hill: University of North Carolina Press, 2004); Lisa Lindquist Dorr, *White Women, Rape, and the Power of Race in Virginia, 1900–1960* (Chapel Hill: University of North Carolina Press, 2004); Peter Wallenstein, *Tell the Court I Love My Wife: Race, Marriage, and Law—An American History* (New York: Palgrave Macmillan, 2002); and Suzanne Lebsock, *A Murder in Virginia: Southern Justice on Trial* (New York: Norton, 2003).
27. Henry's court-appointed defense counsel was J. C. King, a lawyer working in Alleghany County and based in Clifton Forge. *The American Lawyer: A Monthly Journal Serving the*

Business and Professional Interests of the American Bar (New York: Stumpf & Steurer, 1899), 598.
28. *Commonwealth v. Henry Magruder*, Alleghany County, VA (1896); from *CFR:* "Lust and Murder," Apr. 17, 1896; "Magruder Guilty," May 8, 1896; "Magruder Hanged," June 19, 1896.
29. "Magruder Hanged," *CFR*, June 19, 1896; *Commonwealth v. Henry Magruder*, Alleghany County, VA (1896).
30. Note that all newspapers except one reported Bowles was both a recent C&O hire and a recent arrival in town. The *Evening News* (Apr. 6, 1904) reported Bowles lived in Clifton Forge for seventeen years and had worked for the C&O for five years, but it is possible the report conflated Bowles's and Ruff's experience.
31. "Bowles v. Commonwealth, Supreme Court of Appeals of Virginia, 29 Sept. 1904," *Virginia Law Register* 10, no. 7 (Nov. 1904).
32. At least two other Black men in Huntington, WV, and Roanoke, VA, were also arrested on mistaken identity. "How the Fiend Killed Him," (Roanoke) *Evening News*, Mar. 22, 1904; "John A. Ruff Dies of His Wounds," *Richmond Times-Dispatch*, Mar. 23, 1904; "Ruffs Murderer May Be in Custody," *Evening News*, Mar. 25, 1904; "Held on Suspicion," *Evening News*, Apr. 2, 1904; "Virginia News," *Alexandria Gazette*, Apr. 5, 1904; "Bowles Captured," *Staunton Spectator and Vindicator*, Apr. 8, 1904; "Bowles Caught in West Virginia," *Highland Recorder*, Apr. 8, 1904; "Mob Threatens to Kill Negro Who Is in Jail at Lynchburg," *Indianapolis Journal*, Apr. 5, 1905.
33. "Bowles v. Commonwealth"; "How the Fiend Killed Him," (Roanoke) *Evening News*, Mar. 22, 1904; "Slayer of Fireman John Ruff," *Evening News*, Apr. 6, 1904.
34. "Robert Bowles to Hang," *Lexington Gazette*, Apr. 20, 1904; *Highland Recorder*, Apr. 29, 1904.
35. "Bowles v. Commonwealth"; "Many Cases Are Decided," *Richmond Times-Dispatch*, Oct. 1, 1904.
36. *Lexington Gazette*, June 8, 1904; "Criminal Cases at Covington," *Staunton Spectator and Vindicator*, Dec. 30, 1904.
37. "Robert Bowles to Hang," *Lexington Gazette*, Jan. 18, 1905; *Bedford Democrat*, Mar. 9, 1905; "Dark Outlook for Bowles," *Richmond Planet*, Mar. 18, 1905.
38. "Bowles Hung," *Richmond Times-Dispatch*, Mar. 18, 1905.
39. "Robert Bowles Hanged Friday at Covington," *Lexington Gazette*, Mar. 22, 1905; "Robert Bowles Hanged," *Bedford Democrat*, Mar. 23, 1905; "Bowles Hung," *Staunton Spectator and Vindicator*, Mar. 24, 1905.
40. *Richmond Times-Dispatch*, April 5, 1906.
41. *Staunton Spectator and Vindicator*, July 27, 1906; *Richmond Times-Dispatch*, June 26, 1906; (Roanoke) *Evening News*, July 26, 1906; "Commutations," Senate Document 3, *Journal of the Senate of the Commonwealth of Virginia Begun and Held at the Capitol in the City of Richmond on Wednesday January 8, 1908*, 41. "Respites," Senate Document 3, in ibid., 46.
42. *Lexington Gazette*, July 4, 1906; *Richmond Times-Dispatch*, June 29, 1906.
43. Reprinted in (Newport News, VA) *Daily Press*, Feb. 23, 1909.
44. "Negro Sentenced to Death Penalty," *Sacramento Union*, Feb. 20, 1909; "A Speedy Trial," *Alexandria Gazette*, Feb. 20, 1909; "Prompt Justice for this Negro," *Richmond Palladium*, Feb. 20, 1909; "Swift Justice," *Bluefield Daily Leader*, Feb. 20, 1909; *Atlanta Georgian and News*, Mar. 22, 1909.

45. "Colored Boy Shoots into Crowd of White Boys," *Richmond Planet*, Jan. 1, 1921; *World News*, Feb. 23, 1921; *World News*, Dec. 22, 1920; "Thompson Given Death Penalty," *World News*, Mar. 5, 1921.
46. *World News*, Mar. 2, 1921; "Thompson Given Death Penalty," *World News*, Mar. 5, 1921; *World News*, May 2, 1921; "Stay of Execution Granted," *World News*, May 6, 1921; "Colored Boy Shoots," *Richmond Planet*, Jan. 1, 1921; "That Fincastle Case," *Richmond Planet*, May 14, 1921.
47. "Trinkle Refuses to Save Negro," *Norfolk Post*, Feb. 6, 1922; "To Die Tomorrow," *World News*, Feb. 6, 1922; *Alexandria Gazette*, Feb. 7 and 8, 1922.
48. E. M. Beck, "South Polls: Judge Lynch Denied: Combating Mob Violence in the American South, 1877–1950," *Southern Cultures* 21, no. 2 (2015): 134–36.
49. "George K. Anderson," *1930 Annual Reports of the Virginia Bar Association*, 1–4.
50. "Editorial," *Covington Virginian*, Feb. 4, 1930.
51. *Baltimore Sun*, Apr. 4, 1916; *Richmond Times-Dispatch*, Sept. 11, 1911.
52. *Baltimore Sun*, Apr. 4, 1916; *Richmond Times-Dispatch*, Sept. 11, 1911.
53. "Prompt Justice for this Negro," *Richmond Palladium*, Feb. 20, 1909.
54. For more on legal lynching, see George C. Wright, *Racial Violence in Kentucky, 1865–1940* (Baton Rouge: Louisiana State University Press, 1990); Margaret Vandiver, *Lethal Punishment: Lynchings and Legal Executions in the South* (New Brunswick, NJ: Rutgers University Press, 2005); and Melanie S. Morrison, *Murder on Shades Mountain: The Legal Lynching of Willie Peterson and the Struggle for Justice in Jim Crow Birmingham* (Durham, NC: Duke University Press, 2018).
55. From 1787 to 1905, Virginia executed five juveniles—all Black boys—with just one occurring after emancipation. In the first quarter of the 1900s judges began sentencing Black juveniles to death, including ten such instances from 1906 to 1924 (nine boys and one girl). Todd Peppers and Laura Trevvett Anderson, *Anatomy of an Execution: The Life and Death of Douglas Christopher Thomas* (Boston: Northeastern University Press, 2009), 250; M. Watt Espy and John Ortiz Smykla, "Executions in the United States, 1608–2002: The ESPY File," Inter-university Consortium for Political and Social Research [distributor], July 20, 2016, https://doi.org/10.3886/ICPSR08451.v5; Tony G. Poveda, "Geographic Location, Death Sentences and Executions in Post-Furman Virginia," *Punishment & Society* 8, no. 4 (Oct. 2006): 423–42.
56. Stewart Tolnay and E. M. Beck, "'Racialized Terrorism' in the American South: Do Completed Lynchings Tell an Accurate Story?," *Social Science History* 42, no. 4 (Winter 2018): 677–701; Charles Seguin and David Rigby, "National Crimes: A New National Data Set of Lynchings in the United States, 1883 to 1941," *Socius* 5 (2019): 1–9.
57. Michael J. Pfeifer, *Rough Justice: Lynching and American Society, 1874–1947* (Urbana: University of Illinois Press, 2004), 7–8.

PART IV
✴
COLLECTIVE MEMORY AND MEMORIALIZATION OF LYNCHING VICTIMS

Lynching and, more generally, racial terror against minorities, has been for the most part expunged from history textbooks,[1] and its role in shaping the post-Reconstruction South is little understood. Since the demise of Lynch Law, a strain of collective amnesia has enveloped media and political institutions, alongside most white communities, regarding the history and legacy of lynching in the United States. The oblivion around the US past of racial terror not only erases the stories and humanity of the people who were killed by lynching mobs; it also provides an implicit absolution of the system of connivence that made mob violence possible and racialized terrorism a lasting feature of southern society.

In Virginia, the history of racial terror is also hardly recognized in current curricula, and Virginians are, for the most part, unaware of the past lynchings that took place in their area. However, in the past few years there have been numerous initiatives from local communities and political authorities to revive the collective memory of lynching victims and to reflect on the legacy of racial terror. In February 2019, the Virginia General Assembly unanimously passed a joint resolution that condemned all the lynchings that took place in the Commonwealth, expressing regret for the failure of state authorities to act promptly and effectively against lynch mobs.[2] At least eleven historical markers to remember lynching victims have been erected thus far throughout Virginia, while several other commemorative projects have also taken place in towns like Culpeper and Alexandria. In 2020 the African American History Education Commission (AAHEC) published a report recommending the inclusion of the history of lynching in Virginia in the K–12 History and Social Science standards.[3]

These initiatives are part of a larger national effort to finally recognize and confront the ubiquity of past racial terror and its enduring legacy today. Several museums, memorials, and digital projects have been established to document the history of lynching and white supremacist violence.[4] In 2015 the Equal Justice Initiative (EJI) sparked a public debate on the role of lynching in shaping the African American experience under Jim Crow when it released its report *Lynching in America: Confronting the Legacy of Racial Terror.* Three years later, EJI inaugurated the National Memorial for Peace and Justice in Montgomery, Alabama, a site "dedicated to the legacy of enslaved black people, people terrorized by lynching, African Americans humiliated by racial segregation and Jim Crow."[5] In 2022 the US Congress finally passed the Emmett Till Antilynching Act,[6] a law that classifies lynching as a federal hate crime. Local and national initiatives meant to remember lynching victims and reckon our uncomfortable past of racial terrorism are part of the conversation about race and justice that the Black Lives Matter movement has sparked in the past few years. In this final section of the volume, three essays discuss how local communities in Charlottesville and Alexandria are facing their past of racial terror today.

Writer and editor Brendan Wolfe's contribution, "The Train at Wood's Crossing," is a narrative essay in which the author interweaves the story of the 1898 lynching of John Henry James with his own movements through Charlottesville's landscape today. James was accused of raping a young white girl; after his arrest and indictment, he was spirited out of town and then seized from a train by a white mob and hanged. These events are set against the larger backdrop of post–Civil War racial violence and the narratives that justified it. Such narratives are still written into the modern landscape in statues, street names, and segregated neighborhoods, while the lynching, until recently, had been erased. Taking a walk through the city with his daughter, Wolfe contemplates how the city has absorbed the trauma of this violence both through remembering and forgetting. The turmoil of the past few years—the Unite the Right rally in 2017, police violence against Black people, and the Black Lives Matter movement—has begun to alter that landscape, opening up opportunities for new, more inclusive narratives.

Andrea Douglas, art historian and Executive Director of the Jefferson School African American Heritage Center in Charlottesville, has contributed "Public History as Activism: Helping a Community Come to Terms with Racial Violence." This essay looks at the public and private rhetoric associated with the lynching of John Henry James and the subsequent history of disenfranchisement of African Americans in Charlottesville, culminating in the 1920s with the rewriting of history in the public realm. Douglas further describes the process taken by the Albemarle/Charlottesville Community Remembrance project to urge the local community to reckon with the notion that the murder of Heather Heyer during the Unite the Right rally in 2017 was not an anomaly but part of a long history of white supremacist violence deployed to intimidate the local African American community. In 2019 a historical marker to memorialize John Henry James was unveiled in Charlottesville's Court Square; Douglas argues that this marker "points out the failures of the system represented by the courthouse in front of which it sits. It calls into question the very notion of justice for all."

The Alexandria Community Remembrance Project Research Group authored the final essay, "Restoring History: Writing the Narratives of Alexandria's Two Documented Lynchings." In 1897 Joseph McCoy, a Black teenager, was accused of assaulting three white girls and taken into police custody. On the night of his arrest McCoy was dragged from the cell by a white mob, bludgeoned, and then hanged by his neck from a light post a block from the jail. Two years later a mob hauled sixteen-year-old Benjamin Thomas from the city jail, after which they stabbed, shot, and then hanged him within sight of city hall. A key difference between the first and second lynching lies in the response of Black Alexandrians to the sudden seizure of Benjamin Thomas. A group of local Black men attempted to protect Thomas, but the local police arrested and fined some of these men; in some cases, police sent them to the chain gang. Officials and the press even blamed these Black men for enflaming white anger and essentially causing the lynching. In addition to doing justice to Benjamin Thomas, it was the story of the arrested Black men that the Community Remembrance Project wished to uncover and restore, with the goal to honor, advocate for, and do justice by Benjamin Thomas, Joseph McCoy, their families, and the individuals who stood up against mob violence.

Notes

1. Anthony L. Brown and Keffrelyn D. Brown, "Strange Fruit Indeed: Interrogating Contemporary Textbook Representations of Racial Violence toward African Americans," *Teachers College Record* 112, no. 1 (2010): 31–67; Anthony L. Brown and Keffrelyn D. Brown, "'A Spectacular Secret': Understanding the Cultural Memory of Racial Violence in K–12 Official School Textbooks in the Era of Obama," *Race, Gender & Class* 17, no. 3/4 (2010): 111–25.
2. H. J. Res. 655 (V.A., 2019), Legislative Information System, accessed Oct. 22, 2023, https://lis.virginia.gov/cgi-bin/legp604.exe?191+ful+HJ655.
3. Virginia Department of Education, "Board of Education Approves African American History Edits," accessed Oct. 22, 2023, https://content.govdelivery.com/accounts/VADOE/bulletins/2a6341f. The 2023 History and Social Science Standards of Learning now includes the study of lynching, racial terror and Ida B. Wells' antilynching campaign: https://www.doe.virginia.gov/teaching-learning-assessment/k-12-standards-instruction/history-and-social-science/standards-of-learning.
4. Gianluca De Fazio, "Can Critical Digital Archives Address 'Archival Amnesty' towards Lynching? The Racial Terror: Lynching in Virginia Project," in *Transforming the Authority of the Archive: Undergraduate Pedagogy and Critical Digital Archives*, eds. Andy Gustavson and Charlotte Nunes (Amherst, MA: Lever Press, 2023).
5. "The National Memorial for Peace and Justice," Legacy Museum and National Memorial for Peace and Justice, Equal Justice Initiative, accessed Oct. 22, 2023, https://museumandmemorial.eji.org/memorial.
6. Emmett Till Antilynching Act, H.R. 55, 117th Cong. (2022), Congress.gov, accessed Oct. 22, 2023, https://www.congress.gov/bill/117th-congress/house-bill/55.

THE TRAIN AT WOOD'S CROSSING

BRENDAN WOLFE

I

On Monday morning, July 11, 1898, Julia Hotopp rode into Charlottesville to have her horse shod. She left between eight and nine o'clock and returned a short time later, following the Earlysville Road out past Cochran's Mill and then through a patch of woods to the family farm. It was still cool out, or at least as cool as a midsummer's morning in Virginia allowed. But as she approached the gate, she likely had to wipe a little sweat from her brow.[1]

The sun was beginning to climb.

Up until this moment—it was still before ten—everything about Hotopp's short errand had been routine. Charlottesville had been quiet because, let's face it, Charlottesville was always quiet. There'd been a lawn party on Ridge Street over the weekend, and a businessman had been thrown from his buggy on West Main Street Friday morning. Both events had made the front page of the local newspaper.[2] And of course the Spanish-American War was on, but most folks assumed it would end in short order. As Hotopp approached the farm, she noticed something out of place. Rather than fastened with a latch, the gate was bound with wire. Why? What was the point of that? She turned in her saddle and looked around for farm hands, for anyone, but the area was deserted.

After dismounting, she unwound the wire and freed the gate.

"As she turned to remount," the *Daily Progress* reported in that afternoon's edition, "someone approached her from behind and struck her, and then grasped her by the neck, forcing her to the ground, when she became unconscious."[3]

When she came to, it was about ten o'clock. Her assailant had disappeared and so had her horse. A few minutes later, though, she spied her brother Carl running in her direction, the riderless mount having tipped him off. She scrambled to her feet and walked gingerly in his direction.

"Upon meeting her brother," the paper wrote, "she swooned again."

Back at the house and off her feet, Julia Hotopp was finally able to describe what had happened to her. Her assailant, she said, had been "a very black man, heavy-set, slight mustache," who had worn dark clothes. His toes, she recalled, had stuck out of his shoes.

"After making this relation," the *Daily Progress* told its readers, "Miss Hotopp again became unconscious, and was still in that condition, attended by several physicians, at last accounts."[4]

By this time, the sun was beating down.

II

Hotopp was twenty years old that summer and living with her mother and several siblings at Pen Park, one of the oldest homesteads in Albemarle County.[5] Julia's father, Wilhelm Friedrich Hotopp, had immigrated from Germany, bringing with him a love of wine. He planted grapes on several dozen acres of the estate and in 1873 cofounded the Monticello Wine Company.[6] The four-story brick headquarters stood on Charlottesville's north side, with the manager living on what is still known as Wine Street.[7] "Hotopp's wines were very popular," one memoirist, R. T. W. Duke Jr., recalled of his time at the university, "& quite in evidence at our caucuses."[8] Hotopp was also a director of the Woolen Mills and built the Jefferson Auditorium for the city.[9]

Sadly, though, Herr Hotopp had died only two months earlier, on May 4, 1898. His widow and their thirteen surviving children erected an impressive white obelisk in the estate's private graveyard, a marker that still stands[10]— although these days it is surrounded by a golf course. I took my daughter there recently after picking her up from school.

Pen Park, as it happens, is now a city park, at 280 acres the largest in Charlottesville.[11] Aside from the cemetery, which is south of the clubhouse and therefore invisible to most visitors, there is no sign that this ground had once been a plantation worked by enslaved people, or that a crime had allegedly occurred here that would, the next day, provoke another crime—this one so awful that most Charlottesvillians would rather not remember it at all.

People played tennis, toddlers climbed on the playground equipment, and a group of middle-aged women in white visors chatted around a golf cart.

"Daddy, I'm too old for Pen Park," my second grader complained. When I told her we were there for history, not the slides and swing sets, she perked up. But I had trouble explaining what had happened here.

Does she really need to know this? I wondered.

III

John Henry James had lived in Charlottesville for the previous five or six years, working odd jobs such as selling ice cream[12] while otherwise keeping his head down. Where he came from, who his people were, what his story was—no one seemed to know, or even much care.

"John Henry James is not a resident of Charlottesville," the *Daily Progress* declared, before admitting that James had, in fact, been living in the city for years. Labeling him a "tramp,"[13] however, conveniently distanced the city from James while shackling him to the still-potent stereotype of the "idle negro." *Why won't these people work harder?* wondered generations of slaveholders, their cat-o'-nine-tails at the ready. *Why won't they work longer, work happier?*

When Union cavalry arrived in Charlottesville in March 1865, thousands of enslaved people quit their labor to follow the blue-clad troopers to freedom. Frederick Denison, of the First Rhode Island Cavalry, remembered being met by African Americans singing the praises of Union troops and even offering freshly cooked biscuits.[14]

And yet, when an enslaved man similarly fled from John B. Minor, who taught law at the university, the professor wrote in his diary that the man would have been better off a slave: "I lament [his escape] more on his account than my own."[15]

Why won't they understand what's good for them? wondered generations of slaveholders, their cat-o'-nine-tails frayed from use.

After the abolition of slavery, Black people crowded the dirt roads of Virginia. While a few stayed on the plantation, many went off in search of family members from whom they had been separated, either by the auction block or the Underground Railroad. Some preferred just to wander.

"Their freedom," the historian Brent Tarter writes, "overturned a centuries-long racial hierarchy and left many whites concerned about public safety and, more importantly, white social and political supremacy."[16]

In response, the General Assembly in Richmond passed a law that condemned anyone who seemed to be without residence or steady employment to either jail or forced labor.[17] Most historians agree that this amounted to a kind of legalized pseudo-slavery, and if the Vagrancy Act didn't result in the actual arrest of many freed people, it did help prompt the drafting of the 14th Amendment. It also likely increased the speed by which African Americans left areas like Albemarle County for places of greater safety, with jobs and family.[18]

In 1860 the federal census counted 14,522 Black people in the county, or 54.5 percent of the total population. By 1900, even with the total population rising, the number of African Americans had dropped to 10,337, or just 36.3 percent.[19]

In 1898 it still was not safe for a Black person such as John Henry James to be seen as "idle," as a "tramp," as someone without a fixed address. It was an unwelcome reminder of social chaos, and it placed him outside of the (white) community's control.

Of course, none of this tells us what James did on the morning of July 11—where he woke up, what if any errands he accomplished. It is possible he was staying in a boardinghouse or with friends. Perhaps he paid rent somewhere. He may have had regular work, or perhaps he lifted a hammer only when it damn well suited him.

For that matter, it's possible that he preyed on young women. He may have spent the morning devising a plan and then walking the two and a half miles from Charlottesville out to Pen Park, where he hid among the trees and vines, waiting for his moment.

Come noon, though, he was in Dudley's bar on East Main Street. That is where the authorities found him and determined, according to the *Daily Progress,* that he "answer[ed] somewhat the description of Miss Hotopp's assailant. He was taken to jail to await further developments."[20]

Directly overhead by now, the sun saw it all.

IV

He answered somewhat the description.

You can't help but wonder which parts fit and which parts didn't. Perhaps James's skin was "very black," but he was tall and big-chested more than heavy set. His clothes were dark, sure, but could you really say whether a mustache was coming in? And what about his shoes? Did the toes stick out?

You might think the paper would have noted. The victim claimed to have scratched her attacker on the neck, but there was no mention of that, either.

More than one hundred twenty years later, such details matter. We play detective, but we also play novelist. We want to know these characters, to picture them, to chart their pasts and explain their fates. To get inside their heads. In 1898, however, it was different. There was a script to be followed, and the identities of the players mattered not one bit.

In example after example, the script played out like this:

- A violent crime is alleged to have been committed, often against a white woman.
- The attacker is identified as a Black man, often with little other description.
- He is demonized by the press and often situated in some way outside the community.
- And because its sense of justice has been so profoundly betrayed, the (white) community decides that it must respond with like violence.

What happened in Roanoke, just six years earlier, was pretty typical. The newspaper there reported that a white girl had been assaulted and described the assailant as a "very black" man wearing a light gray suit and rubber boots. The next day, amidst criticism of the police for not acting quickly enough, a suspect was publicly identified. "His name is Allen Stevens," the *Roanoke Times* wrote, "and he loafs around Cave Spring."[21]

Except that the day after *that*, a different man was accused, this one described as being "thick-lipped and black." He wore a gray suit and rubber boots—as had the previous day's suspect.[22]

The play, not the players, was all that mattered.

In this sense, the entire ritual—from the purported crime to the identification of a perpetrator and his subsequent murder—reflected a need not for individual justice but for white catharsis and group bonding. Lynching both affirmed the white community's racial values and acted them out.[23] It sought to purify the community of sin and so resembles the Spanish Inquisition's auto-da-fé, whose elaborate ceremonies combined the Church and the bullfight, all with the aim of expunging the heretic. The individuality of that heretic mattered little for the tens of thousands who watched. In fact, the Spaniards tended to believe that such sins lived in a person's blood, and so visited punishment to the condemned children and grandchildren, as well.[24]

In Charlottesville, John James comes off as little more than a dime-novel villain. Upon waking up in custody the morning after his arrest, having been accused of a brutal sexual assault, he "professed to have rested well and smoked a cigarette with cool indifference." I am reminded of a scene from my own family's history, when a relative was shot dead and set afire on the western plains in 1882. The accused murderer hastily fled only to be found later in a saloon, "with no apparent thought of the blood upon his hands, engaged in a game of cards."[25]

The roles here are big and archetypal because that's what the script called for. It existed, again, not in service of individual justice—"he answered *somewhat* the description"—but as a hedge against the chaos of Emancipation and Reconstruction, of an entire social and racial hierarchy having been turned on its head. If the cat-o'-nine-tails no longer obtained, then why not the noose?

Of course, it was important to continue to observe certain legal niceties. After James was arrested at Dudley's, police officers transported him to Pen Park, where Julia Hotopp positively identified him as the man who had attacked her. "They also carried him to the scene of the outrage," the *Daily Progress* reported, "and ascertained by trying his shoes in the tracks found there that they could have been made by no other."[26]

But what about whether his toes stuck out of his shoes? What about the deep scratch on the alleged perpetrator's neck?

"He was then brought back and lodged in jail," the paper tells us, "a large crowd following the entire way. The officers were chary of admitting that he had been identified, but the crowd could not be deceived, and angry mutterings and threats of lynching were heard on every side."[27]

V

The play, not the players, was all that mattered.

VI

"Did something happen here in history?" my daughter wanted to know as we tromped around Pen Park. "Did it have to do with Pocahontas or George Washington?"

She's eight—well, eight and three-quarters by her own more impatient accounting—and still naïve, in many respects still helpless. She's mine and I would do anything to protect her.

This strikes me as normal. When you immerse yourself in stories like the ones involving Julia Hotopp, or "Little Alice Perry" of Roanoke, you can't help but imagine your own daughter. You think that making it personal in this way might help you better understand what happened.

Here's the thing, though. It doesn't.

I searched for images of James and Hotopp and found nothing, but still I yearned to picture them, to see their faces. So, when first researching this online, I downloaded substitutes—the convict Clifton Roberts and the spinster Elizabeth Henry.

It soon occurred to me that this was not only an offense against history (they had nothing to do with the events of July 11 and 12); it was also deeply unfair. Whatever crimes Clifton Roberts may have committed, he did not rape Julia Hotopp. Nor was Miss Henry any kind of victim, at least not in this case. Featuring their portraits implies that they were something they were not, no matter what caveats you write into the captions.

And yet another thought occurred to me: in some respects, this inaccuracy, this clever bit of conflation is the very point. If I really wanted to understand what happened that summer of 1898, then these words—*the play, not the players*—must be my guide. Clifton Roberts or John Henry James? What mattered to the (white) people of Charlottesville is that they were Black men. Liz Henry or Julia Hotopp? They were young white women. No more, no less.

When Julia Hotopp was attacked by a Black man on the morning of July 11, all white women were attacked. By all Black men.

FIGURE 1. Mugshot of Clifton Roberts, no. 18699. (Records of the Virginia Penitentiary, Series II, Prisoner Records, Subseries B, Photographs, Box 43, Accession 41558, State Records Collection, Library of Virginia)

According to one scholar's count, almost 30 percent of all lynchings in Virginia between 1866 and 1932 involved accusations of assault, rape, or attempted rape against white women.[28] Whites believed that African Americans were particularly prone to commit this crime, an attitude borne out of two longstanding white southern traditions—demonizing Blacks and defending white womanly honor. In the postemancipation South, Black men were often caricatured as subhuman, ruled by their appetites and disposed to commit violent crimes. The definition of rape was broad, so that the mere presence of a Black man with a solitary white woman might generate an accusation and possible punishment. The repeated suggestion that, given the opportunity, Black men were likely to rape white women has been described by Michael Ayers Trotti as a "fixation"[29] and by numerous other historians as a myth, one that dated back to slavery and, in particular, a romanticizing of white womanhood and a paranoid distrust of enslaved African Americans. Still, enslavement had at least placed the Black man firmly under his master's control. What could the white man expect now that his former slave walked free?

FIGURE 2. Miss Elizabeth Henry by Rufus W. Holsinger. (Albert and Shirley Small Special Collections Library, University of Virginia)

"There is something strangely alluring and seductive to [Black men] in the appearance of a white woman," wrote the Virginia historian Philip Alexander Bruce in *The Plantation Negro as Freeman* (1889); "they are aroused and stimulated by its foreignness to their experience of sexual pleasures, and it moves them to gratify their lust at any cost and in spite of every obstacle."[30] The Virginia writer Thomas Nelson Page claimed that while enslaved, African American men better understood their proper relationship to white women. Only during Reconstruction, he argued, did they become infected with the idea of equality. "This was followed," Page wrote, "by a number of cases where members of the Negro militia ravished white women; in some instances in the presence of their families."[31]

The slave preacher Nat Turner rose up in 1831, and what followed was a paroxysm of violence; blood spilled across Southampton County. That the one person Turner himself killed should have been a white woman tapped into a deep well of fear and anxiety that was then used to justify decades of more horrific violence. This helps explain why many African Americans fiercely objected to the way in which William Styron's Pulitzer Prize–winning novel imagined a sexual connection between the Black rebel and his white victim.[32] And why white communities such as in Charlottesville themselves rose up to defend what they considered to be a young white woman's honor.

The commonwealth's attorney—apparently contradicting an early report that the attacker had "failed of accomplishing his foul purpose"—now told the *Daily Progress* that what had happened to Miss Julia Hotopp "was one of the most atrocious rapes ever committed, the circumstances of such a character and so revolting that he was unwilling to state them in detail—of a character to stir any community to its deepest depths."[33]

VII

It's interesting what stirs a community to its deepest depths and what doesn't.

VIII

On the ride home, my daughter asked whether he did it. I had just finished explaining to her that a young woman had been hurt at Pen Park a long time ago and that a man had been arrested for the crime.

"Was he guilty?" she asked.

"I'm not sure."

"But what's your opinion?"

The novelist in me wants to connect with these characters as real people, while the detective in me wants to grasp the truth of what happened. The truth, though, is that we have no idea. Not that it matters, of course. Trials ought to make those judgments, not mobs. When I told all this to my daughter, she was confused, and I don't blame her. Even for a second grader it seems intuitive that we should know whether John Henry James actually raped Julia Hotopp. It shapes how we see James and also how we see his accuser—whose finger pointed in his direction as surely as if it were the barrel of a loaded gun.

IX

As the sun sank in the western sky, those "angry mutterings and threats of lynching" began to worry the chief of police, Frank P. Farish, and the county sheriff, Lucien Watts. A mob had surrounded the old jailhouse and violence seemed less like a threat than just a matter of time. "In consequence of this," the *Daily Progress* reported, "it was thought best to remove the prisoner to Staunton for safety."[34]

At about eight thirty that evening, James was pushed up and over the north wall of the jail yard, then through a private home and out a wine cellar. At Union Station he boarded a westbound freight belonging to the Chesapeake & Ohio, which left at nine and was off, the paper wrote, "before the people knew anything about it." The crowd remained until past eleven, "and it became necessary to take some of them through the jail to satisfy them that the negro was really taken away."[35]

Although he was the county sheriff, Watts took responsibility for the custody of prisoners even in the independent city of Charlottesville. Another incident in Roanoke, in 1893, provides a sense of what was at stake for Sheriff Watts and Chief Farish. An African American man, Thomas Smith, had been arrested and charged with assaulting a white woman, at which point the city's mayor, Henry S. Trout, ordered the entire police force and members of the local militia to protect the jail. A mob was formed and initially rebuffed. During the second attack on the jail, however, authorities opened fire, killing eight and injuring a few dozen others, including the mayor, who was shot in the foot.

The white mob, which numbered between fifteen hundred and four thousand citizens, still managed to capture its man, possibly with the help of the police. After Smith was lynched, the crowd hung a sign from his neck: "Mayor Trout's Friend."[36]

Play this thing wrong, I imagine Watts and Farish thinking as the C&O rumbled west to Staunton, *and we could end up shot or worse.*

What's worse than being shot? you ask. Being seen to betray your community in defense of a man the script has dismissed as a mere brute, a beast, a ravisher of young white women.

"Sheriff Watts's Friend."

The terrifying possibility must have run through his mind that night.

After pulling into Staunton at eleven thirty, the sheriff arranged for his prisoner to be locked in a cell at the county jail. Chief Farish rounded up sandwiches, and a grateful James mentioned that it was the first food he'd had since the sun was still rising.

X

The next morning came. It had been twenty-four hours since Julia Hotopp had run her errand into Charlottesville only to return and find the gate mysteriously bound with wire. It was July 12 now, and events had begun to move quickly.

At the courthouse a grand jury of seven white men had been empaneled to consider whether to indict John Henry James for assault. After being sworn in at ten forty-five, they heard from two witnesses, Miss Hotopp and her sister. The jurors then retired to deliberate.[37]

Across the mountain in Staunton, Chief Farish and Sheriff Watts accompanied James back to the train station. "He didn't seem disposed to give the officers any trouble," the *Daily Progress* wrote, "and when they boarded the train this morning, for Charlottesville, it was not considered necessary to handcuff him."[38]

It was a local train, with stops. An express was scheduled, but they decided against taking it. A few minutes before eleven thirty the train approached a spot known locally as Wood's Crossing. About four miles west of Charlottesville, it was there, according to the paper, that "officers noticed a crowd at the station, and at once took in the situation."[39] According to one report, a letter from local housewife Florence Bishop to her husband, a man in the crowd who was "dressed in womans clothes signaled the Train & stopped it before any body knew what they even wanted."[40] Chief Farish raced back to the car where his prisoner was located, and as he did so he could feel the train heave and begin to slow. The screeching of brakes pierced the air.

Charlottesville historian Jane Smith has analyzed maps, train timetables, and aerial photos and concluded that Wood's Crossing was located on what is now the property of Farmington Country Club, land that had once belonged to the slave-owning Peyton family.[41] At the crossing, when the train didn't drown it out, you could hear the rhythmic banging of a nearby blacksmith's shop.

A story that began on a former plantation will now end on one.

XI

The mob, numbering between one hundred and one hundred fifty white citizens, was large for its kind, and its members were fired up by the gruesome details they had read about in the paper.[42] They took to the tracks and crowded around the train as it made its scheduled stop. The editor of the Waynesboro *Herald* witnessed the event and later described how "a number of men crowded in at each door of the car with grim, determined faces and[,] flourishing revolvers[,] demanded the officers in unmistakable tones, 'Gentlemen, we want this negro.'"[43]

Here the editor notes that Chief Farish and Sheriff Watts "made a stout show of resistance," although not stout enough. Perhaps not even particularly stout, because "in less than two seconds three ropes were around the negro's neck and[,] pleading, praying and fighting, he was dragged from the car."[44]

In front of the blacksmith's shop the mob spied a small but sturdy locust tree with a limb hanging about ten feet off the ground. "Under this tree the doomed man was dragged and the end of the rope thrown over the limb," the editor wrote. "Above the hoarse shouts of the enraged men arose the leader's voice in stentorian tones informing the doomed wretch that he had but two seconds to live and asking him if he was guilty of the crime."[45]

This all went perfectly to script. The lynching ritual calls for an opportunity of atonement, again reminiscent of the Spanish Inquisition's auto-da-fé. Penitence lay at the stony heart of that ceremony: only unrepentant heretics (and those who had lapsed) faced the stake, and those who sought forgiveness for their sins were "mercifully" strangled before the fires were lit.[46] One scholar has gone so far as to describe the entire ritual as a symbolic reenactment of the biblical Last Day, when sinners faced their God.[47] Back in 1892 the Roanoke press had described how the prisoner, with a noose around his neck, uttered "an almost incoherent jumble of denial," until a half-hanging brought on "a rambling confession."[48]

According to the Waynesboro editor, James skipped the denial: "In wailing accents he answered yes, that he did it."[49] The *Daily Progress* told a slightly different story. "Before God, I am innocent," James said; the paper went on to explain, "Some reports declare that he avowed his guilt, and hoped to be forgiven, but when the officers pleaded with the mob, to let him come to a trial, he grasped at the hope thus extended and made the above declaration."[50]

The noose, the Waynesboro editor wrote, was tightened and James given a moment for one final prayer. He was subsequently pulled up, screaming and swinging and choking for perhaps twenty seconds. "Then the leader again gave the signal and twenty or thirty revolvers rang out on the morning air and the body of the wretch was perforated with perhaps forty or fifty bullets."[51]

Who was this leader? Did anyone ever attempt to identify him?

The play, not the players, was all that mattered.

"In eight minutes from the time the train stopped," the Waynesboro reporter wrote, "the ghastly deed was done and the avengers of Virginia women's lives and honor mounted their horses and vehicles and drove quietly away, leaving the body of the black brute swaying gently in the morning breeze, a fearful example of swift and sure retributive justice."[52]

XII

The Lexington *Gazette* reported that Carl Hotopp arrived about ten minutes late and emptied his revolver into the dead body. He is the only participant ever identified—yet he was never formally investigated, let alone tried.[53]

XIII

All of this was happening as the Charlottesville grand jury sat behind closed doors to consider charges against John Henry James. News soon arrived that the deliberations had been rendered moot, but the gentlemen of the jury continued in their work. The proper application of justice, or at least the appearance of it, was of paramount concern to everyone.

With John James still hanging from the locust tree they issued a true bill of indictment.

XIV

It's interesting what stirs a community to its deepest depths and what doesn't. The citizens of Charlottesville and Albemarle who lynched John Henry James, mutilated his body, and left it to dangle until three thirty that afternoon did so in the open, their faces uncovered. And not a single one of them was brought to justice. This was typical, of course, and summoned the indignation of only a few people in the area.[54] The *Staunton Spectator and Vindicator,* angry that some in Charlottesville had suggested violence was in the offing in that town too, mocked its neighbor to the east: "The jury summoned by the coroner to sit upon the body of the late James [. . .] found that 'deceased came to his death by the hands of persons unknown to the jury.' The rule in society in Albemarle is such that one frequently has to be introduced to another several times there before he can be said to *know* him. The jury had not had a formal introduction, you see."[55]

R. T. W. Duke Jr., that same memoirist who once had binged on Hotopp's wine at the university, was more succinct. In a diary entry dated July 12, 1898, he wrote: "The negro who ravished Julia Hotopp lynched at Wood's Crossing today. Horrible crime—both him & the lynchers—."[56]

In telling her husband of the events, Florence Bishop describes a town ready to explode with violence. "The whole town *negroes* & white rushed up there," she wrote, referring to Wood's Crossing, "and we expected to have a fight, but the whites were in a perfect frenzy—and I believe if it had commenced—there would have been a battle equal to what is going on in Cuba." That didn't happen, though; no Nat Turners here. "The black devils," she wrote, "soon slunk out of sight when they smelt the 'brimstone in the air.'"[57]

The crimes, both the alleged one and the very real one, were reported in newspapers across the country, from Virginia to Alabama, North Dakota, Kansas, Indiana, Ohio, Connecticut, Delaware, California, Pennsylvania, and even the German-language press of Baltimore, Maryland. The *Richmond Planet,* the African American paper led by the antilynching crusader John Mitchell Jr., issued its usual, full-throated protest.

After noting that James had claimed innocence, that the authorities had not done enough to protect their prisoner, that the lynchers had acted with seeming impunity, and that the criminal justice system had been operating as it should, without any need of mob intervention, Mitchell observed:

"The lynching of John Henry James will be far more damaging to the community than it will be to the alleged criminal."[58]

XV

But was it? Has it been?

John Mitchell's statement implied, I think, that this lynching represented a kind of trauma, one that would haunt Charlottesville long after the authorities cut John James's body down. Long after the sun finally set on that awful day.

In his research, the psychologist Gilad Hirschberger argues that a community's memory of an event such as a lynching persists over time—not as straightforward history but as narratives fashioned specifically to make sense of whatever happened, and to make use of it. A normal occurrence can be explained, justified, and safely stored away. With something like racial violence, however, we must rely on stories to reflect, and across generations even construct, our understanding of the traumatic event and our relationship to it.[59]

We do this, of course, to protect ourselves. For the white perpetrators of lynchings, and those who sympathized with them, safeguards were already in place against the individual and group disruption their actions might cause. They had justifications, in other words. Mob violence was a necessary, if unfortunate, means of upholding community standards of justice, they told each other and themselves.

The crude version came from the pen of Florence Bishop, who scolded her husband, "You see I *told* you that the *South* needed *her* men to look after the black devils that the North 'pitied' so much—and let loose upon us. Therefore it behooves the Virginia men to be on their guard at all times."[60]

A more sophisticated version arrived in the words of Hallie Erminie Rives, who just a year before John Henry James's murder published the prolynching novel *Smoking Flax*. Rives hailed from a well-known central Virginia family: her father, a Confederate veteran, had been born in nearby Amherst County and her cousin, the novelist Amélie Rives, had until recently lived in Albemarle. In *Smoking Flax*, Hallie Rives imagines a conscientious opponent of lynching, only to have logic and circumstances prevail on him to change his mind.

The slave trade, his neighbors insist, was Great Britain's doing, but even so, "slavery was a lifting force to the negro race during the whole period of its existence here." The white race has always educated African Americans in reading, writing, and religion, at great cost, and yet are thanked only by an ever-increasing string of "outrages against our homes." When white women are the victims, "man, if man he be, cannot but choose to avenge it." This, the lynching apologists emphasize, reflects anger against criminals and crime, not against a race—although it happens to be true that if former slaves were to behave with more kindness, loyalty, and respect, and were less inclined to fall victim to their "manifold temptations," then they would have less to fear from the mob's righteous anger.[61]

The novel's protagonist falls in love with a beautiful young woman who is subsequently raped and murdered. Tragically, our hero is not there to protect his love, and although the attacker is captured, tried, and convicted of the crime, his "affected nonchalance and thinly veiled defiance" in the courtroom prove almost too much to bear. He is not so much a criminal as something much, much worse: "The passions of raging fear and terror had driven from his low-browed face every trace of intellectuality or culture, leaving only the cunning cruelty and ferocity of the animal."[62]

This provides the ultimate and, for many, the most forceful defense of lynching: the inhumanity of the lynched. It is why I desperately wish that James was not such an enigma. I want to go back to Dudley's saloon, at noon on July 11, when the authorities came through the door looking for their man.

Who was he and what must he have been thinking? Did someone wait for him at home that night, someone who had been too afraid to go looking? When the historical record tells us nothing, it commits against John James a violence mimicking that of his lynchers. It strips him of his humanity.

In *Smoking Flax*, the governor issues a reprieve of the attacker's death sentence, at which point the novel reaches its denouement. Handcuffed to the sheriff, the man is placed on a train. "The engine was ready to start," Rives writes. "Snorting, trembling, as if in frightened pain, she moved off slowly, slowly..."[63]

—but allowing just enough time for vengeance to accomplish its terrible work.

XVI

On May 29, 1899, or about a year after John Henry James himself was pulled trembling from a train—and not, as Rives would have it, from a trembling train—the *Daily Progress* editorialized against lynching. Surprisingly, perhaps, the paper blamed whites and Blacks equally for mob violence. The African American community had not done enough to control criminal offenders, instead making "martyrs of the assaulter of innocent and defenseless women." The white community, meanwhile, "shields and justifies the mob that takes the law into its own hands."[64]

As much as the paper's editor, James H. Lindsay, recognized the rule of law, he also well understood the importance of white supremacy. He reflected on that point in a discussion of lynching and politics that appeared in the same edition. Absent the "negro question," he said, most votes would go to the Republican Party just on policy grounds. "We are forced to vote with the Democratic party to continue white supremacy and to protect our property."[65] Like Philip Alexander Bruce, Thomas Nelson Page, and Hallie Erminie Rives, the editor felt certain that nothing would be safe until the Black man understood his proper place.

Lindsay served as a delegate to the 1901–2 constitutional convention and voted with the majority for a new state constitution, a document that almost completely disfranchised African Americans in Virginia. Whether by cat o' nine tails, noose, or pen, the object was the same.

"I am a friend of the colored man," Lindsay is quoted as saying on May 29, 1899, and that, I suppose, is how he justified himself, how he personally avoided the trauma of lynching.[66]

It may have been enough for him. The Hotopp family had more difficulty moving on, however. In 1900 the wine company caught fire under what authorities believed to be suspicious circumstances.[67] A year later, Carl Hotopp apparently jumped to his death from a speeding train, which had been traveling west from Charlottesville.[68] A year after that, Carl's younger brother Heinrich died in an equally mysterious manner. According to the Richmond *Dispatch*, while at Pen Park he "attempted to jump out of the window" and became entangled in the sash, which wrapped around his legs and held him "suspended head downward" until he died.[69]

Then, in 1911, Julia Hotopp made the headlines again. Thirty-three years old and still unmarried, she was living in Washington, DC, and working as an artist. According to the *Washington Times*, she called police headquarters on December 20 "and asked for protection from persons she said annoyed her whenever she tried to paint." She "also wanted the police to assist her in getting a position with Buffalo Bill's Wild West, so she could travel around the country and sketch horses."

Miss Hotopp's behavior became so erratic that she was hospitalized and later institutionalized.[70]

Perhaps some form of mental illness ran through the Hotopp line, and John Henry James was only the first of several victims. Or perhaps his violent death had unhinged something in the family. Over the years, the papers noted the state of Miss Hotopp's health but never mentioned the attack that may or may not have happened or the lynching that definitely did.[71]

XVII

What, then, of Charlottesville?

Until recently, Charlottesville and Albemarle County had chosen not to remember John Henry James at all, or to reckon with what a mob did to him here. Historians have preserved the record, of course, and written scores of books about lynching in all its gruesome detail. But the landscape of our community—from the rolling fields of Pen Park to the manicured lawns of Farmington—have remained free of any reminders of that history, or of any hints at all.

Amnesia has always been part of the ritual. Recall the editors in Staunton mocking their Charlottesville counterparts for refusing to acknowledge that they knew anyone in the mob: "The rule in society in Albemarle is such that one frequently has to be introduced to another several times there before he can be said to *know* him." For the white men, women, and perhaps even children present that day at Wood's Crossing, forgetting was essential. They went home and back to their lives, not troubling themselves with the murderous violence they had helped to perpetrate. Remembering was a responsibility that belonged to the Black community. In fact, forcing them to remember—their place and the fearsome consequences that came with straying from it—was the entire point of a lynching. Its effect was powerful enough that, while the memory of racial violence has lived on in the oral tradition of Black communities, African Americans do not often speak of these events with white people, "perhaps mirroring the times when speaking out on lynching could be very dangerous," as one historian put it.[72] Lynching, at least of the sort done to John Henry James, no longer occurs, but its impacts are still with us. The defense found in *Smoking Flax* has faded from polite society, and yet echoes can still be heard in appeals to George Floyd's criminal record, or Trayvon Martin's hoodie. The stories we construct die hard.

The mob, in other words, had largely disappeared from our collective memory—or at least it had until the weekend of August 11–12, 2017. That's when it returned, as terrible as it ever was. White men with tiki torches and automatic weapons traveled to Charlottesville in defense of Confederate statues and the Lost Cause, a narrative that glorifies the same values that demanded James's lynching. (And protects its adherents from the same acknowledgment of guilt.) Suddenly, polite society felt complicit again, rife with updated versions of "I am a friend of the colored man." Members of the community, meanwhile, continued their project of revising, even completely rewriting, the old public narrative. The University of Virginia erected a memorial to enslaved laborers, while new attention was paid to an easy-to-miss plaque downtown that marked the spot of an auction block. "On this site slaves were bought and sold," it read. At various points, activists painted "humans" over the word "slaves," asking us to *think for once about the players and not the play*. Then, the plaque disappeared altogether. Years earlier, the highway marker recalling the Union occupation of Charlottesville had been stolen. Had it happened again? No, or at least not exactly. A seventy-five-year-old white man, whose ancestors had been slaveholders, publicly confessed to tossing the slave-auction plaque into the James River because he found the story it told to be "insulting."[73] By his calculations, silence was more respectful than difficult history.

Many local activists and historians disagreed with this approach, though. And when the National Memorial for Peace and Justice opened in Montgomery, Alabama, it inspired them to research the story of James's murder. They gathered soil from Wood's Crossing and in July 2018 journeyed to Montgomery to deposit it at the memorial. A year later, on the 121st anniversary of the lynching, a historical marker commemorating the event was unveiled in the city. "We take this opportunity to right an old wrong," one of the speakers said that day, "a wrong perpetuated because the nation refused to name it wrong—to look at our history and tell the truth."[74]

What would it take for people to know their history?

I've thought about that question a lot over the years. The problem, though, is not whether we know this history. We do, or at least we could. The problem is whether we *choose to remember.* Important, too, is who we allow to do that remembering in public. And how.

Hirschberger explains that the stories we tell about long-past events such as the lynching of John Henry James are not designed to reflect the historical truth, or at least not only that. Instead, they combine fact and myth as a means of forming and maintaining group identity. For many citizens of Charlottesville, their deepest sense of self rests in opposition to the violence of 2017 and 1898, either because, on another day, in another time, they might have been victims or simply because it's indefensible. For other white people, such as those who loudly objected to the removal of Confederate statues, the act of remembering hundreds of years of racial violence can be threatening. "It leaves the group forever guilty of the past," Hirschberger writes, "with each generation carrying the burden of their ancestors' crimes; it also forestalls any process of change, as changing the inner essence of the group is near impossible."[75]

History can only get us so far, in other words. What we require—not instead of responsible, accurate history, but in addition to it—is a new collective story. A popular history, a narrative not by which professional historians understand us but by which we understand ourselves. It must encompass the enslavement of African Americans, the Civil War, and the terrorism that followed it, as well as the city's more recent history. In fact, that history, including another brutal murder perpetrated by a white supremacist, can be seen as an almost frantic attempt at making sense of the past. Of integrating memory with the urgent needs of the present.[76]

Traumatic memories can sometimes master their keepers. What we are searching for when we seek to build a new public narrative is authority—authority over those memories, the authority to craft them into a story that helps us to acknowledge and even explain these awful parts of our history and the condition in which they have left our community.

What has this lynching wrought, not simply on white folks but on the Black people who knew John Henry James, or lived near him, or simply had the same color skin? What part of it do we carry around with us today, those who shout, "Black Lives Matter!" and those who find excuses to reject the proposition?

Can we avoid the damage predicted by John Mitchell Jr., or is it already too late?

And what, I wonder, do we tell our kids?

"Daddy, I don't really understand," my daughter said as we pulled into the drive.

Which is fair, honestly, because I am struggling, too—not with what happened, but with where we go from here.

Notes

1. "Atrocious and Outrageous," (Charlottesville) *Daily Progress*, July 11, 1898, 1.
2. "Odds and Ends," (Charlottesville) *Daily Progress*, July 8, 1898, 1.
3. "Atrocious and Outrageous," (Charlottesville) *Daily Progress*, July 11, 1898, 1.
4. "Atrocious and Outrageous," (Charlottesville) *Daily Progress*, July 11, 1898, 1.
5. Dr. George Gilmore acquired the property in 1786 and called it Pen Park after the English estate of his friend, the slave trader John Harmer. The farm, which coerced labor from scores of enslaved men, women, and children, stretched across more than five hundred acres. By the time the Hotopps arrived, slavery had been abolished and the estate reduced to just more than four hundred acres. Albemarle County Deed Book 9:309, Clerk's Office, Albemarle County Courthouse, Charlottesville, VA; John Gilmer Speed, *The Gilmers in America* (New York: privately printed, 1897), 73; Ruth D. Gilmer, Pen Park, 2–3, Gilmer Family file, Albemarle Charlottesville Historical Society, Charlottesville, VA; Catherine Hawes Coleman Seaman, *Tuckahoe and Cohee: The Settlers and Cultures of Amherst and Nelson Counties, 1607–1807* (Sweet Briar, VA: Sweet Briar College Printing Press, 1992), 35; Albemarle County Personal Property Tax Records, 1787, Library of Virginia, Richmond; Albemarle County Deed Book, 61:305, 64:210. In 2019–20 archaeologists discovered unmarked graves in the Pen Park family cemetery that they believe represent the burial places of enslaved and later free Black men, women, and children at the estate. See Benjamin, P. Ford, "The Pen Park Cemetery Survey" (City of Charlottesville and Rivanna Archaeological Services, October 15, 2020), i, 7.
6. Ford, "The Pen Park Cemetery Survey," 11–13.
7. Historical Highway Markers: Monticello Wine Company, Virginia Department of Historic Resources, accessed Oct. 12, 2020, https://vcris.dhr.virginia.gov/HistoricMarkers/.
8. Richard Thomas Walker Duke Jr., Recollections, 1899–1926, III:77, Accession #9521-o, Duke Family Papers, Albert and Shirley Small Special Collections Library, University of Virginia, Charlottesville.

9. "The Late Mr. Hotopp," (Charlottesville) *Daily Progress,* May 5, 1898, 1.
10. "The Late Mr. Hotopp," (Charlottesville) *Daily Progress,* May 5, 1898, 1.
11. "Pen Park," City of Charlottesville, accessed Nov. 10, 2020, https://www.charlottesville.gov/Facilities/Facility/Details/Pen-Park-26.
12. Letter from Florence A. Bishop to Jonathan A. Bishop, July 14, 1898, Box 1, Folder 2, Jonathan A. Bishop Papers, 1897–1924, Albert and Shirley Small Special Collections Library, University of Virginia, Charlottesville. In the letter Mrs. Bishop describes James as "That Negro who used to sell 'Hokey-pokey' ice cream," a square bar that street vendors sold from carts for a penny.
13. "He Paid the Awful Penalty," (Charlottesville) *Daily Progress,* July 12, 1898, 1.
14. Frederic Denison, *Sabres and Spurs: The First Regiment Rhode Island Cavalry in the Civil War, 1861–1865* (Central Falls, RI: First Rhode Island Cavalry Veteran Association, 1876), 443.
15. Diary of John B. Minor, March 6, 1865, Accession #3114, Papers of John B. Minor, 1843–1892, Albert and Shirley Small Special Collections Library, University of Virginia, Charlottesville.
16. Brent Tarter, "Vagrancy Act of 1866," *Encyclopedia Virginia,* accessed July 1, 2018, https://www.encyclopediavirginia.org/Vagrancy_Act_of_1866.
17. "Chap. 28.—An ACT providing for the punishment of Vagrants, Passed January 15, 1866," in *Acts of the General Assembly of the State of Virginia, Passed in 1865–1866* (Richmond: Allegre & Goode Printers, 1866), 91–93.
18. Tarter, "Vagrancy Act of 1866."
19. Joseph C. G. Kennedy, *Population of the United States in 1860; Compiled from the Original Returns of the Eighth Census* (Washington, DC: Government Printing Office, 1864), 500–525.
20. "Atrocious and Outrageous," (Charlottesville) *Daily Progress,* July 11, 1898, 1.
21. "The Police Force Wakes Up," *Roanoke Times,* Feb. 11, 1892, 1.
22. "Judge Lynch!," *Roanoke Times,* Feb. 12, 1892, 1.
23. W. Fitzhugh Brundage, *Lynching in the New South: Georgia and Virginia, 1880–1930* (Urbana: University of Illinois Press, 1993), 17.
24. Henry Kamen, *The Spanish Inquisition: A Historical Revision* (New Haven, CT: Yale University Press, 1997), 202–10, 234. Kamen writes, "The ceremony of an auto de fe has a literature all to itself" (204).
25. "Murder and Suicide," Wheeling (WV) *Register,* Nov. 16, 1882, 1. This is not quite what actually happened, which only underscores the point. The newspaper report faithfully followed the script.
26. "He Paid the Awful Penalty," (Charlottesville) *Daily Progress,* July 12, 1898, 1.
27. "He Paid the Awful Penalty," (Charlottesville) *Daily Progress,* July 12, 1898, 1.
28. Racial Terror and Lynching in Virginia, James Madison University, accessed May 20, 2021, https://sites.lib.jmu.edu/valynchings/. The database includes 115 lynchings.
29. Michael Ayers Trotti, "What Counts: Trends in Racial Violence in the Postbellum South," *Journal of American History* 100, no. 2 (Sept. 2013): 375.
30. Philip Alexander Bruce, *The Plantation Negro as Freeman: Observations on His Character, Condition, and Prospects in Virginia* (New York: G. P. Putnam's Sons, 1889), 83.
31. Thomas Nelson Page, *The Negro: The Southerner's Problem* (New York: Charles Scribner's Sons, 1904), 95.

32. Scot French, *The Rebellious Slave: Nat Turner in American Memory* (Boston: Houghton Mifflin, 2004), 238–53.
33. "He Paid the Awful Penalty," (Charlottesville) *Daily Progress*, July 12, 1898, 1.
34. "He Paid the Awful Penalty," (Charlottesville) *Daily Progress*, July 12, 1898, 1.
35. "He Paid the Awful Penalty," (Charlottesville) *Daily Progress*, July 12, 1898, 1.
36. Ann Field Alexander, "'Like an Evil Wind': The Roanoke Riot of 1893 and the Lynching of Thomas Smith," *Virginia Magazine of History and Biography* 100, no. 2 (April 1992): 192.
37. "He Paid the Awful Penalty," (Charlottesville) *Daily Progress*, July 12, 1898, 1.
38. "He Paid the Awful Penalty," (Charlottesville) *Daily Progress*, July 12, 1898, 1.
39. "He Paid the Awful Penalty," (Charlottesville) *Daily Progress*, July 12, 1898, 1.
40. Letter from Florence A. Bishop to Jonathan A. Bishop, July 14, 1898, Jonathan A. Bishop Papers.
41. Lisa Provence, "Confronting a Shameful Past: Search for 1898 Lynching Site Narrows," *C-VILLE Weekly* (Charlottesville,), accessed Nov. 10, 2020, https://www.c-ville.com/confronting-shameful-past-search-1898-lynching-site-narrows/; "Death of Warner Wood," *Richmond Times*, Aug. 26, 1902, 9.
42. Brundage, *Lynching in the New South*, 36. Fewer than half of the lynchings Brundage counted were carried about by what he calls "mass mobs," or mobs of more than fifty people. Smaller mobs responded to more personal grievances, Brundage argues, while mass mobs formed in the wake of particularly heinous alleged crimes or those that seemed to strike in particular at the white community's deepest values.
43. "From an Eye Witness," (Charlottesville) *Daily Progress*, July 16, 1898, 1.
44. "From an Eye Witness," (Charlottesville) *Daily Progress*, July 16, 1898, 1.
45. "From an Eye Witness," (Charlottesville) *Daily Progress*, July 16, 1898, 1.
46. Kamen, *The Spanish Inquisition*, 203. Kamen also notes that once condemned by the Church, a prisoner was "relaxed" to the custody of local officials, who carried out the execution, which the Holy Office of the Inquisition was forbidden to do itself. This mimics the way in which prisoners in the custody of police were, in some sense, "relaxed" to the white mob (202).
47. Maureen Flynn, "Mimesis of the Last Judgment: The Spanish Auto de Fe," *Sixteenth Century Journal* 22, no. 2 (Summer 1991): 282.
48. "Judge Lynch!," *Roanoke Times*, Feb. 12, 1892, 1.
49. "From an Eye Witness," (Charlottesville) *Daily Progress*, July 16, 1898, 1.
50. "He Paid the Awful Penalty," (Charlottesville) *Daily Progress*, July 12, 1898, 1.
51. "From an Eye Witness," (Charlottesville) *Daily Progress*, July 16, 1898, 1.
52. "From an Eye Witness," (Charlottesville) *Daily Progress*, July 16, 1898, 1.
53. "The Negro Lynched," (Lexington, VA) *Gazette*, July 13, 1898, 2.
54. Brundage, *Lynching in the New South*, 182. Brundage notes that Virginia authorities were more likely to prosecute lynchers than their counterparts in Georgia but still faced reluctant juries and social ostracism if they did so.
55. *Staunton Spectator and Vindicator*, July 21, 1898, 2.
56. Diary of R. T. W. Duke Jr., July 12, 1898, Duke Family Papers, 1845–1983, Accession #9521-h, 9521-i, Albert and Shirley Small Special Collections Library, University of Virginia, Charlottesville.
57. Letter from Florence A. Bishop to Jonathan A. Bishop, July 14, 1898, Jonathan A. Bishop Papers.

58. "Another Virginia Lynching," *Richmond Planet*, July 16, 1898, 4.
59. Gilad Hirschberger, "Collective Trauma and the Social Construction of Meaning," *Frontiers in Psychology* 9 (Aug. 2018): 1–14. Hirschberger focuses on genocide and does not mention lynching, but he explicitly defines collective trauma—traumatic events that affect an entire group and create a collective memory that transmits down through generations—in a way that would include it.
60. Letter from Florence A. Bishop to Jonathan A. Bishop, July 14, 1898, Jonathan A. Bishop Papers. Rather than identifying as a "swooning" body in need of defending, Bishop, like many white women, including Hallie Erminie Rives, was an ardent defender of racist myths and racial violence.
61. Hallie Erminie Rives, *Smoking Flax* (New York: F. Tennyson Neely, 1897), 75, 78, 79, 81.
62. Rives, *Smoking Flax*, 214.
63. Rives, *Smoking Flax*, 232.
64. "Lynching," (Charlottesville) *Daily Progress*, May 29, 1899, 2.
65. "Letters from Albemarle," (Charlottesville) *Daily Progress*, May 29, 1899, 1.
66. "Letters from Albemarle," (Charlottesville) *Daily Progress*, May 29, 1899, 4.
67. "The Hotopp Fire," *Richmond Dispatch*, May 1, 1900, 5.
68. "Hotopp's Death a Mystery," *Richmond Dispatch*, May 29, 1901, 6.
69. "The Strange Death of William Hotopp," *Richmond Dispatch*, Nov. 6, 1902, 3. The headline mistakes Heinrich Hotopp for his father, William Hotopp.
70. "Artist-Walker in Capital Hospital for Observation," *Washington Times*, Dec. 20, 1911, 2. The headline refers to Hotopp's "title of champion woman pedestrian about three years ago, when she walked from Atlanta, Ga., to Chicago."
71. E.g., a listing headed "Supreme Court, District of Columbia," published in the *Washington Post* on Aug. 28, 1920, page 9, reads: "In re lunacy Julia Hotopp: auditor's report ratified."
72. Manfred Berg, *Popular Justice: A History of Lynching in America* (Lanham, MD: Rowman and Littlefield, 2011), 192.
73. Laura Longhine, "'Why I did it': County resident confesses to taking slave auction block," *C-VILLE Weekly*, accessed Nov. 10, 2020, https://www.c-ville.com/why-i-did-it-county-resident-confesses-to-taking-slave-auction-block/.
74. Norah Mulinda, "Historical marker unveiled for lynching victim John Henry James," *Charlottesville Tomorrow*, accessed Oct. 12, 2020, https://www.cvilletomorrow.org/articles/historical-marker-unveiled-for-lynching-victim-john-henry-james/; "Charlottesville Dedicates Historical Marker Remembering Lynching," Equal Justice Initiative, accessed May 19, 2021, https://eji.org/news/charlottesville-dedicates-historical-marker-on-lynching/. The marker reads: "In 1898, a black man named John Henry James lived and worked in Charlottesville as an ice cream vendor. He had only been a resident of the area for five or six years before July 11th, 1898, when he was falsely accused of assaulting a white woman and arrested. The police transferred Mr. James to Staunton that evening to avoid a potential lynching, but officers escorted him back to Charlottesville the next morning by train. While en route, an armed mob of 150 white men stopped the train at Wood's Crossing in Albemarle County, and seized Mr. James. Learning of the mob's attack, a group of black men tried to stop the lynch mob but were outnumbered and forced to retreat. The white mob threw a rope over Mr. James's neck and dragged him about 40 yards away to a small locust tree. Despite his protest of innocence, the mob hanged Mr. James and riddled his body with dozens of bullets. *The Richmond Planet*, an

African American newspaper, reported that as his body hung for many hours, hundreds more white people streamed by, cutting off pieces of his clothing, body, and the locust tree to carry away as souvenirs. The grand jury, interrupted by news of the lynching, issued a posthumous indictment, as if Mr. James were still alive. Despite the presence of the Charlottesville police chief and Albemarle County sheriff, no one was ever charged or held accountable for the murder of John Henry James."

75. Hirschberg, "Collective Trauma and Meaning," 8.
76. Nikole Hannah-Jones's *The 1619 Project: A New Origin Story* (New York: One World, 2021) is fast becoming the archetypal example of such a narrative.

PUBLIC HISTORY AS ACTIVISM

Helping a Community Come to Terms with Racial Violence

ANDREA DOUGLAS

In 2012, during an interview at the Virginia Film Festival, Kristin Szakos, then a Charlottesville, Virginia, city councilor, proposed that the city's three Confederate monuments be removed from its public spaces. The response from sectors of the white public was immediate and viciously negative. Nonetheless, Szakos was stalwart in her insistence that these objects continued to "represent something hateful to a small but vocal subset of our community."[1] Despite her assertions, the councilor was dismissed as a heretic for daring to question the ever-present "Lost Cause" narrative that drove the installation of the city's three Confederate statues in the first decades of the twentieth century. Although primary documents from the period revealed that their *mise en scène* was meant to solidify the presence of white social dominance, those opposed to the removal of the statues in 2012 lauded them as objects of art, their presence positioning the city as urbane. Four years later Szakos, still on the city council, would again lead the call to remove Confederate statues. This time, however, her assertions would begin a process that in 2017 resulted in a brutal murder and injury of twenty-nine additional people during the Unite the Right rally organized by neonationalists.

Since the Unite the Right rally in August 2017, the community of Charlottesville has been earnestly engaged in a series of public history projects that hope to redress the raced-based inequities at the core of the economic, legal, and social life of this southern town—these inequities being even more prevalent because it is a college town. The founding and subsequent growth of the University of Virginia is commensurate with the development of the ideology of white supremacy—white faculty and students served as a percolator for white supremacy and eugenical sciences until at least the 1960s. This racist history collided with Charlottesville's desire to address its racist past on August 11 and 12, 2017, through the rally organized by UVA graduate Jason Kessler and his neonationalist cronies.

In the aftermath of this tragic event, the myth of the region as a historic Arcadia—which had been promoted by such institutions as the region's tourism board and, until recently, the various historic homes in the area—was dispelled. City residents were forced to reconcile themselves with the reasons why groups they believed to be outsiders would see Charlottesville as a symbolic sacred ground that needed to be protected to the extent of murder. Ultimately, the community's participation in the Equal Justice Initiative Community Remembrance project and the associated lifting up of the 1898 murder by lynching of John Henry James proved to be a significant tool for Charlottesville to come to terms with its racial past. It opened the door for a greater cross section of the community to share in restorative justice conversations and creating a place for community healing.

The Lynching

On July 11, 1898, the *Daily Progress*, Charlottesville's local paper, reported that John Henry James had attacked Julia Hotopp, a twenty-year-old white woman, outside her family estate located at what is now known as Pen Park. Newspaper accounts further established that James was later arrested by local law enforcement, who put him on a train to Staunton, Virginia, because they feared mob violence. The next day, while traveling back to Charlottesville, he was violently removed from the Wood's Crossing depot by a mob of 150 unmasked whites. He was then dragged forty yards into the woods, allowed to pray and beg for his life for twenty minutes before being hung from a locust tree and his body riddled with over seventy bullets. James's body hung in the tree for several hours as white community members collected pieces of his clothing and body as souvenirs. The Albemarle County sheriff and the Charlottesville chief of police were present at the time of the lynching but did nothing to stop the crime, and no one was prosecuted for it. The grand jury who would have reviewed James's initial case issued a posthumous indictment of him.

Just a week after James's death, an article in the *Staunton Spectator* under the heading "Mob Law" posited two justifications for the mob action against James: the first was to prevent the offended woman from having to endure the indignity of a trial; and the second was that the perpetrator had "forfeited his right to life, that he is classed as a brute, a wild beast, an outlaw and the 'Hue and Cry' have been raised as soon as the crime is known, and no man has been guilty of an offense who rids society of such a creature.... There is one sure way to end such trouble and the power is in the hands of those who commit such crimes. Let them cease their crime and lynching will cease, not before."[2] This was not the only murder by mob violence in the vicinity, and white residents of the area continued to publish their thoughts on lynch mobs in the local paper for years. One article published a year after his murder warned against the potential lawlessness that would ensue if both races did not do their part to end mob violence: "While there can be but one result to a race war, to which such a course inevitably leads, the pathway to such an end will be strewn with the blood of the innocent and helpless and succeeded by all the horrors which follow in a reign of lawlessness and disregard for the protection and restraining influence of the law."[3] The author walked a fine line as they tried to persuade the community to lessen the mentality of mob violence. While not denouncing the actual practice of lynching, they instead advocated for the humanity of innocent people who could be inadvertently killed due to lawlessness.

After his torturous murder, James's body was removed from the lynching site by local Black undertaker James Kesler. There is no record of a public burial witnessed by friends and family. In 2019 additional accounts of the lynching were found in an unpublished letter written by Florence Bishop to her husband, who was away fighting in the Spanish-American War. Bishop's letter suggests that the train was flagged down by a man dressed as woman and that the African American community attempted to come to James's aid but were scared away "when they smelt the brimstone in the air."[4]

Why a Lynching

The violence meted out to the African American community through James's lynching was punctuated ten years later with the installation of *At Ready*, also known as the Johnny Reb statue, formerly located in front of the Albemarle Charlottesville courthouse. The need to situate this and subsequent Confederate statues in the public space was consonant with the institutional development of the Black middle class. In 1890 the population of Albemarle County was 32,379; of that number 14,126 were Black. In July 1890 the *Richmond Planet* described the establishment in Charlottesville of the Piedmont Industrial Land and Improvement Co. (PILIC) as a major step forward for the African American community. The reporter wrote: "Even the Company's greatest enemies, the kickers including many whites, acknowledge the Company's progressive merits.... It also proves that colored men can do something if they try."[5] The PILIC's original nine members, employed as undertakers, builders, pastors, and shop owners, represented the burgeoning Black middle class. The organization's influence could be seen with home purchases occurring all along Dice Street in the neighborhood now known as Fifeville, as well as other parts of the city. Formerly enslaved individuals like John West invested heavily in real estate. He acquired his first property in Vinegar Hill in 1870 and ultimately owned nearly one hundred properties between 1872 and 1924.[6] Black community success was further evidenced by the expansion of Black churches founded thirty years earlier: First Baptist Church, Mount Zion First African Baptist Church, Ebenezer Baptist Church, and Zion Union Baptist Church all saw new buildings between 1888 and 1907.

The *Richmond Planet* extolled the sense of Black optimism in its description of a successful county fair organized by Black residents. The Rev. J. Francis Robinson, pastor of Mount Zion First African Baptist Church, wrote:

> The Afro-American people of the city in the holding of said County Fair have not only excelled the state, but the whole Southland by giving the first Fair having the prefix "county" before it.... The general verdict is that it was the grandest and most successful race undertaking in this section of the state.... The Fair was a grand success financially and commercially. It was a credit to Charlottesville and a great boom for the Piedmont Industrial Land and Improvement Company, and a proof positive of the asserted fact that the Afro-American is HERE TO STAY and share in the benefits accruing from a land of plenty and abundant prosperity.[7]

The Black community had its first lawyer, Harrison Ferrel, and its first doctor, George Ferguson. The construction of the Southern Railroad Line in 1894 spurred in-migration of both whites and Blacks, and opportunities abounded with the increase in population. By 1894 the Jefferson Graded School had moved from its location on West Main Street to an expanded space on Commerce Street, and Vinegar Hill continued to grow into a vibrant commercial area. African Americans were active in Charlottesville's interracial Republican Party, albeit the relationship became more and more tenuous. Black Republican George Inge held party leadership into the 1920s, despite growing racist backlash. By the time of James's lynching, the number of African Americans in the city proper was almost half the number of whites.

As the Black community prospered, the white community began to mobilize against them. The Confederacy remained alive and viable in Charlottesville; the Lost Cause narrative held sway with the founding of the local chapter of the Sons of Confederate Veterans in 1893, and the ladies' equivalent, the Daughters of the Confederacy, in 1894. Fear became an important weapon in the war whites waged to regain their perceived lost supremacy. An 1890 article entitled "A Word to Young Virginians" published in the *University of Virginia* magazine sums up the sentiment of the times. The author, identified only by the initials L.B.E., suggests that as a consequence of defeat in the Civil War, "four million ignorant people of African descent were made equal to Whites, who were then through the Reconstruction period subjected to an unequal struggle against negro supremacy and carpet-bag misrule."[8] The obsession with Black inferiority was certainly the justification for the lynching of Black people in Central Virginia between 1885 and 1915.

Fear is one thing, but terror is fear taken to its highest level. Author Michael Eric Dyson suggests that there is an ever-present, pervasive, anxiety associated with crimes against Black bodies. The fear of random acts of violence brings with it a sense of constant terror that is transmitted generationally. Dyson makes the distinction between fast terror and slow terror. According to Dyson, "Fast terror is explosive and expected; it is the spectacle of unwarranted Black deaths at the hands of the state or displays of violence directed against defenseless bodies. Slow terror is masked yet malignant; it stalks Black people in denied opportunities that others take for granted."[9] Lynching is an act of fast terror, while slow terror is generational trauma derived from the knowledge that at any moment, because of any arbitrary transgression, someone can decide whether you live or die. Lynching is just one form of racial terror the African American community was subjected to.

Coupled with this violence was the constant demoralization caused by racist ideologies promoted by the University of Virginia, beginning with founder Thomas Jefferson's own assertions about Black inferiority.

We are only just beginning to understand the impact of these assertions on race and how they became inculcated into the postemancipation ethos of the university and, concomitantly, into the community that it so thoroughly influenced. The notion of southernness established at the university by Jefferson and others included the sentiment that Black people were of a different, lower order. Much of this information was the subject of inquiry by the President's Commission on Slavery and the University (PCSU), which began its work in earnest in 2013.[10] Interestingly, it was at this same time that the city began its conversation regarding removal of Confederate statues. The PCSU's work made clear that the university and, ultimately, Albemarle County created a system of racial capitalism that allowed the area to grow into the fourth most successful slave economy in the state. African American people were not just subject to the whims of a single owner but were an integral part of an ecosystem that left them vulnerable to the vagaries of men or women who thought them to be subhuman.

The PCSU research describes a longer history of racial terror suffered by both enslaved and free Black people in the community. Most telling is the commission's documentation of grave robberies suffered by both groups well into the 1870s.[11] African Americans were only too aware that the research demand of the university medical school meant that recently buried family members faced a real threat of being stolen from their graves under the cover of night. PCSU cochair Kirt von Daacke opined that such a reality "created a palpable fear for both enslaved and free families."[12] And yet this was only one aspect of the fear that was a significant part of Black life in postemancipation Charlottesville. The university's twentieth-century eugenics research, grounded in the presupposed inferiority of the Black population, flourished in concert with the urbanization of the city's Black community.[13]

Against this historical backdrop Szakos's demand for the removal of Confederate monuments should be considered. By suggesting that their presence was harmful to African Americans in Charlottesville, she echoed arguments at the forefront of the Equal Justice Initiative's (EJI) 2015 report entitled *Lynching in America* that documented lynchings in the twelve most active states in the United States: Alabama, Arkansas, Florida, Georgia, Kentucky,

Louisiana, Mississippi, North Carolina, South Carolina, Tennessee, Texas, and Virginia. These documented lynchings were defined specifically as acts of terrorism since they were carried out with impunity, sometimes in broad daylight, often on the courthouse lawn. The report includes the June 12, 1898, lynching of John Henry James in Charlottesville.

EJI makes a direct connection between racial terror lynching and white supremacist ideology—the same ideology that fostered the placement of over three hundred Confederate monuments in Virginia, seventy of which stood in front of courthouses. The report asserts that "many of the communities where lynchings took place have gone to great lengths to erect markers and monuments that memorialize the Civil War, the Confederacy, and historical events during which local power was violently reclaimed by White Southerners. These communities celebrate and honor the architects of racial subordination and political leaders known for their belief in white supremacy."[14] Most of Charlottesville was unaware of the connections between the extralegal act of lynching and the Confederate monuments they held dear.

In 2016 Virginia governor Terry McAuliffe (2014–18) vetoed House Bill 587, which would have prevented localities from removing their Confederate war memorials. Simultaneously, ninth grader Zyahna Bryant in a school project addressed the impact that Confederate statues had on her ability to fully enjoy the city's public parks. As a class project she circulated an online petition wherein she called for the removal of a statue of Robert E. Lee. Bryant outlined the harmed caused by the presence of the statue in this way:

> Nevertheless, let's not forget that Robert E. Lee fought for perpetual bondage of slaves and the bigotry of the South that kept most black citizens as slaves and servants for the entirety of their lives. As a result, legislatures of the south chose to ignore and turn a blind eye to the injustices of African Americans from Jim Crow and anti-black terrorism to integrated education. These are all some things that this statue stands for. It is about more than just an individual, but rather what that individual believes in and the things that he stands for.

Bryant's petition received 726 signatures and contributed to a standoff at Charlottesville's Lee Park between African American leaders and neo-Confederates. Quickly thereafter, in hope of avoiding the violent confrontations that had occurred elsewhere in the country (e.g., in Berkeley, California, and Portland, Oregon), the Charlottesville City Council assembled the Blue

Ribbon Commission on Race, Monuments, and Public Spaces (BRC). The commission was charged with providing the city council with recommendations for how "public spaces are used, or could be used, to address race." Their proceedings engaged the city in a renewed conversation about statues that was last held in the 1920s: only at that time, the conversation was one-sided and celebrated symbols of racial dominance on the heels of anti-Black violence and disenfranchisement.

The Blue Ribbon Commission

Over the course of six months and twelve meetings, the nine-member commission—made up of historians, lawyers, and social activists—heard from the public. Deliberations revealed a fractured city: opposition along racial, generational, and ideological lines was apparent at every meeting. While the often-acrimonious debate seemed to center the dichotomy between history and heritage, the meetings further exposed a deeper discussion about truth, mythology, and social authority.

Despite the city's ambition to avert violence through public hearing, the world watched as Charlottesville became the epicenter of racial conflict. What exploded on Charlottesville's doorstep on August 11, 2017, was precipitated by Richard Spencer, another graduate of the University of Virginia. Spencer returned to Charlottesville in 2016 to head the racist think tank National Policy Institute and to recruit young white males to his ideology of white supremacy. Commentators opined that his capacity to do so was largely owed to his ability to reflect the desires of a newly disenfranchised middle class. However, activists rebutted this theory with their claim that his rhetoric mirrored that of nineteenth-century Lost Causers who, during Reconstruction, bemoaned their "niggardly" treatment; these malcontents were joined by twentieth-century Anglo-Saxons, who feared miscegenation would lead to the erasure of the white race.

The BRC presented its recommendations in December 2016. Most of the attention in the ensuing year focused on the disposition of statues. One recommendation, however, proved to be truly significant, as it exposed the community to its own violent history: the decision in March 2018 to participate in EJI's Community Remembrance Project. Involvement with this project heralded Charlottesville's reckoning with its racial past, which included acknowledging the connection between that past and present social inequities.

To this point, the acceptance of Charlottesville's complete racial narrative had proved slow. Any understanding the community had was facilitated in the early 1990s, in part by university professors who, along with local scholars, uncovered histories about Vinegar Hill.[15] While these histories were known in the Black community, they were not part of the majority discourse or the city's wider collective memory. The professors had their own goals for their community engagement, including educating UVA students and furthering their research. For years these lay scholars had been amassing their own public history through genealogical research. Their subsequent partnership in the 1990s with UVA to produce films and oral history projects meant access to research tools they had lacked until then. Concurrent with this work, Monticello launched its Getting Word African American Oral History Project "to preserve the histories of the African American families at Thomas Jefferson's plantation." In 2011 the restoration of the Jefferson School, the former Black elementary and high school, and the creation of the African American Heritage Center resulted in highlighting the site's vernacular history and completing the collection of oral histories of its alumni.

At the national level, several museums that focused on African American history were opened. The specificity of story offered by sites such as the A. Phillip Randolph Porter Museum, founded in 1997, or the African American Civil War Museum in Washington, DC, founded in 2002, suggests that the appetite for information about the Black experience was growing. Even with these changes, there was lingering resistance to the idea that the African American experience was relevant in the narrative of American history. Resistance to this idea grew with the rise of Black activism. The Black Lives Matter movement, for instance, was countered with an All Lives Matter movement that universalized social history and whitewashed America's violent racial past. Hence, when the BRC made its recommendations, it was within the space of an increased interest in the telling of America's authentic truth.

The city's participation in EJI's Community Remembrance Project ended up without direct city leadership. An injunction that prevented the immediate removal of the Robert E. Lee statue and a lawsuit brought against individual council members forced a trio of African American women to take charge. Dr. Andrea Douglas, Executive Director of the Jefferson School African American Heritage Center; Dr. Jalane Schmidt, a professor at UVA; and Siri Russell, then manager for policy and special programs and liaison to Albemarle County's Board of Supervisors, created a public collaboration that included the city, the county, and the University of Virginia.[16]

A Community Remembers

The Community Remembrance Project began the recognition of John Henry James's lynching on July 7, 2018, with the collection of soil from the site of his murder. From there began a pilgrimage that would lead physically from this site to Alabama and back and would intellectually link the violence, 120 years apart, of John Henry James's murder and the tragedy of the Unite the Right rally. The discerning of historical similarities, however, would have been a hollow goal without concomitant community education to promote understanding and reconciliation.

Ritual acts are key elements of community identity building since they tend to create a sense of shared experience. The ceremonial act of collecting soil from the lynching site ritually afforded James the respect of a burial by loved ones. According to EJI, by collecting soil, they "aim to transcend time and altered terrain to bear witness to this history and the devastation these murders wrought upon individuals, families, communities and our nation as a whole."[17] On that July day in 2018, a group of about thirty people walked the forty yards over which James's body was dragged from the train tracks to a grove of trees. Prayers were offered, songs were sung, and a libation poured. For a community that had endured three months of racial intimidation in 2017, nearly one year later this simple service was cathartic on many levels.

The proceeding was conducted under the watchful eye of law enforcement. Despite the peaceful nature of the event, participants were apprehensive: the specter of recent violence weighed heavily, and there was real fear that the harmony would be spoiled by white supremacists. The irony of the moment was not lost. James lost his life because the police officer and sheriff who accompanied him on the train failed to protect him from an angry mob. In fact, they utterly failed to do their duty when shooting started and no person was ever arrested for participation in this murder.

Five days before the 120th anniversary of James's death, 108 people boarded two buses for the trip to EJI headquarters in Montgomery, Alabama. The organizers took great pains to ensure a diverse group according to age, gender, race, and financial ability. Funds were raised to ensure that a third of the group could come from the ranks of the economically disenfranchised. A third of the group was able to afford the trip on their own. The final third was composed of teachers, students (the youngest in grade 9), librarians, and city and county officials.

The route south took the pilgrims to significant locations in the history of this country's racial violence. One could imagine that the atmosphere on the buses echoed that of the Freedom Rides of the Civil Rights era—people singing and bonding over a shared understanding of a life-changing experience. However, any emotional high that might come from personal interaction with like-minded people was not destined to last during a trip through the American South if that like-mindedness was born of a desire to right racial injustice.

Emotional release turned to dismay and anger on the first stops at Appomattox Court House National Historical Park and Danville's Museum of Fine Arts and History. The Danville stop proved to be a particularly emotional low point. The group had expected to hear from the victims of Bloody Monday, June 10, 1963—the day that Martin Luther King described as the most violent he had encountered to that point in the civil rights movement. Apparently, the speakers had been delayed, and the museum staff suggested that the group watch a film produced in 1990 about the life of William Sutherland, a rich, slave-owning tobacco planter. Perhaps surprisingly to the museum staff, but not to this audience, the film white-washed history, making only passing mention of the enslaved people who effectively created Mr. Sutherland's wealth.

Many in the group felt it irresponsible to present this account to people interested in engaging with the country's racial harm. It is true that this reaction may have been heightened by a similar experience at Appomattox, the famed location of Confederate surrender. The history of African Americans at Appomattox was relegated to a former out-kitchen, a room of just over 900 square feet—in stark contrast to the vistaed landscape meant not only to describe the three days of surrender of Lee to Grant but also to highlight the history of the town. On day one of their pilgrimage to "equal justice," the group learned a sobering lesson about the difficulty in twenty-first-century America of developing a national narrative that included African Americans as active agents in the creation of place.

The pilgrimage headed next to the Beloved Community Center in Greensboro, North Carolina, to meet with Nelson and Joyce Johnson, cofounders of the Greensboro Truth and Reconciliation Commission. The Johnsons described the November 3, 1979, murder of five, and wounding of ten, communist worker activists by forty proclaimed neo-Nazi and Ku Klux Klan members. Local news reporters who covered the violence published video evidence of the attack. Collusion between the Klan and police prohibited any convictions. In 2004 the Johnsons led the movement to create the Greensboro Truth and Reconciliation Commission in response to Dr. King's call for a beloved community.

Atlanta was the next stop, where the group toured the Sweet Auburn Historic District, Dr. King's birthplace. Then on to Birmingham and the Civil Rights Memorial Center. Drs. Douglas and Schmidt engaged in a filmed conversation with the Southern Poverty Law Center's former president, Richard Cohen, about events in Charlottesville and the importance of confronting white supremacists. The SPLC originally took the position that direct engagement with extremists should be avoided, but after Charlottesville, their position changed.[18] Both Douglas and Schmidt argued that it is important to respond to neofascism in order to signal to the larger community the very real threat to Black lives that white supremacist groups represent.

Those who witnessed the proverbial burial of John Henry James defined their weeklong experience in similar ways. Many chose to embark on the journey because they hoped to have opportunities to consider their own racial biases. As they traveled south, they found the constancy of anti-Black hatred to be oppressive. However, there was solace in the conversations they had with elders on the trip. Many commented on how meaningful it was for them to hear about the experiences of people who lived through harrowing times in Charlottesville and elsewhere. The youngest participant, a ninth-grade student traveling with her mother, expressed pride in learning about her heritage. She described the opportunity afforded by the trip as a "privilege that not all black students get."[19] Back in Charlottesville, the Community Remembrance Project began to engage the city's broader community, holding as many as seventy public meetings to describe the experience. High school students were engaged in the discussion through participation in an essay contest. One hundred fifty-seven students in the eleventh grade wrote about the area's racial history. The soil collected at the site of the James lynching became part of two exhibitions, one at the Albemarle County office building and the other at the Jefferson School African American Heritage Center.[20]

Community engagement, or perhaps more correctly, education and enlightenment, continued through Confederate monument tours given by Douglas and Schmidt. Developed largely from research Schmidt had conducted to respond to the Blue Ribbon Commission, the monument tours described both the historic and symbolic import of Charlottesville's Confederate statues. The tour's starting point was Court Square, the county seat where in the eighteenth century commerce and judicial business were conducted, including the buying and selling of enslaved people. Schmidt began giving the tours in advance of the first anniversary of the Unite the Right rally. Consequently, the early audiences included national and international reporters. Over time, the audiences included the broader community. There was no regularity to when the tours were offered. Social media advertising produced audiences that varied from one person to one hundred fifty. Over two years, at least 2,500 people experienced the tour, some multiple times. In 2019 the tour was recorded by a local radio station, which opened it to an even broader public.

As it moved from one location to another, the tour's underlying sentiment was the pervasiveness of Black erasure and the systematic devaluation of Blackness in a supposedly egalitarian space. It began at the plaque memorializing the slave auctions. In 2018 this was the only referent to the existence of Black people in the area. In addition, the plaque, embedded in the ground, is the only memorial without a vertical presence. It sits embedded in the brick: it is easily traversed and, therefore, missed. This is in stark contrast to the various other memorials and markers to Charlottesville's colonial, Confederate, and Jim Crow histories. Missing from this narrative altogether is the fact that a portion of this property was once a community known as McKee Row and that it was owned by John West and other members of the Black middle class. In 1914 the city confiscated the property through eminent domain and sold it to philanthropist Paul Goodloe McIntire, who then commissioned and had erected the Stonewall Jackson statue.[21] The idea of a statue as central to a leisured vista derives from the City Beautiful Movement of the 1920s, in which an ordered city plan was in keeping with the ideals of southern progressiveness. The tour's reinsertion of the narrative of Blackness into Court Square was a jarring moment for the mostly white audiences. The possibility that McKee Row could have been a locus of Black success, rather than a place of described ill repute, created a historical dissonance that once again left people feeling deceived. Like the pilgrimage to Montgomery, the monument tours became an opportunity to reclaim history.

The Court Square site was organized to deliberately place Charlottesville within a larger national history. Markers there tell the story of Jack Jouet, the local Paul Revere, who informed Jefferson of the coming of British soldiers. A rock holds a plaque that highlights the fact that three presidents, Jefferson, Madison, and Monroe, frequented the area. Another innocuous object commemorates the placement in 2008 of a bust of Meriwether Lewis in the House of Delegates. Not far from the slave auction plaque is one that describes the four fountains bought by the city in the 1800s for the purpose of providing water to residents and horses. Nowhere in this topography of historical references is there mention of the Monacans, the area's Indigenous people, or of the gallows and whipping post that once stood there. Instead, the site is a series of symbols that celebrate the accomplishments of white men. The statuary, both monumental and otherwise, describes a history that attaches Charlottesville to the Revolutionary War, the Civil War, and, finally, to the successful war waged by former Confederates to overtake the historical narrative. White control is glorified here and in neighboring Lee Park, home of the now-infamous statue of Robert E. Lee.

At the end of the year-long Community Remembrance Project, two markers were planned to commemorate the lynching of John Henry James. One would be placed on the Route 250 Bypass proximate to the actual site of the lynching. The other was placed in front of the courthouse, reminding people of the extralegal activity perpetrated by mob violence. This second marker was installed on July 12, 2019, at an event attended by a hundred people, many of whom were on the pilgrimage. Speakers at the event included Kiara Boone from EJI, Albemarle supervisor Diantha McKeel, Andrea Douglas, and Charlottesville mayor Nikuyah Walker. Virginia governor Ralph Northam was in attendance but did not speak. In her remarks, Boone noted the importance of truth telling as a means of acknowledging the pain of racial injustice. She spoke of the purpose of the soil collection as part of the story of the blood, tears, and sweat of those who were oppressed in the community. Mayor Walker's speech was particularly moving as she asked the audience to consider James's humanity—to see him as a lost son, brother, husband, or father. She admonished the crowd that to achieve real change, one had to be intentional to ensure that what happened to James could not be repeated. The reactions to the comments of Boone and Walker were mixed. While applauding the placement of the marker as a positive move toward reconciliation, some felt that their words were divisive and accusatory and was representative neither of King's "beloved community" nor of racial reconciliation. Others suggested, however, that such a criticism infers an equitable relationship and ignores the ongoing power struggle between whites and Blacks. Activist Don Gathers remarked that the ceremony was powerful and moving, albeit surreal, and caused him to reflect on what brought us to this moment—the reality of man's inhumanity to man. The marker reminds us of where we have been as a country and the amount of healing still to be done.[22]

At the conclusion of the speeches, the marker's text was revealed.[23] As with all EJI markers, one side discussed the history of lynching. The other recounted in detail James's murder. In Court Square's field of white exceptionalism, the marker is disruptive. It is accusatory in pointing out the failures of the system represented by the courthouse in front of which it sits. It calls into question the very notion of justice for all. Prior to its installation, the site's narrative read like the Bible's Genesis. The bravery of Jouet led to the greatness of Jefferson that carried through to Lewis and finally Jackson. All the while these figures are protected by Johnny Reb, whose statue is decorated with Virginia's state seal as if conferring a benediction. Nearby sits another marker describing Monticello that points in the direction of the plantation. The blue-hued EJI marker mirrors this directional nod, tying Jefferson to the racial terror described thereon. Together these objects suggest two protagonists of Charlottesville's racial history, the famous president and the violated Black body. The Monticello marker reads: "Monticello: Three miles to the southeast. Thomas Jefferson began the house in 1770 and finished it in 1802. He brought his bride to it in 1772. Lafayette visited it in 1825. Jefferson spent his last years there and died there, July 4, 1826. His tomb is there. The place was raided by British Cavalry June 4, 1781." Certainly, a discussion about Jefferson as racist or enslaver would not have been part of the text; however, today the presence of the EJI marker recalls these facts for the visitor, subsequently complicating Jefferson's progenitor biography described in the Monticello marker.

Charlottesville has changed considerably since 2016. The unexpected violence of 2017 forced introspection by city and county residents and the University of Virginia community alike. In the last four years the list of initiatives aimed at creating a more authentic recounting of the area's history has become considerable. The list includes a community engagement process crafted by members of the President's Commission on Slavery at the University of Virginia that ultimately resulted in the building of the Monument to Enslaved Laborers; the creation of Liberation and Freedom Day to commemorate the March 3, 1865, liberation of the city by Union troops, which replaces Jefferson's birthday as a recognized paid holiday; projects like Mapping Cville, which exposes racist covenants in property deeds; the changing of park, street, and school names that were weighted with names of Confederates and known racists; and the emphasis on African American history in student and teacher education at the city and county levels through programs that emphasize cultural competency. Both the city and county now recognize July 12 as John Henry James Day. The activists who attended the Blue Ribbon Commission meetings continued their work to remove monuments with results. Activists were instrumental in crafting Senate Bill 183 and House Bill 1537, which allows localities to determine the outcome of their statues. Albemarle County removed its 1909 Johnny Reb statue from the front of the courthouse in 2021. In 2022 Charlottesville rid itself of both its Confederate monuments and those that celebrate native genocide.

Even with the drastic changes that have taken place, Charlottesville continues to wrestle with its social inequities. In 2018 Zyahna Bryant was featured in a *ProPublica, New York Times* article entitled "Charlottesville's Other Jim Crow Legacy: Separate and Unequal Education," which outlined the race-based disparities in the city's public schools.[24] Also in the same year, activists began to challenge city government about the true meaning of affordable housing in a city with rampant development. It was reported that four thousand units of affordable housing are needed to offset the impact that expensive developments have on those of average median income.[25] Disparities in health care also impact the city's African American community.[26] The process of revealing Charlottesville's racist past has allowed for this uneasy, often messy, move towards racial equality.

Typically, commission reports are placed on shelves waiting for their suggestions to be addressed (or often forgotten). Charlottesville's activist community happily includes historians who have little patience with this dead-end potentiality. These historians have taken leadership in educating the community by constantly inserting history into every social conversation. The process that began in 2018 to engage with the history of racial terror lynching has galvanized a significant swath of the community, resulting in a ripple effect that is driven by collective knowledge. The new projects, which effected significant change in the city's lived environment through elevation of the role played by Black people in the creation of the city, were advocated by and executed by many who participated in the pilgrimage. Their unique shared experience energized them for the considerable work ahead. As the Charlottesville's white majority pushes to reclaim a status quo that continues to see Jefferson as a source of collective identity, the revelation of racial terror as an element of a racist ethos that begins with him, is necessary. One must continue to indict the system of white supremacy that allowed the lynching of John Henry James and that continues to render powerless that historic 52 percent of the population.

Notes

1. Graham Moomaw, "Szakos Decries Response to Statue Comments," *Charlottesville Daily Progress*, April 2, 2012.
2. *Stanton Spectator and Vindicator*, July 21, 1898, 2
3. *Daily Progress*, May 29, 1899.
4. In the letter Bishop writes, "The whole town, negroes and white rushed up there and we expected to have a fight, but the whites were in a perfect frenzy—and I believe if it had commenced there would have been a battle equal to what is going on in Cuba." Unpublished letter, dated July 14, 1898, from Florence Bishop to her husband Jonathan A. Bishop, Albert and Shirley Small Special Collections Library, University of Virginia.
5. *Richmond Planet*, July 22, 1890, 2.
6. Jordy Yager, "John West and South Hall's Meadow," *Mapping Cville*, accessed Nov. 28, 2020, https://mappingcville.com/2019/03/.
7. J. F. Robinson, "The Charlottesville Fair," *Richmond Planet*, Nov. 7, 1891.
8. "A Word to Young Virginians," *Virginia University* magazine, Nov. 1890, 1.
9. Michael Eric Dyson, "Racial Terror, Fast and Slow," *New York Times*, April 17, 2015.
10. The PCSU engaged its public in a process that resulted in the naming of new buildings after formerly enslaved people, the commemoration of an African American burial ground at the university, and the building of a monument to enslaved laborers.

11. President's Commission on Slavery and the University, *Report to President Teresa A. Sullivan*, University of Virginia, 2018, 45.
12. Kirt Von Daacke, "Anatomical Theater," in *Educated in Tyranny: Slavery at Thomas Jefferson's University*, (Charlottesville: University of Virginia Press, 2019), 192.
13. See P. Preston Reynolds, "UVA and the History of Race: Eugenics, the Racial Integrity Act, Health Disparities," *UVA Today*, Jan. 9, 2020, https://news.virginia.edu/content/uva-and-history-race-eugenics-racial-integrity-act-health-disparities.
14. EJI.org, *Lynching in America: Confronting the Legacy of Racial Terror*, accessed Oct. 23, 2023, https://lynchinginamerica.eji.org/report/.
15. Vinegar Hill was, until 1964, the center of Black commerce. Its origins date to the 1870s, and by 1965, when it was leveled through the city's urban renewal plan, it included 129 homes and 29 businesses. The twenty-acre evidence of Black success and white neglect sat undeveloped until the 1980s.
16. Because of the Community Remembrance Project, Albemarle County realized they would have to contend with their racial narrative. In November 2018 Ms. Russell was appointed director of the county's newly founded Office of Diversity, Equity and Inclusion.
17. EJI.org, Community Remembrance Project, accessed Oct. 23, 2023, https://eji.org/projects/community-remembrance-project/.
18. Point no. 6 in the SPLC community resource guide entitled *Ten Ways to Fight Hate* suggests a person should not attend hate rallies. Instead, one should create an alternative event. That tactic was used in Charlottesville when events were held around the city to try and divert people away from the June 8, 2017, Ku Klux Klan rally.
19. Unpublished interview with Andrea Douglas, Nov. 18, 2019.
20. Mtamanika Youngblood and Donell Woodson from Atlanta's Sweet Auburn Historic District Development Corporation came to consult about the possibility of creating a similar historic development corporation for Vinegar Hill, the once-vibrant Black neighborhood whose destruction cauterized Black upward mobility and economic success. The Johnsons were invited to Charlottesville to begin discussions about a truth and reconciliation process for the city. They recommended that the Unite the Right rally be the catalyst for bringing together city and county residents to consider the area's racist past. A truth and reconciliation process is still being considered.
21. What allowed for the razing of McKee Row was its description as an unsightly felon rookery; once removed from the area, racial covenants ensured that Blacks would not return.
22. Unpublished interview with Andrea Douglas, Nov. 3, 2019.
23. The marker's text is purposefully stark. It is intended to be both revelatory and a reminder of the outcomes of extralegal mob activity. It reads: "Thousands of African Americans were the victims of lynching and racial violence in the United States between 1877 and 1950. During this era, racial terror lynching of African Americans emerged as a stunning form of violent resistance to emancipation and equal rights for African Americans, intended to intimidate black people and enforce racial hierarchy and segregation. Racial terror lynching was most prevalent in the South and was used to uphold white supremacy and enforce decades of political, social, and economic exploitation. Racial terror lynching became the most public and notorious form of subordination directed at black people and was frequently tolerated or even supported by law enforcement and elected officials illustrating the failure of the criminal justice system to afford black people equal

justice under law. White mobs were usually permitted to engage in brutal violence with impunity. Many black people were pulled out of jails or given over to mobs by law enforcement officials who were legally required to protect them. Even without any evidence, Whites' allegations against black people often sparked violent reprisal. Terror lynchings often included burnings and mutilation, sometimes in front of crowds numbering in the thousands. Many of the victims of these acts of violence were not recorded by name and remain unknown, but over 84 victims were documented in Virginia alone." Equal Justice Initiative, 2019, https://www.hmdb.org/m.asp?m=166184.
24. Annie Waldman and Erica Green, "Charlottesville's Other Jim Crow Legacy: Separate and Unequal," *ProPublica* and *New York Times,* Oct. 16, 2018, https://www.propublica.org/article/charlottesville-other-jim-crow-legacy-separate-and-unequal-education.
25. Bryan Kralik, "City Faces Uphill Battle with Affordable Housing," *Charlottesville Tomorrow,* June 20, 2018.
26. Ebony Hilton et al., "The Flaw of Medicine: Addressing Racial and Gender Disparities in Critical Care," *Anesthesiology Clinics* 38, no. 2 (June 2020): 357–68, https://doi.org/10.1016/j.anclin.2020.01.011.

RESTORING HISTORY

Writing the Narratives of Alexandria's Two Documented Lynchings

MADDY MCCOY, FARAR ELLIOTT, SUSAN K. FLINN, ANN MARIE HAY,
ELIZABETH LOCKWOOD, CHRISTOPHER MILKO, AND ROB TAYLOR

> No other city in the United States has as many historical points of interest as the old City of Alexandria, "Washington's home town." Volumes could be written in regard to them, and yet the whole story would not half be told.
> —A. J. Wedderburn, *1607–1907: Souvenir Virginia Tercentennial of Historic Alexandria*, 1907

The city of Alexandria trades on its history, small-town charm, and proximity to the nation's capital. Located just across the Potomac River from Washington, DC, tourism drives the Virginia town's economy. Along tree-lined streets of million-dollar row houses, plaques and tourism brochures speak of the many places George Washington ate, slept, and strolled. But these same streets housed one of the largest domestic slave traders in the country. And just over one hundred years ago, in the heart of the historic district, white Alexandrians dragged two Black residents from cells and tortured and murdered them. Knowing Alexandria's whole story, including its history of racial violence, is vital to understanding its past, as well as navigating our future.[1]

In 2019 Alexandria put out a call for citizens interested in participating in an Equal Justice Initiative Community Remembrance Project. The Equal Justice Initiative (EJI), based in Montgomery, Alabama, collaborates with communities to memorialize victims of racial violence and create meaningful dialogue about issues of race and justice. As concerned residents of Alexandria, the members of the authoring group volunteered for the research committee, one of several committees working on this project. We were tasked with uncovering and analyzing the truth of Alexandria's two documented lynchings. Our work was intended to serve as the foundation for the other committees, which would produce educational content, create historical markers, and conduct outreach to the community. By 2021 the city's program had been renamed the Alexandria Community Remembrance Project (ACRP). ACRP defined its mission as "a city-wide initiative dedicated to helping Alexandria understand its history of racial terror hate crimes and . . . creating a welcoming community bound by equity and inclusion." The narratives of Alexandria's two lynching victims are published on the city's website and form the basis of ongoing community remembrance initiatives.

Researching and writing the narratives of the two lynchings meant confronting Alexandria's historic prejudices and America's systemic, institutionalized racism. It meant challenging our own biases as a group that was predominantly composed of white volunteers. With 2020's nation-shaking protests as a backdrop, we found ourselves confronting the same script in the present day that was emerging from our historical research.

The project's core challenge was uncovering and restoring the truths that had been masked by racist journalism and deliberately misleading official statements. The two lynchings occurred during a short time span, and this allowed a "script" to emerge within the white community of our city in response to the murders. In both cases, white authorities praised police as heroic public servants overwhelmed by a massive anonymous mob and determined the deaths were at the hand of a "person or persons unknown." Newspapers alleged the presence of "outsiders" and refused to report that white Alexandrians were in the mob. White residents, journalists, and city officials all pointed to Black Alexandrians who attempted to prevent attacks as the very reason a lynching became "inevitable."

Black-run newspapers like the *Richmond Planet* and the *Cleveland Gazette* provided valuable keys to decode the events misrepresented in the dominant white press. Their counternarrative provided what little insight exists into the Black community's response and a small window into the truth behind the official scripts. Their reporting was invaluable in deconstructing the official white narrative.

The Lynching of Joseph McCoy

> As the people killed him, they will have to bury him.
> —Joseph McCoy's aunt, name omitted by
> the *Alexandria Gazette*, April 24, 1897

In the early morning of April 23, 1897, a Black teenager named Joseph McCoy was lynched in Alexandria. Beginning in the late evening on April 22, a white mob attacked the police station where he was being held. On their second attempt, the mob seized McCoy from his cell, then shot, bludgeoned, and hanged him from the lamppost on a corner near the police station. Virginia governor Charles T. O'Ferrall was highly critical of Alexandria's failure to anticipate and prevent the lynching and immediately launched an inquiry.

Events began when a white resident named Richard Lacy alleged that Joseph McCoy, who had long worked for Lacy, had sexually assaulted three of Lacy's daughters. Alexandria police lieutenant James Smith arrested McCoy without a warrant and detained him in the station house. Joseph McCoy denied the charge. Later, Smith interrogated McCoy and reported that the prisoner confessed, despite the earlier denial.[2]

As the evening progressed, a white crowd gathered outside the station house. Later, in the aftermath of the lynching, Leonard Marbury, commonwealth's attorney and a lieutenant in the Alexandria Light Infantry (ALI), and Alexandria mayor Luther Thompson testified that they had believed there was no danger of attack at the station house. They both reported speaking with people they knew in the crowd but denied that these Alexandria residents had anything to do with lynching Joseph McCoy.[3]

The *Washington Post* reported that a crowd of at least five hundred gathered near city hall. Ordered to disperse, they remained in the area. Sometime around midnight, the mob attacked the front doors of the brick station house using a piece of lumber as a battering ram. The doors were broken open and several men entered. Officers reportedly fired their pistols in the air and drove the crowd back. Four members of the mob were detained. The police closed and braced the station house doors.[4]

Lieutenant Smith, who had arrested and detained McCoy, addressed the crowd in a tone suggesting familiarity: "Gentleman, I hope and pray that each and every citizen will go home; this man will be dealt with according to law and be given a fair and impartial trial, and I hope if he is guilty he will get his just desserts, and I am satisfied he will."[5]

Despite the attack on the station house, officials later, implausibly, claimed that the initial crowd had no intention of lynching McCoy. At the same time, they professed not to know who the people in the crowd were. The governor's investigator asked many of the white witnesses, including police officers, members of the ALI, and the mayor, "Did you recognize any of the men that were in the mob?" The answer, repeated by these witnesses almost verbatim, was: "Not a one of them sir."[6]

Mayor Thompson stated that he was awakened after midnight by a court constable who reported the first attack. The constable claimed that no further trouble was expected, so Thompson went back to sleep. Although slumbering only five blocks from the station house, the mayor also claimed not to hear the alarm bell that Lieutenant Smith later ordered be rung. Lieutenant Marbury heard the alarm and proceeded to the station. He claimed the mob assembled there was, "as a whole," composed of different men from the first attack.[7]

An hour later, the mob attacked the station house and gained entrance despite another fusillade of warning shots from officers. Police captain James Webster reported: "By the time I got down there the place was full of men; they had come through the doors and windows on all sides."[8]

Again, officials later claimed to recognize no one in this mob. Lieutenant Smith said, "There were a great many strangers" and "the lights were turned out and many of the men in the crowd had their hats pulled down over their eyes, which obscured their features."[9] This statement conflicts with initial newspaper reports that "many of the leading citizens of the town were among the crowd" and that "most of the members [of the Alexandria Light Infantry], however, were in the crowd about the station-house."[10]

The officers were quickly overpowered. The attackers broke down McCoy's cell door and carried him into the street. He was beaten and dragged a city block from the station house to the corner of Cameron and Lee streets. Here, the mob hanged Joseph McCoy from a lamppost, shot him several times, and bludgeoned him with an axe.[11] The *Alexandria Gazette* added that "other indignities [were] heaped upon his quivering remains."[12] The *Washington Post* reported: "The body of McCoy was left hanging to the lamppost for fifteen minutes before it was cut down. Three bullet holes were found, one in the left shoulder and two bullets in the left thigh. The left eye was much swollen. As he was strung up to the lampost he was struck on the head with a cobblestone. . . . A pool of blood was found near the base of the post."[13]

The postmortem on Joseph McCoy occurred on the morning of April 23 at Demaine and Son Funeral Home. The coroner's jury, composed of prominent Alexandria citizens, stated that McCoy's cause of death was "strangulation at the hands of a person or persons unknown."[14] The jury also determined that the "officers of the police force did all in their power to protect the prisoner."[15]

Among the white population that day, there was approval of the mob's action as well as a stated fear of an uprising from the Black community. Rumors swirled of mobs bent on revenge. Crowds of armed white men, including ALI members, gathered around the Lacy house. No actual threat from the Black community emerged, despite a false report "that a mob of negroes had surrounded" the Lacy house and was "endeavoring to burn it."[16] As is also apparent in the second lynching two years later, these false reports justified further white violence against the Black community.[17]

On the evening of April 24, rumors spread that more than two hundred "negroes were congregating near Arlington [an adjacent county] with the avowed purpose of marching on Alexandria and wreaking their revenge upon its [presumably white] inhabitants." The authorities' reaction ran counter to their response the night of Joseph McCoy's lynching. Military alarms were rung. The ALI gathered at the armory. The "whole white male population of the city was upon the street by this time, and began to arm themselves." Mayor Thompson even accepted the services of the Confederate veterans and the Alexandria Fire Department.[18]

After this and other "alarming rumors" turned out to be unsubstantiated, the militia was recalled and the white male citizens of Alexandria went home to bed. Nonetheless, several local Black citizens were arrested "on suspicion."[19]

Joseph McCoy's body was buried in a "common pine coffin" in Penny Hill Cemetery, Alexandria's burial ground for the indigent.[20] McCoy's relatives refused to pay the costs of the funeral. His aunt stated, "As the people killed him, they will have to bury him."[21] Her powerful statement lays the blame for the death squarely on the shoulders of the city of Alexandria and its white citizens.

Local Black pastor Rev. William Gaines conducted the funeral service: "We cannot indorse mob violence and lynch law. Nor do we believe that the best citizens of this city approve of such. I trust that the time will soon come when all people will realize the fact that the same judgment which they measure to others will be measured to them at the bar of God."[22]

Following the investigation, Governor O'Ferrall chastised the Alexandria police officers for dereliction of duty and failure to protect their prisoner. The governor did not, however, question the accusations against the untried Joseph McCoy, stating:

> In the city of Alexandria I regret to say that in my opinion there was dereliction of duty somewhere. . . . There may be no doubt the prisoner was guilty of a most heinous crime, committed under the most diabolical circumstances, and deserved death, but he was in the custody of the law officers, safely confined, and yet a mob was permitted in a city of 18,000 population, with a strong military force at the command of the Mayor, to bid defiance to the law and trample down the authority of the Commonwealth. There can be no possible excuse offered for the success of the mob.[23]

The Black editors of the *Richmond Planet* expressed outrage:

> Almost within the shadow of the capitol at Washington, within a few minutes ride of the official residence of the President of the United States and the halls of Congress, with Virginia militia as spectators, and the United States troops a few steps away, a murderous mob, composed of men who knew better on Friday, April 23, 1897, took from the station-house at Alexandria, Va., the crouching, trembling form of Joseph McCoy and hanged him to a lamp-post. . . .
>
> It was murder pure and simple and as it was premeditated, executed with precision, it was murder in the first degree.
>
> Every citizen, white or black, young or old who took part in this disgraceful proceedings is as guilty of as heinous a crime as the one with which McCoy stood charged.[24]

Many in the region's white community did not share the outrage. There were reports of a festive, celebratory atmosphere, as the sites involved in McCoy's lynching drew crowds from the city and surrounding area. The station house and the street corner where the lynching occurred were visited by "2,000 strangers" and, on the lamppost itself, "an enterprising tobacco firm had placarded cigarette advertisements."[25] The reported atmosphere reflected no sense of regret, disapproval, or shame. An article in the *Alexandria Gazette* reported: "SUMMER WEATHER.—Yesterday was a summer day with the temperature too high for comfort. It was generally conceded that there were more visitors in the city than on any Sunday in the city's history. Several hundred went to the station house for the purpose of seeing the damage inflicted by Thursday night's mob, and the lamp post from which McCoy was hanged was also an object of interest. Hundreds came here on bicycles and spun through the streets. The electric cars and boats were crowded on each trip."[26]

The Lynching of Benjamin Thomas

> One hundred willing hands dragged him out . . .
> —*Washington Times*, August 9, 1899

Emboldened by the anemic official response to the murder of Joseph McCoy, white Alexandrians lynched Black teenager Benjamin Thomas two years later. On August 8, 1899, a mob attacked the city jail on St. Asaph Street and dragged Thomas half a mile to the city's main thoroughfare. They hanged him from a lamppost on a prominent corner opposite city hall. Since Joseph McCoy's murder in 1897, some things had changed in Alexandria. A different mayor and governor held office, and members of the ALI had left town to fight in the Spanish-American War.[27]

Alexandria police had arrested Benjamin Thomas on August 7, on the charge of attempted criminal assault on Lillian Kloch, an eight-year-old white girl who lived next door. Sixteen-year-old Thomas asserted his innocence at the time of his arrest.[28]

Mayor George L. Simpson directed officers to confine Benjamin Thomas "quietly" in the police station house, although the *Alexandria Gazette* reported that Thomas's arrest had "caused some excitement in the community."[29]

Alexandria's Black residents soon became aware of Thomas's arrest. Neighborhood conversations revolved around the memory of McCoy's violent murder in 1897. As concerns grew, some Black men organized in an attempt to aid police in defending Benjamin Thomas. One man, James Turley, was confronted by a group of white men loudly threatening a lynching. Turley then sought to organize Black citizens to prevent another murder. Albert Green, another Black Alexandrian, also sought to gather a group for the same purpose. Furthermore, a delegation of Black men visited Simpson's house around midnight to plead for the protection necessary to prevent Benjamin Thomas's lynching. They reiterated the Black community's fear of another murder.[30]

In contrast, Mayor Simpson and police lieutenant James Smith both implausibly stated that they perceived no danger to the prisoner's safety. Despite the murderous white violence in 1897, and the obvious danger to Thomas, the mayor denied the Black residents' requests and threatened the concerned men with arrest for being out on the street. White newspapers also disingenuously portrayed this desire to aid the accused as an affront to the white community and a threat of direct violence against white Alexandrians.

Later, Lieutenant Smith visited the mayor's home. He did not report the concerns voiced *by* the Black community. Instead, Smith expressed concerns *about* the Black community. He told the mayor that officers and white residents were increasingly fearful about the growing numbers of Black men gathering downtown. The mayor ordered Smith to direct officers to clear the streets and arrest the Black residents.[31]

The officers confronted the group led by Albert Green, who once again tried to express the community's fears of an impending lynching. Green and his men "proposed to offer their lives in his [Thomas's] defence" and aid the police. Lieutenant Smith discounted their fear and arrested Albert Green and others for being "very insolent."[32] Nearby, officers and white residents accosted and arrested other Black citizens, including James Turley and Richard Washington, who expressed their desire to help protect Thomas. Over the course of the night, police arrested a total of twelve Black men. Even though they were earnestly offering to assist the police, the men were all charged with various offenses, including carrying concealed weapons, disorderly conduct, and inciting a riot.[33]

In marked contrast, police recruited white vigilantes to help patrol Alexandria's Black neighborhoods. These white vigilantes were empowered and encouraged by the police officers to detain Black residents. This informal deputization reinforced Alexandria's racial hierarchy and its implied precept that white citizens had unchecked extrajudicial power over Black bodies.

Newspaper articles in the white press consistently depicted the Black community's attempt to defend Benjamin Thomas as "demonstrations against the whites."[34] The *Richmond Planet* presented a different perspective: "We are pleased to notice the attitude of the colored men of Alexandria in organizing to prevent a lynching. Our only regret is that they did not go further, and be more combative. . . . Oh, what a pity that the colored men dispersed and failed to re-assemble again! . . . However, they acted manfully. Let colored men in other sections do likewise. Let them defend colored men threatened with lynching even if they have to sacrifice a dozen lives in so doing."[35]

The next morning, following the Black community's organized protection efforts for Benjamin Thomas, white Alexandria was in an uproar. Exaggeration, falsehoods, and distortion served to inflame violent sentiment. Wild stories circulated. They described hundreds of armed Black men attempting to break Thomas free, threatening to lynch a white man, and desiring to kill white residents. In the face of the Black community's explicit pleas for protection, local authorities and journalists accused them of roiling white residents. While newspaper articles claimed that no white citizens knew about the case prior to the organized effort to defend Benjamin Thomas, white Alexandrians in the street spoke openly of lynching him.[36]

That day, Mayor Simpson convened the court before a large crowd at city hall to consider the cases of the Black men arrested the previous night. Lieutenant James Smith testified first, recounting his version of Monday night's events. Most tellingly, he claimed the town was quiet and there was no gathering of white men. Smith testified that, shortly before midnight, several Black men passed the police station house together. This, along with reports of Black residents congregating in their neighborhoods, was apparently enough for Smith to report to the mayor's house; there, he had received his orders to clear the streets.[37]

Other officers testified, describing the Black men as "obdurate" and "bent on mischief," and stating that "there seemed to be no corner in the eastern part of town without its squad of rioters." Calling the Black men "rioters" contradicts reports of the officers' own accounts of their encounters with the Black community.[38]

Although lynching was openly discussed on the streets outside the court, the police, the mayor, and several white citizens all testified according to script that "no threats of lynching were heard on the part of the whites."[39]

Of those arrested, the only man to speak was James Turley, who pled innocent to the charge of causing disorder. He testified that he had heard several white men threatening violence.[40]

Mayor Simpson berated the accused men and the Black community for a "boisterous display of regard for the safety of one of their own race," where they "noisily congregate and recklessly invite a catastrophe." He again described Alexandria's white community as having been completely unaware of any imminent trouble. The men were found guilty and either fined or sentenced to the local chain gang.[41]

The *Richmond Planet*, reflected upon the proceedings: "Was there ever a greater parody upon justice than the sight of citizens of Alexandria—colored citizens hauled before a white mayor and fined $20 for doing their duty? Mayor Simpson is a disgrace to the office. He, a sworn official of the law fining other citizens who were anxious to see the laws upheld."[42]

Sixteen-year-old Benjamin Thomas's hearing came next on the mayor's docket. According to the *Alexandria Gazette,* on the day of the hearing, Lillian Kloch "was the only witness examined" and she provided the only evidence offered to the court. She accused Thomas of attempting to take "indecent liberties" with her but said that "he committed no assault."[43] There is no record that Thomas testified in his own defense. Mayor Simpson remanded Thomas into the city sergeant's custody until a trial by the grand jury for a capital offense that under Virginia law meant he could be hanged. Thomas was taken immediately from the court and transported to the Alexandria jail "followed by a crowd of whites and blacks."[44]

The city's turbulent atmosphere did not subside after court adjourned. Following the hearing, Mayor Simpson was handling a confiscated pistol when he accidentally fired the weapon into the office wall, alarming people in the street. This incident fed white anxiety and inspired multiple rumors, including one of an attempted escape by Benjamin Thomas.[45]

Journalists circulating through the city saw small groups of white men gathering and heard "threats of lynching had been freely made" all day.[46] Lieutenant Smith made a similar report. An observer from Washington, DC, described crowds of white men and said, "I do not believe there was a man in those little groups who had not bought or borrowed a firearm."[47] The *Richmond Planet* reported that "the stock of firearms and ammunition in this city was exhausted, and expeditions were made to Washington to increase the supply."[48]

Although he was "apprehending no trouble," Mayor Simpson ordered Police Chief Webster to fortify the jail with additional personnel for the evening to assure citizens that "every means will be resorted to in order to protect the prisoner."[49] Additionally, officers removed Thomas from his cell and hid him in the jail's cellar.[50]

Later that evening, the white mob gathered in front of the jail. A witness observed, "There was a leadership . . . of the highest ability. . . . The first movement on the jail was orderly, and not until the engagement with the police did the fury of the mob, which had now become lawless and uncontrollable, show itself."[51] Sometime before midnight, the "enraged white citizens," who numbered between 500 and 2,000, demanded that Benjamin Thomas be handed over to them.[52]

Official statements and newspaper articles presented conflicting reports about the composition of the crowd. In an interview the next day, Mayor Simpson said that "legal proceedings could be instituted against those who took part in the lynching. He said when he reached the jail, he recognized several prominent citizens as leaders of the mob." In the same interview, he backtracked and said, "These very men were the most prominent in advocating the rule of law and order, and others assumed leadership."[53] His continued indecision, at a minimum, confirms that Simpson knew and recognized many members of the mob. This is confirmed by his statement: "I did all I could by persuasion and force to disperse the mob. My efforts seemed of no avail. I was trampled upon in defending the dignity of the city. My friends, however, stood by me and all of the respectable citizens who were in the mob did the same, but the lawless element overpowered them. The mob element, although it may be composed of some of my friends, will be prosecuted as far as I am able to the fullest extent of the law."[54]

From the jailhouse steps, Mayor Simpson addressed the crowd, urging them to return home: "Fellow citizens, if you will disperse and go away quietly, I will promise you that a court will be convened today and a true bill found by the grand jury. If this is not done, I will give you my word, as a man of honor, that I will personally lead a mob tomorrow night to lynch Thomas."[55]

The mayor clearly stated that he would lead the lynch mob himself if Thomas was not found guilty by the courts. Although this may have been his attempt to maintain control of the crowd, the mayor used Thomas's life as a pawn to appease the armed mob, while openly interfering with the legal process and validating the mob's worst impulses. This was also an attempt to avoid the same civic embarrassment previously generated by the governor's investigation into Joseph McCoy's lynching. Simpson's only stated concern was "defending the dignity of the city."[56]

Despite the mayor's promise, Simpson's fellow citizens were undeterred by his words. Once again, a white mob used a battering ram to break through the jail door. Chief of Police Webster was knocked over and injured during the attack.[57]

Inside the jail, the mob "overpowered"[58] the officers and used axes to beat down the heavy, interior iron door.[59] The enraged crowd demanded that the guards turn Thomas over to them, but newspapers reported that the guards refused. Members of the mob wrested the cell keys from the jail wardens and began searching for Thomas. Every cell and room in the jail was "invaded by the frenzied people," who assaulted two other Black prisoners in their pursuit of Thomas.[60] The *Wilkes-Barre Times* wrote that "a great shout went up when Thomas was found and one hundred willing hands dragged him out and up the stairs" onto the street.[61]

The *Evening Star* reported, "A dozen stalwart hands now fastened their grip upon him."[62] The excited mob bound Thomas with a rope around his neck, in his mouth, and under his arms. The hooting and jeering mob dragged the young man, his head bumping over the rough cobblestones.[63] The *Richmond Planet* wrote that "thousands of spectators" followed close behind.[64]

The *Alexandria Gazette* reported that "the excitement at this time was at fever heat."[65] Later, numerous white newspapers described, with exhilaration and relish, the brutalization of Benjamin Thomas. The frenzied mob pelted him with stones and bricks. They struck him with pieces of iron. They stabbed him, kicked him, and fired "bullet after bullet"[66] into his body.[67] Wounded and bleeding, Thomas "cried in vain for his mother."[68]

The *Evening Star* reported: "The outspreading limbs of a convenient tree presented themselves and a halt was called, but it was soon decided to seek another place. Vainly Thomas strove to free himself. He fought with the ferocity of a demon. But the rope had so caught over his head as to make him powerless. In the struggle every particle of clothing was torn from his body, so that his feet alone were protected. His cries and moans were heartrending but the mob was relentless. Down to King street the crowd proceeded, shouting and firing pistols in the air."[69]

The mob dragged Thomas half a mile to one of the most prominent intersections in the city, known as Leadbeater's Corner. At that point, Thomas's head "was crushed and battered by the terrible drag over the stones, while his breast and legs were a mass of bullet holes."[70]

Across from the market square at city hall, the mob fashioned a noose, and threw the rope over a lamppost. "Willing hands pulled at the loose end, and in a few moments Thomas's life went out."[71] One participant proudly reported snatching souvenirs, including bloody scraps of clothing, a bit of rope, and part of a bullet casing that went through Thomas's head.[72]

The white terror mob, "after being satisfied that he was dead, dispersed," "leaving the body suspended as a terrible warning."[73]

The next morning, the *Alexandria Gazette* reported that "the streets gradually resumed their normal quiet."[74] With a tone of ghoulish sensationalism, newspapers reflected the mood of many of the white citizens, using phrases such as "exciting scenes" and "theatre."[75] The prevailing white sentiment was that the Black community's actions caused the behavior of the white mob and the subsequent lynching. The *Baltimore Sun* reported, "The popular feeling had culminated in the idea that a class of negroes were carrying things with a high hand" and that "this led to the lynching."[76]

The *Alexandria Gazette* also reported that "the authorities have taken decided steps to prevent any further breach of the peace."[77] These actions were clearly taken only to constrain the Black community, as the white mob had already achieved its purpose.

The next morning, the city coroner conducted the inquest, as he had following Joseph McCoy's murder. The verdict stated: "We, the jury, find that Benjamin Thomas came to his death at the hands of a mob unknown to the jury."[78]

The idea that the members of the white mob were "unknown to the jury" clearly contradicted earlier reports that prominent citizens were present and involved. It mirrors, however, both the inquest conclusion following Joseph McCoy's murder and the language commonly used to describe lynchings throughout the country. In both Alexandria lynchings, white citizens, officers, and officials refused to name the white men who took part in the murders.[79]

Denials of white Alexandrians' participation appeared in the white press immediately. The *Baltimore Sun* falsely declared, "It is a fact that strangers led the lynching party." The paper instead asserted that "while nearly a thousand Alexandrians were congregated on the occasion, more of them endeavored to restrain the crowd and to uphold the law than participated in the lynching."[80] However, the Black press confirmed the presence of well-known white Alexandrians.[81]

The denials had grown bolder in the two years since Joseph McCoy was killed. After the 1897 lynching, the lack of identification of the mob members was blamed on the night being dark, faces being obscured, and the crowd being largely composed of outsiders. In 1899, the white community did not rely on similar excuses. The *Times* of Washington, DC, stated that "the lynchers wore no masks," and that the mayor and police officers were certainly close enough to have identified members of the mob.[82] The crime was committed with full confidence that the perpetrators would never be brought to justice.

Cementing the violent assertion of white dominance over the Black community, Mayor Simpson ordered the Alexandria Light Infantry to "hold themselves in readiness for any emergency."[83] White citizens feared retaliation from their Black neighbors. In response, a shipment of rifles and ammunition was sent from Richmond for the infantry's use. This concern for law and order did not manifest the previous night when an armed mob attacked the jail. The state only acknowledged and acted upon the fear of anticipated violence against the white community. One newspaper reported that the lynching "has awakened the State to its unprotected condition."[84] As was often the case, the irrational white fears were unjustified; there were no attacks from the Black community.

In reality, although Black Alexandrians were both afraid and angry, "there was no suggestion of an uprising." The *Washington Times* quoted one Black resident, who lamented, "What have we to be violent with? You have the arms and the wealth. We have neither. The law is with you and against us. We would simply invite our annihilation were we to provoke a conflict."[85]

Instead of direct agitation, the Black community protested through passive resistance; the *Times* reported that "numerous colored servants have refused to return to their work in the homes of white families."[86]

On Thursday, August 10, 1899, following a simple service, Benjamin Thomas was laid to rest at Penny Hill Cemetery. Hundreds passed through the funeral home where the body lay, but none was his mother. The *Evening Star* of Washington, DC, reported "Elizabeth Thomas, his mother, refused to receive the remains at her home. She could not bear to look upon her boy, she said, and would have nothing to do with his funeral."[87]

Later that month, a large crowd, estimated at six hundred, attended a memorial service at Alexandria's Shiloh Baptist Church. Rev. Henry H. Warring and clergy from three other local Black churches eulogized Benjamin Thomas. Reverend Warring spoke of Thomas as a moral, honest boy, innocent of any crime, and condemned the city for failing to protect him. He advocated charging anyone guilty of the lynching with criminal assault. He exhorted the congregation to boycott businesses of those who participated in the lynching, offering evidence that the Black community knew who was in the white mob. He cautioned them: "Men stand behind counters selling you goods whose hands are stained with the blood of Ben Thomas. Don't spend another dollar with them."[88] He continued: "Who can tell how this poor innocent boy felt as he crouched in the cellar at the jail and listened to the howling mob crying for his life's blood; when the rope was placed about his neck and into his mouth; when he was dragged mercilessly through the streets and bullets were being poured into his body by his heartless persecutors, as he cried in vain for his mother?"[89]

The Script Emerges

> A new generation has appeared who have been taught to believe that they are entitled to equal rights, politically, socially and otherwise.
> —Prominent Alexandria businessman Thomas Risheill,
> *Alexandria Gazette*, August 16, 1899

Alexandria's two known lynchings followed a script common not only to each other but also to lynchings across America. This script developed and spread across the South from rural areas to urban centers such as Alexandria.[90] As Ida B. Wells pointed out, "It has left the out of the way places where ignorance prevails, has thrown off the mask and with this new cry stalks in broad daylight in large cities."[91]

In both known Alexandria lynchings, white officials—including the mayor, the governor, and the commonwealth's attorney—claimed to be distressed and promised investigations. Although the governor did order an inquiry into the McCoy lynching, and testimony was taken, no arrests were made or punishments handed down. In the case of Benjamin Thomas, there was no investigation, let alone any consequences. In contrast, Thomas's Black defenders were arrested, tried, and punished for trying to prevent his murder.[92]

In both cases, newspaper accounts painted a mythology of police officers as white saviors overwhelmed by impossible odds. They claimed authorities "made a heroic resistance" and used every means in their power to defend the Black youths. However, in the case of Thomas's murder, reports stated that "no man in the mob was injured by a policeman and no policeman was hurt by any man in the mob."[93] Additionally, some contemporaneous articles denounced Alexandria's response, reporting that the police "practically surrendered the prisoner without protest."[94]

In both cases, city officials and newspaper accounts acknowledged that prominent Alexandrians were leaders of the mobs and simultaneously emphasized that anonymous outsiders were responsible for the violence. Later press reports stated that it was a fact that "strangers" led both lynching parties. These convenient scapegoats were conjured up to exonerate the city's white residents and deflect blame or responsibility away from Alexandria.[95]

By contrast, in both instances, white officials and media weaponized the concept of "strangers" against the Black community. Newspaper reports and false eyewitness accounts detailed large numbers of Black men descending upon Alexandria to take revenge. These false reports intentionally incited white fear and anxiety and provoked a militarized response from armed residents, local police, and the militia.[96]

In both cases, there was an immediate presumption of the victims' guilt—by the white press, the white authorities, and the white community. Even the governor's investigation into Joseph McCoy's murder was grounded in a presumption of McCoy's guilt. Two years later, the Alexandria mayor promised to lynch Benjamin Thomas himself, regardless of proven guilt. It was a common tactic by white authorities to blame the victims and use their presumed guilt to justify the murders.[97]

In both cases, the lynching script dehumanized and devalued Black bodies. The reports lied about Joseph McCoy's and Benjamin Thomas's ages, physical appearance, and aggressive behavior to fuel white fear and justify white violence. The press used words like "ravisher," "demon," and "brute" to describe the two teenagers.[98]

The absence of accountability following Joseph McCoy's murder sent a clear message to all involved: Do not fear repercussions for violence or dereliction of duty. The refusal of the coroner and the coroner's jury to lay blame confirmed what the white community already knew—no one would be held accountable. In both cases, the white community was complicit in allowing the lynchings to occur or actively engaged in supporting or perpetrating the murders.

The bold and blatant murders of two Black teenagers highlighted the overwhelming power of Alexandria's state-sanctioned racism. Nonetheless, and in the face of violence, the Black community articulated a counternarrative and found concrete ways to resist white supremacy. During the bleak, dark hours before Benjamin Thomas's lynching, Black members of the community mobilized in an attempt to prevent his murder, and in the immediate aftermath, domestic workers reportedly refused to come to work. Meanwhile, Black religious leaders advocated boycotting the businesses of mob members and spoke out against the failures of civic authorities to prevent and then subsequently prosecute the crimes. Following both attacks, family members refused to pay for the funerals of the murdered youths.

Lynchings were used to control and suppress Black communities in Alexandria and elsewhere, maintaining a social and racial hierarchy. Prominent businessman Thomas Risheill clearly articulates the control that the white community wielded over the Black community. One week after Thomas's murder, on the front page of the *Alexandria Gazette,* he advocated candidly for the role lynching played in creating a "well ordered" society:

> During the time that slavery existed in the south and for twenty years after the negro was freed, lynching was not thought of or practised in the south. During the civil war when the father, husband and son left home for the battlefield, the mother, wife and children were placed under the protection of the slave and they knew they were safe. But since that time a new generation has appeared who have been taught to believe that they are entitled to equal rights, politically, socially and otherwise. From this generation we get the criminals who merit the rope and shot gun. . . .
>
> Lynching is not approved of by the great mass of people in the south. But so long as the attorney can put in evidence that the criminal is not responsible for his acts, and so long as the courts postpone trials indefinitely, and so long as the unmentionable crime is committed, no man who takes part in the lynching bee will be punished.[99]

Restoring History and Moving Forward

> The answer always is: "Tell the world the facts."
> —Ida B. Wells-Barnett, *The Red Record*, 1895

In 1897 and 1899, Joseph McCoy and Benjamin Thomas were murdered while in police custody in Alexandria. Today, these murders echo loudly as we watch police killings of Black Americans.

Our research group began work in October 2019 under the auspices of the Equal Justice Initiative and the Office of Historic Alexandria. The city of Alexandria charged us with researching these acts in order to provide information for use in commemoration of the lynchings and the creation of historical markers.[100]

We continued the work in the summer of 2020, as protests around the murders of Black Americans rose above the nation's continued efforts to ignore them. More than a century after Benjamin Thomas called for his mother with a noose around his neck, George Floyd used his dying breath to do the same.[101] The brutality is ongoing, the script pushes back, and history repeats itself.

Reactions to today's racial justice protests mirror official statements and white press coverage of Alexandria's lynchings over a century ago. They continue to echo Thomas Risheill's words to denigrate those who feel "entitled to equal rights" during Black Lives Matter protests.[102] In contrast, after a predominantly white mob of armed citizens attacked the US Capitol in January 2021, US senator Ron Johnson (R-WI) indicated he was never concerned for his safety. He stated that the mob was composed of "people that loved this country" who "truly respect law enforcement, would never do anything to break the law, so I wasn't concerned."[103] His comment explicitly illustrates the belief that, while Black protesters and their allies are a threat to America, a white mob can attack the Capitol and still be labeled patriotic. In Virginia's classrooms, and throughout the country, educators face serious political opposition to teaching the full facts of America's racial history.

We worked hard to deconstruct Alexandria's lynching narratives, to make hidden history visible, and to move closer to overriding systemic racism's official script. Our research established the complicity of Alexandria's white citizens, law enforcement, and government during the lynchings of Joseph

McCoy and Benjamin Thomas. This complicity has not yet been fully acknowledged. We hope commemorations and historical markers will help our community begin to reflect, as the Equal Justice Initiative puts it, on the "deeply-rooted, violent resistance that upheld the racial caste system for so long."[104] As Andrea Douglas argues in this volume, truth telling can become an act of activism.[105] This mirrors Ida B. Wells's sentiment when asked what can be done to help the cause. "The answer always is: 'Tell the world the facts.'"[106]

Since we completed our assignment, the city of Alexandria has worked to acknowledge and spread the facts by creating markers memorializing the lynching victims, collecting soil to bring on the community pilgrimage to the Legacy Museum and National Memorial for Peace and Justice in Montgomery, and conducting further research regarding other incidents of racial terror in Alexandria. The ACRP continues efforts to identify living descendants of the McCoy and Thomas families.[107]

While our nation's continued reckoning with racial violence illustrates the need to confront the history that contributes to the present, markers and monuments are only the first step. To begin to dismantle the systems that maintain white supremacy, we must address the lasting effect of these crimes on our community. The creation of monuments will be performative and devoid of meaning without the city engaging in real and significant change demanded by an affected community. Monuments removed are insufficient. Monuments erected are only part of the work.

Scholar, lawyer, and activist, Sherrilyn Ifill suggests that the bottom-up, community-driven truth and reconciliation process is essential to achieve that reckoning.[108] Local institutions must confront their complicity in the terror that lynchings held, and hold, over the Black community. This is especially important in Alexandria—where descendants of victims and perpetrators still live shoulder-to-shoulder.

As a citizen-based research group, we hope that confronting this history and acknowledging our culpability and complicity will help move the community into uncomfortable, honest public discussions. If Alexandria and, indeed, America are ever to become more just and equitable, our government, civic bodies, faith organizations, and fellow citizens need to engage with the racist complicity in our past and strive to fully understand and reject the script that is still followed today.

Notes

1. At the time, Alexandria's population was about 14,500; 31 percent were Black: see Krystyn Moon, "The African American Housing Crisis in Alexandria, VA, 1930s–1960s," *Virginia Magazine of History and Biography* 124, no. 1 (2016): 28–68; Joshua D. Rothman, *The Ledger and the Chain: How Domestic Slave Traders Shaped America* (New York: Basic Books, 2021).
2. (Washington, DC) *Evening Star,* April 23, 1897; Amy Bertsch, *Alexandria Police Department* (Charleston, SC: Arcadia, 2006); Virginia, Governor (1894–98: O'Ferrall), executive papers of Gov. Charles T. O'Ferrall, 1894–97, Accession 43210, Box 3, Folder 7, State government records collection, Library of Virginia, Richmond, https://ead.lib.virginia.edu/vivaxtf/view?docId=lva/vi01956.
3. Executive papers of Gov. Charles T. O'Ferrall.
4. *Washington Post,* April 23, 1897; *Alexandria Gazette,* April 23, 2897; executive papers of Gov. Charles T. O'Ferrall.
5. *Alexandria Gazette,* April 23, 1897.
6. Executive papers of Gov. Charles T. O'Ferrall.
7. Executive papers of Gov. Charles T. O'Ferrall.
8. Executive papers of Gov. Charles T. O'Ferrall.
9. Executive papers of Gov. Charles T. O'Ferrall.
10. *Washington Post,* April 23, 1897.
11. Executive papers of Gov. Charles T. O'Ferrall; *Alexandria Gazette,* April 23, 1897.
12. *Alexandria Gazette,* April 23, 1897.
13. *Washington Post,* April 24, 1897.
14. *Washington Post,* April 24, 1897.
15. Demaine and Son Funeral Home was located at 817 King Street. *Virginia State Gazetteer and Business Directory 1897–98* (Richmond, VA: J. L. Hill Print. Co., 1896); *Washington Post,* April 24, 1897.
16. *Alexandria Gazette,* April 24, 1897.
17. *Salt Lake Semi-Weekly Tribune,* April 27, 1897.
18. *Washington Post,* April 25, 1897.
19. *Washington Post,* April 25, 1897.
20. (Washington, DC) *Evening Star,* April 26, 1897.
21. *Alexandria Gazette,* April 24, 1897.
22. *Washington Post,* April 25, 1897.
23. *Washington Post,* Dec. 2, 1897.
24. *Richmond Planet,* May 1, 1897.
25. *Washington Post,* April 26, 1897.
26. *Alexandria Gazette,* April 26, 1897.
27. *Cleveland Gazette,* Aug. 26, 1899; *Sun and New York Press,* Aug. 10, 1899. The *Richmond Planet* stated that the mob consisted of "thousands" (Aug. 12, 1899).
28. *Washington Times,* Aug. 8, 1899. (This paper was published from 1894 to 1939 and should not be confused with the current publication by that name.)
29. *Alexandria Gazette,* Aug. 8, 1899.
30. *Alexandria Gazette,* Aug. 8, 1899; *Washington Times,* Aug. 8, 1899; *Baltimore Sun,* Aug. 11, 1899.

31. (Washington, DC) *Evening Star*, Aug. 8, 1899.
32. *Washington Times*, Aug. 9, 1899.
33. The arrested men were Edward Gibson, Robert Buckner, Allen Carter, John Haskins, James Alexander, Edward Payne, and Thomas Elzie (also spelled "Elsey"), Alfred Mason, Harry McDonald, and James Turley. *Alexandria Gazette*, Aug. 8, 1899; *Richmond Planet*, Aug. 12,1899. Many were active leaders and organizers in Alexandria's Black community. *Alexandria Gazette*, June 12, 1896, Aug. 6, 1896; (Washington, DC) *Evening Star*, Sept. 15, 1888, Aug. 8, 1899; *Washington Times*, Aug. 9, 1899; (Washington, DC) *Evening Star*, Aug. 9, 1899, Aug. 9, 1898, Sept. 15, 1888; *Alexandria Gazette*, April 6, 1900; *Washington Times*, Aug. 22, 1902; *Alexandria Gazette*, Oct. 18, 1907, July 3, 1912, April 6, 1900, Oct. 18, 1907, July 3, 1912; *Richmond Planet*, Aug. 12, 1899.
34. *Washington Evening Times*, Aug. 9, 1899.
35. *Richmond Planet*, Aug. 12, 1899.
36. *Democratic Advocate* (Westminster, MD), Aug. 12, 1899; *Alexandria Gazette*, Aug. 8, 1899; *Washington Times*, Aug. 8, 1899; *Southern Aegis* (Bel Air, MD), Aug. 11, 1899; *Washington Evening Times*, Aug. 9, 1899; (Washington, DC) *Evening Star*, Aug. 8, 1899; *Washington Times*, Aug. 9, 1899; *Baltimore Sun*, Aug. 11, 1899.
37. (Washington, DC) *Evening Star*, Aug. 8, 1899; *Alexandria Gazette*, Aug. 8, 1899; "The Mayor's Court," *The Charter and Laws of The City of Alexandria and an Historical Sketch of Its Government* (Alexandria, VA: City Council, 1874).
38. (Washington, DC) *Evening Star*, Aug. 8, 1899.
39. (Washington, DC) *Evening Star*, Aug. 8, 1899.
40. (Washington, DC) *Evening Star*, Aug. 8, 1899.
41. *Alexandria Gazette*, Aug. 8, 1899.
42. *Richmond Planet*, Aug. 12, 1899.
43. *Alexandria Gazette*, Aug. 8, 1899.
44. *Washington Times*, Aug. 9, 1899. The jail was located on the northeast corner of St. Asaph and Princess Streets: Sanborn Map Co., "Sanborn Fire Insurance Map," *Alexandria, Independent Cities, Virginia*, Aug. 1896, Library of Congress Geography and Map Division, Washington, DC; *Richmond Planet*, Aug. 12, 1899.
45. *Alexandria Gazette*, Aug. 8, 1899.
46. *Wilkes-Barre* (PA) *Times*, Aug. 9, 1899.
47. *Washington Evening Times*, Aug. 9, 1899.
48. *Richmond Planet*, Aug. 12, 1899.
49. *Alexandria Gazette*, Aug. 8, 1899.
50. *Baltimore Sun*, Aug. 9, 1899.
51. *Washington Evening Times*, Aug. 9, 1899.
52. *Richmond Planet*, Aug. 12, 1899; *Washington Times*, Aug. 9, 1899.
53. (Washington, DC) *Evening Star*, Aug. 9, 1899.
54. *Washington Evening Times*, Aug. 9, 1899.
55. *Washington Times*, Aug. 9, 1899.
56. *Washington Evening Times*, Aug. 9, 1899.
57. *Richmond Planet*, Aug. 12, 1899; *Alexandria Gazette*, Aug. 9, 1899.
58. *Shepherdstown* (WV) *Register*, Aug. 10, 1899.
59. *Washington Times*, Aug. 9, 1899.
60. *Alexandria Gazette*, Aug. 9, 1899.

61. *Wilkes-Barre (PA) Times,* Aug. 9, 1899; *Alexandria Gazette,* Aug. 9, 1899; *Washington Times,* Aug. 9, 1899; *Baltimore Sun,* Aug. 9, 1899; *Washington Times,* Aug. 10, 1899; *Daily Press* (Newport News, VA), Aug. 8, 1899; *Sun and New York Press,* Aug. 10, 1899; *Richmond Planet,* Aug. 12, 1899.
62. (Washington, DC) *Evening Star,* Aug. 9, 1899.
63. *Alexandria Gazette,* Aug. 9, 1899.
64. *Richmond Planet,* Aug. 12, 1899.
65. *Alexandria Gazette,* Aug. 9, 1899.
66. *Washington Evening Times,* Aug. 9, 1899.
67. *Cleveland Gazette,* Aug. 26, 1899; *Washington Times,* Aug. 9, 1899; *Alexandria Gazette,* Aug. 9, 1899.
68. *Washington Times,* Aug. 29, 1899.
69. (Washington, DC) *Evening Star,* Aug. 9, 1899.
70. *Washington Times,* Aug. 9, 1899; *Richmond Planet,* Aug. 12, 1899.
71. *Richmond Planet,* Aug. 12, 1899.
72. *Washington Evening Times,* Aug. 9, 1899; *Alexandria Gazette,* Aug. 9, 1899; *Washington Times,* Aug. 10, 1899.
73. *Baltimore Sun,* Aug. 9, 1899; *Washington Times,* Aug. 9, 1899.
74. *Alexandria Gazette,* Aug. 9, 1899.
75. (Washington, DC) *Evening Star,* Aug. 9, 1899; *Alexandria Gazette,* Aug. 9, 1899.
76. *Baltimore Sun,* Aug. 11, 1899.
77. *Alexandria Gazette,* Aug. 9, 1899.
78. *Alexandria Gazette,* Aug. 9, 1899.
79. *Alexandria Gazette,* Aug. 9, 1899; Alexandria Community Remembrance Research Group, *The Lynching of Joseph H. McCoy: April 23, 1897* (Alexandria, VA: Alexandria Community Remembrance Project, 2020). Similar verdicts were rendered in most lynchings in America: see Philip Dray, *At the Hands of Persons Unknown: The Lynching of Black America* (New York: Modern Library, 2003).
80. *Baltimore Sun,* Aug. 11, 1899.
81. *Richmond Planet,* Aug. 12, 1899.
82. *Washington Times,* Aug. 10, 1899.
83. *Alexandria Gazette,* Aug. 9, 1899.
84. *Sun and New York Press,* Aug. 10, 1899.
85. *Washington Times,* Aug. 10, 1899.
86. *Washington Times,* Aug. 11, 1899.
87. (Washington, DC) *Evening Star,* Aug. 10, 1899; *Washington Evening Times,* Aug. 9, 1899.
88. *Alexandria Gazette,* Aug. 29, 1899; *Washington Times,* Aug. 29, 1899; *Alexandria Gazette,* Aug. 28, 1899.
89. *Washington Times,* Aug. 29, 1899.
90. Sherrilyn A. Ifill, "Creating a Truth and Reconciliation Commission for Lynching," *Law & Inequality: A Journal of Theory and Practice* 21, no 2 (2003): 263, https://scholarship.law.umn.edu/lawineq/vol21/iss2/2/.
91. Ida B. Wells-Barnett, *Southern Horrors: Lynch Law in All Its Phases* (Aberdeen, Scotland: Thomson & Duncan, Printers, 1892), 18.
92. (Washington, DC) *Evening Star,* Aug. 9, 1899; *Norfolk Virginian,* Aug. 10, 1899; *Washington Times,* Aug. 9, 1899.

93. *Washington Times,* Aug. 10, 1899.
94. *Washington Times,* Aug. 10, 1899, Aug. 15, 1899.
95. *Cleveland Gazette,* Aug. 26, 1899; *Washington Times,* Aug. 10, 1899; (Washington, DC) *Evening Star,* Aug. 8, 1899; *Southern Aegis* (Bel Air, MD), Aug. 11, 1899; *Baltimore Sun,* Aug. 9, 1899.
96. *Washington Times,* Aug. 10, 1899.
97. *Richmond Planet,* Aug. 12, 1899.
98. *Alexandria Gazette,* April 23, 1897; *Washington Post,* April 23, 1897; *Washington Evening Times,* April 23, 1897; *Baltimore Sun,* Aug. 10, 1899.
99. *Alexandria Gazette,* Aug. 16, 1899.
100. Office of Historic Alexandria, Alexandria Community Remembrance Project, City of Alexandria, no date, accessed Oct. 24, 2023, https://www.alexandriava.gov/historic/blackhistory/default.aspx?id=106501.
101. Jack Uldrich, "We Want a More Peaceful World, But It Starts from Within," (Minneapolis) *Star Tribune,* May 28, 2020.
102. Amy B. Wang, "GOP Sen. Johnson Says Capitol Rioters Didn't Scare Him—but Might Have Had They Been Black Lives Matter Protesters," *Washington Post,* March 14, 2021; Donald J. Trump, White House Executive Order 13950, Combating Race and Sex Stereotyping, Sept. 22, 2020, https://en.wikisource.org/wiki/Executive_Order_13950.
103. Wang, "GOP Sen. Johnson."
104. Equal Justice Initiative (EJI), *Lynching in America: Confronting the Legacy of Racial Terror,* 3d ed. (Birmingham, AL: EJI, 2017), https://eji.org/reports/lynching-in-america/.
105. See Andrea Douglas, "Public History as Activism: Helping a Community Come to Terms with Racial Violence," in this volume.
106. Ida B. Wells-Barnett, *The Red Record: Tabulated Statistics and Tabulated Causes of Lynchings in the United States* (Chicago: Donohue & Henneberry, 1895).
107. Office of Historic Alexandria, Alexandria Community Remembrance Project.
108. "Americans must begin to confront the history of lynching and its continued effect on blacks and whites in communities throughout the United States. Such an examination should be focused principally on the role of local institutions, state officials, and ordinary people in condoning and promoting the public torture, killing, and dismemberment of thousands of black people. Most importantly, in towns where lynchings occurred, such a process should provide Blacks and whites with the opportunity to find appropriate forms of reparation and avenues toward reconciliation." Ifill, "Creating a Truth and Reconciliation Commission for Lynching," 309.

CONCLUSION
THE LEGACY OF LYNCHING IN VIRGINIA TODAY

GIANLUCA DE FAZIO

One of the overarching goals of this book is to try to restore the dignity of the lives that were lost at the hands of violent mobs in Virginia. The essays in this volume tell numerous lynching stories that have too often been erased from the collective memory of many Virginian communities; it is time that we remember and honor the victims of lynching mobs. In telling these stories, this volume discusses many different themes related to racial terror: from the virtual impunity granted to white mobs to the role of the death penalty in furthering racial terror, from the role of newspapers in legitimizing lynching to the active resistance of Black communities to white supremacist oppression. In this conclusion, I will briefly discuss why these themes are still relevant today, indicating how the legacy of lynching is still shaping society in Virginia and United States at large.

One of the central themes in this volume is *white mob violence against Black people,* a constitutive element of past racial terror lynchings. While white-supremacist violence has changed shape over time, it is still an ongoing threat today. In addition to traditional white terror groups like the KKK, other forms of reactionary violence are emerging, such as those behind the Unite the Right rally in Charlottesville in 2017 and the attacks on Black Lives Matter protesters during the summer of 2020. Perhaps the most egregious example took place on January 6, 2021, when an almost exclusively white mob descended on the US Capitol in Washington to subvert the electoral results and declare the outgoing president of the United States, Donald Trump, as the winner of the November 2020 presidential elections. The insurrectionists waved Confederate flags and nooses and even built makeshift gallows, while chanting threats to hang "traitor" politicians like Vice President Mike Pence, who refused to change the outcome of the elections. This was not accidental; as political scientist Hakeem Jefferson argues, the failed insurrection, with its open display of symbols of white supremacy, clearly represented an attempt to "maintain white power in America." Echoing the spirit animating lynching mobs in the past, the insurrectionists represented "a dangerous mob of grievous white people worried that their position in the status hierarchy is threatened by a multiracial coalition of Americans."[1] Rather than an aberration, armed white mobs have a long tradition in US history, as the practice of lynching reminds us.

Another central theme in this volume regards the *system of complicity* that made the practice of lynching persist for several decades.[2] This system included federal, state, and local authorities, as well as the press, churches, and local communities; violent mobs could count on the tacit or explicit support of this system to act with impunity against Black communities. It was only when this system of complicity started to crumble under the pressure of antilynching activists and public opinion that lynching became unacceptable and lethal mob violence increasingly rare. Today, the legacy of this system is still recognizable in certain institutions, especially the death penalty. More generally though, the legal system of punishment is still bent to criminalize African Americans and deny them basic defendants' rights. It is well known that mass incarceration and the death penalty disproportionately affect Black communities, a legacy of the harsh punishments that were deemed necessary to control "fiendish Black criminals" during the lynching era. After lynch law disappeared from the streets, the criminal justice system eagerly became the apparatus through which the threat of "Black criminality" could be dealt with legally, meting out harsh sentences that rendered vigilante mob justice obsolete. Police brutality against African Americans, and its nearly guaranteed impunity, is also in part the prosecution of white mobs' purpose to control, intimidate, and subjugate Black citizens, with the implicit or explicit complicity of public officials.[3]

Most recently, the murder of George Floyd in full daylight by a white police officer and his colleagues in Minneapolis needs to be understood within the larger history of what criminologist Geoff Ward calls "state organized race crime,"[4] wherein state agents routinely fail to protect Black people, while committing or abetting the violence against them.[5] Again, the resilience of state-sanctioned racial violence and the lack of accountability that complements it today is part of the legacy of the history of lynching.

Finally, *Black resistance and activism* against lynching is the third theme that emerges throughout the volume. The antilynching campaign by editor John Mitchell Jr. and the *Richmond Planet* constantly denounced the barbarism of mob violence and challenged the narratives that justified lynching in the white press. In Alexandria, a group of Black men tried to protect the jail where sixteen-year-old Benjamin Thomas was held when a white mob threatened to lynch him in 1899. After Thomas's murder, the local Black community engaged in various acts of protest against the lynching and the official impunity shown towards the lynchers. Today, local activists and organizations across Virginia are working to revive the collective memory of lynching victims while denouncing the system of silence that has kept those stories from being publicly discussed and remembered. It is our hope that this volume will help in disseminating these stories and further our understanding of racialized terrorism in Virginia as part of a process of racial healing and reconciliation.

Notes

1. Hakeem Jefferson, *Storming the U.S. Capitol Was about Maintaining White Power in America*, FiveThirtyEight.com, Jan. 8, 2021, https://fivethirtyeight.com/features/storming-the-u-s-capitol-was-about-maintaining-white-power-in-america/.
2. Historian Charles Chavis describes the system of silence that suffused white mob violence and its impunity in his book *The Silent Shore: The Lynching of Matthew Williams and the Politics of Racism in the Free State* (Baltimore: Johns Hopkins University Press, 2022).
3. Margaret A. Burnham, *By Hands Now Known: Jim Crow's Legal Executioners* (New York: Norton, 2022).
4. Geoff Ward, "The Slow Violence of State Organized Race Crime," *Theoretical Criminology* 19, no. 3 (2015): 299–314.
5. The fact that the police officer who killed George Floyd has been indicted, tried, and found guilty is extraordinary in its rarity. Virtually every legal expert and scholar of police violence agrees that without the video evidence of the murder and the huge wave of protest around this case, there would have been no legal consequences for the police officers involved in the killing.

AN AFTERWORD

W. FITZHUGH BRUNDAGE

The history of lynching is a confounding riddle. Like other murders, lynchings were discrete events, each with its unique setting, chronology, characters, and backstory. Yet each lynching was also part of a web of social violence that had recognizable patterns and, often, common rituals. Therein lies the challenge for the historian of lynching. For a century after the American Civil War, anyone anywhere in the United States might fall victim to a lynch mob, but more often than not only some people in some places in the United States did so. To render this phenomenon comprehensible, a historian has to trace deep, seemingly inexorable forces at work in lynchings while also accounting for the play of contingency in the phenomenon.

This volume underscores the crucial importance of place in the history of lynching. Recognizing the geographical variation of lynching over time is an important step in distinguishing those traits that defined the practice in the United States in general and Virginia specifically. Americans, after all, have not been unique in their resort to lethal vigilante violence, as the deeds of present-day mobs in India, South Africa, Mexico, the Philippines, and elsewhere underscore. Because of the work of scholars who have charted the tragic toll of lynch mobs from Duluth, Minnesota, to Waco, Texas, from California to Delaware, we can discern that in important regards the pattern of lynching in Virginia was tragically typical. As elsewhere, Black people, especially men, were the targets of most mobs. Most lynch mobs in Virginia, as was common across the South, seized their victims from law officers. Contemporary newspapers both inside and outside the state played an outsized role in legitimizing lynching and interpreting its meaning.

But neither Virginia nor any single state can serve as a representative microcosm of the phenomenon of lynching in the United States. Lynching was far more commonplace in Virginia than in many midwestern or mid-Atlantic states even while the Commonwealth hosted fewer lynchings than any of the other states that had joined the Confederacy. Unlike public officials in many southern states, authorities in Virginia took meaningful steps to stifle lynching, including passing a substantive antilynching law. Most of the lethal lynchings in the state, moreover, occurred during the late nineteenth century and tapered off rapidly during the early twentieth century, whereas extralegal mobs plagued many states further to the south well into the twentieth century.

In light of the horrific toll and grim persistence of lynch mobs elsewhere, we may be tempted to assume that lynching weighed less heavily on the institutions and public life of the Old Dominion. To do so would be to ignore one of the most important lessons of this collection, which demonstrates the deep and enduring impact of lynching in Virginia, and, indeed, throughout the nation.

Certainly, John Mitchell Jr., the fearless Black editor of the *Richmond Planet* from 1884 to 1929, would be pained if we underestimated the impact of lynching on his state. In the columns of his newspaper, especially during the 1890s, Mitchell traced the devastation wrought by lynch mobs and inveighed against white state and local officials for their failure to protect all Virginians from extralegal violence. Mitchell methodically and tirelessly dismantled white justifications and excuses for lynchings. The precise degree to which Mitchell's activism influenced white officials and editors in the state is impossible to measure, but we can be certain it was considerable. With each unvarnished news report of a lynching, editorial cartoon, and column that Mitchell published, he demonstrated that anti-Black violence had failed to cow Black Virginians even while it eroded all prospects for progress and social peace in the state.

The waning of lynching in Virginia, as these essays affirm and Mitchell well understood, in no way presaged a loosening of white supremacy in the state. Yes, a reverence for law and order motivated some influential white Virginia officials and jurists to suppress lynching. But their opposition to extralegal violence was not complemented by a commitment to justice for all Virginians. For these white champions of law and order, the popular justice of the lynch mob represented indefensible anarchy. In its place, they preferred the methodical, merciless, and relentless redress of the courts. Their devotion to law and order translated into replacing the violent terror of the lynch mob with the ritualized theater of the courtroom. That Black Virginians were often the scapegoats in these legal theaters was of no special concern to them.

Another especially significant contribution of this collection is the revelation of the prevalence and persistence of the practice of lynching. The decline in the incidence of "successful" lethal lynchings, we learn, did not coincide with a decline in the impulse to lynch in Virginia. Groups of Virginians, composed almost exclusively of white men, continued to muster to pursue alleged suspects, attack jails, and seize prisoners from law officers well after state and local officials had displayed resolve to stifle extralegal violence. Although these attempted lynchings did not add to the state's record of lethal mob violence, they delivered a clear message. State and local officials who ignored local white preferences risked unleashing violent retribution not just against targeted Blacks but also the apparatus of the law. Some of the attempted lynchings may have been mere public theater, but even they affirmed that substantial numbers of white Virginians reserved the power to resort to vigilantism if the courts failed to provide satisfaction when punishing Blacks.

The persistence of attempted lynchings had especially sinister significance for Black Virginians. They could never rest secure that they were safe. No matter how infrequently lynchings occurred in Virginia, no Black person in police custody could have confidence that white law officers and officials would not succumb to the mob's demands or even actively aid the lynchers. No Black person could take solace in the capriciousness of the lynch mob: Who could know which mob would have sufficient resolve or bloodlust to succeed in its murderous violence? In this regard, we do well to remind ourselves of novelist Richard Wright's keen observation in his memoir *Black Boy* (Harper & Brothers, 1945): "The things that influenced my conduct as a Negro did not have to happen to me directly; I needed to but hear of them to feel their full effects in the deepest layers of my consciousness. Indeed, the white brutality that I had not seen was a more effective control of my behavior than that which I knew" (151).

Readers who are encountering this history for the first time may not appreciate the importance of the new knowledge about attempted lynching in Virginia presented in this collection. During the decades between 1870 and

1940, when most lynchings occurred in the United States, no one compiled a definitive inventory of both lethal and attempted lynchings. The Tuskegee Institute in Alabama and the National Association for the Advancement of Colored People (NAACP) made a conscientious effort to do so, but they depended largely on news clipping services that collected newspaper accounts of mob violence. These services typically gathered stories about lethal lynchings published in major urban daily newspapers. But these newspapers often overlooked attempted lynchings. Until recently, locating reports of attempted lynchings in all extant historical newspapers, including especially small-town and rural newspapers, was a painstaking, time consuming, exhausting, and inevitably incomplete undertaking. But thanks to digitized newspapers and digital searching tools we can now collect news accounts of attempted lynchings with unprecedented thoroughness in seconds. Our understanding of the history of lynching is certain to deepen as scholars follow in the footsteps of this book and mine the nation's historical newspapers.

What is to be done with the grim history recounted within the covers of this book? This history is sure to inform the work of Virginians who seek to address longstanding inequities in the state's criminal justice system. So, too, jurists in the Old Dominion have much to ponder in the history told here. Journalists in Virginia may now be inspired to both investigate and draw lessons from the role their predecessors played in legitimizing lynching. And those in the Commonwealth who are committed to acknowledging and commemorating the historical record of lynchings in their communities will soon dogear their copies of this book. For others, whether or not they live in Virginia, this collection is a timely and sobering reminder of the violence that is inextricably woven into the fabric of American life.

CONTRIBUTORS

CHARLES T. BLAIR is an attorney in private practice in Washington, DC. He holds a JD and BA (English) from the University of Virginia. Growing up in Rockingham County, Virginia, he developed an abiding interest in Civil War and Reconstruction-era history. In 2019 he contributed the essay "The Lynching of Charlotte Harris" to the Racial Terror: Lynching in Virginia website.

DALE BRUMFIELD is a journalist and the author of twelve books, including *Closing the Slaughterhouse: The Inside Story of Death Penalty Abolition in Virginia* (Abolition Press, 2022). He is the former Field Director and Executive Director for Virginians for Alternatives to the Death Penalty, a Richmond-based nonprofit, and was a recipient of the 2021 Frederick Douglass Human Rights Award from the Southern Center for Human Rights in Atlanta for his work helping abolish Virginia's death penalty.

TOM COSTA has taught in the Department of History and Philosophy at the University of Virginia's College at Wise since 1992. He was recently named Interim Dean of Faculty Affairs. Trained in early American history, he directs the website The Geography of Slavery in Virginia. He is currently working with a team memorializing lynchings in Wise County. The essay in this volume is the product of their research.

ZOE CRIHFIELD is a recent graduate of the University of Tennessee, where she obtained a master's degree in Public Policy and Administration. She is a student fellow for the 2022–23 Appalachian Leadership Institute. She currently lives in Knoxville, Tennessee, where she will begin a career in public service. Before moving to Knoxville, she was part of Southwest Virginia's Community Remembrance Project, where she helped research the three lynchings that occurred in Wise County. She credits this project as the groundwork for much of her academic and professional success.

GIANLUCA DE FAZIO is an Associate Professor in the Justice Studies Department at James Madison University. He has compiled the website Racial Terror: Lynching in Virginia, documenting with primary resources each known lynching that took place in the Commonwealth between 1866 and 1932. Professor De Fazio is also a member of the History of Lynching Work Group at the Virginia General Assembly.

DOLORES FLAMIANO is a professor in the School of Media Arts and Design at James Madison University, where she teaches media literacy and media criticism. Her research and writing focus on photography history, and she is the author of *Women, Workers, and Race in Life Magazine: Hansel Mieth's Reform Photojournalism, 1934–1955* (Routledge, 2016).

ANDREA DOUGLAS is the Executive Director of the Jefferson School African American Heritage Center, in Charlottesville, Virginia. She holds a PhD in art history from the University of Virginia. She was curator of collections and exhibitions and curator of contemporary art at the University of Virginia Art Museum from 2004–10. She has taught graduate and undergraduate classes in African American and contemporary art and art theory and has published exhibition catalogs and scholarly articles. Douglas's scholarship considers the cultural and social connections in the biographies of twentieth- and twenty-first-century artists of the African Diaspora. She has been a Chair of the City's PLACE Design task force, and a member of the Blue Ribbon Commission on Race and Monuments and the University of Virginia's President's Commission on Slavery at the University, where she sat on their monument and community outreach committee.

JAMES WILLIAM HAGY, a resident of Abingdon, Virginia, has a PhD in history from the University of Georgia and is a retired professor of history at the College of Charleston. He is the author of ten books, including *History of Washington County, Virginia to 1865* and about fifty articles in historical journals, mostly about Southwest Virginia and Charleston, South Carolina.

JIM HALL is a native of Virginia, a resident of Fredericksburg, and retired after a thirty-six-year career as a newspaper reporter and editor. He studied lynching coverage by Virginia newspapers while earning a master's degree at VCU. He is the author of *The Last Lynching in Northern Virginia: Seeking Truth at Rattlesnake Mountain* (History Press, 2016) and *Condemned for Love in Old Virginia: The Lynching of Arthur Jordan* (History Press, 2023).

KEVIN HEGG is the Head of Digital Projects within the Libraries at James Madison University. He designed and implemented the Racial Terror: Lynching in Virginia website and is currently completing his master's in Public History at James Madison University.

JOSH HOWARD is an applied historian with Passel LLC, a historical consulting company based in Virginia's Shenandoah Valley. His other work includes *Hell's Not Far Off: Bruce Crawford and the Appalachian Left* (West Virginia University Press), official historical reports for the National Park Service, and articles in journals such as the *Journal of Sport History, Virginia Magazine of History and Biography,* and *West Virginia History.*

MADDY MCCOY, FARAR ELLIOTT, SUSAN K. FLINN, ANN MARIE HAY, ELIZABETH LOCKWOOD, CHRISTOPHER MILKO, and **ROB TAYLOR** served as the volunteer research group for the Alexandria Community Remembrance Project (ACRP). ACRP is a project inspired by the Equal Justice Initiative (EJI) and dedicated to helping the City of Alexandria, Virginia, understand its history of racial terror hate crimes and create a welcoming community bound by equity and inclusion. The authors arrived at this project from a variety of professional backgrounds and with a drive to contribute to this important initiative. Their hope was to create the foundation of historical understanding necessary for the community of Alexandria to continue having honest discussions that will challenge our government and citizens to affect real change.

BRENDAN WOLFE edited *Encyclopedia Virginia* at Virginia Humanities from 2008 until 2019. He lives in Charlottesville and is the author of *Finding Bix: The Life and Afterlife of a Jazz Legend* (2017) and *Mr. Jefferson's Telescope: A History of the University of Virginia in 100 Objects* (2017). His essays have appeared in *The Morning News, Colorado Review*, and *VQR*.

INDEX

Italicized page numbers indicate figures. Locations are in Virginia unless another state is indicated.

Abernathy, Mary, 163–64
A. Phillip Randolph Porter Museum (Chicago), 261
ACRP. *See* Alexandria Community Remembrance Project
Adkins, Mrs. Ira, and her husband Z. T., 81
African American Civil War Museum (DC), 261
African American History Education Commission (AAHEC), 223–24
Afro-American Press Association, 140
Akers, Thomas, *92, 94*
Albemarle/Charlottesville Community Remembrance project, 225, 260–61, 262–69, 270n16
Albemarle County: Black migration from, 230; Black population (1890), 256; James lynching (1898), 14, 228, 240–42; racial capitalism based on slavery in, 258
Alexander, Ann Field, 17n26, 40, 130
Alexander, Michelle, *The New Jim Crow,* 184
Alexandria: Black population in 1890s, 291n1; coerced confession of Henry Smith (1910), 154–55; McCoy lynching (1897), 274–78; O'Ferrall criticizing lynchings in, 144, 274,

277; public place chosen for lynching to ensure maximum intimidation, 35; shared script of lynchings in, 286–88; Thomas lynching (1899), 1–3, 278–86
Alexandria Community Remembrance Project (ACRP), 5, 15, 223, 272–94; background, 272–73; McCoy and Thomas family living descendants, search for, 290; purpose of, 273; Research Group, 15, 225, 273, 289; two lynching victims, publishing narratives of, 273; white authorities' complicity in lynchings, 273
Alexandria Gazette: on Bailey's mental condition (1913), 191; encouraging lynchings and mob violence, 165; on Guynn lynching (1902), 106; on Jordan and Corder's interracial romance and Jordan's lynching (1880), 29, 39, 41; on McCoy lynching (1897), 275, 277–78; on O'Ferrall's unpopularity (1896), 129; Smith's death row poetry published, revealing coerced confession (1910), 155; on speed of Bailey trial (1913), 190; on Suits lynching (1898), 83; on Thomas lynching (1899), 278, 281, 283, 284, 288

{307}

308 INDEX

Alexandria Light Infantry (ALI), 274–76, 278, 285
Alleghany Commission on Racial Equality, 213
Alleghany County: Anderson practicing law in, 203–4, 216n8; Anderson's legacy of racial injustice, 211–15; Black population growth in, 53, 55; courthouse dedication (1911), 212. *See also* Anderson, George K.; Clifton Forge
Allentown (Pennsylvania) *Morning Call* on Falls lynching (1897), 167
All Lives Matter movement, 261
Ames, Jesse, 40
Amherst County, 38; white man fined for rape of Black woman (1950), 158
Anderson, George K. (Alleghany and Botetourt County Courts judge), 14, 127, 197–219; anti-Black legislation drafted by, 202, 212; background of, 199; Bowles murder case against Black C&O railroad worker (1904), 197, 206–8; character of, 212; Christian's protection from lynching and speed of trial for legal hanging (1909), 209–10, 213; Confederate nostalgia and, 212–13; as defense attorney for white clients, 203–4, 216n8; Hubbard murder case (legal hanging 1906), 197, 208–9; jury instructions given by, 204, 207, 217n25; legacy of, 211–15; Lewis hanging commuted to life imprisonment (1906), 208; Magruder case of Black itinerant executed for attempted rape (1896), 197, 203–6; perpetuation of racial injustice and terror, 199, 211–15; replacing mob lynchings with legal executions, 209, 211–12, 213; speed of capital trials of Black defendants, 197, 209–10, 211, 213
Anderson, Robert, 157
antilynching campaign: American citizenship and, 63; lynching postcards and imagery use in, 64; system of complicity crumbling under pressure of, 296. *See also* Mitchell, John, Jr.; NAACP; Wells, Ida B.
antilynching laws: Emmett Till Antilynching Act (federal law, 2022), 64, 119, 224; Virginia (1928), 9, 17nn29–30, 71, 88, 111–12, 117, 118, 162, 300
Appalachian South. *See* Southwest Virginia
Appomattox County, Wright execution thwarting lynching mob (1912), 155
Appomattox Court House National Historical Park, 263
arson allegations, 9–10, 134
Ashby, Turner, 41
assault accusations: beating and rape of white woman (1893), 81–82; confession triggering speedy trial and execution of Breckenridge (1909), 158–59; frequency of charge against lynching victims, 88; mentally disabled man sentenced for (1908), 156; robbing and assault on white woman (1899), 55; sixteen-year-old white girl in Tazewell County (1920), 74; speedy trials in early 1900s resulting in executions, 190; twelve-year-old white girl in Wise County (1902), 84, 103, 105, 106–7; white storekeeper in Wise County (1920), 110–11; white woman in Richmond (1909), 150; white woman in Sussex County (1925), 165; white woman in Wise County (1920), 86, 105, 109–10; white woman in Wythe County (1888), 77; white women, attempted assault or assault on, 70. *See also* rape accusations
Atlanta Constitution spurring lynching of Sam Hose (1899), 47, 54
attempted lynchings. *See* threatened lynchings
Augusta County, 34; Hart executed for attempted rape (1922), 161
averted lynchings. *See* prevention of lynchings; threatened lynchings

Bailey, Amy Kate, 189
Bailey, Benjamin (executed 1913), 190, 191
Baker, Sam, 85
Baldwin-Felts Detective Agency, 90, 156
Ball, Sarah, 86
Baltimore Afro-American on Woods lynching (1920), 116
Baltimore Sun on Thomas lynching (1899), 284–85
Bardwell, Kentucky lynching (1893), 62–63
Barnes, Mary (served two of ten-year sentence 1895), 163–64
Barnes, Pokey (exonerated by courts 1895), 163–64
Barns, Sam (lynching victim 1893), 79–80
Barrett, Albert (saved from lynching 1917), 156–57
Barwell, Taylor B. (Black man shot in Clifton Forge 1881), 200
Battaile, Gabriel (legal hanging 1906), 191
Battle, John S., 157
Baxley, Henry and Mamie, 118
Beardshall, Ann Hardy, 99n12
Beavers, Thomas (first white person executed for murder of Black woman 1997), 161
Beck, E. M., 8–9, 16n10, 17n33, 184–86, 211; *A Festival of Violence* (with Tolnay), 17n26, 97, 177, 184, 189. *See also* statistics
Bedau, Hugo, *The Death Penalty in America*, 168
Bedford County, lynching of Spinner prevented (1909), 156
Bedford Times on multiple lynchings in Tazewell County (1893), 81
Belote, Ida, 159
Big Stone Gap Post: on court docket's number of criminal and civil cases (1921), 96; on Foy probable lynching (1901), 108; on Foy sentencing (1902), 108; on Guynn lynching (1902), 106; on Hurst lynching (1920), 110; sensationalism in reporting lynchings, 164

Bishop, Florence, 238, 241, 255, 269n4
Black community: disproportionate effect of mass incarceration and capital punishment on, 296; middle class, rise of, 256–57; mobilizing in attempt to prevent Thomas lynching (1899), 288; monument tours reclaiming history, 266; newspapers creating racial identity for, 48; passive resistance after Thomas lynching (1899), 288; resistance and activism against lynching, 297; response to lynchings, 273, 286, 288; white exclusion from society, 217n16; white fear of revenge violence from, 201, 285, 287. *See also* Black men
blackface ruse to gain access to jail to seize lynching victim, 35–36, 134
Black Lives Matter movement, 224, 261, 289, 295
Black men: increased racial tensions following World War I return of Black soldiers, 109; as main target of attempted rape law resulting in death penalty, 11, 128, 157, 162, 176, 184, 186, 201–3, 212; as main target of lynching, 8, 299; migrating from Clifton Forge area, 201; other crimes resulting in death penalty for, 177; racial code of acceptable conduct for, 54–55, 107, 119; stereotyped descriptions of, 40, 53–54, 150–51, 166, 243, 280, 287. *See also* itinerant Black men; statistics
Black newspapers: civic belonging rhetoric of, 63; on Clifton Forge lynchings of three Black miners (1891), 23, 40, 48, 53; counternarratives on lynchings, 47, 50, 64; in early twentieth century, 163; racial identity, creation of, 48, 63; short-lived, 163. *See also Richmond Planet*
Black rebellion, white fears of, 54
Black society, 217n16
Blair, Charles T., 14, 126
Bland, Peter (lynching victim 1884), 166

Bland County, 73; Jackson lynching (1885), 76–77
Blankenship, Thomas, accused lyncher (1896), 81
Bloody Monday (June 10, 1963), 263
Blow, Sam (lynching victim 1893), 79–80, 89, 100n19
Boone, Kiara, 266
Boswell (Lebanon mayor), 10
Botetourt County: Anderson's legacy of racial injustice, 211; show trials in, 14, 127–28; speedy trial of Aurelius "Felix" Christian (1909), 159, 209–10
Bowles, Robert (legal hanging 1904), 197, 199, 206–8, 214, 218n30
Bowles, Thomas, 200–201
Branch, Spencer (lynching victim 1893), 79–80, 89
Braxton, Carter, 158–59
Breckenridge, Clifton (executed 1909), 158–59
Bristol, 73, 74; Clark lynching (1891), 78–79
Bristol, Tennessee, alleged assault on white girl by Black man (1925), 84
Bristol Herald Courier (Tennessee) reporting news from Southwest Virginia, 74
Brown, Jerry (lynching victim 1893), 79–80
Brown, Robert, 208
Bruce, Philip Alexander, 244; *The Plantation Negro as Freeman*, 235
Brumfield, Dale, 14, 127, 150, 184, 185
Brundage, Fitzhugh, 15, 299; on anomaly of collective racial violence in Southwest Virginia, 69, 73; on Black leaders meeting with whites to work out compromise to lynching, 121n26; on economic problems as contributing factor to lynchings, 97, 104; *Lynching in the New South: Georgia and Virginia*, 8–9, 73, 154; on Mitchell's antilynching campaign, 22; on more prosecutions of lynchers in Virginia than in Deep South states, 250n54; on O'Ferrall's legacy of antilynching as government policy, 130, 145; on pervasiveness of extralegal violence, 15, 250n42; on reduced lynchings during O'Ferrall's term, 162; on threatened lynchings, 154; on white newspaper bias in lynching coverage, 52
Bryant, Zyahna, 259, 268
Buchanan County: anti-Black animus in, 95; attempted lynchers, Little protected from, 91; Brown lynchers from (1893), 80; Pennington lynching (1909), 85–86; population increase in, 97
Buffalo Evening News on Falls lynching (1897), 167
Bunch, Linwood (last man executed for rape in Virginia 1961), 173
Burgess, Nathan (lynching victim 1892), 79
Burton, Robert (lynching victim 1891), 45, 53, 56, 200, 216n13. *See also* Clifton Forge lynchings of three Black miners
Butler, Corder, 32
Byrd, Harry, 71, 87, 88, 111–12, 117–19, 162, 169
Byrd, Raymond Arthur (lynching victim 1926), 86–87, 89, 112, 115, 117; miscegenation as grounds, 86, 88, 112

Campbell, Arthur, 94
Canter, James and Luther (saved from lynching 1915), 91–94, 92
capital punishment, 161–63, 214; abolished in Virginia (2021), 152, 170, 194; Anderson sentencing of executions, 209, 211–12, 213; Beavers as first white person executed for murder of Black woman (1997), 161; Black female Virginia Christian as sole female executed between 1896 and 2010, 159; Black men sent to electric chair for rape-related crimes (1908–61), 177; Black men sent to electric chair or gallows

for rape-related crimes (1877–1961), 180–84, *181, 183;* Black men vs. white men executed in Jim Crow era, 180–81, *181;* cadavers sent to Virginia medical schools for anatomy classes, 193; discouraging mob lynching by offering "legal lynching," 168; electric chair use, 170, 177, 182–85, *183,* 190, 191, 210; female executions, rarity of, 178, 180; lynching justified as speedier alternative, 169; as evolution of mob lynching into "legal lnyching," 14, 15, 151, 168–69, 173–75, 182, 192, 211–12, 296, 301; number of cases resulting in, 91; persons who escaped lynching in Southwest Virginia (1883–1922), 91, *92–93;* as racial repression, 5, 12; for rape or attempted rape, 12, 14, 146, 155, 157, 160–62, 173–74, 176, 180, 182–84, 193; ritual of execution day, 193; show trials, 14; slave or free Black Virginian sentenced to, 161

Capitol insurrection (January 6, 2021), 15, 289, 295–96

carnival game "The African Dodger," 158

Carroll County, Howlett lynching (1898), 83–84

Carter, James (lynching victim 1902), 166

Cashin, Sheryll, 34

Charleston, South Carolina, lynchings of eight Black men (1890), 166

Charlotte County, Barrett saved from lynching (1917), 156–57

Charlottesville: Albemarle/Charlottesville Community Remembrance project, 225, 260–61, 262–69; Black churches, expansion of, 256; Black middle class, rise of, 256–57; Black population (1890s), 257; Blue Ribbon Commission on Race, Monuments, and Public Spaces (BRC), 259–62, 265, 268; Civil War history of, 229; Confederate monuments, proposals for removal of, 253, 258; disenfranchisement of African Americans in, 225; Goodman murder case against white killer found not guilty (1895), 204; grave robberies in, 258; historical markers of slave trade, 246, 265; initiatives to address race-based inequities, 253, 261, 268; initiatives to memorialize lynching victims in, 5, 15; July 12 recognized as John Henry James Day, 268; Lost Cause keeping Confederacy alive in, 257; lynchings in, 14; McKee Row, razing of, 265–66, 270n21; Pen Park, 228–29, 248n5; racial terror in, 256–58; remembering and forgetting trauma of violence, 224, 245–47, 254, 261; Vinegar Hill neighborhood, 256–57, 261, 270n20. *See also* Confederate monuments; James, John Henry; Unite the Right rally

Charlottesville Messenger, as Black newspaper in early twentieth century, 163

Chavis, Charles L., Jr., *The Silent Shore,* 90, 297n2

Chicago Defender (Black newspaper), 48, 62

Chicago Tribune on Harris lynching (1878), 136

Christian, Aurelius "Felix" (death penalty by electrocution 1909), 197, 199, 213, 214; speed of trial, 159, 209–10

Christian, Joseph (Virginia Supreme Court justice), 34–35

Christian, Virginia (executed 1912), 159

Cincinnati Commercial on Harris lynching (1878), 136

Civil Rights Memorial Center (Birmingham), 264

Clark, Robert "Bob" (lynching victim 1891), 78–79

Cleveland Gazette offering counternarrative on Alexandria lynchings, 273

Clifton Forge: Anderson's court making a dangerous place for Black men, 215; Barwell shot by Pugh (1881), 200; Bowles case originating in (1904), 206; Christian

Clifton Forge (*continued*)
case, prevention of lynching in (1909), 213; departure of Black men to better and safer jobs in Pennsylvania, 201; description of town in 1890s, 199–200; Hubbard murder trial (legal hanging 1906), 208–9; Jones escape from lynching (1934), 107; Magruder lynch mob (1896), 205; murders of Black men as commonplace in, 200

Clifton Forge lynchings of three Black miners (1891), 13, 23, 40, 45–64, 128, 197, 198–203; Black community's memory of, 198, 215n6; image of lynched men used by *Richmond Planet* in antilynching campaign, 49, 59–62, 60–61; mayor handing over the prisoners for lynching, 200–201; political leaders in 2020 ignorant of, 198; posse formed to hunt down men, 200; *Richmond Planet*'s (black newspaper) coverage, 53, 55, 56–59, 60–61; trope of the hunt in white press coverage, 55–56; white newspapers' coverage, 50–64, 50–52, 201

Clifton Forge Review (previously *Clifton Forge and Iron-Gate Review*): on Clifton Forge lynchings of three Black miners (1891), 58; on Downey as white rapist (1894), 203; on threatened lynching of unnamed Black man (1891), 201

Clinch Valley News: on difficulty of identifying lynchers, 90; encouraging lynchings through reporting, 164–65; on frequency of murder cases on court docket (1891), 96; on Kirkpatrick lynching (1893), 80–81; on Peters lynching as falsehood (1920), 74; on Rippey trial and execution (1908), 165, 190; on Williams legal hanging (1904), 185

Coalfield Progress on Woods lynching (1927), 113–15

coal workers. *See* miners and mining

Cohen, Richard, 264

collective memory: Black community's memory of lynchings, 198, 215n6, 242, 245; initiatives to revive memory of lynchings, 297; lynchings overlooked and purged from, 3, 15, 223, 224, 245. *See also* Albemarle/Charlottesville Community Remembrance project; Alexandria Community Remembrance Project

collective trauma, 224, 242, 244, 247, 251n59. *See also* racialized terror and intimidation

Combs, Perry, 78

Commission on African American History Education (Virginia), 3

community support of and complicity in lynching, 7, 35, 46, 84, 296

Compromise of 1877, 174

Confederate monuments, 5, 256–59; in Alleghany County, 213; Charlottesville's Blue Ribbon Commission on Race, Monuments, and Public Spaces (BRC), 259–62, 265, 268; Charlottesville's Lee Park standoff between Black leaders and neo-Confederates, 259; courthouse placement of, 259; Johnny Reb statue in front of Albemarle Charlottesville courthouse, 256, 267, 268; Jordan hanging near, 37; racial violence's connection with, 247; removal proposed in Charlottesville (2012), 253, 258; Stonewall Jackson statue on land formerly owned by Black freed man, 265; tours in Charlottesville to explain significance of, 265; White supremacy and, 246

Confederate nostalgia and Lost Causers, 135, 144, 212–13, 246, 253, 257, 260; Capitol insurrection (2021) and, 295

confessions of accused men, 80, 89, 127, 136, 152–55, 157, 274; recanting at trial, 155, 192

Cooper, Robert, Jr., 92, 94

Corder, A. P., 70, 110–11, 119, 120–21n24

Corder, Elizabeth, 25, 26

Corder, Elvira, 22, 25–33, 37, 39, 41

Corder, Nathan, 25–26, 28, 31–32, 35

coroners' complicity in lynching reports, 38, 82
Corron, Elizabeth, 198
Costa, Tom, 14, 70, 103
court system. *See* judicial system
Covington Virginian praising Judge Anderson (1930), 212
Crawford, Bruce (editor/publisher *Crawford's Weekly*), 115–17, 119
Crebs (Winchester judge), 31
Crihfield, Zoe, 14, 70, 103
Crockett, William M. (white lynching victim 1883), 75
Culpeper commemorative project, 223

Daily Progress: editorial against lynching (1899), 244; on James as Black assailant of Hotopp (1898), 227–32, 236–38, 254; on James lynching (Woods Crossing 1898), 240
Daily Worker on Martinsville Seven case (1949), 157
Danville Bee on reprieve to examine sanity of Percy Lee (1925), 190–91
Danville Register on lynching as response to Black conduct (1893), 166
Danville's Museum of Fine Arts and History, 263
Darst, Major, 160
Daughters of the Confederacy, 257
Davis, Charles, 78
Davis, Westmoreland, 211
death penalty. *See* capital punishment
Death Penalty Information Center, 160
Deaton, Herschel, 87, 103, 112–13, 116–17, 119
Deep South: Border States lynchings compared to, 97; lynching as phenomenon associated with, 7, 8; Virginia lynchings compared to, 5, 8–9, 11, 13, 94, 300
De Fazio, Gianluca, 295
Democratic Party, linkage to white supremacy, 244

"desperado" term applied to Black lynching victims, 51–52, *51*, 54
Dickenson, A. M., 82
Dickenson County, 73; population increase in, 97
display of lynched victims: in Alexandria, 275, 284; in Charlottesville, 241; in Roanoke, 139–40; in Rockingham County, 135, 178; in Wise County, 104, 107, 110, 115. *See also* drawings of lynching victims; photographs
Dobbs, Mary, 209–10
Dotson, W. G. G., 85, 107, 109, 119
Douglas, Andrea, 15, 225, 253, 262, 264–66, 290
Douglass, Frederick, 48, 150
Downey, George, 203–4
drawings of lynching victims: Gustavus R. B. Horner's sketch of Jordan's hanging body, 38; *Richmond Planet*'s pen-and-ink drawings of Clifton Forge lynching victims, 55, 59, 65n14
Drysdale, Duncan, 155
Du Bois, W. E. B., 64
due process, disregard for, 7, 63, 176. *See also* speedy trial
Duke, R. T. W., Jr., 228, 241
Dyson, Michael Eric, 257

electric chair use in executions, 170, 177, 182–85, *183*, 190, 191, 210
Ellerson, Sam (lynching victim 1893), 79–80
Elliot, Farar, 272
Emmett Till Antilynching Act (2022), 64, 119, 224
Equal Justice Initiative (EJI): background and purpose, 272, 290; Charlottesville's participation in Community Remembrance project, 254, 260–69, 289; *Lynching in America: Confronting the Legacy of Racial Terror*, 224, 258–59; National Memorial for Peace and Justice (Montgomery, Alabama), 224

Ergenbright, James, 134–37
eugenics, 214, 258
Evening News on petition to commute Robert Lewis's execution to life sentence (1906), 208
Evening Star: on Smith's confession to murder (1910), 154; on Thomas lynching (1899), 283, 285
extralegal trials: lynchings as result of, 5; in Revolutionary War, 6
eyewitness accounts, 35, 40, 48, 56, 77, 138, 208, 287

failure to open door as cause of lynching, 82–83, 88
Fain, Sarah Lee, 162, 163
Falls, Peb (white female lynching victim 1897), 8, 167–68
false reports of lynchings, 74–75
Farish, Frank P., 237–39
Fauquier County: as agricultural center in Piedmont region, 32; Jordan lynching (1880), 13, 22–26, 35; Thompson lynching (1932), 17n30, 118
fear tactic. *See* racialized terror and intimidation
Feimster, Crystal N., 32
Ferguson, George, 256
Ferrel, Harrison, 256
Fields, George Washington, 159
Fields, William J., 116–17
Fifteenth Amendment, 31
Finley, Noah (executed 1899), 159–60
Finney, William (commutation of death sentence to life imprisonment 1908), 156
Fisher, Mrs. Robert, 84
Flamiano, Dolores, 13, 23, 45
Flinn, Susan K., 272
Floyd, George, 246, 289, 296, 297n5
Floyd, Ruby, 157
Fourteenth Amendment, 31, 230

Foy, Robert: escape from prison, capture, and hanging (1902), 108–9; Guynn lynching as possible consequence of, 109, 119; imprisoned for shooting two white men (1901), 108; lynching prevented by law enforcement, 109
Foy, Robert (delays in court case 1919), 70
Frankland, proposed as state (1780s), 94–95
Frank Leslie's Illustrated Newspaper, 164
Franklin, John Hope, 109
Franklin County, Finney saved from lynching in (1908), 156
Freedmen's Bureau, 133, 145, 147n14
Freeman (Indianapolis Black newspaper), 48
Furman v. Georgia (1972), 160–61

Gaines, William, 276–77
Garrett, Haney (Black female imprisoned for arson 1890), 9–10, 92
Gathers, Don, 267
Georgia: compared to Virginia, for number of lynchings, 8–9; compared to Virginia, for prosecution of lynchers, 250n54
Gillespie, Charles (executed 1909), 150–53, 190
Gilmer, Dan, 157
Gilmore, Jim, 169
Glass, Carter, 162, 202
Gleason, Paul, 200
Goldsby, Jacqueline, 62
Goodman, Thomas, 203–4
Goods, R. (Alexandria police chief), 154–55
Goodwin (Richmond judge in Wilson case 1901), 192
Gore (Middletown sheriff), 174
government officials, role of, 4–5, 10, 15; complicity in lynchings, 289–90, 296. *See also specific mayors, governors, etc.*
Grayson, Francis D., 157
Great Migration, 95
Green, Albert, 278–79

Green, Alice, 103, 106–7, 109
Green, William and Otto (unsuccessful attempt to lynch 1903), 201–2
Green Pastures (US only historically segregated recreation area), 215n6
Greensboro Truth and Reconciliation Commission (North Carolina), 264
Grubb, Grover Cleveland, 86, 112
Gwynn/Guynn, Wiley: background of, 105; Foy's treatment leading to lynching of, 109, 119; shooting victim (1902), 70, 84–85, 103–4, 106–8, 118

Hagy, James William, 13–14, 69–70, 73
Hairston, Frank, Jr., 157
Hairston, Howard Lee, 157
Hairston, James L., 157
Hall, Jim, "Impossible Love: An Interracial Romance in Post-Reconstruction Virginia," 13, 22, 25
Halsey, George (lynching victim 1893), 81–82
Hamilton, William, 41
Hampton, James Henry, 157
Hannah-Jones, Nikole, *The 1619 Project: A New Origin Story*, 252n76
Harris, Charlotte: lynching victim (1878), 3, 8, 126–27, 134–35, 178; memorializing (2020), 3; newspaper reporting of lynching, 135; O'Ferrall conducting lynching inquiry, 126–27, 135, 137, 142
Harrisonburg, 3; O'Ferrall practicing law in, 133–34, 178
Hart, Harry, 161
Hart, Henry (death by electric chair 1921), 185
Hart v. Commonwealth (1921), 161
Hatchell, Robert, 152
hate crime, lynching as, 119
Hatfield-McCoy feud, 96
Hay, Ann Marie, 272
Hegg, Kevin, 14, 127, 146, 173

Henry, Elizabeth, 233, *235*
Heuser, H. M., 87
Heyer, Heather (murdered 2017), 225
Higginbotham, A. Leon, 33
Hill, Oliver, 9
Hinton News, "Railroad Recollections" column displaying ignorance of lynchings (1989), 198
Hirschberger, Gilad, 242, 247, 251n59
historical markers, placement of, 223, 246, 265, 267, 290
history and truth telling: Black community's monument tours reclaiming, 266; community-oriented public history, 4, 262; Monticello's Getting Word Oral History Project, 261; oral history on lynchings and their impact on victims' families and Black communities, 24n3; political opposition to teaching America's racial history, 289; racial identity created by, 247; systemic racism confronted by, 289; teaching in Virginia's K–12 schools, 16n9, 224, 226n3, 289; Wells on, 290
Hodes, Martha, 30, 34
Horner, Gustavus R. B., sketch of Jordan's hanging body, 38
Hose, Sam: burning of, 48; lynching victim (1899), 8, 47, 54; religious meaning attributed to lynching of, 58
Hotopp, Carl, 228, 240, 244
Hotopp, Heinrich, 244
Hotopp, Julia, 227, 228–30, 232–33, 236, 238, 241, 245, 254
house breaking crime exaggerated to assault and rape, 118–19
How, W. Storer, 132–33
Howard, Josh, 14, 127–28, 179, 197
Howlett, Floyd McP. "Mack" (lynching victim 1898), 83–84
Hubbard, Ben (legal hanging 1906), 197, 199, 208–9

Huddle, Howard, 87
Hundley (Virginia Circuit Court judge), 155
Hurst/Hunt, David (J.H.): arrest and imprisonment of some lynchers of, 18n38, 70–71, 119; background of, 105, 120n7; breaking and entering exaggerated into attempted rape, 119; lynching victim (1920), 70, 86, 103–4, 109, 118–19; name confusion, 120n7
Hurt, Joseph, 75

Ifill, Sherrilyn, 290, 294n108
impunity of lynchers, 7–8, 10, 11, 104, 296; anonymity of lynchers, 82, 241, 274–75, 284–85, 287; Harris lynching (1878), 135, 178; James lynching (1898), 241, 252n74, 262; Jordan lynching (1880), 37; legacy in impunity of police for brutality, 296; McCoy lynching (1897), 286, 287–88; possible violence and threats against prosecuting attorneys and sheriffs, 90–91; in rapists' lynchings, 255; Thomas lynching (1899), 285, 287, 297; white newspapers' assumption of 48, 37
Inge, George, 257
interracial romance: Byrd lynching (1926), 86, 88, 112; pre-Civil War, 34; social condemnation of, 25–42. *See also* miscegenation laws
itinerant Black men: Anderson targeting, 197, 203–6, 214; John Henry James characterized as, 229, 230; as lynching victims, 89, 105

Jackson, Alvy (lynching victim 1885), 76–77, 89, 99n12
Jaffé, Louis, antilynching editorials by, 119, 121n42
jailers: Byrd lynchers threatening in Wythe County (1926), 86–87; Corder's commendation for averting lynching of Williams (1920), 111; cowardice and complicity of, 36, 111, 114; intimidation as reason to turn over prisoners, 91, 134; refusal to turn over Howletts (1898), 83
James, John Henry (lynching victim 1898), 14, 224, 254–56, 259; Alabama trip to commemorate 120th anniversary of death of, 263–64; Charlottesville Community Remembrance Project and, 262–64; Charlottesville using to come to terms with racial past, 254; collection of soil from site of his lynching (2018), 262, 265, 266; evidence ignored, 231, 232; historical marker in Charlottesville, dedication of (2019), 225, 246–47, 251n74, 266–69, 270n23; impunity of lynchers, 241, 252n74, 262; July 12 recognized as John Henry James Day, 268; lynch mob, efforts to save James from, 237–38, 254, 262; national newspaper coverage, 241, 254; newspaper labeling as itinerant ("tramp"), 229, 230; rape accusation against, 224, 229–33, 236, 254; reaction of local community to, 233, 241, 255; taken off train in Wood's Crossing for lynching, 239–40, 254
Jean, Susan: "'Warranted' Lynchings: Narratives of Mob Violence in White Southern Newspapers, 1880–1940," 21, 166
Jefferson, Hakeem, 296
Jefferson, Thomas, 258, 261, 266, 267, 269
Jenkins, Woods lynching prevented in and moved to Kentucky (1927), 103, 113–15, 117
Jim Crow era: legacy of, 4; racial code of acceptable conduct for Black men, 54–55, 107, 119; Virginia Constitution (1870) legitimizing, 162. *See also* "legal lynching"; lynchings, history of; racialized terror and intimidation; statistics; white supremacy
Johnson, Andrew, 132
Johnson, Burrell (death sentence 1902), 190, 191
Johnson, James Weldon, 109

Johnson, John (lynching victim 1893), 79–80
Johnson, Nelson and Joyce, 264
Johnson, P. L., 85
Johnson, Ron, 289
Johnson, Walter (legal hanging 1891), 191–92
Jones, Philip, escape from lynching (1934), 107
Jones, Suzanne, 30
Jones, William Henry (lynching victim 1888), 77
Jordan, Arthur: background and character of, 28–30; interracial romance with Elvira Corder, 25–28, 30–32; lynching victim (1880), 13, 22–23, 25, 29–30, 34, 35–38; newspaper coverage of lynching, 22–23, 39–42
Jordan, James (lynching victim 1925), 165
Jouet, Jack, 266, 267
judicial system: coming to terms with role in history of lynching and legal lynching, 302; criminal justice system targeting Black population, 9, 193, 299, 301; duty of officials in, 90–91; jurors under pressure from lynching threat to accused, 159–60, 184; "let law take its course" assurances, 79, 85, 127, 133, 151; lynchers considering as capricious and unpredictable, 37, 156, 176; role of, 4–5, 10; search of court records for proceedings against lynchers, 75; Virginia's capital punishment as fastest judicial approach in US, 169. *See also* speedy trial
judicial system, role of, 4
Justus, Elizabeth Baker, 85
Justus family members involved in Pennington lynching (1909), 85

Kamen, Henry, 250n46
Kansas, anti-Black mob violence in, 6
Kellis, Lawrence, 116
Kentucky: anti-Black mob violence in, 6; dispute with Virginia over Woods lynching (1920), 112, 116; mob lynchings transformed to state-sanctioned legal lynchings in, 192
Kesler, James, 255
Kessler, Jason, 254
Kilpatrick, James J., 154
Kincer, W. C. (Wythe County sheriff), 86
King, F. W., 212
King, J. C., 217n27
King, Martin Luther, 263, 264, 267
King William County: Bland lynching (1884), 166
Kinney, Andrew, 34
Kinser, Charles, 75
Kirkpatrick, Sam (lynching victim 1893), 79–81
Kloch, Lillian, 278, 281
Knights Templar, 82, 113
Kopytoff, Barbara K., 33
Ku Klux Klan (KKK), 113, 115, 116, 264, 295

Lacy, Richard, 274
Lambert, Thomas, white man accused of murder (1893), 80
Lavender, Will (lynching victim 1892), 165
law enforcement: complicity in lynchings, 82, 289–90; evidence not found of active participation in lynchings, 89; lynching influence on, 152–58; prevention of mob violence by, 70, 94, 104; Southwest Virginia lynchings and, 90–94. *See also* jailers; posses
lawyers, representation by. *See* right to counsel and adequate counsel
Lebanon News on outlaws in Clinch Valley Division (1889), 97
Lebsock, Suzanne, *A Murder in Virginia,* 130
Lee, Harper, *To Kill a Mockingbird,* 33
Lee, Percy (execution 1925), 190–91
Lee, R. E. (grandson of Robert), 213

Lee, Robert E., 133; statue in Charlottesville, 259, 261
Lee County: ignored by state legislature, 94; white outlaw gang in, 96
"legal lynching": capital punishment replacing mob lynching, 14, 15, 151, 168–69, 173–75, 182, 192, 211–12, 296, 301; coming to terms with judicial and press role in history of, 302; due process paid lip service, 176, 189; hallmarks of lynching in, 176; O'Ferrall passing law to make attempted rape punishable by death, 12, 14, 146, 155, 157, 160–62, 179, 182–84, 193; statistics of mob lynchings vs. legal lynchings (1877–1961), 182–84, 183; trials resulting in (Jim Crow era), 189–92
Letcher County: Kellis leaving due to "KKK conditions" in, 116; population growth between 1910 and 1920, 106
Lewis, Meriwether, 266, 267
Lewis, Robert (sentence commuted to life imprisonment 1906), 199, 208, 214
Lexington *Gazette* on Carl Hotopp arriving at lynching venue (1898), 240
Lindsay, James H., 244
Liscomb (Staunton police chief), 158
Little, Howard (saved from lynching 1909), 85, 91, 92
Litwack, Leon, 29
local historical societies as source for information on lynchings, 74–75, 99n12
local histories omitting lynchings, 88
Lockwood, Elizabeth, 272
Loewen, James W., *Sundown Towns*, 98
Lomax, John (legal hanging 1902), 191
Long, Daniel (lynching victim 1900), 84
Long, Roy C., 198
Lost Cause. *See* Confederate nostalgia
Louisville Courier-Journal on Moore's report on Woods lynching (1920), 116
Loving v. Virginia (1967), 34

Lowery, Marguerite, 161
Lucas, Sherman (lynching victim 1892), 79
Lunenburg County: Marable lynching (1895), 163–64; O'Ferrall preventing lynching of three Black women (1895), 142–43, 146
Lynch, Charles, 6
Lynchburg, as safe location for Bowles to avoid lynching while awaiting trial (1904), 206
Lynchburg militia, prevention of Barrett lynching (1917), 156
lynchers: arrest of, 70–71; conviction in Hurst lynching (1920), 110; Harris lynchers (1878) never indicted, 135, 178; indictment and trial of, 79; indictment but no one guilty in Wood lynching (1894), 83; indictment but no trial reported for Pennington lynchers (1910), 85–86; justice system's capricious and unpredictable outcomes as motivating factor, 37; newspaper treatment of, 13, 21–23, 39–42, 48, 51, 53, 64; number of inquiries before official bodies, but rarely ending in convictions, 88; pardons of, 86, 88, 91, 110; reward for arrest and conviction in Byrd lynching (1926), 87; search of court records for proceedings against, 75; unknown or masked, 82, 89; Woods lynchers (1920) unprosecuted due to multiple factors, 117. *See also* impunity of lynchers
lynching postcards, 45, 47, 49–50, 63, 64
lynchings. *See* threatened lynchings; *specific names of victims and locations*
lynchings, history of: age of lynching victims, 89; decade with highest number of lynchings, 88; definition and elements of lynching, 7, 198; disposition of persons who escaped lynching (1883–1922), 91; initiatives to restore truth of racialized terrorism and dignity of those murdered, 4, 15, 223–24, 295; intertwined with

INDEX 319

history of Virginia, 6; legacy of, 5, 13, 223, 289, 297; lynching, origins of term, 6; no documented lynchings after 1928 in Virginia, 117; not unique to the South, 6; number in Jim Crow Virginia, 6, 8, 16n10, 17n26, 46; overlooked and purged from collective memory, 3, 15, 223, 224; place as important feature of, 299; as popular justice, 6; Revolutionary War background in Virginia, 6, 8; similarities among and rituals common to lynchings, 103–4, 299; teaching in Virginia's K–12 schools, 16n9, 224, 226n3; undercounting, 8; Virginia General Assembly condemnation and regret (2019), 223; white victims in majority in first half of nineteenth century, 6. *See also* racialized terror and intimidation; statistics; *specific counties, crimes, and victims*
Lynch Law, 6

Magruder, Henry (legal hanging 1896), 197, 199, 204–6, 214, 217n23, 217n25, 217n27
Manassas, O'Ferrall ordering troops to prevent lynching (1894), 237
Mann, William Hodges, 191
Mapping Cville, 268
Marable, William (lynching victim 1895), 163–64
Marbury, Leonard, 274, 275
Marion, 81–82
Martin, Trayvon, 55, 246
Martinsville Seven case (1949–51), 157–58, 194
mass incarceration, 5, 184, 193, 296
Matthews, George (executed 1915), 190
McAuliffe, Terry, 259
McCorkle, C. R., 86, 110
McCoy, Joseph (lynching victim 1897), 1, 15, 225, 274–78; ACRP working to identify living descendants of McCoy family, 290; arrest for rape and alleged confession, 274; burial in indigents' cemetery, 276; compared to Thomas lynching two years later, 284; lynching, shooting, and bludgeoning with axe, 275; lynching mob and anonymity of lynchers, 274–75; officials exonerated by coroner's jury, 276; officials not expecting lynching to proceed, 274–75; possible uprising from Black community feared due to false rumors, 276; postmortem, 276; white community's complicity in lynching, 289–90; white community's reaction to, 276, 277
McCoy, Maddy, 272
McGhee (Bedford County deputy sheriff), 156
McIntire, Paul Goodloe, 265
McKinney, Philip, 58, 202
Meadows family massacre (Buchanan County 1909), 85
medical schools' use of Black bodies, 193, 258
mental disability of defendant, 156, 190–91, 205–6
Metcalfe, Mrs., 77
Mexicans/Mexican Americans as targets of lynchings, 6
Miles, Columbus, as lynching victim (1880), 38
militias: armed white militias, 15; Clifton Forge mayor requesting to protect town from possible Black retribution, 201; protection of Black prisoners, 11, 138; reimbursement for protection of prisoners from lynchings, 161
Milko, Christopher, 272
Miller, Charles W. (lynching victim 1891), 45, 53–57, 59, 200–201, 216n13. *See also* Clifton Forge lynchings of three Black miners (1891)
Miller, C. J. (lynching victim 1893), 62–63
Miller, Dayton, 108
Miller, Hugh Gordon, 192

Miller, Mahala, 34
Millner, Booker T., 157
Milton, Mrs. (alleged rape victim 1895), 173–74
miners and mining: coal boom generating demographic change between 1910 and 1920, 106; coal companies in partnership with law enforcement to apply rule of law, 105; coal companies recruiting Black and immigrant workers (1890s), 97; conflicts with owners, 90
Minor, John B., 229
miscegenation laws, 33–35. See also interracial romance
Mississippi compared to Virginia, for number of lynchings, 8–9
Mitchell, John, Jr.: antilynching campaign of, 7, 12, 22, 45, 47–49, 61, 130, 198, 297, 300; Clifton Forge lynchings photograph received by, 59; on cowardice and complicity of jailers, 36; fearless in confronting racism, 163; influence of, 300; on James lynching in Charlottesville (1898), 241–42; on legalized lynching by passage of Virginia code Section 3888, 180; on newspaper coverage of lynchings, 40; praise for O'Ferrall on antilynching stance, 130, 140–41, 146, 163–64, 175; as self-defense advocate, 61, 64, 83; unapologetic for publishing lynching images, 63; on Wood lynching (1894), 83
mob violence: acts of cruelty toward victims, 9, 47; in Alexandria (1899), 1–2; Brundage distinguishing from smaller mobs, 250n42; in Clifton Forge, 46; history of, against Blacks, 6, 295; incidents in Virginia (actual and threatened 1865–1940), 174, 175; justification for, 242; newspapers on how to curtail, 255; recent events of 2017 and 2021 as, 15, 260; respectability of the mob lending legitimacy to, 22, 66n31. See also newspapers (white) for press coverage; statistics
mock lynchings, 81
Montague, Andrew Jackson, 108
Montgomery, Alabama: Equal Justice Initiative based in, 272; National Memorial for Peace and Justice, 224, 246, 290; pilgrimage from site of John Henry James lynching to, 263
Montgomery County, decline in Black population in, 101n43
Monticello: African American Heritage Center, 261; Getting Word Oral History Project, 261; historical marker for, 267, 268
Moore, C. F. (Alleghany County judge), 203, 204
Moore, Harry, 106, 112–13, 116–17
Moore's Ford quadruple lynching (1946), 8
Morgan, Charles (lynching victim of Black lynchers 1893), 81, 88, 101n44
Morgan, Rush, 96
Morgan County: O'Ferrall as clerk of circuit court of, 177; O'Ferrall's Civil War actions in, 131–32
Morton, Miller, 200–201
Moss, Thomas (lynching victim 1892), 52
murder accusations, 70, 75, 77–81, 83, 85–87, 142, 161; in Anderson's Alleghany County court, 206–11; Beavers as first white person executed for murder of Black woman (1997), 161; Black female Virginia Christian executed for (1912), 159; coerced confession of Henry Smith (1910), 154; exoneration of Rogers after serving prison sentence (1943–51), 152–54; "legal lynching" for, 177; lynching of Barrett averted (1917), 156–57; as most frequent accusation against lynching victims, 88; self-defense of Bowles not persuasive in Anderson's court (1904), 206–8; white man killing another white man (1894),

203–4; Williams saved from lynching and legally hung (1904), 185
Museum of Jim Crow Memorabilia, 170n13

NAACP: antilynching stance of, 12, 22, 63, 64, 125; compiling number of lynchings and attempted lynchings, 302; *The Crisis* (magazine), 62; definition and elements of lynching set forth by, 7, 35; investigation of suspicious deaths of Blacks after antilynching law, 118; praising Sheriff Corder for averting lynching of Williams (1920), 111, 119; on Woods lynching (1920), 116
Napier, A. L., 18n38, 110
national guard, governor calling upon, 91
National Memorial for Peace and Justice (Montgomery, Alabama), 224, 246, 290
National Policy Institute, 260
Nation on Hurst lynchers' conviction (1923), 110
neonationalist event (Charlottesville 2017). See Unite the Right rally
Newport News Daily Press: on dangers of eliminating death penalty (1913), 169; on Gillespie assault on Stumpf (1909), 150–51
Newsome, Joseph Thomas, 159
newspapers (white): on Alexandria lynchings, 273, 279; anti-Black stereotypes built into reporting by, 13, 21, 40, 47, 50–51, 63–64, 66n31, 166, 177, 190, 198–99, 229, 279–80; Black paper coverage compared to white coverage, 21, 40, 48, 164; Blacks identified by "col." or "colored" following names in, 199; on Clifton Forge lynchings (1891), 50–64, 50–52; complicity in characterizations of lynchers and their victims, 13, 21–23, 39–42, 53, 64, 296; duty of journalists to tell truth, 163; errors in original lynching reports, 104, 287; errors in reporting confessions, 189–90; gossip as basis of coverage, 89; historical reliance on mostly white Southern newspapers, 21; Jordan lynching (1880), coverage of, 22–23, 39–42; lynching influence on, 163–68; racial bias of white newspapers, 48, 51, 164, 166, 198, 287; sensationalism in reporting, 56, 164; as source for information on lynchings, 7–8, 21, 74, 302; on speed of legal process in trying and executing Black men for crimes against white women, 189–90; spurring mob violence and lynchings, 47, 63, 108, 115, 164–65; threatened lynchings, coverage of, 152; trope of the hunt in, 55–56; voicing opposition to lynchings, especially after 1920, 22, 115; yellow journalism, 164. *See also* Black newspapers; *specific newspapers by name*
New York Globe (Black newspaper), 47
New York Herald on Harris lynching (1878), 135
New York World telegram from O'Ferrall (1894), 141
Noell, Charles, 156
Norfolk Black community endangered by Virginia Christian trial (1912), 159
Norfolk Journal and Guide: as Black newspaper in early twentieth century, 163; on white man's rape of Black woman, punishment for (1948), 158; on Woods lynching (1920), 116
Northam, Ralph, 170, 194, 266
Norton: KKK active in, 113; newspapers on Woods lynching (1927), 114–15. *See also* Crawford, Bruce

O'Ferrall, Charles Triplett, 14, 129–49, *139*, 177–79; Alexandria lynching of McCoy, criticism of, 274, 277; attempted rape made crime punishable by death penalty, 12, 14, 146, 155, 157, 160–62, 179, 182–84, 193; autobiography of, 129, 131–34, 144,

O'Ferrall, Charles Triplett (*continued*)
178; character of, 130–31, 133, 145, 178; as Confederate officer, 131–32, 177–78; as congressman (1882–94), 137–38, 179; Conservative party orthodoxy embraced by, 134; contradictory and unpredictable approach to lynching, 18n40, 126–27, 130, 136–37, 140, 144, 145, 174, 179; criticizing Alexandria lynchings, 144, 274, 277; as defender of white supremacy, 129–30, 178; early life of, 131–34, 177; fall from public favor, 129, 144, 148–49n45; final years and death (1905), 129; as governor, 138–44, 179; Harris lynching inquiry conducted by, 126–27, 135; as hotel manager in Staunton, 132, 147n11; as judge (1874–80), 134–37, 178; Lawson saved from execution (1875), 178; as lawyer, 133, 178; legacy of, 146; Lunenburg County, preventing lynching of three Black women in (1895), 142–43, 146; opposition to and reduction of lynching and civil disorder, 11, 130, 140, 143–44, 161, 163–64, 175, 179, 182, 184, 186, 202; Parker executed under new law making attempted rape punishable by death (1895), 193; political ambitions of, 133–34; posthumous reputation of, 14, 130; refusal to endorse Democratic party candidate for president (1896), 129, 144; Roanoke Riot (1893), response to, 140, 145; telegram to *New York World* (1894) on lynching as appropriate response to crime of rape, 141–42; Wells opposed by, 127, 141; West Virginia governor declaring as "enemy of the State," 132

O'Ferrall, Plunkett, 132–33, 147n16
oral history on lynchings and their impact on victims' families and Black communities, 24n3
Ore, Ersula J., 63
"outraging" accusations, 78, 94, 99n6

Page, Thomas Nelson, 235, 244
Paige, Richard G. L., 38–39
Panic of 1893, 97
pardons by governor, 18n38, 86, 88, 91, 94, 101n40, 110
Paris, Texas, lynching of Henry Smith (1893), 8
Parker, Thornton (first man executed under new law making attempted rape punishable by death 1895), 173–74, 180, 193
Parsons, Henry, 202–3
paternalism, 32, 161, 167
Pattie, Caldwell, 36–37
Pattie, Horace, 35–36
Paul, John, 137
Payne, William Henry Fitzhugh, 39
Pendleton, William C., *History of Tazewell County and Southwest Virginia*, 88
Pennington, Henry (white lynching victim 1909), 85–86
Perkins, John (legal hanging 1868), 195n20
Perrow, R. L. (Campbell County sheriff), 156
Perry, Alice, 165, 233
Peters, John (falsely purported to be lynching victim 1920), 74
Pfeifer, Michael J., 37; *Rough Justice: Lynching and American Society, 1847–1947*, 168, 169, 176, 192, 214
Phillips, V. N. "Bud," *Pioneers in Paradise: Legends and Stories from Bristol Tennessee/Virginia*, 74–75, 99n16
photographs: Miller, Scott, and Burton (three black Clifton Forge miners), 45, 46, 200; Smith's body after lynching and shooting, 139–40; Woods' body after lynching, shooting, and burning, 115
Piedmont Industrial Land and Improvement Co. (PILIC), 256
Plessy v. Ferguson (1896), 174
police brutality, 5, 15, 193, 289, 296
police state, Virginia as, 9, 13
Pollard, Lucy, 163

posses: in Clifton Forge to capture Black men (1891), 200; defined, 41; payment by O'Ferrall for Harris lynching (1878), 135; suspects caught by, treatment of, 153; word choice to imbue lynchers with legitimacy as law enforcement authorities, 42, 46, 55–56
Pound Gap (Virginia/Kentucky border), site of Woods lynching (1927), 70, 114, 117
pre–Civil War: castration of slave convicted of attempted rape (1765 statute), 160; interracial romance, 34; Southwest Virginia during, 73–74
press. *See* Black newspapers; newspapers (white); *specific names of newspapers and editors*
prevention of lynchings: Anderson replacing mob lynchings with legal executions, 209, 211–12, 213; Dotson attempting to dissuade angry mob (Gwynn lynching 1902), 85; law enforcement's role, 156–57; methods for, 155–56; possibilities of, 11–12; refusal by officials, 4–5; refusal to prevent, 4–5; speedy trial and execution as means for, 151, 158–59; in Virginia, 11. *See also* threatened lynchings
Priddy, J. C. (Charlotte County sheriff), 156
Printing Hate digital project (Howard Center for Investigative Journalism), 24n6
Privitt, Sam (Jenkins sheriff), 114
property disagreement, 83–84
Protestantism of Southwest Virginia, 95
Puckett, Lee (white lynching victim 1899), 18n38
Pugh, J. Andrew, 200, 216n10
Pulaski County, decline in Black population in, 101n43

racial identity: Black newspapers helping to forge, 48, 63; history's combination of fact and myth to create, 247

racialized terror and intimidation: Anderson's perpetuation of, 199, 211, 214–15; Anderson's role in, 199, 211, 214; in Charlottesville, 225; demoralization of racist ideologies and, 258; fast vs. slow terror, 257; fear compared to, 257; lynchers as capricious and unpredictable factoring into, 37, 301; lynchings/threatened lynchings as, 3–5, 7–14, 47, 58, 105, 109, 152, 154, 165–66, 246, 257, 259, 301; mob violence as, 10, 159; national effort to recognize and confront, 224; newspapers' role in, 13; persistence of, 301; prevalence in Virginia shown by research, 189; public place chosen for lynching to ensure, 35; redefinition of "racialized terrorism" to include threatened lynchings, 177, 184; state-sanctioned, 111, 117, 175–76, 192, 193, 288, 296–97. *See also* capital punishment; *specific lynching victims and locations*
racial justice, 15, 150
racial mixing: Falls lynching and (1897), 167–68; prohibition against, 33–35; white suprematists' fear of, 260. *See also* interracial romance; miscegenation laws
Racial Terror: Lynching in Virginia project, 3, 8, 182
rape accusations: in Alexandria, 274; in Anderson's Alleghany County court, 204–6; beating and rape of white woman (1893), 81–82; Black men accused of rape against white women, special criminal status during Jim Crow, 7, 21, 126, 141, 169, 176, 193, 233; broad definition of "rape," 234; fifty-seven Black men sent to electric chair for (1908–61), 177; inadequate representation by counsel, 189–91; "legal lynching" for, 177–96; lynching as way of sparing women from testifying in trial, 37, 255; Martinsville Seven case (1949–51), 157; mental disability or insanity of defendants,

rape accusations (*continued*)
156, 190–91; number of Black vs. white Virginians executed for (1626–1961), 180; punishable by death penalty in Virginia, 12, 14, 146, 155, 157, 160–62, 173–74, 176, 180, 182–84, 193; show trials for, 180; slave castration for (1765 statute), 160; white father accused of rape of daughter, not guilty (1894), 203–4; white girl eight-years old, allegations against Black teen (Thomas case 1899), 1–2, 281; white men's rape of Black women, punishment for, 158, 160. *See also* assault accusations

Raper, Arthur F., 176

Raper, Franklin, *Southern Commission on the Study of Lynching*, 166–67

Ratliff, Alexander, 79–80

Reconstruction: anti-Black mob violence in, 6; Black people's equality as issue for whites during, 235, 257; withdrawal of troops at end of, 174. *See also* Confederate nostalgia and Lost Causers

Reed, Kiz, 81

Religious Herald on Jordan lynching (1880), 41

religious meaning attributed to lynchings, 48, 58

Republican Party, 244, 257

Revolutionary War, 6, 8

Reynolds (sheriff in Whitesburg, Kentucky), 114

Richardson, James, 140

Richlands lynchings (Tazewell County 1893), 79–80, 90

Richmond: Gillespie execution (1909), 150–53

Richmond Afro-American on Martinsville Seven case (1951), 157

Richmond Daily Press on Gillespie at trial (1909), 151

Richmond Dispatch (formerly *Richmond Daily-Dispatch*): on Bland lynching (1884), 166; on Clifton Forge lynchings (1891), 51, 51, 54–57; on Guynn lynching (1902), 106; on Hotopp family tragedies (1900–1902), 244; letter commending O'Ferrall's rebuke of Black conduct (1894), 142; on pro se Black defendant Walter Johnson (1892), 191–92; sensationalism in reporting lynchings, 164

Richmond Planet: antilynching campaign of, 12, 13, 40, 45–49, 63, 163, 297; on arrests of Black men for offering to help police protect jailed Black teen (1899), 1; on Barnes's early release from prison (1897), 164; as Black newspaper published 1883–1938, 47, 163, 173, 273; on Clifton Forge lynchings of three Black miners (1891), 13, 23, 40, 48, 50, 53, 55, 56–59, 62, 64; compared to white newspapers' coverage, 48, 99n7, 273; counternarrative on Alexandria lynchings, 273; on Downey as white rapist (1894), 203; on Finley verdict of death sentence (1899), 160; on Hart conviction requiring two jury trials (1923), 185; on James lynching in Charlottesville (1898), 241–42; lynching images and broadside advertisement as form of protest, 49, 50, 55, 59–62, 60–61; on McCoy lynching (1897), 277; on Mitchell's praise of O'Ferrall, 130, 175; on O'Ferrall as opponent to lynching, 130, 140; on O'Ferrall's prevention of lynching of three Black women in Lunenburg County (1895), 142–43; on Parker as first Black man executed under new law making attempted rape punishable by death (1895), 173–74, 180, 193; on Piedmont Industrial Land and Improvement Co. (1890), 256; "The Reign of Lawlessness" column, 61–62, 61; rule of law, commitment to, 61, 62; on self-defense necessary for Black people, 83; on sentencing of William H. Wilson (1901), 192; on Thomas lynching and Black men who attempt to protect jailed Thomas (1899), 279–81, 283, 291n27; on Thompson's death

verdict and sentence (1922), 211; wrongly attributed 1894 lynching to Lebanon, Virginia (actually Lebanon, Indiana), 99n6. *See also* Mitchell, John, Jr.
Richmond Times: on Kirkpatrick lynching (1893), 81; on O'Ferrall's fall from public favor (1896), 149n45; on Parker as first Black man executed under new law making attempted rape punishable by death (1895), 173; on Peters lynching in Tazewell County (1920), 74
Richmond Times Dispatch: comparing Virginia's use of electric chair to lynching (1908), 170; on lawyers' inadequate representation of Black defendants (1904), 191; on sanity examination of Percy Lee and his danger to community (1925), 190–91; on trial and execution of Burrell Johnson (1902), 190; on trial and execution of Matthews and Rollins (1915), 190; on trial and sentencing of William H. Wilson (1901), 192
Rigby, David, 168
right to counsel and adequate counsel: Anderson's court's failure to provide, 210, 211; Black defendants acting pro se, 191; failure to defend, 191; neglected for black defendants, 142, 153, 177, 191; white attorneys reluctant to take Black defendants, 158, 189, 191
Rippey/Ripply, Walter (legal hanging 1908), 92, 165, 190
Rise, Eric, *Race, Rape, and Radicalism: The Case of the Martinsville Seven, 1949–51*, 157
Risheill, Thomas, 286, 288, 289
Rives, Hallie Erminie, *Smoking Flax*, 242–43, 244, 246
Roach, W. T., 156
Roanoke, 17n29; authorities shooting into lynching mob of Thomas Smith (1893), 237; Black population (1890 and 1900), 216n7; Stevens charged for assault on white girl (1892), 231, 233. *See also* Roanoke Riot (1893)
Roanoke Evening News on Finney sentenced to death (1908), 156
Roanoke Light Infantry, 138
Roanoke Riot (1893), 11, 17n29, 55, 138–40, 145, 198, 202
Roanoke Times: on Clifton Forge lynchings (1891), 52, 52, 54, 56, 57, 59; on Guynn lynching (1902), 106; praising Sheriff Corder for averting lynching of Williams (1920), 111; on Stevens as Black assailant of white girl (1892), 231
robbery allegations, 79–81; "legal lynching" for highway robbery, 177
Roberts, Clifton, 233, *234*
Robinette, Creed, 110–11
Robinson, J. Francis, 256
Rockbridge County, Downey as white rapist (1894), 203–4
Rockingham County, 3; Falls lynching (1897), 167–68; Harris lynching (1878), 134–35, 178; O'Ferrall as county judge in, 126; women as lynching victims in, 8, 134
Rockingham County Court, O'Ferrall as judge of, 134–37, 178
Rockingham Register denying lynching of Peb Falls (1897), 168
Rogers, Silas (exonerated after serving prison sentence 1943–51), 152–54
Rogers v. Commonwealth of Virginia (1943), 152–53
Rollins, John Lewis (executed 1915), 190
Rollins, Martin (lynching victim 1889), 78
Ruff, John, 206–7, 218n30
rule of law: Clifton Forge preferring vigilantism to, 51; coal companies in partnership with law enforcement to apply, 105; in conflict with white supremacy, 244; O'Ferrall as defender of, 130; *Richmond Planet*'s commitment to, 61, 62

Russell, Siri, 262, 270n16
Russell County: Black female imprisoned for arson (1890), 9–10; Burgess and Lucas lynchings (1892), 79; in coal country, 97; cruelest lynching of Black boy (1884), 76, 88; Ellerson arrest in (1893), 80; prevention of Howard Little's lynching, 91; unnamed Black man (lynching victim 1890), 78, 89; violence as frequent occurrence in, 96

Schmidt, Jalane, 262, 264, 265
Schultz, Walter, 154
Scott, John (lynching victim 1891), 45, 53, 56, 59, 200–201, 216n13. *See also* Clifton Forge lynchings of three Black miners
Scott County: in coal country, 97; Wood lynching (1894), 82
Seguin, Charles, and David Rigby article on capital punishment as direct legacy of lynching (2021), 168
self-defense, 61, 64, 83, 116, 197, 206–8
sham trials. *See* show trials
Shenandoah Herald: on Gillespie trial and execution (1909), 190; on lynchings of eight Black men in Charleston (1890), 166; on Parker protected from lynching (1895), 174; on Peters lynching as falsehood (1920), 74
Shortridge, Benjamin, 79–80
show trials, 12, 14, 126, 153, 161, 177, 180, 189. *See also* speedy trial
Shuman, Edwin L., *Practical Journalism: A Complete Manual of the Best Newspaper Methods*, 163
Simpson, George L., 1–2, 278–83
slavery: abolition of, 230; Albemarle County's system of racial capitalism based on, 258; Alexandria as large domestic slave trade site, 272; castration for attempted rape (1765 statute), 160; historical markers of slave trade, 246, 265; keeping Black man in his place, 234; Union calvary freeing enslaved people in Charlottesville, 229
Smångs, Mattias, 31
Smith, Bluford (lynching victim 1882), 75
Smith, Douglas, 17n30, 121n46
Smith, Henry (executed 1910), 154–55
Smith, Henry (lynching victim 1893), 8
Smith, James, 274–75, 279–81
Smith, Jane, 238
Smith, Thomas: burning of body of, 140; display and photographs of lynched victim, 139–40; lynching victim, associated with Roanoke Riot (1893), 11, 17n29, 55, 138–40, 198, 237
Smyth County: Canter brothers, prevention of lynchings of, 91; Halsey lynching (1893), 81–82
social transgressions as crime, 166
Sons of Confederate Veterans, 257
Southampton County, Nat Turner rebellion in (1831), 235
Southern Poverty Law Center (SPLC), 264, 270n18
Southern Railroad Line, 256–57
Southwest Virginia, 69–121; agriculture in, 73–74, 95; Black people, distribution by county, 98n4; concentration of lynchings in, 5, 69, 73, 94–95; demographic changes in, 95; Far Southwest Virginia lynchings, 70; geographic definition of, 73, 95, 98n2; Hatfield-McCoy feud in, 96; mountainous nature of, 98n3; newspapers as information source for, 74; political, economic, and social factors motivating lynchings in, 70, 95–96, 104; Protestantism of, 95; Republicans as dominant political party in, 95; shootings in, prevalence of, 96; threatened lynchings in, 70; transportation options limited in, 95; white supremacy in, 95. *See also specific counties*

INDEX 327

Spanish Inquisition, 232, 239, 250n46
speedy trial, 151, 155, 158–59, 165, 169, 174, 177, 190; Anderson's court and, 197, 209–10, 211, 213
Spencer, Richard, 260
Spinner, Thurman (saved from lynching 1909), 156
S. S. Griffith & Co. (photographer), 45, 46, 49, 50
Stanford (Kentucky) *Interior Journal* on Falls lynching (1897), 168
statistics: actual and threatened mob violence in Virginia by race of victim (1865–1940), 174, *175;* census of Black population in Virginia counties, 215–16n7; Charlottesville's Black population growth (1890s), 256–57; comparison of Virginia for number of lynchings to Black belt states, 8–9, 189; decade with highest number of lynchings, 88; estimates of lynchings in Jim Crow South, 6, 8–9, 16n10, 17n26, 46; Jim Crow trials resulting in legal lynchings, 189; juvenile executions (1787–1905), 219n55; legal executions in Virginia by race (1877–1961) and compared to population by race (1880–1960), *181, 182;* mob violence against Black men, by outcome and nature of accusation (1877–1932), *188;* mob vs. legal lynchings in Virginia (1877–1961), 182–84, *183;* persons who escaped lynching in Southwest Virginia (1883–1922), 91, *92–93;* rape accusations, number of Black vs. white Virginians executed (1626–1961), 180; Southwest Virginia lynchings, 88; threatened lynchings between 1866 and 1955 (Beck inventory), 17n33, 185–86, *187,* 189; threatened lynchings between 1880 and 1929 (Beck inventory), 184; Virginia as mid-Atlantic state with most lynchings, 300; Virginia lynchings (1880–1917), 144;

Virginia number of lynchings compared to Deep South, 5, 8–9, 11, 13, 94, 300
Staunton, 50; Black population in (1880–1900), 216n7; Breckenridge saved from lynching and legally executed (1909), 158; James moved to jail in to avert lynching, 238; O'Ferrall as hotel manager in, 132; O'Ferrall ordering troops to prevent lynching (1894), 140
Staunton Dispatch and News on restraint of lynching mob in case of Aurelius "Felix" Christian (1909), 209
Staunton Leader on speedy conviction of Wright (1912), 165
Staunton Spectator: on Clifton Forge lynchings (1891), 50–51, *50,* 53–54, 56–58; on mob action against James (1898), 255; on O'Ferrall's discriminatory treatment of Black people (1866), 133; on O'Ferrall's ejection of Black people from hotel he managed, 132
Staunton Spectator and Vindicator on anonymity of lynchers of James (1898), 241
Steiker, Carol and Jordan, 168
stereotypes and tropes: on Black inferiority, 257–58; in Black men's descriptions, 40, 53–54, 150–51, 166, 243, 280, 287; to dehumanize and demonize Black people, 158, 234, 242–43, 258, 287, 296; hunting, trapping, and killing of Blacks as trope to normalize lynching practice, 55; newspapers employing in reporting on lynchings, 13, 21, 40, 47, 50–51, 63–64, 66n31, 166, 177, 190, 198–99, 229, 279–80; white catharsis by lynching of victim that fit Black stereotype of criminal, 232; white womanly honor, 47, 234, 236
Stevens, Allen, 231
Stumpf, Marie Louise, 150–51
Styron, William, 236
Suits, Paris (lynching victim 1898), 83

328 INDEX

sunset towns, 98
Sussex County, Jordan lynching victim (1925), 165
Sutherland, Horace (judge), 87
Sutherland, Oak, 79
Sutherland, William, 263
Swanson, Claude, 156, 208
syphilis allegations against lynching victim, 78
Szakos, Kristin, 253, 259

Tarter, Brent, 230
Tate, Shayler, 18n38, 110
Taylor, John, 157
Taylor, Rob, 272
Tazewell County, 17n29; Brown, Kirkpatrick, Johnson, Branch, Ellerson, Blow, and Barns lynchings (1893), 17n29, 79–81, 88, 99n18, 165; in coal country, 97; false newspaper accounts of lynching (1920), 74; law enforcement personnel in 1890s, 90; lynchers tried three years later for multiple 1893 lynchings, 81, 88; Morgan lynching (1893), 81, 89; omission of lynchings in local histories, 88; Smith lynching (1882), 17n29, 75
Tennessee, emergence as state, 95
terrorism against Blacks. *See* racialized terror and intimidation
Thirteenth Amendment, 31
Thomas, Benjamin (lynching victim 1899): ACRP working to identify living descendants of Thomas family, 290; Alexandria mayor's court sentencing Black residents seeking to protect Thomas, 281; Alexandria remembrance ceremony (2020), 3; anonymity and impunity of lynchers, 284–85, 287, 297; arrest for criminal assault on eight-year-old white girl, 278; arrest of Black men gathering to protect Thomas, 279–80; Black men attempting to protect from white mob violence, 225, 278–79, 297; Black passive resistance after, 285, 288; burial of Thomas, 285; compared to McCoy lynching two years earlier, 284; in jail awaiting grand jury hearing, Thomas dragged out for lynching, 283; lynching victim (1899), 1–3, 15, 225; mayor promising lynching if grand jury failed to indict Thomas, 282; memorial service at Shiloh Baptist Church, 286; officials seeing no potential danger to jailed Thomas, 279; only testimony from eight-year-old girl, 1–2, 281; rumor of attempted jail escape by Thomas, 281; shooting and battering of, 284; trophies taken from lynching scene, 284; white community's complicity in lynching, 289–90; white fear of Black violence in revenge, 285, 287; white reaction to Black residents seeking to protect Thomas, 279–80, 284
Thomas, Elizabeth, 2–3
Thompson, Edmund (executed 1922), 197, 199, 210–11, 214; mob lynching averted, 210, 213
Thompson, Luther, 274–76
Thompson, Shedrick (lynching victim 1932), 17n30, 118
threatened lynchings: change of law to legal lynching, effect on, 193; effective method of racial oppression and coercion, 3–5, 7–14, 47, 58, 105, 109, 152, 154, 165–66, 246, 257, 301; including in count of "racialized terrorism," 177, 184, 185–86, 189, 301–2; influence on courtroom procedures, 151–52, 158–60; influence on legislation, 151–52, 160–63; influence on press coverage, 152, 163–68; law enforcement, effect on, 152–58; Martinsville Seven case (1949) at dawn of civil rights movement, 157–58; number between 1880 and 1929, 17n33, 184; in Southwest Virginia, 70; victims

primarily Black men, 186; Virginia with highest number in the South, 9, 11, 13, 14, 17n33, 301. *See also* statistics
Tinsley, Fred (lynching victim 1902), 166
Tolnay, Stewart, 8–9, 16n10; *A Festival of Violence* (with Beck), 17n26, 97, 177, 184, 189
Tom's Creek. *See* Gwynn/Guynn, Wiley
trials resulting in legal lynchings (Jim Crow era). *See* "legal lynching"
Trinkle, Elbert Lee, 18n38, 86, 110, 190, 211
tropes. *See* stereotypes and tropes
trophies from lynchings and legal hangings, 47, 116, 140, 185, 254, 284
Trotti, Michael Ayers, 234
Trout, Henry (Roanoke mayor), 138–40, 237
True Index on interracial romance of Jordan and Corder (1880), 33
truth and reconciliation process, 290. *See also* history and truth telling
Tulsa Massacre (1921), 63
Tulsa Tribune, role in Tulsa Massacre (1921), 63
Turley, James, 278–80, 292n33
Turner, Nat, 235–36
Tuskegee Institute compiling number of lynchings and attempted lynchings, 302
Tyler, J. Hoge, 162

United Daughters of the Confederacy, 213
Unite the Right rally (Charlottesville 2017), 15, 224, 246; alternative events held at time of, 270n18; as catalyst for community to consider racist past, 270n20; Heyer murder during, 225, 247; James lynching (1898) and, 262; reaction to proposals to remove Confederate monuments, 253; Spencer as leader, 260; violence perpetrated by, 295
University of Virginia: community engagement of, 260–62; Liberation and Freedom Day, 268; magazine on Reconstruction rise of Black people despite their inferiority (1890), 257; medical school's use of Black bodies taken from graves, 258; Monument to Enslaved Laborers, 246, 268, 269n10; President's Commission on Slavery and the University (PCSU), 258, 269n10; white supremacy and, 253–54, 258

Vandiver, Margaret, *Lethal Punishment*, 155–56
vigilante justice, 6, 23, 59, 81, 126, 130. *See also* mob violence; *specific lynching victims*
Virginia Board of Education, 3
Virginia Citizen: on Carter lynching (1902), 166; on speed of Christian conviction (1909), 159
Virginia Constitution: revision (1870), 162; Section 7 (1870), 90; Section 34 (1902), 91, 212
Virginia legislation: antilynching law (1928), 9, 17nn29–30, 71, 88, 111–12, 117, 118, 162, 300; death penalty abolition bill (proposed 1928), 162–63; House Bill 587 (2016) to stop removal of Confederate monuments, 259; ignoring lynching for decades, 152; Senate Bill 183 and House Bill 1537 on local determination of removal of Confederate monuments, 268; Vagrancy Act (1824), 230; Virginia code, Section 3888, 160, 179
Virginia Pilot on Peters lynching in Tazewell County (1920), 74
von Daacke, Kirt, 258

Walker, Nikuyah, 266–67
Ward, Geoff, 296
war on drugs, 184, 193
Warren, Earl (Supreme Court chief justice), 34
Warren, Mrs. John, 78
Warring, Henry H., 286
Washington, Richard, 279

Washington County: Black population in, 101n43; Canter brothers protected from lynching (1915), 91–94
Washington County, Maryland, 27, 30
Washington Post on McCoy lynching (1897), 274, 275–76
Washington Times on Thomas lynching (1899), 285
Watkins, Mrs. W. T., 192
Watts, Lucien, 237–39
Waverly Dispatch on Jordon lynching providing lesson to Black men (1925), 165
Waynesboro *Herald* on James dragged off train for lynching (1898), 239–40
Webster, James, 2, 275, 281–83
Wedderburn, A. J., 272
Weekly Louisianian on Jordan lynching (1880), 41
Wells, Ida B.: antilynching campaign of, 7, 22, 48, 52, 61, 198, 226n3; on interracial romance as nonexistent in minds of white men, 27; on Miller lynching (Bardwell, Kentucky 1893), 62–63; on Moss lynching (1892), 52; on newspaper coverage of lynchings, 40; O'Ferrall's opposition to, 127, 141, 142; *A Red Record* (pamphlet), 61; *Richmond Planet*'s depiction of lynchings and, 64; on shared script of lynchings across the South, 286; on truth telling, 289, 290; on unmarked graves of lynching victims, 42
West, John, 256, 265
"What's Your Story?" oral history initiative, 215n6
Wheeler, Ellen, 205, 217n25
White, Albert, 206–7
White, Gilmer, 208
White, Walter, 11, 35, 111, 116
white men: interracial romance as nonexistent for, 27; as lynching victims (1866–1932), 8; number executed in Jim Crow era, 180–81, *181*; saved from lynching, 91–94, *92*; sentenced for rape or attempted rape, 158, 160
Whitesburg, Kentucky, jail holding Woods (1927), 103, 113–14, 117
white supremacy: "Black rapist" image as justification for violence, 21, 193; Capitol insurrection (2021) and, 15, 289, 295–96; Confederate monuments linked with, 253; death penalty as form of, 215; Democratic Party's linkage to, 244; fear of newly freed Black enslaved people and, 230, 257; importance of confronting, 264, 269, 290; impunity of, 15; justice demanded by, 176; lynching as form of, 7, 259; lynching postcards in support of, 45, 50, 64; miscegenation laws and, 33–35; neo-Confederates and, 260; in Southwest Virginia, 95; threat of lynching as form of, 9; violence associated with, 3, 5, 11, 247, 295; Virginia Constitution (1870) and, 162; waning of lynching not indicating ending of, 300. *See also* racialized terror and intimidation
white women: "Black rapist" threat to, 21, 235–36; lynching promoted as way to defend from "Black rapists," 7; stereotype of white womanly honor, 47, 234, 236; subordination of Southern white women, 32. *See also* assault accusations; rape accusations
Wilkes-Barre Times on Thomas lynching (1899), 283
Willard, Floyd, 87
Williams, Charles, 108
Williams, Henry (legal hanging 1904), 185, 191
Williams, John, martial law declared upon arrest of (1916), 165
Williams, Sydney (near lynching of 1920), 109, 110–11, 119
Williamsport, Maryland, interracial romance as socially unacceptable in, 30–31

INDEX   331

Wilson, Lizzie, 77
Wilson, William H. (imprisoned 1901), 192
Wilton, Glen (threatened lynching 1909), 154
Winchester, 31, 41; Parker execution by hanging for rape (1895), 173–74
Wise County, 14, 103–21; court docket (1921), 96; demographic and economic changes in, 70, 97, 105; Gwynn/Guynn shooting (1902), 84–85, 103–4; Hurst/Hunt lynching (1920), 70, 86, 103–5; increased racial tensions following World War I return of Black soldiers, 109; lynchings and racialized mob violence in, 70; number of lynchings in, 88; prevention of lynching (1920), 11–12; Suits lynching (1898), 83; Woods lynching (1927), 17n29, 70, 87–88, 103, 111–19
Witte (Richmond Circuit Court judge), 151
Wolfe, Brendan, 14, 224, 227
women: executions of, rarity of, 178, 180; independent and capable women in yeomen farmers' families, 26; lynching as way of sparing women from testifying in rape trials, 37, 255; as lynching victims (1866–1932), 8, 134, 142–43, 195n24. *See also* rape accusations; white women
Wood, Cecil, as last man given death sentence for rape (1972), 160–61
Wood, Samuel (lynching victim 1894), 82–83, 88
Woods, Leonard: antilynching legislation (1928) precipitated by, 17n29, 71, 111, 117–19; background of, 106; lynching victim shot and burned (1927), 17n29, 70, 71, 87–88, 103, 111–19
Wood's Crossing. *See* James, John Henry
World War I, Black soldiers returning from, 86, 109, 112
Wright, Alfred (executed 1912), 155, 165
Wright, George C., 176, 192
Wright, Richard, *Black Boy*, 301
Wythe County: Byrd lynching (1926), 86–87, 112; Crockett lynching (1883), 75; decline in Black population in, 101n43; Jones lynching (1888), 77; Long lynching (1900), 84; number of lynchings in, 88

yellow journalism, 164

Recent books in
The American South Series

Justice for Ourselves: Black Virginians Claim Their Freedom after Slavery
JOHN G. DEAL, MARIANNE E. JULIENNE, AND BRENT TARTER

After Emancipation: Racism and Resistance at the University of Virginia
KIRT VON DAACKE AND ANDREA DOUGLAS, EDITORS

Driven to the Field: Sharecropping and Southern Literature
DAVID A. DAVIS

The Princess of Albemarle: Amélie Rives, Author and Celebrity at the Fin de Siècle
JANE TURNER CENSER

In the True Blue's Wake: Slavery and Freedom among the Families of Smithfield Plantation
DANIEL B. THORP

Against the Hounds of Hell: A Life of Howard Thurman
PETER EISENSTADT

Facing Freedom: An African American Community in Virginia from Reconstruction to Jim Crow
DANIEL B. THORP

Capital and Convict: Race, Region, and Punishment in Post–Civil War America
HENRY KAMERLING

The Uplift Generation: Cooperation across the Color Line in Early Twentieth-Century Virginia
CLAYTON MCCLURE BROOKS

The Risen Phoenix: Black Politics in the Post–Civil War South
LUIS-ALEJANDRO DINNELLA-BORREGO

Designing Dixie: Tourism, Memory, and Urban Space in the New South
REIKO HILLYER

A Deed So Accursed: Lynching in Mississippi and South Carolina, 1881–1940
TERENCE FINNEGAN

Radical Reform: Interracial Politics in Post-Emancipation North Carolina
DEBORAH BECKEL

Religion and the Making of Nat Turner's Virginia: Baptist Community and Conflict, 1740–1840
RANDOLPH FERGUSON SCULLY

From Yeoman to Redneck in the South Carolina Upcountry, 1850–1915
STEPHEN A. WEST

What Reconstruction Meant: Historical Memory in the American South
BRUCE E. BAKER

Black, White, and Olive Drab: Racial Integration at Fort Jackson, South Carolina, and the Civil Rights Movement
ANDREW H. MYERS

Murder, Honor, and Law: Four Virginia Homicides from Reconstruction to the Great Depression
RICHARD F. HAMM

South by Southwest: Planter Emigration and Identity in the Slave South
JAMES DAVID MILLER

A Way out of No Way: Claiming Family and Freedom in the New South
DIANNE SWANN-WRIGHT

The Lynching of Emmett Till: A Documentary Narrative
CHRISTOPHER METRESS, EDITOR

Ladies and Gentlemen on Display: Planter Society at the Virginia Springs, 1790–1860
CHARLENE M. BOYER LEWIS

Forgotten Time: The Yazoo-Mississippi Delta after the Civil War
JOHN C. WILLIS

Bloody Promenade: Reflections on a Civil War Battle
STEPHEN CUSHMAN

Slave in a Box: The Strange Career of Aunt Jemima
M. M. MANRING

Haunted Bodies: Gender and Southern Texts
ANNE GOODWYN JONES AND SUSAN V. DONALDSON, EDITORS

www.ingramcontent.com/pod-product-compliance
Lightning Source LLC
Chambersburg PA
CBHW030605230426
43661CB00053B/1850